The Panama Canal: An Engineering Treatise. a Series of
Papers Covering in Full Detail the Technical Problems
Involved in the Construction of the Panama Canal
- Geology, Climatology, Municipal Engineering;
Dredging, Hydraulics, Power Plants, Etc. Prepared

George Washington Goethals, International
Engineering Congress, San Francisco

THE
PANAMA CANAL

AN ENGINEERING TREATISE

—— — —

A Series of Papers Covering in Full Detail the Technical Problems
Involved in the Construction of the Panama Canal — Geology,
Climatology, Municipal Engineering, Dredging, Hydraulics,
Power Plants, etc. Prepared by Engineers and other
Specialists in charge of the various branches of
the work and presented at the International
Engineering Congress, San Francisco,
California, 1915

UNDER THE DIRECTION OF

GEORGE W. GOETHALS, Major General, U. S. Army

Member American Society of Civil Engineers
Governor of the Canal Zone
Formerly Chairman and Chief Engineer, Isthmian Canal Commission

·

—— ——

VOLUME II

·

McGRAW-HILL BOOK COMPANY, Inc.
239 WEST 39TH STREET, NEW YORK
6 BOUVERIE STREET. LONDON. E. C.
1916

CONTENTS

PAPERS

Paper No. 14

GENERAL DESIGN OF THE LOCKS, DAMS AND REGULATING WORKS OF THE PANAMA CANAL.

By

Brig. Gen. H. F. HODGES, U. S. Army
M. Am. Soc. C. E.
Formerly Member and Assistant Chief Engineer, Isthmian Canal Commission
Fort Totten, N. Y., U. S. A.

The actual work of building the Panama Canal began before it had been finally decided whether the sea-level or lock type would be adopted. Much of the necessary plant had been acquired, a large force of employees collected, adequate measures for feeding, housing and recruiting the force initiated, sanitary work organized and the excavation undertaken, before Congress, by act approved June 29, 1906, ordered that a lock canal be built, following the general plan proposed by the minority of the International Board of Consulting Engineers in its report of 1906. This report fixed the alignment of the canal and the approximate location of the principal structures, but the design of the latter had not then been carried beyond the stage of study needed for comparison between the two rival types of canal.

In the latter part of 1906, a designing force was organized, under the Principal Assistant Engineer, in the Washington Office of the Isthmian Canal Commission. This force prosecuted studies for the lock masonry, the gates, and the emergency dams. A portion went to the Isthmus of Panama after the reorganization of the work in the spring of 1907, and continued there the studies for the masonry, under the Head of the Department of Lock and Dam Construction. The studies for the lock gates and emergency dams were continued in Washington, under the supervision of the Chief of the Washington Office. In July,

1908, the designing of the locks, dams and regulating works was consolidated and placed in charge of the Assistant Chief Engineer. The part of the force then in Washington was brought to the Isthmus, and remained there until disbanded upon completion of its work.

It was not until January, 1908, that the width of the locks was fixed at 110 feet (33.53 m.); and the final location of the locks and dam at Miraflores was not determined until about the same time. Naturally the designing up to then had been tentative, and mainly for the purpose of settling which of the several available plans should be adopted for the different structures and moving parts. Careful investigation had been made of the foundations at the different localities and, without waiting for the completion of the designs, the work of excavation at the lock sites was pushed vigorously. This resulted in the loss of some little work, but in the saving of much time; and compelled the designing force to direct its energies to catching up with the field work. When this had been done it was still by no means easy to keep ahead of it.

When the force was finally consolidated, under the supervision of the Assistant Chief Engineer, preliminary designs had been made for locks 100 feet (30.48 m.) wide, and estimates for locks of other widths up to 125 feet (38.10 m.); the investigations of the foundations had been made, and important data in regard thereto had been collected; but the structural designs had not in other respects passed beyond the preliminary stage, the important questions of the foundation plan and wall sections not having been settled. The design of the gates had reached a point where the type to be used had been fixed, the general arrangement of the leaf in compartments had been blocked out, and many details of the quoin posts and bearings had been determined; the swinging type of emergency dam had been adopted, and studies made of a truss of a system afterwards discarded; and the plan for the earth dam at Gatun was in essentials complete, according to the sections then adopted.

The office force engaged upon the designs was organized in 1908 into subdivisions as follows:

Masonry and locks, including valves, under Mr. L. D. Cornish, Designing Engineer.

Lock gates and protective devices, under Mr. Henry Goldmark, Designing Engineer.

Operating machinery and electric installations, under Mr. Edw. Schildhauer, Electrical and Mechanical Engineer.

Emergency Dams, under Mr. T. B. Mönniche, Designing Engineer.

Two other subdivisions were added later—

Spillways, under Mr. E. C. Sherman, Designing Engineer.

Aids to Navigation, under Mr. W. F. Beyer, Assistant Engineer.

The details of the work done in these subdivisions are treated elsewhere by the gentlemen in immediate charge.

DESIGN OF LOCKS.

The general design adopted for the Canal provided for overcoming differences of water level at three places, namely, at Gatun, 7 miles (11.25 kilom.) from the Atlantic end, where the total lift was to be 85 feet (25.91 m.) at ordinary stage, and where a flight of three locks was proposed; at Pedro Miguel, 40 miles (64.37 kilom.) from the Atlantic end, where the ordinary lift was to be 30-1/3 feet (9.23 m.), and a single lock was proposed; and at Miraflores, 42 miles (67.60 kilom.) from the Atlantic, or 8 miles (13.42 kilom.) from the Pacific end, where the average lift was to be 54-2/3 feet (16.67 m.), and where a flight of two locks was proposed. In the original plan of the minority Board of Consulting Engineers, the lock flight at the Pacific end had been placed at La Boca, now Balboa, close to the shore of the bay. The difficulty and expense incident to the construction of the dams on the soft and unstable soil, and the desirability, from a military point of view, of having the structures further inland, caused a change of the site to Miraflores. The designs of the locks, with the elevations and dimensions of the principal parts, will be found in Plates II, III and IV. In describing them it will be convenient to mention first the features common to all the locks, for outlines of which Plate I may be consulted as typical.

Features Common to All the Locks.

Dimensions of Locks: The Act of Congress approved June 28, 1902, which authorized the construction of an Isthmian

Canal, provided that it should be of sufficient capacity and depth to afford convenient passage for the largest vessels then in use or reasonably to be anticipated. The report of the minority of the Board of Consulting Engineers, which fixed the general plan of the Canal, recommended locks 900 feet (279.32 m.) long and 95 feet (28.96 m.) wide. Before the designs were well under way, it was known that vessels 795 feet (242.41 m.) long and 88 feet (26.82 m.) in beam were soon to be afloat; before the designs were finished, these dimensions had increased to 892 feet (271.88 m.) and 92 feet (28.04 m.); and before the locks were used, the "Imperator" appeared with a length of 883 feet (269.13 m.) and beam of 98 feet (29.87 m.). At first the Commission contemplated locks 1000 feet (304.80 m.) long and 100 feet (30.48 m.) wide; but, upon the suggestion of the General Board of the Navy, which was evidently influenced by the relatively large beam given to battleships, the width was finally increased to 110 feet (33.53 m.), and the adopted dimensions stand, therefore, at 1000 ft. (304.80 m.) by 110 feet (33.53 m.).

The depth of the canal was fixed at the equivalent of 40 feet (12.19 m.) in salt water, or 41-2/3 feet (12.71 m.) in fresh water. In the locks it is nowhere less, when the pools have their normal level. To provide for continuity of traffic when a lock might be out of service, and to facilitate simultaneous movement in both directions, it was determined to build the locks with twin chambers, side by side, separated by a middle wall.

Walls: Concrete was adopted as the material of the walls. The main walls of the locks have a gravity section, not depending upon reinforcement for stability. Certain of the wing walls and approach walls, as well as certain subsidiary parts, such as operating tunnels, are of reinforced concrete. Above the level of the roof of the culvert the main part of the middle wall consists of two retaining walls, the space between being back-filled with earth and rock. At the valve chambers and gate buttresses the earth fill is omitted, and the wall built of solid concrete. The further details of the masonry design are described in another paper.

The freeboard of the terminal locks of the summit level was assumed at 5 feet (1.52 m.) above high water of Gatun Lake, placing the coping of upper Gatun and Pedro Miguel locks at elevation +92 feet (+28.04 m.) above mean tide. The assumption was guided by the thought that waves of some height might develop in Gatun Lake, and that floods coming down the Chagres might bank up the water in the Culebra Cut from Gamboa to Pedro Miguel. The stated freeboard places the sill of the opening through which the gate-operating strut protrudes, 1 foot 5½ inches (0.45 m.) above the Gatun Lake high level of +87.

At Miraflores, 4 ft. (1.219 m.) freeboard was assumed as sufficient for the upper lock, as the level of the small lake above can be regulated rapidly; and no waves of any considerable height can develop.

The freeboard in the intermediate locks of the Gatun flight varies with the size of the lock and the stage of water. It is approximately 5 feet (1.52 m.) in ordinary service. At Miraflores some water must be wasted, or the walls of the lower lock will be flooded, at certain stages of the tide, by the prism let down from the upper 1000 or 900 ft. lock.

Gates: Steel was adopted as the material for the gates, the great size forbidding the use of timber. The shape of the leaves in vertical elevation, and the magnitude of the pressures which they must withstand, indicated that the type of the gate with vertical members, dividing the pressure between the sill and a strong upper girder, a type which has great merit, was not applicable to the conditions to be met; accordingly the main members were placed horizontally, with a sufficient number of vertical girders to give the desired rigidity. The horizontals were designed as girders rather than arches, principally because of the additional unit cost of curved gates, and the deeper recesses which they would have demanded, which would have been objectionable, especially in the middle wall.

Detailed information as to the gates is given in another paper. The accompanying illustration (Fig. 1) shows the downstream side of the upper gates in the upper lock at Gatun, under a head of 70 feet (21.34 m.) against the upstream face. The leakage at the gates is insignificant.

There are 92 gate leaves in the canal, with a total weight of 60,000 net tons (54,432 met. tons). If piled on top of each other, end for end, they would make a tower more than a mile and a quarter (1998.6 m.) high.

Intermediate Gates: The prisms drawn from the summit level, at each lockage, with full chambers of the adopted dimensions, measure nearly 4,000,000 cubic feet (113,200 c. met.). As the water-supply during the dry season may be small, it was regarded as highly important to reduce the loss through lockage as much as practicable. To this end, intermediate gates were planned, to divide the main chamber into two shorter ones, one of which might be used with vessels of ordinary size. These

Fig. 1.   Ladder Dredge "Corozal" and "C" Class Submarines Dry-docked in Upper East Chamber, Gatun Locks.

intermediate gates were introduced in all the locks, except the lower Miraflores lock, where tidal conditions rendered them inadvisable. In the upper locks of each flight and in the Pedro Miguel lock they leave available chambers 550 feet (167.6 m.) long and 370 feet (112.8 m.) long. The difference of 80 feet (24.4 m.), between the total of these lengths and the available length of the single large chamber, is lost by the introduction of a fender chain to guard the intermediate gates. By using one of these smaller chambers, a considerable saving in water can be effected.

As a precaution against the obviously disastrous results which would ensue, if the gates separating the upper and lower pools should be rammed and broken down, it was deemed justifiable to require that a vessel should always have double gates ahead of it, at points where the destruction of the barrier might join the two levels—that is, at the upper and lower end of the upper lock in each flight, and of the Pedro Miguel single-lift lock. While the destruction of a gate at other points in the lock-flights would have very serious consequences, it would not let the upper pool down into the lower one. The duplication of the locks, and the possibility of operating with chambers of different length, provide sufficiently against the consequences of accidents at the less vital points of the system. At the upper end of the locks mentioned are placed the guard gates, with sill on top of the lift wall, and the upper operating gates, with sill at the same level as the sill of the lower gates, that is, a foot or two above the lock floor. The full length of 1000 feet (304.8 m.) for the entire chamber is measured from the fender chain above the lower gates to the soffit of the vertical arch of the lift wall, on which the upper guard gates are placed. A vessel requiring the full 1000 feet (304.8 m.) in length of the chamber, on a down-lockage, would be stopped with its bow at the fender chain above the lower locks, having in front of it, in the direction of its motion, the safety and lower gates at the foot of the lock. The stern of the vessel would project into the space between the upper operating and the upper guard gates. Only the upper guard gates would be closed behind the vessel, which would have available a chamber 1000 feet (304.8 m.) long. On an up-lockage, on the other hand, the lower fender chain would necessarily be out of use on the bottom of the lock, and the vessel would have available a chamber extending from the safety gates below to the upper operating gates above, viz, 1008.5 feet (307.4 m.), measured between hollow quoins. At the same time, all four pairs of gates would be in use. Placing the sill of the upper operating gates near the floor level, rather than on top of a lift wall, leaves the full length of the lock to the upper guard gate still available when needed for very large ships.

The chamber with length of 908.5 feet (276.9 m.) between the upper operating gate and the lower fender chain will accommodate, even on down-lockages, vessels of the largest size liable to use the canal for many years; so that both upper guard gates and upper operating gates may be swung at practically every down-lockage, and the full 1000 feet (304.8 m.) prism of lift will seldom, if ever, be taken out of the summit level.

It is possible to save a certain amount of water by cross-filling from one lock to its twin through the middle wall. This results in carrying a smaller prism of lift down to the lower level, and consequently reduces the available depth in the lower locks of the flights.*

With the summit level at elevation +85 ft. (+25.91 m.), Miraflores Lake at elevation +54-2/3 ft. (+16.67 m.), and the oceans on both sides at mean level, or elevation +0.0, the prisms of lift of the locks are as follows, expressed in thousands of cubic feet:

1	2	3	4	Total loss from summit level[†]	
Lock	Gatun	Pedro Miguel	Miraflores	Sum of Cols. 2 and 4	Col. 5 in second feet
1000 ft.	3,545	4,065	3,716	7,259	84.0
900 ft.	3,446	3,730	3,484	6,930	80.2
550 ft.	2,300	2,500	2,690	4,990	57.8

or, expressed in cubic metres:					Col. 5 in metres[2] per sec.
304.8 m.	100,325.	115,141	105,175	205,500	2.378
274.3 m.	97,533	105,569	98,608	196,141	2.271
167.6 m.	65,090	70,760	76,138	141,228	1.636

Sill Levels: The sills of the upper guard gates are placed from one foot to two and one-half feet (0.31 to 0.76 m.) below the bottom level of the pool just above them, and are thus guarded against blows from any vessels which can reach them. The sills

---

* For discussion of saving due to use of intermediate gates and cross-filling, see Annual Report, Isthmian Canal Commission, 1910, pp. 65 et seq.

† The total loss is measured at Gatun and Miraflores, since, at the single-lift lock at Pedro Miguel, the consumption can always be cut in half, if desired, by cross-filling or by alternating up- and down-lockages.

of the remaining gates are placed one or two feet (0.31 to 0.62 m.) above the general floor level of the lock, to facilitate circulation of water under hulls of vessels and to prevent injury from small obstacles which may fall or drift into the chamber. A raised sill of concrete, a short distance above the miter sill, is intended to guard the latter against injury, and sumps are placed immediately above all gates, to catch sunken objects and prevent their lodging against the sills.

Filling and Emptying System: In designing the system of filling and emptying the locks, the chief aim was to secure one which, with due economy in construction, would permit equalization of levels in a reasonable time, would not create dangerous disturbance in the locks or approaches, and would not allow excessive waste through leakage. Economy made it desirable not to go too far below the floor level with any part of the system. The other considerations required a very large flow; an unobstructed admission and discharge in the fore- and tailbays; a distribution of flow over the horizontal area of the lock chamber; and the use of reasonably tight valves, with possibility of access for examination and repair.

To fill or empty the large locks in fifteen minutes was regarded as satisfactory in point of time. With reasonably good flow this would require an opening of at least three or four hundred square feet (27 to 37 sq. met.) in area under the usual heads. It was clearly impracticable to pass such a stream through the gates, and a system of culverts was indicated. After study of various locations for the main culverts, it was decided that all conditions could best be met by locating them in the lock walls, with suitable auxiliary culverts for distributing the flow throughout the lock chamber.

To secure a reasonably even distribution of flow when filling the lock, it was thought desirable to admit water from culverts on both sides. This consideration required that the middle wall should be prepared with culvert discharge into either lock chamber. No satisfactory disposition of two culverts of the size desired could be found in the middle wall, without increasing the width very considerably beyond the limits required for stability. As such an increase would necessarily extend through the full length of all lock chambers and middle approach walls, it would

have entailed serious expense. Accordingly, it was determined to adopt for the middle wall a single culvert, equipped for discharge into either lock chamber at will.

The system adopted is as follows (see Plate I) : Near the base of each lock wall there is placed a culvert, running the entire length of the lock flight and connecting the upper and lower pools. The main culverts communicate with the chambers through lateral culverts, at right angles to the main culverts, spaced at approximately equal intervals along the length. The laterals run under the chamber floor and discharge upward through openings spaced uniformly across the lock floor.

The main culverts are closed by valves at each lift. The laterals from the side wall culverts, which communicate with only one chamber, are open freely. The laterals from the middle-wall culvert, which may discharge into either of the twin lock chambers, are closed by individual valves, permitting the flow to either chamber to be established or interrupted.

The main culvert valves are gate valves of the Stoney type, moving vertically on frames of live rollers, against which they are pressed by the operating head. This type was chosen because it permitted the use of large valves under high head, without too great friction; and because it can be made reasonably watertight. For the smaller lateral culverts, where the flow may come from either direction, cylindrical valves were chosen, packed with leather gaskets against exterior and interior pressure. As this type of valve is balanced, the friction does not increase with the head. They have been much used in the United States as the main valves for small locks, but have been used there only when the head is always on the same side. With careful installation they can be made very tight, so long as the packing lasts; and can be re-packed readily, if installed in an accessible position. The details of the valves are described in another paper.

The side-wall culverts draw from the upper pool through three openings, each 8 ft. by 18 ft. (2.44 m. by 5.49 m.) in sectional area. Each opening is closed by one Stoney valve, operated through chains by a winding engine above. These valves are called guard valves, but may be used for operating the lock, in case the operating valves next below them should be out of commission for any cause. Screens are placed above the guard valves, to prevent drift from entering the culvert. All the other Stoney valves are operated through a rigid stem, raised and lowered by a cross-head actuated by screws. Except at the entrance, the main culvert valves are installed in pairs, each closing one-half of the culvert, which divides at the valve chambers into two branches separated by a central pier. Each branch is 8 ft. by 18 ft. (2.44 m. by 5.49 m.) in cross section.

The valves above each lift wall are installed in duplicate, one set being raised out of the way and held in reserve, while the other is in use. The guard valves form one of the sets which separate the upper chamber from the upper pool, the set next below being used ordinarily in operating the lock. The side-wall culverts have each a set of valves above the intermediate gates, to permit the use of the smaller chambers into which these gates divide the main chamber. These valves are not needed in the middle wall, as the cylindrical valves serve to establish communication with the smaller chambers separately.

The middle-wall culverts draw through three rectangular openings, which lead from the forebays on each side and are suitably screened against drift. These openings are each 8 ft. by 15 ft. (2.44 m. by 4.57 m.) in dimensions, and are provided with slots in which regulating valves can be installed, in case it should be found that the cross-draught creates too much disturbance in the forebay of one lock while the other is being filled. The masonry has been prepared to receive the machinery of these valves, which may be so arranged as to balance each other, and close the openings on one side while the others are left open.

The discharge of the middle culvert is similar to the intake, but without screens. Here, also, provision has been made for the installation of balanced regulating valves, which will probably be necessary when the volume of shipping becomes sufficient to require simultaneous operation of both locks.

Access may be had to the interior of the main culverts, through wells from the coping, and tunnels at or near the floor level. Above the upper gate there is one well or shaft 3 feet (0.92 m.) in diameter, leading into each of the three main culverts. Below the upper gates the side-wall culverts have open tunnels 7 ft. by 3 ft. (2.13 m. by 0.92 m.), leading from the floor of the lock into the valve chambers above the intermediate gates and above the lower gates, there being two such tunnels in each chamber. The middle-wall culverts' have also openings into the lock chambers, at the level of the floor of the culvert, or 10 to 10½ ft. (3.05 to 3.20 m.) above the floor of the lock. These openings are closed by tight bulkheads, and are 12 ft. by 5 ft. (3.66 m. by 1.52 m.) in clear dimensions, or large enough to admit any part of a cylindrical valve. There are two such tunnels leading into the middle culvert of each lock, one from the chamber on each side. It is not intended to remove the bulkheads except in case of damage to one of the valves. For examination of the culvert, access can be had through vertical shafts, similar to those in the side walls, which lead from the coping to the tunnels just mentioned.

Between the intake and the upper set of Stoney valves, each main culvert has a sectional area of 333 sq. ft. (30.94 sq. m.), with flat floor and arched roof. At the valve chambers the two branches of the culvert have a total sectional area of 288 sq. ft. (26.76 sq. m.). Between valve chambers the side-wall culverts are circular in cross section, with radius of 9 ft. (2.74 m.) and area of 255 sq. ft. (23.69 sq. m.). The middle-wall culvert retains the form with flat floor and arched roof, with total sectional area of 255 sq. ft. (23.69 sq. m.).

Each side culvert communicates with the lock chamber through eleven laterals. The middle-wall culvert has ten laterals on each side.

The cross section of the laterals is elliptical, with sectional area of 41 sq. ft. (3.80 sq. m.). The throats of the laterals, where they lead from the main side culverts, have edges rounded off to a maximum sectional area of 55 sq. ft. (5.11 sq. m.). The throats of the laterals from the middle-wall culvert are formed by the bed-plates of the cylindrical valves, and are circular in plan, with a minimum section of 33.2 sq. ft. (3.08 sq. met.), enlarged by rounding the edge to permit freer flow. The openings from the laterals into the chamber have a minimum sectional area of 12.24 sq. ft. (1.14 sq. met.), also with rounded edges to facilitate flow in either direction. There are five such openings in each lateral.   The course of the water in filling the lock with the side culvert lies through (a) intake, 432 sq. ft. (40.13 sq. met.); (b) large culvert, 333 sq. ft. (30.94 sq. met.); (c) valves, 288 sq. ft. (16.76 sq. met.); (d) main culvert, 255 sq. ft. (23.69 sq. met.); (e) throats of laterals, 605 sq. ft. (56.20 sq. met.);

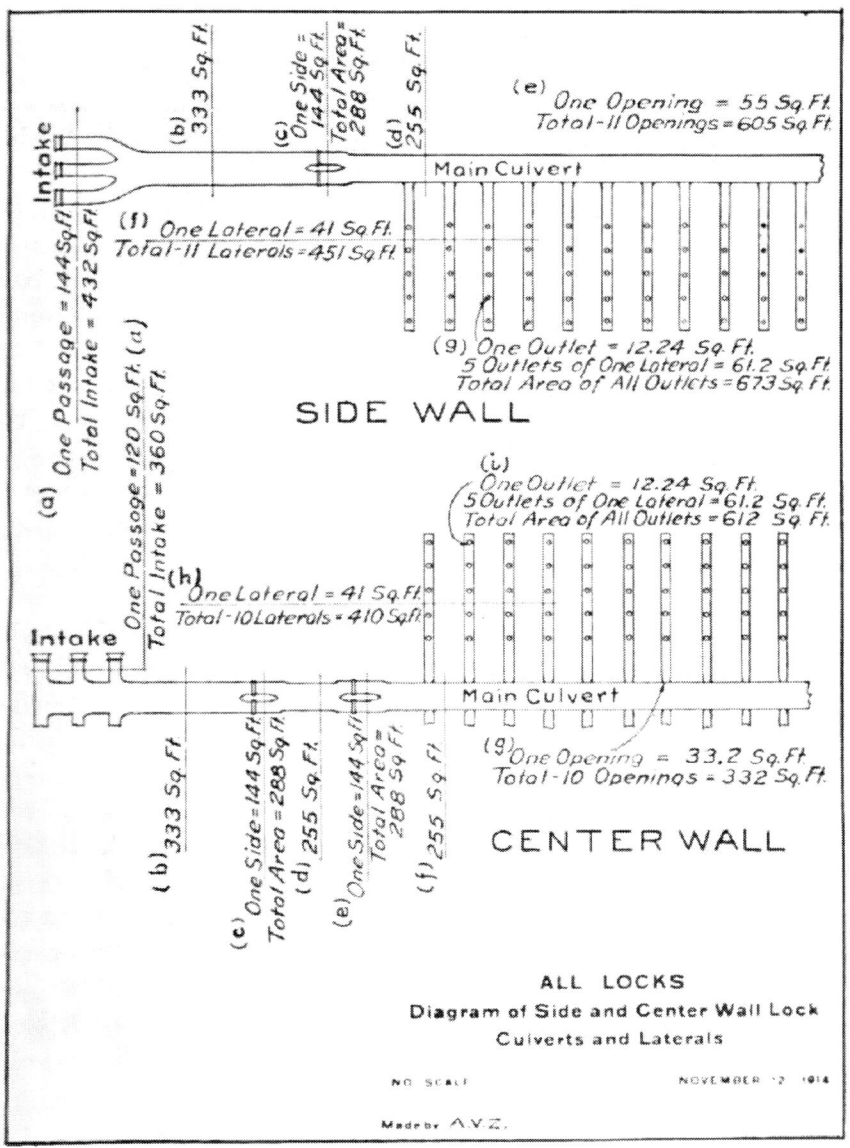

Fig. 2.

(f) laterals, 451 sq. ft. (41.90 sq. met.) ; (g) outlets in floor of chamber, 673 sq. ft. (62.52 sq. met.).

For the middle culvert the course lies through (a) intake, *360 sq. ft. (33.44 sq. met.) ; (b) large culvert, 333 sq. ft. (30.94 sq. met.) ; (c) valves, 288 sq. ft. (16.76 sq. met.) ; (d) main culvert, 255 sq. ft. (23.69 sq. met.) ; (e) valves, 288 sq. ft. (16.76 sq. met.) ; (f) main culvert, 255 sq. ft. (23.69 sq. met.) ; (g) cylindrical valves, 332 sq. ft. (30.85 sq. met.) ; (h) laterals, 410 sq. ft. (38.09 sq. met.) ; (i) outlets in floor of chamber, 612 sq. ft. (56.86 sq. met.).   The course is shown diagrammatically in Fig. 2.

Action of Water in Locks: It may be of interest to note at this point what actual results have been reached through the design just described.   By trial, repeated many times, it has been found that, with normal pool-levels and using both side and middle culverts, it takes from 7.5 to 8 minutes to fill the upper 900-ft. (274.3 m.) lock of a flight, or the Pedro Miguel 900-ft. (274.3 m.) lock; 6.5 to 7 minutes to equalize consecutive locks of a flight; 7.5 to 8.5 minutes to empty the lower lock of a flight; and 7.5 to 8 minutes to empty the Pedro Miguel lock.

When the side culvert only is used, with both valves open, these intervals become about 13.5 minutes, 12.5 minutes, 17.5 minutes and 15 minutes, respectively.

The coefficient of flow is very favorable for the side-wall culverts.   For example, it took 14.0 minutes to fill Pedro Miguel 900-ft. (274.3 m.) lock from elevation +50.9 (+15.51 m.) to elevation + 84.4 (+ 25.84 m.), the level of the forebay.† Of this time 1 minute was occupied in raising the valve, during which time the area of cross-section of the waterway at the valves was increasing from 0 to its final value of 255 sq. ft. (23.69 sq. met.), and the water in the lock was observed to rise from elevation 50.9 (15.51 m.) to elevation 51.7 (15.76 m.).   For the remainder of the time, viz., 13.0 minutes, the full area of the waterway was available, viz., 255 sq. ft. (23.69 sq. met.), at the most contracted point.   These observed data give a value of the coefficient of flow, for the time when the entire waterway was available—

---

* Assuming one side closed by regulating valves.

† See Fig. 10 of "Hydraulics of the Locking Operations of the Panama Canal" by R. V. Whitehead.

$$* \ c = \frac{2 \times 123,000 \times \sqrt{33.1}}{13.0 \times 60 \times 255 \times \sqrt{64.4}} = 0.886$$

If the entire time consumed after the first movement of the valve be reckoned, leaving out of consideration the fact that the culvert does not reach its full capacity until the valve is raised, the coefficient still remains large, having the value of $c = 0.833$.

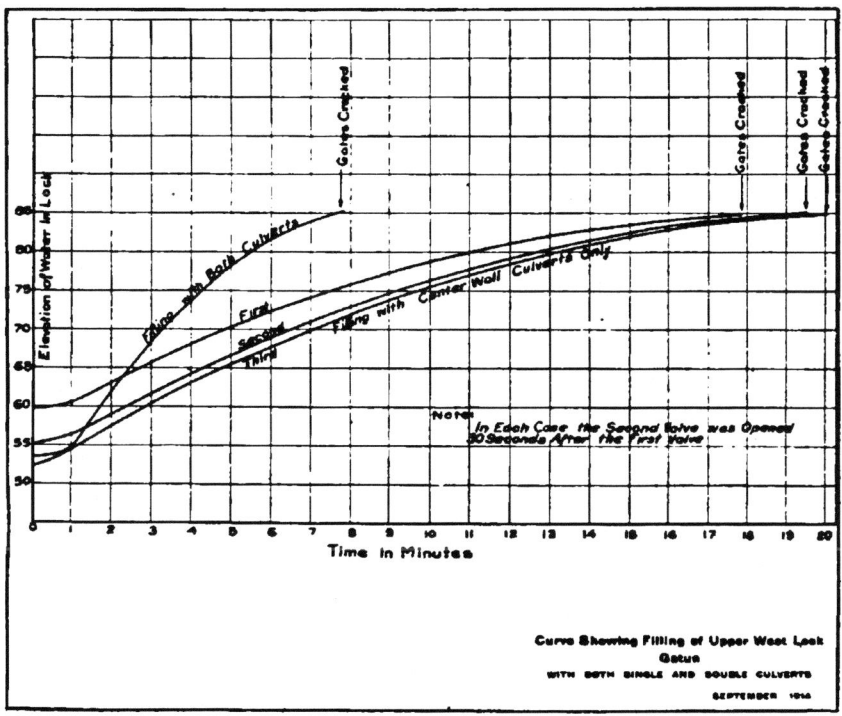

Fig. 3.

This result is much better than had been anticipated, and makes it possible to pass vessels without undue loss of time, even when only the side culvert is available.

For the middle culvert the coefficient is less favorable,

---

* In formula for time of filling single-lift lock.

$$t = \frac{2A(\sqrt{H} - \sqrt{h})}{c\,a\,\sqrt{2g}}$$

$t =$ time in seconds
$A =$ area of lock in plan
$a =$ cross-section of culvert
$H =$ original difference in level
$h =$ remaining difference in level
$g =$ acceleration of gravity.

doubtless because the flow is cramped at the cylindrical valves and their recesses. At the upper Gatun lock a value of $c =$ 0.587 was found as the mean of three observations. (Fig. 3.)

A rather remarkable result is found when the chamber is filled through the side culvert only, using but one valve. (Fig. 4.)

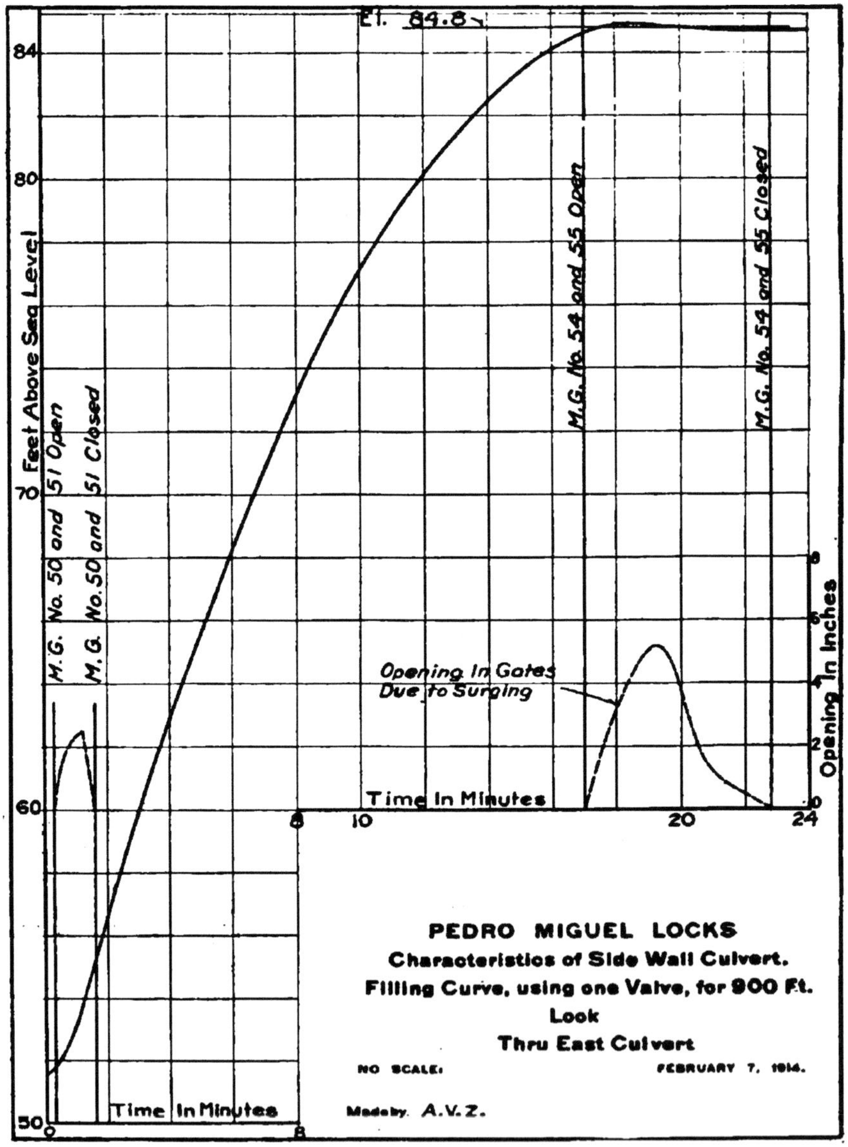

PEDRO MIGUEL LOCKS
Characteristics of Side Wall Culvert.
Filling Curve, using one Valve, for 900 Ft.
Lock
Thru East Culvert
NO SCALE.   FEBRUARY 7, 1914.
Made by A. V. Z.

Fig. 4.

The most contracted area of the culvert is then at the valve and measures 144 sq. ft. (13.38 sq. met.). A natural prediction would be that the time of filling would be increased, over that consumed when the side culvert is used with both valves, about in the ratio of $\dfrac{255}{144}$.

It actually takes 18 minutes to equalize Pedro Miguel lock from Miraflores Lake level of $+51.5$ ft. ($+15.7$ m.) to Gatun Lake level of $+84.8$ ft. ($+25.84$ m.) through the one valve. During the first minute, when the section of the waterway at the valve is increasing from 0 to 144 sq. ft. (13.38 sq. met.), the water in the lock was observed to rise from $+51.5$ ft. ($+15.70$ m.) to $+53.0$ ft. ($+16.16$ m.). For the remaining time of filling, the value is found—

$$c = \frac{2 \times 123{,}000 \times \sqrt{31.8}}{17 \times 60 \times 144 \times \sqrt{2g}} = 1.177, \text{ or, greater than unity.}$$

If the entire time from the first movement of the valve be considered, neglecting the diminished area of flow during the first minute, c will be found equal to 1.086, or still greater than unity. It appears, therefore, that, during the time of filling with only one valve, the average velocity through the most contracted section of the culvert is greater than that due to the head producing it. This result was confirmed by observations at the upper Gatun lock, where, under similar conditions, the coefficient c was found to have the value 1.272, when corrected for the time while the valve was rising.

For the combination of side-wall and middle-wall culverts, observations indicate values about as follows:

For filling upper lock.. $c = 0.78$
For equalizing consecutive locks .... $c = 0.60$
For emptying lower lock to sea............................... $c = 0.69$
For emptying Pedro Miguel lock........................... $c = 0.79$

The coefficient for equalization between consecutive locks has not been found the same for all cases. Repeated observations indicate that it takes longer to equalize the same difference in level between the middle and lower lock at Gatun than between the upper and middle lock, perhaps because the water in the lowest chamber is denser, having more sea water than that in the middle chamber. The conditions are otherwise identical, so far as we know. The value given above of $c = 0.60$ is an approximate mean of those found for the different cases.

The flow in filling the lock is reasonably uniform over the area of the chamber, even when only one culvert is used. In that case, however, it is noticeable that the greatest discharge comes from those openings in the laterals which are farthest from the culvert in use. Thus, when the side-wall culvert is used, the discharge is very evidently greatest from the openings nearest the middle wall, giving a slight slope to the surface, which tends to

Fig. 5.   Filling Pedro Miguel Lock, Using Side and Middle Culverts.   All Valves Open.

draw a vessel away from the middle and toward the side wall. This is not strong enough to prevent holding the vessel central in the lock by the towing locomotives, aided usually by hawsers. The effect of the side pull is much more noticeable in the lowest locks of the Gatun and Miraflores flights than it is in the upper ones. When the lowest locks are filled from the side culvert only, the locomotives can not hold a large vessel central in the lock, unless aided by manila lines; and sometimes the vessel's chocks, through which the towing lines are passed, suffer damage under the strain. In the upper locks, however, the towing locomotives have little difficulty in keeping the vessel central during filling from one side only; although, as a measure of precaution, manila lines are usually held in readiness. When both side and middle culverts are used there is no tendency to draw the vessel to either side, and the water surface remains sufficiently quiet to suit even a small boat. In no case has any tendency been noted to draw a vessel lengthwise of the lock.

Figure 4 of Mr. Whitehead's paper and Fig. 5 illustrate the operation of filling through the side culvert and through both culverts.

In emptying the lock, the surface remains absolutely placid, whether one or both culverts are used.[*]

Auxiliary Culverts: As the upper locks of both flights, and the Pedro Miguel lock, have double gates at each end, some means had to be provided to regulate the water levels in the spaces between these gates; otherwise unequal leakage might cause serious trouble in operation.

The space between the upper guard gates and the upper operating gates is connected with the upper pool by a culvert 5 feet (1.52 m.) in diameter, and with the lock chamber by a culvert 3 feet (0.92 m.) in diameter. These culverts are in the side wall, and have valves so arranged that the space between the gates may be made part of the upper pool or of the lock chamber. Either of the two upper gates may therefore be used in locking, in case the other gates are out of commission; or, as is usually the case, both may be used, one gate carrying the main pressure.

The space between the two gates near the lower end of the lock, which are called the "safety gates" and the "lower gates", is regulated by an auxiliary culvert under the lock floor, known as the "T culvert", which places it in communication with the lock chamber above the gates, the connection being made in the side-culvert below the lowest lateral. The T culvert has a valve which may be used to cut off this communication, in case it should become necessary to use the safety gates alone as the lower barrier.

It is observable at all the locks that, when the upper valves

[*] For more extended discussion of action of water in locks, see Professional Memoirs, Corps of Engineers, U. S. Army, No. 31, Jan.-Feb., 1915.

are opened to fill the chamber, there is a drop in level of the water in the forebay. This drop is most noticeable at Pedro Miguel, doubtless because there the water is drawn from the canal instead of from a lake. It has been observed as 0.8 ft. (0.244 m.) at the last-named lock. The water in the space between the upper gates and the upper guard gates does not respond instantly to this drop, and there is consequent reverse pressure against the upper guard gates, which opens them slightly at the miter posts. This condition soon ceases, the gates close again and remain closed until near the end of the operation of filling. The water in motion in the culverts continues its flow after the head producing it has ceased, causing the water in the lock to rise slightly higher than the water above the gates. Reverse pressure is then produced on the upper operating gates, which crack at the miter posts. Thus, in Fig. 10 of Mr. Whitehead's paper, the original level of the water in the forebay was + 84.8 (+25.84 m.). The drop, subsisting to the end of the operation, was 0.8 ft. (0.244 m.). The upper operating gates cracked when the level in the lock reached + 84.0 ft. (+ 25.60 m.), but the flow in the culvert still continued and the water in the chamber finally rose to + 85.0 ft. (+ 25.91 m.), two tenths of a foot (0.061 m.) higher than the original level of the water in the forebay, and one foot (0.305 m.) higher than the level at which the upper gates cracked from backpressure. The phenomenon is noticed at all the locks, but is particularly observable at Pedro Miguel. It apparently results from the over-travel of the water in the culverts, and is not to be confounded with the wave due to the motion of the water in the canal, which occurs much later.*

The space between the safety gates and the lower gates feels a marked effect upon the admission of the water through the side culvert. When the T culvert is unobstructed, the water in the space rises faster than that in the chamber, producing back-pressure on the safety gates and opening them to the full compression of the strut springs in the operating gear, parting the miter posts about six inches. This condition was not permissible, and the valve was therefore used to throttle the culvert. It would not do to throttle it too much, however, since then the water between the gates would lag behind the water in the chamber, when the

* See p. 37, and Fig. 9.

latter was lowered, and would again produce back-pressure against the safety gates. By trial, a position was found at which the space between the gates, controlled by the valve, would fill more slowly than the chamber, and empty faster. Positive pressure would therefore be maintained on both gates under both conditions; in practice, however, it is usual to start the safety gates to open before lowering the level of the water in the chamber, and after the vessel has been brought into position in the lock; this, because otherwise the position of the T culvert valve would have to be changed according to the number of main culvert valves to be used in emptying the lock. In filling the lock, positive pressure on the safety gates can be maintained, without changing the valve according to the number of main culverts used.

In emptying the lower locks of the flights and the Pedro Miguel lock, the effect of over-travel of the water in the culverts is also noticeable. The water in the lock is observed to lower beyond the point where the pressures on the two sides of the lower gates equalize, and the latter tend to open under reverse pressure from the tailbay. Similar effect is produced in equalizing consecutive locks of a flight. The opening of the gates at the miter is so reliable that, in operating the locks, it is taken as an indication of the proper time to apply the power to the gate opening gear.

Precautions Against Accident: The gravity of the results which might follow a serious accident to the locks or gates was regarded as warranting the adoption of extraordinary precautions to guard against the occurrence and the effect of such an accident. The first of these precautions, viz., the introduction of double gates at the most vital points, has already been mentioned. As a second precaution, the gates at the approaches and at the most vital points are guarded by fender chains, which rest on the floor, when not in use, and are raised by hydraulic cylinders to the surface of the water, when needed as a protection. They are placed above the upper guard gates, the middle gates and the safety gates in each upper lock, and in the Pedro Miguel lock, and below the lower guard gates of all locks. It is expected that they will absorb the energy of any vessel striking them, before the gates themselves can be reached by the blow.

The chief reliance is placed upon the fact that vessels are towed through the locks, the motive power being electric locomotives running on tracks in the coping of the walls. The details of the towing system are described in another paper. In its practical use it has been found that the control of the vessels by the locomotives is nearly perfect, and that passage of the locks is made in rather less time than had been anticipated. A vessel of ordinary size, say, 5000 tons net register, can be taken through the Gatun flight of three locks in 60 to 70 minutes, including the time used in making fast and casting off the towing cables and passing out of the last lock. The towing speed of two miles (3.22 km.) per hour is well suited to vessels of ordinary size, and has proved adequate for a collier of 19,000 tons displacement. For a battleship of nearly twice that tonnage a slower speed may be desirable. By altering the connections of the motors on some of the locomotives, it has been made possible to tow with them either at one mile (1.61 km.) or at two miles (3.22 km.) per hour; and the corresponding alteration of all locomotives is now in hand.

The practice at present is for the vessel to come up to the middle approach wall of the lock at very slow speed, and to take the lines from the middle-wall locomotives, usually without coming to a stop if the gates are open; to move along the middle approach wall under tow and with the aid of her own engines, taking the lines of the side-wall locomotives by means of hauling lines passed on board by a skiff; to pass through the locks under tow, being held near the center by the locomotives assisted, if necessary, by manila lines on each side; and to drop the locomotives on signal after the last gate has been opened and steerage way gained. The propeller is used in the locks, as a rule, only in starting and stopping, when it relieves the strain on the locomotives very advantageously. Six locomotives are used in general—three on each side, one fast to the bow, one nearly amidships, and one at the quarter. Many lockages have been made with four locomotives, two ahead and two astern.* The writer believes that, except for very large vessels, four locomotives will in the end be found adequate.

* See Figs. 20 and 21 of ''Electrical and Mechanical Installations of the Panama Canal'' by Edward Schildhauer.

To keep the towing lines of the locomotives so far as possible from chafing, the upper three feet of the wall have a slope, withdrawing the edge one foot from the plane of the face. The edge is finished as an arc with radius of 6 inches.

In order to avoid unnecessary curves in the towing track, and at the same time to keep it as near the edge of the coping as practicable, it is carried over the gate recess on beams corbelled

Fig. 6.   Corbel Over Gate Recess.

out from the top of the wall. The recess cover leaves only enough of the top of the gate exposed to form a convenient footpath when the gates are closed. (See Fig. 6.)

Snubbing hooks are inserted in the faces of the lock walls, and snubbing posts and buttons in the coping. The posts are placed in the approach walls and at a few points in the lock walls, and the buttons at intervals of about fifty feet along the walls.

The foregoing precautions have been taken to prevent accident. A further safeguard in the form of the emergency dam has been introduced, to minimize the effect of an accident, should one occur.

Above the upper guard gate at each lock is placed a drawbridge, which can be swung across the lock, and which carries wicket girders pivoted to the horizontal truss system at their upper extremities. These girders can be lowered until the lower ends rest in a sill prepared for them in the floor of the forebay; and upon the runway thus formed by their upstream flanges, panel gates can be lowered, closing the waterway progressively. The details of the structure are described in another paper. The object is to check the flow which would take place through the lock were the gates to be carried away. One dam has been tested with the full head against it, and has shown leakage which would not prevent the closing of any gate below it.

The middle wall of each lock flight is prolonged up and down stream, to form a quay for vessels to moor against, or to touch when approaching to take the tow lines. At Miraflores and Pedro Miguel these approach walls extend 1200 feet (365.76 m.) beyond the angles of the splay of the side wall, which limit the forebay and tailbay. At Gatun, on account of conditions of foundation, the walls were shortened to 1000 feet (304.80 m.) beyond the fore and tailbays. The outside ends of the approach walls are provided with fender cribs, or floating fenders secured to piles; and the entire wall is provided, along both faces, with two lines of fender timbers resting against springs held in castings set in the concrete.

Operating Machinery: The details of the different machines are described in a separate paper. Here it is necessary to mention only certain salient features. All the machines are operated electrically, and will ultimately use power generated at the Gatun spillway. The lock machines are placed in chambers below the coping level, opening on operating tunnels, of which there is one in the back-fill of each wall, running the entire length of the lock flight. All maintenance and repair work can be performed under shelter, and the coping of the walls is free from encumbering machinery. The operating tunnels are in three stories—the highest for communication, the middle for the electric cable ducts, and the lowest for drainage.

The machines for moving the valves and fender chains, and for moving and locking the gates, are habitually operated by remote control from a central control house, placed at the lower end of the upper lock. Dummy indicators at the control boards show the response of the different machines to the action of the operator. Means are also provided for operating by local control installed at the individual machines.

The control house operates machines as follows:

At Gatun	204
At Pedro Miguel	108
At Miraflores	146

At each locality there are also 28 machines, at the emergency dams, which are not operative from the lock control board.

Leakage Through Gates and Valves: Careful measurements have been made of the total loss to the summit level by leakage through the gates and valves of the locks and spillway. At the locks the measurements were made by observing the rise or fall of the water in the chambers at upper Gatun and Pedro Miguel, when the gates and main culvert valves were closed, the water being at the low or high level, and the twin chambers in communication through the cylindrical valves of the middle wall. In this way the leakage through the upper or lower gates and valves, under the known head, can be accurately determined. At the spillway the flow in the channel below the concrete dam was collected into a narrow stream, by means of a low earth dam, and the stream was measured as it passed over a weir. The leakage from the summit level, as thus determined under operating heads of 30 and 59 feet (9.14 and 17.98 m.) is—

At Gatun locks	5.93 sec. ft.	(0.1679 m³ per sec.)
At Pedro Miguel lock	4.99 " "	(0.1413 " " "
At Gatun spillway	3.65 " "	(0.1033 " " "
Total	14.57 sec. ft.	(0.4125 m³ per sec.)

In the preliminary estimates of the water supply, the loss through leakage was assumed at 275 second feet (7.78 m³ per sec.).

The lock gates are surprisingly tight at the posts and sill. (See Fig. 1.) The closure at the posts is of steel against steel. At the sill it is wood against wood, with a specially devised rubber packing.

Floating Caisson: The lock chambers may be unwatered for examination and repair, by using the guard gates as coffer dams. The outside faces and bottoms of these gates, their sills, and the sill of the emergency dam would, however, still be inaccessible. To reach these parts a special floating caisson was built, for which seats are prepared in the fore- and tailbays, outside the sills of the emergency dams and lower guard gates. The caisson is provided with a pumping plant having a capacity of 52,000 gallons (198 m^3) per minute, calculated to unwater the Miraflores lock flight from mean tide to sill level in twenty-four hours, liberal allowance being made for leakage.

The main culverts may be unwatered with the assistance of bulkheads prepared for installation in the screen recesses of the intakes, and in special recesses at the outlets.

Setting Temperatures of Concrete: Electrical thermometers were buried in the massive concrete of the east and middle wall of the upper lock at Gatun. Records of the temperature were kept for 14 months, readings of four instruments being taken. The maxima temperatures ran from 127° to 132° F., and were observed between seven and eighteen days after laying the concrete. The temperature thereafter continued to fall for about one year, final values of 80° to 85° being reached in 11 to 13 months after placing the instruments.

Local Differences in Design of Locks:

While the general features of the design are the same at all locks, there are points of difference, due to local circumstances, which merit remark:

Gatun Lock, Special Features (Plate I): The upper lock has greater horizontal area than the others, owing to the double gates at both ends. The areas may be stated as follows:

Lock	1000 ft.	900 ft.	550 ft.
Upper	134,000	123,000	82,500 sq. ft.
Middle	121,000	121,000	80,500 " "
Lower	121,000	121,000	80,500 " "

or, in metric units:

Lock	304.8 m.	274.3 m.	167.6 m.
Upper	12,450	11,430	7,665 sq. m.
Middle	11,240	11,240	7,480 " "
Lower	11,240	11,240	7,480 " "

The total lift of the lock flight may vary from 88 ft. (26.82 m.) to 81 ft. (24.69 m.).

---

* See Annual Report, Isthmian Canal Commission, 1911, p. 118.

With high lake-level of + 87 ft. (+ 26.52 m.) and low tide
of — 1.0 ft. (— 0.31 m.), the lifts of the individual locks are:

Lock	1000 ft.	900 ft.	550 ft.
Upper	27.38	29.02	28.22
Middle	30.31	29.49	28.89
Lower	30.31	29.49	28.89

or, in metric units:

Lock	304.8 m.	274.3 m.	167.6 m.
Upper	8.35	8.85	8.60
Middle	9.24	8.99	8.81
Lower	9.24	8.99	8.81

The dimensions and elevations of the different parts are as
shown on Plate II.

The bed of the foundation of the upper part of the lock
flight at Gatun is less favorable than that of the other locks, but
is of ample strength for the load, and was pronounced satisfactory by a Board of Consulting Engineers which examined it in
1907. The material underlying the forebay and upper part of
the upper lock was soft sandstone, which had to be excavated to a
depth considerably greater than that needed for navigation, in
order to secure a reliable foundation. Even at the final depth it
was found permeable to water; and it was, therefore, thought pru-
dent to guard against the pressure from the lake which might develop under the floor. A trench was excavated through the water-
bearing stratum across the lock pit just above the sill of the
emergency dam, and down the lock just back of the side walls,
as far as the intermediate gates. The trench was filled with concrete, making a cut-off wall 6 ft. (1.83 m.) or more thick. (See
Plate I.) Below the intermediate gates the side walls were back-
drained with broken rock. Between the emergency-dam sill and
the upper-gate sill, the floor of the forebay was made 20 ft. (6.10
m.) thick; between the sills of the upper guard gate and the intermediate gate of the upper locks, the floor was made 13 ft.
(3.96 m.) thick, and was fastened to the bed with discarded steel
rails set vertically 10 to 20 ft. (3.05 to 6.10 m.) deep in the underlying material. Tests of these rails showed great anchoring power,
one 10 ft. (3.05 m.) deep resisting a pull of 237,750 lbs. (107,844
kg.) without movement. Below the intermediate gates, where
the bed is a conglomerate rock of considerable density, the only

precaution taken was to make the floor 3 ft. (0.92 m.) thick. It was intended at first to anchor this part of the floor with rails, but the underlying material, when uncovered, seemed good enough to warrant omitting the anchors. The floor of the middle lock was made 3 ft. (0.92 m.) thick, and that of the lower lock 1 ft. (0.31 m.) thick, the last being drilled with weep holes at intervals of about 10 ft. (3.05 m.). Small sumps were excavated below the floor in six places in the upper part of the upper lock, and these sumps were connected freely with galvanized iron pipes placed vertically in the side walls of the lock. These were intended as tell-tales, to indicate the pressure under the floor by the height of water standing in the pipe. In the autumn of 1914, with the lake at, say, elevation + 85.0 ft. (+ 25.91 m.), the tell-tale pipes indicated heads of from 20 to 40 feet (6.10 to 12.19 m.) under the floor at the sumps, which are approximately at elevation + 0.0.

The middle approach walls at Gatun are placed on a naturally poor foundation. For a short distance above the forebay, the south approach wall rests on rock. For a short distance further it rests on piles driven to rock, and beyond that it rests on piles, driven through an earth fill about 25 feet (7.62 m.) thick, into the soft natural ground underneath. The portion which rests on rock or on piles driven to rock is of massive construction, back-filled with earth and rock. The remainder is cellular, reinforced, and not back-filled.

The wall was stopped when it reached the bed of the old east diversion channel, on account of the expense of extending it over the channel. It is 994.5 ft. (303.1 m.) long, measured from the splay of the wing walls, exclusive of the timber fender crib.

The north middle-approach wall rests on a foundation of piles driven to rock and supporting a series of piers, the openings between which are spanned by bridges of steel girders encased in concrete. The spandrel walls of these bridges form the mooring faces of the approach wall, and are protected by continuous fender strips. The six bays of the wall next to the culvert outlets are provided with curtain walls, to guard against excessive local cross currents through the wall from one forebay to the other, when one lock is emptied.

The south end of the upper approach wall is protected by a

floating timber dolphin, or fender crib, stayed by piles driven into the soft bottom. The level of the lake may vary so much that a floating fender was desirable.

The north end of the lower approach wall is protected by a timber crib resting on a concrete foundation, 25 feet (7.62 m.) above the bottom. The foundation consists of a hollow box with massive walls, back-filled with earth. Piles driven into the back-fill assist in anchoring the crib to its foundation. The concrete foundation rests on piles driven into the underlying material.

The wing walls at the south, or upper, end of the side walls are provided with arched openings, intended to break the force of waves during southerly winds, and thus to prevent a concentration of wave action in the forebay, which might otherwise be caused by the funnel shape of the approach. Similar precautions were not taken at any of the other approaches, as this was the only one where troublesome waves were to be expected.

The north wing-walls have a gravity section. The side walls of the locks are connected with the dam on the west, and the natural hill on the east, by curtain walls at right angles to the axis of the lock, one at the intake of the west wall, extending into the dam, the other at the middle gate buttress of the east wall, extending into the natural hill.

The side wall intakes are placed with their sills at elevation + 24′ .2 (+ 7.38 m.), well above the bottom of the forebay, which is at elevation + 14′ (+ 4.27 m.). Before reaching the first rising-stem valve chamber, the bottom of the culvert drops to elevation + 11′ .17 (+ 3.41 m.), which it holds all through the upper lock. The deep excavation, necessary to reach a good foundation in the forebay, made the walls there the same height as in the upper lock. It was therefore desirable to place the culvert at a low level at once, for economy in wall-section.

The culvert level drops at the lift walls between the locks, the bottom reaching elevation — 48′ 1/3 (— 14.75 m.) in the lowest lock.

The middle-wall culvert has the sill of its intakes at elevation + 24′ .2 (+ 7.38 m.), and the floor at the same level throughout the upper lock. The level drops at each lift, the floor being 10.5 and 10 feet (3.20 and 3.05 m.) above the floor of the locks. In the tailbay the floor level drops to elevation — 50′ .0 (— 15.24

m.), and the culvert discharges through three openings on each side, with sills at that level.

At Gatun, as well as at Miraflores, the lowest lock discharges into salt water. The water in the chamber, when the latter has been filled, is partially fresh. It follows that the lower gates divide waters of different densities, and that, when the lock is emptying, the pressures on the opposite faces of the gates will equalize before the water levels do. The side culverts are placed at a low elevation, the axis being 39 2/3 ft. (12.10 m.) below mean tide. In theory the flow through the culverts should cease when the unit pressures from inside and outside are equal, at the culvert level.*

Calling the density and the height of the water level above the middle of the discharge opening

δ and h, above the gates, and
δ' and h', below the gates,

then the unit pressures at the level of the discharge will be equal when

$$\delta h = \delta' h'$$

The pressures against the two faces of the gates will be equal when

$$\delta (h + a)^2 = \delta' (h' + a)^2$$

a being the distance of the middle point of the discharge above the sill of the lock. In one of these expressions h and h' enter in the first power; in the other they enter in the second power. One equation may be satisfied when the other is not. It appears therefore that the unit pressures at the discharge may equalize and flow cease, while the pressures on the two sides of the gates are still unequal.

Analysis indicated that, with the low level taken for the culverts and the great size of the gate leaves, the discharge might cease while the gates were still kept closed by a force entirely beyond the strength of any practicable opening mechanism. This residual pressure can be lessened by raising the culvert level; and a position can be found where it will reduce to zero for given levels and densities of water above and below the gates.

* For analysis of effect of difference in density of water, see Annual Report, Isthmian Canal Commission, 1911, pp. 85, et seq.

At Gatun (see Fig. 7) and at Miraflores each side culvert
at the lower end is turned upward, discharging through an opening in a horizontal plane at an elevation such that, in theory, the
total pressure at mean tide on the gates will reduce to zero at
the instant when the unit pressures from inside and outside

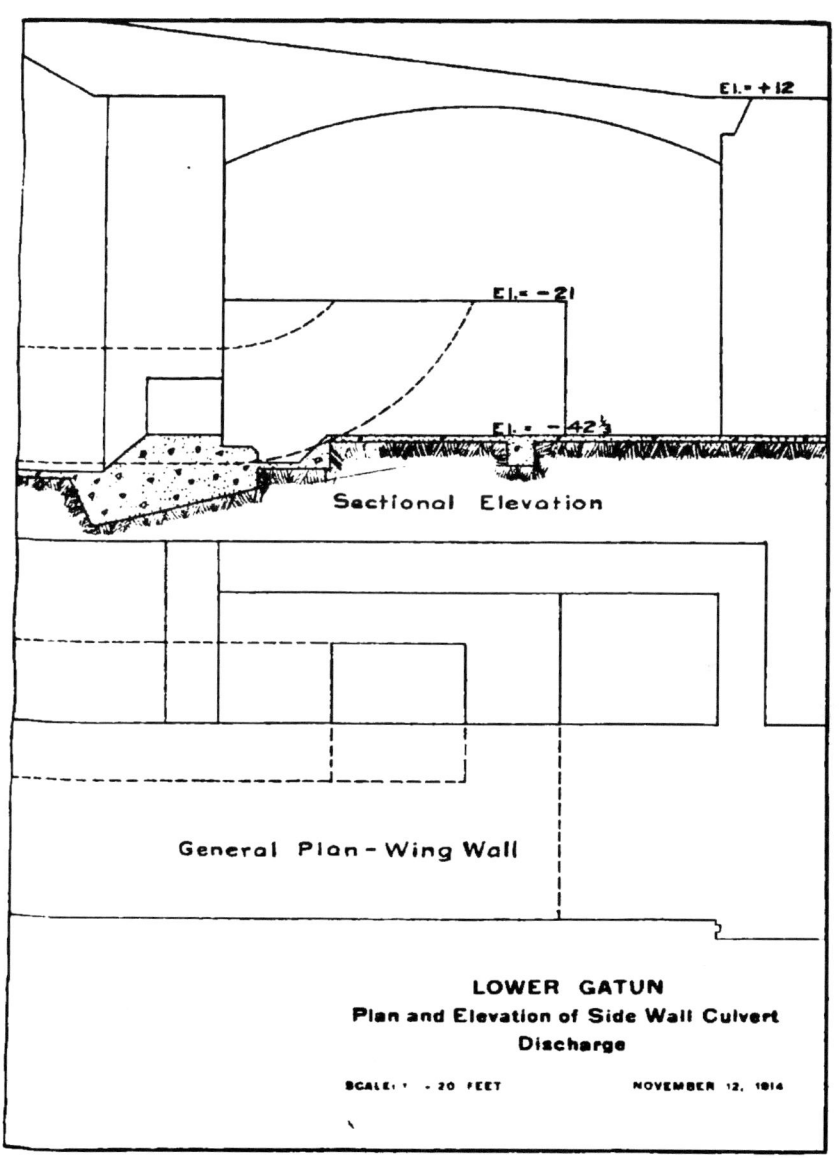

Fig. 7.

become equal at the culvert axis. This should bring the maximum direct and reverse pressures, which occur at high- and low-water respectively, well within the strength of the maneuvering gear. No precaution was taken at the outlets of the middle-wall culverts.

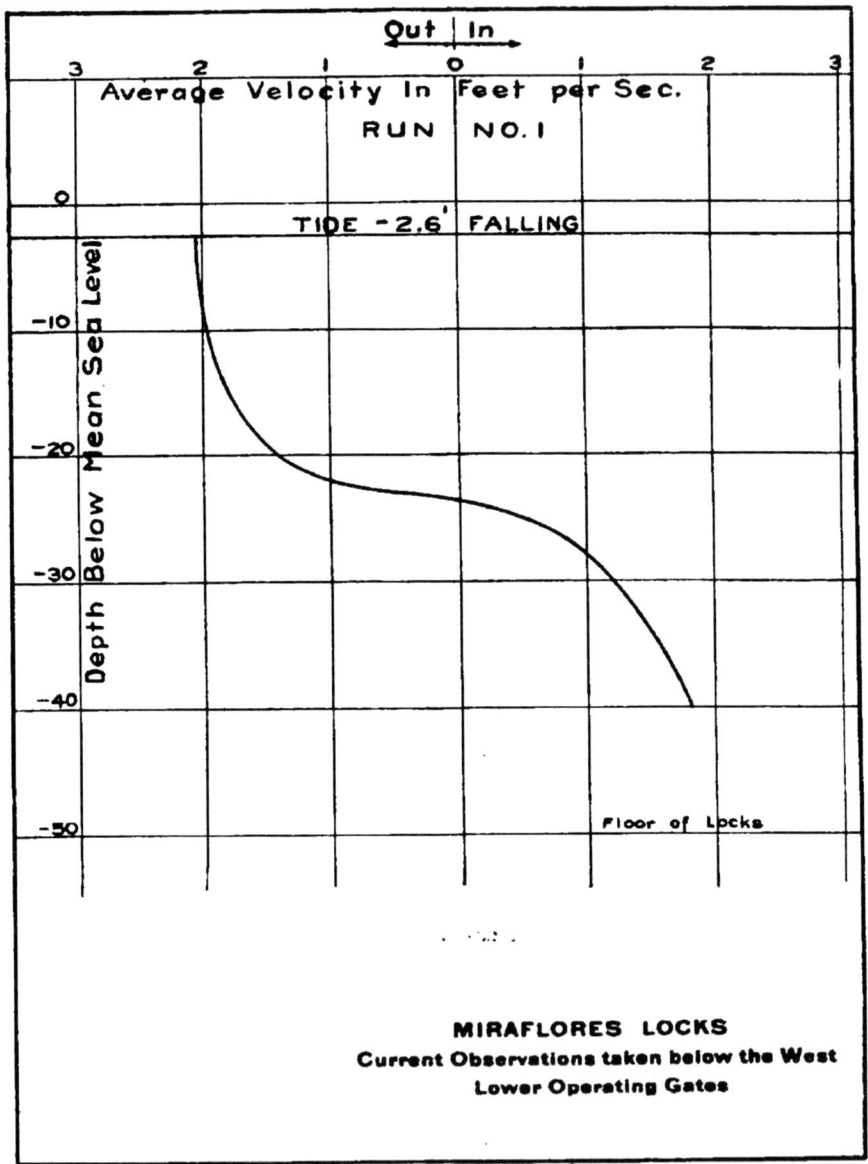

Fig. 8.

Since the locks have been in operation, no difficulty has been experienced in maneuvering the lower gates. As has been noted, (p. 23, ante.) the water continues to flow through the culvert after equalization of pressure on the gates, and the latter open spontaneously from reverse pressure, usually while the fresher water in the lock is still some inches higher than the heavier salt water outside. Whether the over-travel of the water flowing in the culverts would have been sufficient to equalize the pressure on both sides of the gates, had the discharge been placed at a lower level, as at Pedro Miguel, is a matter for speculation. We know only that the trouble, which the design was intended to obviate, is not felt; perhaps because of the form given to the outlet, and perhaps because of the over-travel of the water, which was not anticipated when the design was made.

The difference in density of the water on the two sides of the lower gates produces one marked effect which is worthy of notice. When the lower lock at Miraflores or Gatun has been equalized with the sea and the gates opened, the relatively fresh water in the lock rushes out to sea on top of the relatively salt water in the channel below. An outward surface current is generated which may last for three quarters of an hour, and reach 2 feet (0.61 m.) per second. It is accompanied by an approximately equal inward current of salt water in the lower depths. These currents interfere somewhat, although not seriously, with vessels approaching the locks from downstream soon after the gates have been opened. The direction and intensity of the currents are illustrated by Fig. 8.

A similar effect is felt when the gates separating two locks in a flight are opened, after equalizing levels. The fresher water in the upper lock moves downstream on top of the saltier water in the lower lock and creates a surface current which reaches the lower lock gates. Eventually the waters arrange themselves according to their weight, but motion continues for some time and is felt by the towing locomotives when moving a vessel from one lock to the other.

Pedro Miguel Lock, Special Features (Plate III). * The lift of the Pedro Miguel lock varies with the levels in the Gatun and Miraflores Lakes. With normal levels of + 85

* See also Fig. 1 of Mr. Whitehead's paper.

m.) and + 54 2/3 (16.67 m.), the lift is 30 1/3 feet (9.2

t it may reach 33 feet (10.06 m.) or even more, if Mira

ake be allowed to fall below its usual level when Gatu

high. The areas of the locks are the same as for the uppe

the Gatun flight. The dimensions and elevations of th

t parts are shown on Plate III.

e foundation is on rock throughout, but the rock varies ir

er and hardness. A dyke of trap-rock extended diagon

:ough the lock-pit, being within the limits of the middl

m the upper gates nearly to the safety gates at the lowe

the lock. A core of this, about 40 feet (12.19 m.) thick

t unexcavated, from El. + 10 ft. (+ 3.05 m.), the floo

tion, to about El. + 23.2 ft. (+ 7.07 m.), one foot (0.3

ow the floor of the middle culvert. This core was con

sound enough to incorporate in the middle wall as par

nass below the culvert, and a considerable saving in exca

and concrete was thus effected. Neither at Gatun no

res was the rock considered sound enough to warran

action.

e lock walls rest, in part, on this rock, where they cros

:e, but are founded on an argillaceous sandstone for th

part of their length. This stone, while perishable whei

l to the air, appears to be permanent when covered witl

r concrete, and is of ample strength for its loads.

e bed being firm, no special preparation of foundation o

hening of floors was deemed necessary. The rock wa

d for the lateral culverts, and the floor was made one foo

ierced with weepholes about 10 ft. (3.05 m.) apart.

e middle approach walls rest on argillaceous sandstone

per wall was made of reinforced concrete of cellular con

m, back-filled with any obtainable excavated material. I

feet (365.8 m.) in length, measured from a point oppo

angle of the splay of the guide wall. The lower approacl

as made of massive construction for about one thousanc

04.8 m.), comprising two walls of gravity section, betweer

back-fill was placed, using any convenient material. The

der, about two hundred feet (61.0 m.), could not be buil

he first part was without interrupting certain railroad

nications which it was necessary to retain. The wall was

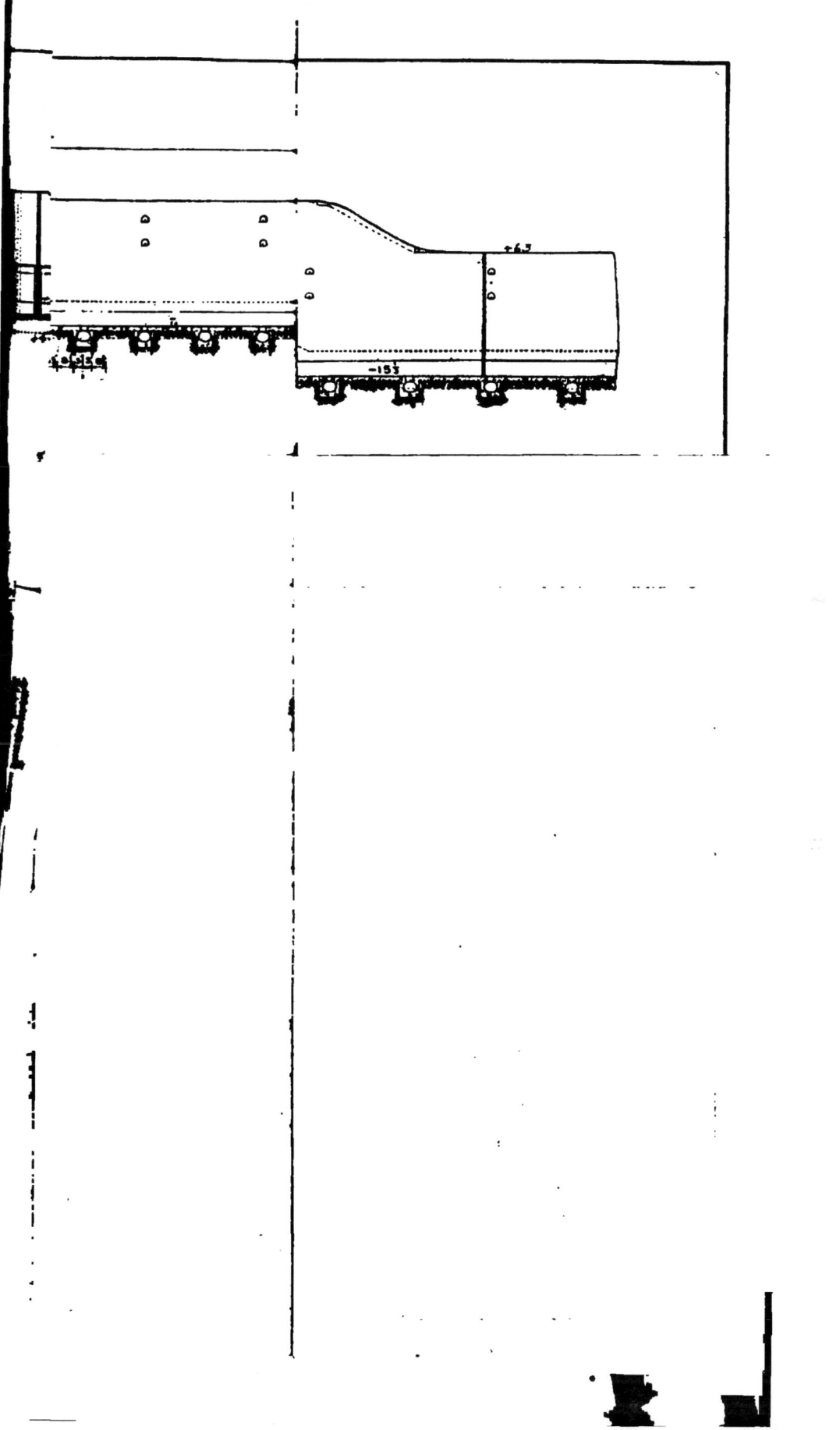

not completed until after the main part of the masonry; and the added length was made of reinforced concrete, cellular in construction and back-filled. As completed, the wall is 1200 feet (365.8 m.) long, measured from a point opposite the angle of splay of the wing wall. Both north and south approach walls have two fender strips along the faces, and are guarded at the ends by floating timber fenders held in place by piles. As it was not practicable to drive piles into the rock on which the wall is founded, a reinforced concrete box or caisson was constructed at the end of the wall. This was made twenty feet (6.10 m.) high above the bottom, and was back-filled with earth into which the piles for the fender are driven.

The part of the lock walls lying above the first rising-stem valve chamber is founded at floor level. At the valve chambers, the foundation must be lowered in order to give sufficient headroom for the rising-stem valve and its mechanism. This required trenching in the foundation for the walls, from just above the valve chambers to the upper miter sill. The culvert consequently takes two drops from the intake to the chamber, one just above the valve chambers and the other at the lift-wall. It continues horizontal, with lowest line at El. $+ 8.5$ ($+ 2.59$ m.), and discharges in prolongation of its length into a bay at the lower end of the wall, the boundary walls of which form a quadrant of a circle in plan. The discharge is baffled and turned across the tailbay by the curved wall. The discharge bay is spanned by an inclined arch, in continuation of a similar one which spans the recess for the lower guard gate. These sloping bridges were introduced in order to carry the towing locomotives over the lift from the lower to the higher level.

The bottom of the middle-wall culvert continues horizontal at El. $+ 24.2$ ft. ($+ 7.38$ m.) from the upper valve chamber to the lower gates, where it drops to El. $+ 5.375$ ft. ($+ 1.64$ m.). The discharge is through three openings on each side, perpendicularly to the axis of the locks.

The Pedro Miguel Lock forms the south end of the Culebra Cut, which is the narrowest part of the canal, being 300 feet (91.44 m.) wide at the bottom. The net section of the Cut, with the theoretical slopes, and with lake level at El. $+ 85.00$ ft. ($+ 25.91$ m.), would contain 13,601.5 sq. ft. (1263 sq. met.).

The valves when opened draw at a maximum rate of about 13,000 sec. ft. (1207 met. per sec.), which would give a current of about 1 ft. per sec. (0.305 met. per sec.) in the Cut, if the water were supplied as fast as drawn. The conditions would be favorable for setting up surges in the Cut which might give

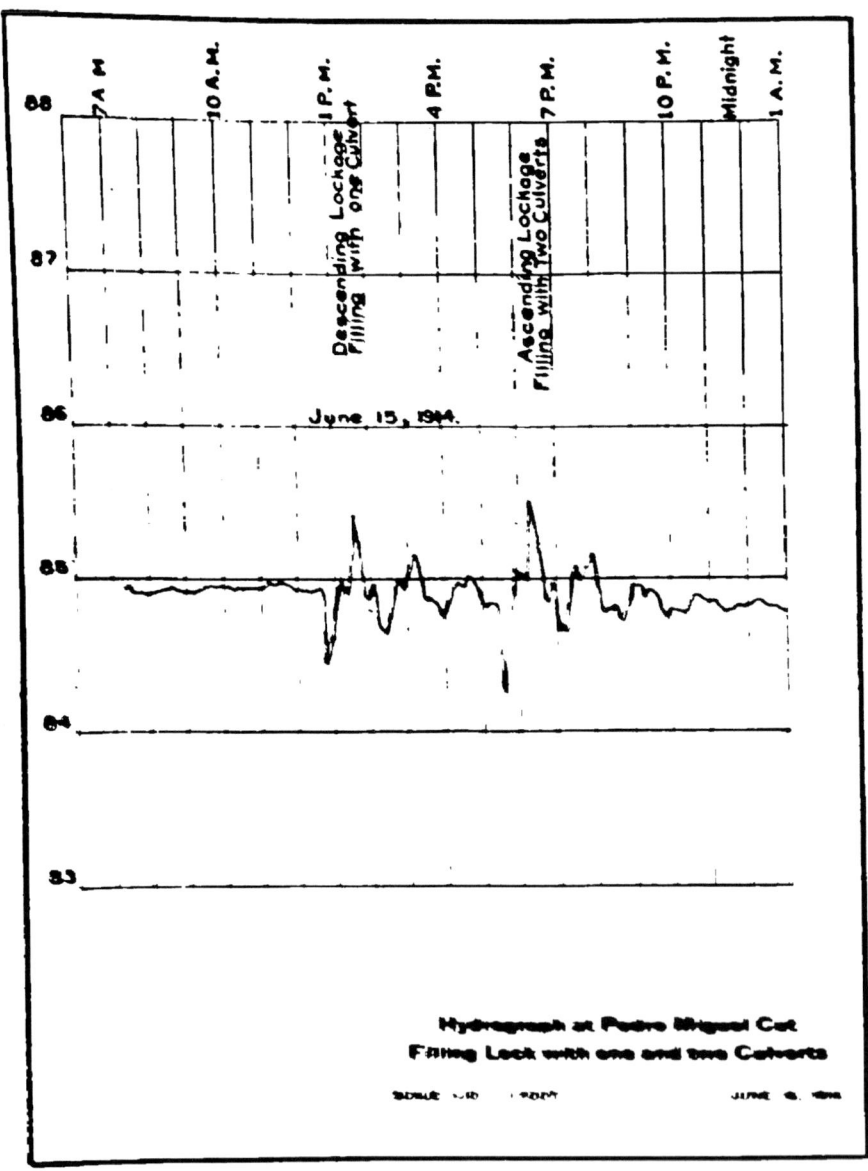

Fig. 3.

trouble. In the effort to guard against these, the Canal just above the lock was made 600 ft. (182.88 m.) wide, reducing to 300 ft. (91.44 m.) at a point about 3400 ft. (1036 m.) north of the upper guard gates. A basin was thus formed from which the first draft required for filling the locks is supplied.

Figure 9 is a hydrograph, taken in the basin, showing the oscillation of the water when the lock is filled through one culvert and through two culverts, the usual times of filling under these conditions being about 13.5 minutes and about 8 minutes respectively. The total vertical oscillation measures about 1.0 ft. (0.305 m.) in the former, and 1.25 ft. (0.380 m.) in the latter case. This is of small moment. The effect recurs for hours, and is felt at the observation station at Juan Mina, on the Chagres, four miles (6.44 kilom.) above Gamboa and about 13 miles (20.92 kilom.) from the lock, and outside the Culebra Cut. The indication on the hydrograph there is made about 45 minutes after the filling valves are opened at Pedro Miguel. The lockage is felt at Gamboa, through 9 miles (14.49 kilom.) of practically still water, in 20 minutes. The effect appears to take 25 minutes more to travel 4 miles (6.44 kilom.) against the current of the Chagres River.

The rise in the forebay has been observed some inches higher than that shown on the hydrograph, which is taken outside the forebay. This increase is probably due to the funnel effect of the wing walls.

The north guide or wing walls at Pedro Miguel are of massive construction and gravity section. The one on the west side has at its north end a return or curtain wall extending into the substance of the dam, and forming the connection on that side. On the east side a similar return or curtain wall forms the connection with the natural hill.

The wing walls at the south end of the lock are made of reinforced concrete resting on rock.

Miraflores Locks, Special Features (Plate IV): The pool above Miraflores lock flight has its normal level 54 2/3 ft. (16.67 m.) above mean tide. The lower pool has a tidal oscillation which may reach a maximum assumed at 20 feet (6.10 m.). The lift of the lock flight may therefore vary from 44 2/3 to 64 2/3 ft. (13.62 to 19.72 m.).

The tidal oscillation complicated the design seriously. Obvious considerations made it desirable, if not necessary, that the main features of the locks should be the same as elsewhere on the canal, and practically forced the adoption of an upper lock with maximum area in plan of 134,000 sq. ft. (12,450 sq. met.). A lower lock of the adopted horizontal dimensions, built with walls high enough to accommodate the prism of lift of the upper lock at low tide, would have its walls and gates flooded by that prism at high tide; while, if built to accommodate the prism of lift at high tide, the resulting height of the gates and walls would have been 87.75 ft. (26.746 m.) above sill level. It was not desired to undertake the construction of gates so much larger than those in the other locks; while the added height of the walls meant additional direct expense, due not only to the height, but also to the accompanying necessity for increasing the thickness of the middle wall as well, an increase which would have extended through the entire lock flight. The possibility of gaining sufficient capacity without raising the walls, by adding to the length of the lower lock, was considered, but the idea was abandoned on account of expense. The decision finally reached was to build the lower lock of the same dimensions as at Gatun, viz., 1085 by 110 ft. (330.71 by 33.53 m.), with walls of height sufficient to retain safely the prism of the 550-ft. (167.7 m.) upper lock at all stages of tide, and of the 900-ft. (274.3 m.) lock at mean tide. This entails wasting water from the 900-ft. (274.3 m.) lock at stages above mean tide, or, to be accurate, above + 0.32 (+ 0.09 m.), and from the 1000-ft. (304.8 m.) lock at stages above — 2.15 ft. (— 0.66 m.). To accomplish even this, the walls and gates had to be built 82 ft. (24.99 m.) high above sill level. To avoid risk of flooding from the 550-ft. (167.4 m.) lock through possible carelessness in operation, it was deemed advisable to leave out the intermediate gates of the lower lock. The area of the lower lock in plan is 120,000 sq. ft. (11,148 sq. met.). The dimensions and elevations are given on Plate IV.

With Miraflores Lake at El. + 55 ft. (+ 16.76 m.), and sea at low-level of — 10 ft. (— 3.05 m.), the lifts are:

Lock	1000 ft.	900 ft.	550 ft.
Upper	30.71	32.10	38.52
Lower	34.29	32.90	26.48

or, in metric units:

Lock	304.8	274.3	167.4 met.
Upper	9.36	9.79	11.74
Lower	10.45	10.03	8.07

The foundation is on rock of varying quality, mainly argillaceous sandstone, containing a good deal of lime in places. Probably none of the rock would last well if exposed to the air, but some was firm and hard when first uncovered, and of sufficiently good character to be used in masses in the thicker portions of the floor, although not in the walls. Some of the rock was poor and decomposed rapidly, unless promptly covered with concrete after exposure. Even the poorest variety proved upon test to be amply strong to carry its load.

The lock walls and the lower approach and wing walls rest on rock directly. The upper approach wall is cellular in construction and founded on cylindrical caissons of reinforced concrete, sunk to rock and filled with concrete. The upper wing walls are of reinforced concrete founded on wooden piles driven to rock.

The lower approach and wing walls are of massive construction founded on rock.

The entrances to the side-wall culverts are at El. — 9.13 ft. (— 2.81 m.), and the bottom line of the culverts continues at that elevation throughout the forebay, dropping at the upper miter wall to El. — 22.83 ft. (— 6.96 m.) in the upper lock and — 53.5 ft. (— 16.31 m.) in the lower lock.

For the same reason as at Gatun, the side culverts are turned up at the outlets and discharge through openings in a horizontal plane at El. — 25.0 ft. (— 7.62 m.).

The entrance to the middle-wall culvert in the forebay has the sill at El. — 9.13 ft. (— 2.81 m.). The bottom of the culvert continues at this elevation throughout the forebay and upper lock. It drops to El. — 35.8 ft. (— 10.91 m.) in the lower lock, and drops again below the lower gates to El. — 41.4 ft. (— 12.62 m.), the elevation of the sill of the discharge openings.

The upper end of the middle approach wall is protected by a timber crib or dolphin secured to piles driven into the lake bed.

The lower end of the middle approach wall is protected by a timber crib resting on a concrete foundation, which is similar to that at the lower end of the Gatun flight, except that it rests on rock instead of piles.

The west side wall of the locks is connected with the dam by a core wall of concrete, extending back at right angles to the axis of the lock, and behind the upper gate buttress. The east side wall is connected with the spillway dam by a return wall above the culvert intake.

The effect of the difference in density of the water above and below the lock has been mentioned in describing the Gatun flight. An effect which is more noticeable at Miraflores than Gatun is the manner in which the salt water climbs up the lock flight and appears in the lake above, the bottom of which is above high tide. In diluted form some is brought in every time the upper gates are opened; and by October, 1914, it had contaminated the lake seriously, the lower layers of water showing 1000 or more parts of chlorine to one million. No effect has been noticeable in the larger Gatun Lake, but doubtless the salt water is present in the lower strata.

DESIGN OF DAMS.

The general design of the dams will be treated briefly, as the papers written by the Division Engineers in charge of the construction cover the important features at length.

Gatun Dam.

Location: The suggestion that Gatun be chosen as the site for the dam forming the northern barrier of the summit level was made even before the French began their work on the sea-level plan. In 1879, Mr. Ashbel P. Welch,* in discussing interoceanic canal projects, referred to the possibility of closing the Chagres valley by a dam at Gatun "such as was advocated by Mr. C. D. Ward"; and, in 1904, Mr. C. D. Ward brought the project up again tentatively in a paper presented at a meeting of the American Society of Civil Engineers.† The site was also advocated by Major C. E. Gillette, in a plan presented by him before the International Board of Consulting Engineers in 1905; possibly others also favored it before its adoption; but the ench selected Bohio as the site for their main dam, when the

---

* Transactions, Am. Soc. C. E., 1879, Vol. VIII, p. 311.
† Transactions, Am. Soc. C. E., 1904, Vol. LIII, p. 36.

change was made from the plans of the first French Canal Company, although not intending that the lake to be formed should necessarily be the summit level. The International Board of Consulting Engineers selected, for comparison with its proposed sea-level plan, a project involving a dam at Gatun with a summit level 60 feet (18.29 m.) above mean tide, and the minority of that Board in its report, which was finally adopted, fixed the location at that place.

Plan of Minority of Board of 1906: The cross section proposed in the minority report is shown on Plate XIII, Fig. 1 accompanying the article by Gen. Sibert. The natural surface of the ground at the site of the dam was generally low, say, from 8 to 10 feet (2.43 to 3.05 m.) above mean tide. The line of the dam crosses two deep gorges, in which the rock is found at a depth of 200 and 260 feet (60.96 and 79.25 m.) respectively, the overlying material being a clayey marine deposit, soft and easily moved, but apparently impervious to water. The very flat section given to the dam in all the designs, was adopted because of the character of the underlying material, which made it necessary to distribute the weight over a wide base, and avoid any abrupt change in the unit load.

The section recommended in the report of the minority of the Board of 1906 was changed somewhat before beginning construction, as the result of preliminary study, the upstream slopes being made more gentle.

A hill on the eastern side of the valley, in which the lock flight is built, forms one abutment of the dam. Near the middle of the length another hill was found, which gave good foundation for the masonry of the spillway. Beyond the spillway were several small hills which were incorporated in the body of the dam, which abuts on the west against the high hills forming the western edge of the Chagres valley.

The great depth of soft material overlying the rock, in the gorges which the dam must cross, made it out of the question to carry down to the rock any water-tight core or diaphragm. The plans upon which work began in 1907 contemplated a central cut-off of wooden sheet piling, at the places where the dam crosses the then-existing river channels.

The first work consisted in dumping two embankments, or

toes, of hard rock, parallel to each other and 1200 feet (365.8 m.) apart; the intention being to raise the upstream toe to El. + 60 ft. (+ 18.29 m.), and the downstream toe to El. + 30 ft. (+ 9.14 m.). The dam was connected with the natural surface by clearing the bed and digging a trench or muck ditch in the soft material. Where the trench crossed the hills in the western part of the dam, the excavation was carried to the natural rock.

Consulting Board of 1909: A slip which occurred in 1908 in the south toe caused the appointment of a second Board of Consulting Engineers, who visited the Isthmus in 1909, and recommended a change in the section* of the dam, placing the crest at El. + 115 ft. (+ 35.05 m). The upstream surface was to have a paving of stone 10 feet (3.05 m.) thick, and the top above El. + 100 ft. (+ 30.48 m.) was to be finished to El. + 115 ft. (+ 35.05 m.) with rock. The sheet piling was omitted.

Before the arrival of the Board on the Isthmus, the Division Engineer of the Atlantic Division had brought up the question of reducing the height of the dam, placing the crest at El. + 105 ft. (+ 32.0 m.), instead of + 135 ft. (+ 41.15 m.), as originally proposed. His views were before the Board when the report in favor of a crest at El. + 115 ft. (+35.05 m.) was made.

On the section proposed by the Consulting Board, the minimum bottom width of the hydraulic fill was placed at 760 feet (231.7 m.), by scale. It sloped to a width of 100 ft. (30.5 m.) at El. + 100 ft. (+ 30.5 m.). The section of the dam outside the hydraulic fill was to be of the "cheapest filling available", rock 15 ft. (4.57 m.) thick being prescribed for the upstream surface and a layer of rock being preferred for the downstream surface. As construction proceeded in accordance with the general plan above outlined, it became manifest that the cheapest filling available was the material furnished by the dredges; and that, to follow the plan exactly, might result in having the greater part of the dam of hydraulic material, with an insufficient amount of dry fill to hold it in place, especially if it should not consolidate promptly. Accordingly, orders were given to increase the amount of dry fill, lessening, if necessary, the hydraulic fill, in order to secure, as outside limits of the latter,

---

* See Fig. 2 of Plate XIV accompanying article by W. L. Sibert.

banks of material against which the pressure of the wet fill before its consolidation would act downward rather than upward.

In the process of construction, dredged material was pumped between the ridges of hard rock, and dry material was dumped from them, inward, on top of the dredged material. Various movements of the substance of the dam indicated the advisability of flattening the slopes near the west end, and of omitting the change in slope at El. + 90 ft. (+ 27.43 m.), continuing the slopes of 1 on 7.67 and 1 on 8 to the top of the dam. The same movements served also as evidence that the great localized weight of the stone, proposed for the upstream surface and the top of the dam, in the section recommended by the last Board of Consulting Engineers, might prove objectionable, by causing movements in the dam or in the soft material underlying it. Accordingly, the armor on the upstream slope was reduced to three feet (0.92 m.) in thickness of hard rock, laid on a bed of spalls, and extending from El. + 74.0 ft. (+ 22.55 m.) to El. + 92.0 ft. (+ 28.04 m.) ; and the rock fill on top of the dam was omitted altogether. Dry material was dumped to form the exterior masses and to drive the more plastic dredged material toward the center and to raise its surface level at the same time. Finally, when the surface of the dredged material was raised nearly to the required height, the distance between the banks of dry fill was about 25 feet (7.62 m.). The top of the core was then finished with red clay, well puddled. A part of the north slope of the dam, east of the spillway, was also modified from the original plan, by omitting the change in slope at El. + 60 ft. (+ 18.29 m.), and carrying a uniform slope of about 1 on 11.11 from El. + 30 ft. (+ 9.15 m.), to the top of the dam.

The general plan and typical cross sections of the dam as finally constructed, are shown on Plate I accompanying Gen. Sibert's paper* and Plate V. It will be noted that effort has been made to avoid sudden changes in the loading on the soft foundation or lower tiers of the dam itself, such as would be occasioned by abruptly steepening the slopes, or by local masses

---

* Construction of Gatun Locks, Dam and Spillway by Brig. Gen. W. L. Sibert.

of heavy material; and to maintain a practically uniform rate of increase in loading from the edge toward the middle of the base.

The dam is about 1½ miles (2.40 km.) long and about 2300 ft. (701.1 m.) wide at the widest part of the base.

The total amount of material in the dam is 22,958,069 cu. yds. (17,552,565 m³), of which 12,229,104 cu. yds. (9,349,261 m³) is dry fill, and the remainder hydraulic fill.

Up to December, 1914, when this paper was written, and when the lake had been standing at full height of from + 85 to + 87 feet (+ 25.91 to + 26.52 m.) above mean tide for one year, the dam, after its completion, had shown no movement beyond that attributable to consolidation; and there had been no appearance of leakage or underflow.

Pedro Miguel Dam.

Plan: The dam at Pedro Miguel is of earth and rock, and forms, with the lock, the southern barrier which closes the old valley of the Rio Grande and restrains the Gatun Lake, or summit, level of the Canal. The design was prepared in the office of the Division Engineer of the Pacific Division, and is illustrated in his article.* The crest of the dam is 20 feet (6.10 m.) above the normal water surface of the summit level. The material was obtained from the excavation of the lock pit and prisms above and below, and was placed by dumping, the core being of selected clay, well puddled.

Foundation: The foundation was, in general, on reasonably hard and impervious material, and required no preparation beyond clearing, except at the crossing of the old bed of the Rio Grande, where a permeable stratum of gravel was found immediately over the rock. This required excavating a muck ditch to the rock for about 300 feet (91.4 m.), the ditch being afterward re-filled with puddled clay.

The dam extends from the upper west wing-wall of the lock—to which it is well connected—to a hill to the northward, and forms practically an extension of the west wall of the lock. It is about 1400 feet (426.7 m.) long, and contains 699,518 cu. yds. (534,800 m³) of material. There is no need for a spillway

---

* Methods of Construction of the Locks, Dams and Regulating Works of the Pacific Division, by S. B. Williamson, Plate XI.

connected with the Pedro Miguel dam, as the summit level can be regulated by the Gatun spillway.

The barrier to the east of the lock is formed by the core wall described in connection with the lock, (page 40 ante.).

Miraflores Dam.

Plan: The lock and dams at Miraflores form a barrier closing the lower Rio Grande valley and retaining the intermediate level of Miraflores Lake, which normally stands at El. + 54 2/3 ft. (+ 16.67 m.). The lake receives directly the flow of the Cocoli, Pedro Miguel, Caimitillo and Cameron rivers, all small streams formerly tributary to the Rio Grande. In the rainy seasons the discharge of these streams may be considerable, but in the dry season it reduces to a small amount, not sufficient to make up for the evaporation from the lake surface and the small leakage through the locks and over the spillway. The main supply of the lake then is the water let down from the summit level when passing vessels through Pedro Miguel lock. The area of the small lake is only 1.65 sq. miles (4.27 km²). One full prism of lift will raise or lower its surface 0.12 ft. (0.037 m.) from its normal level.

The dam at Miraflores locks is in two parts, a masonry dam with spillway, east of the locks, and an earth dam west of the locks. The design for the former will be mentioned later. The design for the latter was prepared in the office of the Division Engineer of the Pacific Division and is illustrated on Plate XII, accompanying his article.*

West Dam: The dam is connected with the west lock wall at the buttress of the upper, or north, gate, and runs nearly south and nearly parallel to the lock wall against which it abuts, being connected with the latter by a concrete core wall reaching to rock. It was made by pumping material, excavated by dredges from the lock pit and channel below the locks, between dumps of spoil excavated in the dry from the lock pit and channel above. It contains 1,758,423 cu. yds. of dry material and about 630,000 cu. yds. of hydraulic fill.

The crest of the dam is at El. + 70 ft. (+ 21.34 m.), or about 15 ft. (4.57 m.) above the normal level of Miraflores Lake.

_____

* Methods of Construction of the Locks, Dams and Regulating Works of the Pacific Division, by S. B. Williamson.

It is about 2700 feet (823.0 m.) long, measured from the connection with the lock wall to the abutment at Cocoli Hill. The foundation is compact and impervious, except where it crosses the bed of the Cocoli. Here a muck ditch 20 feet (6.10 m.) wide was carried down to rock and filled with puddle. Elsewhere the ditch was made 12 feet (3.66 m.) wide and served to bond the hydraulic fill of the dam with the natural surface.

GENERAL DESIGN OF SPILLWAYS.

Gatun Spillway.

Considerations Governing Design: The object of the spillway at Gatun is to regulate the level of the lake and permit the passage of floods without injury to the dam or locks. As the crest of the dam is 12 feet (3.66 m.) above the terreplein of the upper locks at Gatun and of the Pedro Miguel lock, it is clear that the destructive effect of a flood would be felt first in the overflow and washing out of the back-fill of the locks; and this would occur at any stage above El. + 92 ft. (+ 28.04 m.). Furthermore, minor injury to the operating mechanism would be liable to occur at a lower level, since water can enter the machinery chamber of the upper guard gates at stage 3½ feet (1.07 m.) below the coping. It appears, therefore, that the spillway at Gatun should be of dimensions such that the lake can be kept at all times below the level of + 92 ft. (+ 28.04 m.), and preferably below the level + 88.5 ft. (+ 26.97 m.).

Before 1907, estimates of the flood discharge of the Chagres River were based on records of observations taken at Bohio, Alhajuela and elsewhere. Until the closing of the Chagres River at Gatun, actual measurements of the discharge at that place were not satisfactory, owing to the sluggish flow and the influence of the tide. The early measurements indicated that the probable value of the discharge at Gatun was 1.62 times that observed at Bohio. Applying this relation to the measurements taken at Bohio during the flood of 1906 (the greatest about which authentic records are available), a maximum momentary discharge at Gatun results as 108,026 x 1.62 = 175,000 sec-ft. (4955 m³ per sec.); the maximum average discharge for 33 consecutive hours as 84,956 x 1.62 = 137,600 sec-ft. (3896 m³ per sec.); and the maximum average discharge for 48 consecutive hours as 74,371 x 1.62 = 120,500 sec-ft. (3412 m³ per sec.).

The spillway was designed to pass 154,000 sec-ft. (4360 m⁸ per sec.) when the lake is at El. + 87 ft. (+ 26.52 m.).   Assuming the maximum known momentary discharge, the lake would be required to store 21,000 sec-ft. (594 m³ per sec.) during its continuance, which could only be a matter of a few hours.   At El. + 87 ft. (+ 26.52 m.) the lake had an area of 167.4 sq. miles (433.5 km²).   The addition of 21,000 sec-ft. (594 m³ per sec.) would take nearly 50 hours to raise the level of the lake one foot (0.31 m.).   As the maximum calculated discharge for 48 hours is only 120,500 sec-ft. (3412 m³ per sec.), or less than the discharge of the spillway at lake elevation + 87 ft. (+ 26.52 m.), it is thought that the assumed capacity is ample to regulate all floods.

An open spillway, unprovided with regulating works, would require a very great length to discharge the maximum flood before the level of the lake should rise considerably, unless the sill should be placed at a low elevation, to which the level of the lake would itself fall in time of great drought.   Such a plan would necessarily involve either an abnormally long crest or a considerable fluctuation in lake level.   A shorter spillway, with regulating gates, was thought preferable.

The minority of the Board of Consulting Engineers, in 1906, recommended a straight crest for the spillway, with 21 bays, each 30 feet (9.14 m.) wide in the clear, closed by regulating gates.   With the piers, the crest was to be 790 feet (240.8 m.) long.   The water flowing over the crest was to be guided by wing walls into the discharge channel 160 feet (48.77 m.) wide.

Adopted Design: The general design of the spillway as finally adopted is shown on Plates I and II of Mr. Sherman's article.*   The body of the dam and the floor and walls are of concrete, the regulating gates of steel.   The necessary development of crest is obtained by throwing the trace of the dam into the arc of a circle.   By this form the discharge over the crest is directed toward the center, where the energy of the converging streams will partially neutralize itself.   To assist the neutralization, two rows of baffle piers are placed below the dam.   The design is described more fully in another paper.*

---

* "The Design of the Spillways of the Panama Canal", by E. C. Sherman.

The crest of the dam is at El. + 69 (+ 21.03 m.), or 16 ft. (4.88 m.) below normal lake level of + 85.0 ft. (+ 25.91 m.). Its developed length over-all between abutments is 807.96 ft. (246.3 m.), of which 630 ft. (192.0 m.) is available for discharge. It is divided in 14 bays, each 45 ft. (13.72 m.) wide in the clear, and closed by a Stoney gate, counterweighted and raised by lifting mechanism located in the tunnel in the body of the dam. The gates are 19 ft. (5.79 m.) high, and, when fully raised, have their bottoms at El. + 92 ft. (+ 28.04 m.). Taking into consideration the slope which the water assumes in approaching to flow over the crest, the distance from the bottom of the gate to the surface of the stream flowing under it is 9.15 ft. (2.82 m.) when the lake level is at El. + 86.67 ft. (+ 26.42 m.). This has thus far proved ample for the passage of all drift. The current caused by opening the spillway is imperceptible at a short distance, and the motion of drift is determined usually by the wind.

The location of the spillway is in a natural hill about midway of the length of the dam, where the rock came close to the surface. The material was first excavated and the walls and floor of the channel built, the latter sloping from a sill at El. + 10 ft. (+ 3.05 m.), at the upper end, to El. + 2.2 ft. (+ 0.67 m.) at the lower end. Small piers, to be incorporated afterward in the body of the dam, were built close enough to form supports for coffer beams, under the shelter of which the concrete could be placed when the water should flow over the sill. The discharge of the weir was taken through the spillway after the construction of the dam had closed the channels previously existing; the flow at first was between the coffer piers and later through one small and three large culverts, left for this purpose at a low level. These culverts were closed by valves precisely like the lock valves, and were of great value in regulating the lake level during construction. Finally, after completion of the spillway dam, the culverts were bulkheaded, the valves removed, and the openings filled permanently with concrete.

Action of Water: On December 30, 1913, and January 2–6, 1914, the discharge was measured several times with different gates open, the number raised being seven and two. The average discharge per gate was 9740 sec-ft. (275.7 m³ per sec.), the corresponding lake level being + 84.41 ft. (+ 25.73 m.). This average discharge corresponds to a value of C = 3.58 in the Francis formula, neglecting end contraction, which is somewhat more favorable than was assumed in the calculations. If the conditions do not change, the spillway discharge with lake at El. + 87.0 ft. (+ 26.52 m.) should be 12,300 sec-ft. (348.3 m³ per sec.) per bay, instead of 11,000 sec. ft. (311.5 m³ per sec.) as assumed. The gates operate smoothly and reliably, being controlled from the electric generating station located below the spillway. It takes approximately ten minutes to raise a gate.

Fig. 10. Gatun Spillway, One Gate Raised.

When one or two gates near one end of the dam are opened, there is a tendency to throw spray over the opposite wall, near the angle of the channel and guide wall, in such quantities as to produce washing of the fill back of the walls and of the ground surrounding the generating station. This tendency disappears when the discharge is balanced by opening corresponding gates near the other abutment.

The effect of the baffle piers and of the convergence of flow is to arrest the velocity which the water has acquired in flowing over the dam, and to make the stream deepen and assume slope to carry it through the spillway channel. When the gates are raised, a pool forms between the piers and the foot of the dam, which tends to check the flow, to some extent, before it reaches the piers themselves. The pool becomes deeper as more gates are raised. It thus happens that when only one gate is raised the water, on striking the baffle piers, is thrown higher in the air than when more gates are open. (See Figs. 10 and 11.)

After a year of use the baffle piers, which are armored on the upstream face and for part of their width on the sides and

Fig. 11.   Gatun Spillway, Seven Gates Raised.

top, show signs of erosion, which will be repaired in the dry season, when the spillway can be kept closed for a time.

The leakage through the spillway gates is small. It was carefully measured by collecting the entire flow, by a light earth dam, into one narrow channel, where it passed over a weir. The result showed leakage through the fourteen gates varying from 1.34 sec-ft. (0.0379 m³ per sec.) at 7 a.m. to 7.90 sec-ft. (0.2237 m³ per sec.) at 4 p.m., after the heat of the sun had had its full effect on the steel. The average leakage for a period of 49 hours was 3.65 sec-ft. (0.1033 m³ per sec.), or about 0.25 sec-ft. (0.00071 m³ per sec.) per gate. The lake was at normal elevation of + 85 ft. (+ 25.91 m.) during the observations.

The spillway was finished in October, 1913.

Miraflores Spillway.

The determining consideration in the design of the Miraflores spillway was the possibility of an accident at Pedro Miguel lock which should allow free flow, through one of the lock chambers, from the Gatun Lake level into Miraflores Lake. The flow in such a case has been calculated by different computers, with results varying from 85,000 to 125,000 sec-ft. (2407 to 3539 m³ per sec.). If the discharge be taken at 100,000 sec-ft. (2830 m³ per sec.), it would raise Miraflores Lake level one foot (0.31 m.) in 5 1/3 minutes. The lock terreplein at Miraflores would be flooded in twenty-five minutes, if the lake were at normal level when the accident occurred; and great damage would probably result before the emergency dam at Pedro Miguel could be closed and the flow stopped. For this reason, it was thought justifiable to provide a spillway capacity which, when assisted by the lock culverts, would carry off the flow due to such an accident, assuming the volume at 100,000 sec-ft. (2830 m³ per sec.). This discharge is many times larger than would be necessary for the sole purpose of regulating natural floods in Miraflores Lake.

Adopted Design: Obviously it was desirable to adopt the same design for the gates and moving parts as at Gatun. A spillway of eight bays 45 feet (13.72 m.) in the clear, was therefore assumed, since each bay is designed to give a flow of 11,000 sec-ft. (311 m³ per sec.) when the lake is 18 feet (5.49 m.) above the crest of the dam. The lock culverts can be counted on for, say, 25,000 sec-ft. (708 m³ per sec.).

The location first investigated was in the hills to the west of the main dam, and some little distance from the lock. It was finally determined, however, to place it in the immediate vicinity of the lock, to constitute the east dam which would have to be built to close the gap between the locks and hills bounding the valley on the east. As this gap was wider than is necessary for a spillway, a part of it 134 ft. (40.90 m.) wide, between the lock masonry and the west abutment of the spillway dam, is closed by a cut-off wall built up from the rock. The spillway closes the greater part of the gap, and is laid out with its crest straight in plan, and 432 feet (131.68 m.) long. A second cut-off wall is carried from the east end of the spillway dam to an impermeable stratum in the hill against which it abuts. The design adopted is shown on Plates IV and V of Mr. Sherman's paper.

The leakage at the spillway is apparently about the same per gate as at Gatun.

The work was finished in 1914.

Appended is a statement of the Division cost of certain individual items of the work. The figures given include the overhead charges of the construction divisions, but not of the central administrative office. Unless otherwise noted, they give the cost of the different items installed and ready for work.

Total Division Cost of Certain Items of Locks, Dams and Spillways.

Gatun Locks—complete	$28,607,286.51
Pedro Miguel Locks—complete	12,433,768.81
Miraflores Locks—complete	17,975,260.41
Gatun Dam, except spillway	7,570,228.03
Gatun Spillway—complete	3,159,204.49
Pedro Miguel Dam	341,627.72
Miraflores Dam, except spillway	905,032.29
Miraflores Spillway—complete	992,015.73
Lock gates (most of the expense of fixed iron work not included), 46*	6,194,846.17
Spillway gates, 22	126,774.51
Emergency dams (including operating machinery), 6	2,453,430.88
Chain fenders and machines, 24 and 48	1,021,846.37
Lock irons†	2,106,589.55
Towing-track system, except locomotives	1,400,627.08

Electrical distribution system:

Transformer rooms, high-tension switch chambers, power cables, lighting cables and fixtures	$1,317,562.50	
Lamp posts	137,431.27	1,454,993.77

Towing locomotives, 40	598,082.79
Control boards, 3	108,324.33
Miter-gate moving machines, 92	1,005,384.20
Miter-gate forcing machines, 46	69,904.02

* Does not include cost of spare parts or of recess covers.

† Includes purchase and installation of fixed irons for quoin and sills of gates and caissons; snubbing irons, buffer castings, etc.; and, installation of Stoney valve frames and cylindrical and auxiliary culvert valves.

Rising-stem and guard-valve machines, 134.................................$ 1,076,151.47
Cylindrical and auxiliary culvert-valve machines, 132..............   229,267.54
Smaller machines:
     Miter-gate handrail, 92.........................$36,237.95
     Miter-gate sump pumps, 92................... 34,849.65
     Culvert sump pumps, 3......................... 12,746.14
     Drainage sump pumps, 9.......................   4,036.98
     Machinery and cable-pit pumps, 7.......   3,542.04
     Float well, 46................................... 25,298.74   116,711.50
Rising-stem and guard valves, moving parts only, 134.................   448,132.58
Fixed irons for same, contract price, not installed......................   392,600.00
Cylindrical and auxiliary culvert valves, contract price, not
    installed, 132 ....   236,000.00
Spillway-gate machines, 22...   209,924.15
Gatun Locks—masonry .... 2,068,636.4 cu. yds.   14,942,706.17
Pedro Miguel Lock—masonry ....   929,405.15 "   "   5,304,758.46
Miraflores Locks—masonry .... 1,509,469.17 "   "   7,865,085.30
Gatun spillway—masonry ....   231,179.0 "   "   1,740,085.54
Miraflores spillway—masonry ....   74,313.0 "   "   464,751.95

THE DESIGN OF THE SPILLWAYS OF THE PANAMA CANAL.

By

EDWARD C. SHERMAN, M. Am. Soc. C. E.
Formerly Designing Engineer, Isthmian Canal Commission
Consulting Engineer
Boston, Mass., U. S. A.

The adoption of the high-level type of canal at Panama, with the consequent impounding of large quantities of water in lakes which are essentially enormous storage reservoirs, necessitated the construction of spillways of very considerable capacities to provide safe regulation at Gatun and at Miraflores.

GATUN SPILLWAY.

The lake formed by the great dam at Gatun, with surface at 87.0 ft. (26.52 m.) above mean sea-level, has an area of about 167.4 sq. miles (433.5 sq. km.), and receives the discharge of the Chagres, the Trinidad and the Gatun Rivers, draining a watershed of 1,320 sq. miles (3,420 sq. km.). While the Isthmus of Panama is not subject to violent storms accompanied by heavy rains, the ordinary precipitation of the rainy season frequently causes great freshets in the rivers. Records of the discharge of the Chagres at Bohio have been kept for many years, the engineers of the French canal company having secured invaluable run-off data, and from more recent observations it was determined that the discharge of the combined streams, at Gatun, is about 1.62 times that of the Chagres at Bohio.

From the available data, it appeared that the maximum rates of discharge at Gatun which should be considered in designing the spillway were as follows:

	sec-ft.	cu. m-sec.
Maximum momentary rate	175,000	4955
Maximum rate for 33 hours	137,500	3900
Maximum rate for 48 hours	120,000	3400

The area of the lake at its normal level of 85 feet (26 m.) above sea-level is so great that, with a spillway capacity of 120,000 second-feet, an inflow amounting to 183,000 second-feet would cause the surface to rise only one foot (0.3 m.) in 20 hours and an inflow of 137,500 second-feet, lasting 33 hours, would cause it to rise only 0.46 feet (0.14 m.) in all.

On account of the possibility of the occurrence of a freshet exceeding in duration and rate of discharge any of which there is record, it was determined to provide a spillway capacity of 140,000 sec-ft. (3,960 cu. m-sec.) with the lake at its normal level. The designs of the lock walls and gates were based on the assumption that the lake level would seldom be permitted to rise more than 2 feet (0.6 m.) above normal, or, to el. + 87.0 ft. (26.52 m.) ; and, as a simple overfall dam without regulating gates would have to be about 3 miles (4.8 km.) long to discharge 140,000 sec-ft. (3,960 cu. m-sec.) without exceeding a depth of 2 ft. on its crest, it was decided to construct the dam with its crest below the normal lake level and to hold back the water by means of steel sluice gates of the Stoney type. This would permit the construction of a dam of reasonable length to give a large discharging capacity, not only when a freshet might cause a rise in the lake, but also with the lake at its normal level of 85 feet (26 m.) above the sea, so that water might be drawn off in anticipation of freshets.

About midway in the length of Gatun Dam there was a rocky hill outcropping which provided an excellent site for the regulating works, affording a suitable foundation for the heavy masonry structure and being near enough to the locks to be easily defended in time of war.* The extent of this foundation determined in part the length of the spillway dam and, consequently, the elevation of the crest, which was placed at 69 feet (21 m.) above sea-level, or 16 feet (4.9 m.) below normal lake level.

---

* See Plate I of ''Construction of Gatun Locks, Dam and Spillway'', by Brig. Gen. Wm. L. Sibert.

With no data available to assist in the determination of the proper coefficient of discharge for a dam with from 16 to 18 feet (4.9 to 5.5 m.) depth of water on its crest, the effects of the unusual depth, the shape of the crest and the piers necessary for holding the gates were studied, and it was estimated that from a gate opening 45 feet (13.8 m.) in length a discharge of not less than 10,000 sec.-ft. (283 cu. m.-sec.) might reasonably be expected. The spillway dam was therefore de-

Fig. 1. Gatun Spillway. Site of Dam.

signed to have fourteen such openings, making the total clear crest length 630 feet (192 m.).

A cut was made through the hill which had been selected as the site of the spillway and a concrete floor and side walls were put in, except at the site of the spillway dam, where low piers were built in the channel to key the dam to the rock and to serve for supports for such stop-planks or coffer-dams as were necessary to shut off the water and permit the placing of concrete in the dam. (Fig. 1.) When the construction of the Gatun Dam had proceeded far enough to cause the closure of the natural outlets of the rivers, the slowly forming lake found a new one ready in this artificial channel. (Fig. 2.)

While the crest of the dam was made of a form which, while providing seats for the Stoney gates and for the caisson needed to permit repairs to be made, would facilitate the flow of the water, the design of the down-stream face was controlled by the principle that the nappe should adhere to the masonry to prevent air from entering between them to cause chattering

Fig. 2. Gatun Spillway. Lake Discharging Through Channel.

and the consequent lifting action, which, with such an enormous quantity of water, might be dangerous to the structure.

In determining the profile of the dam, it was not considered necessary to use the velocity of flow through the orifice which exists under a gate while it is being opened, as the amount of water would then be too small to do any harm. At the same time it was not considered safe to use the lower velocity of flow over the weir which exists when the gate is fully opened, as a large amount of water would pass during the last stages of opening and the first stages of closing a gate and while the gate was still immersed on its lower edge. It was assumed that the horizontal velocity due to the gate being open 6 feet (1.8 m.) was a reasonable one to use, and the upper part of the downstream face of the dam was made a parabola, convex upward, of the form $h^2 = 42v$.

To turn the water back to the horizontal direction at the toe of the dam without serious disturbance, the lower part of the face was designed to be a circular curve of long radius, concave upward.

The general plan and the cross-section of the spillway dam which was adopted and built are shown in Plates I and II. The crest is divided into openings or bays—each closed by a Stoney gate 19 feet (5.8 m.) high—by piers which extend above the crest enough to permit the gates to be raised clear of the water to allow the safe passage of drift.

The floor of the spillway channel below the dam is 10 feet (3.1 m.) above sea-level so that there is no pool to serve as a cushion for the overflowing water, which, having fallen 75 feet (23 m.) has a velocity of about 60 feet (18 m.) a second. Such a velocity would be dangerous to the lining of the channel and the depth of the stream could not be computed, since, under such conditions, the great initial velocity and correspondingly small cross section may be retained or, without apparent reason, the depth and area of section may increase and a less velocity be assumed, or stationary waves may be formed, the velocity of the stream being different at different points in the channel. It was considered important that some positive check be devised to destroy the high velocity, and the desired result was secured by installing a system of baffle piers in the apron just below the toe of the dam.

The baffle piers are of concrete, like the rest of the structure, but they are heavily reinforced with steel rails and their upstream faces are armored with very thick, ribbed, iron castings, so that such drift as may strike them will not easily destroy them. If they are destroyed or badly damaged, they can be replaced or repaired in the dry season when no water will be discharged from the lake. (Plate III.)

The spillway channel is 285 feet (87 m.) wide and 960 feet (293 m.) long, its length being such that the water is discharged beyond the limits of the earth dam at a point where erosion will do no harm. The concrete floor varies in thickness from 4 feet (1.2 m.) at the upper end to 1 foot (0.3 m.) at the lower end, except that in the apron immediately below the toe of the ogee and around the baffle piers, where the velocity of the overflowing water is reduced and great disturbances are caused, it is 12 feet (3.7 m.) thick.

The water flowing over the face of the dam has a depth of about 6 feet (1.8 m.) when it reaches the baffles. Striking them, it turns vertically upward and much of its energy is used in internal work and converted into heat. When all the gates are open, the stream immediately below the baffle piers has a depth of approximately 20 feet (6.1 m.) and a velocity of about 20 feet per second.

The crest gates are operated electrically by machines installed in a tunnel extending throughout the length of the dam and beyond it, through the earth, to the vicinity of the power house on the east side of the discharge channel, where the control board is located. The gates are lifted by means of chains, attached to the ends, passing over sheaves on the tops of the piers; thence down through pipes in the masonry to the tunnel, where they are attached to vertical stems, threaded and engaged in the operating nuts, which are driven by worms at the ends of the main shaft, back-geared to the motor. Counterweights, traveling in pits under the tunnel floor, are attached to the lower ends of the stems, so that comparatively little power is required for operation.

The openings between the crest piers, above the gates, are spanned by steel foot-bridges, which can be removed, if necessary, for the installation of new gates. Auxiliary hand hoists are provided, to be operated from the tunnel, so that means are available for opening the gates even though the machinery should break down.

MIRAFLORES SPILLWAY.

The construction of the locks and dam at Miraflores has resulted in the formation of a small lake, by backing up the Rio Grande, Rio Cocoli, Rio Caimitillo and the Rio Pedro Miguel. The total discharge of these streams is small, even in the rainy season, and a small spillway would be sufficient to protect the earth dam from being overtopped if there were no other conditions to be considered. In the event of an accident occurring at one of the Pedro Miguel locks by which the water would be permitted to flow unobstructedly from the level of Gatun Lake, through Culebra Cut and the lock into Miraflores Lake, about 31 feet (9.5 m.) below it, the inflow would be at an estimated rate of between 90,000 and 100,000 sec-feet (2550 and 2830 cu. m-sec.). While this may be a remote contingency, considering all the protective devices with which the locks have been provided, it is not an impossibility; and, as its occurrence would result in the total destruction of the earth dam at Miraflores, if there were insufficient provision for disposing of the water, it was deemed advisable to provide a spillway with a capacity of not less than 90,000 sec-ft. at the highest allowable lake level, which corresponds to a depth of 18 feet (5.5 m.) on the crest of the spillway dam.

The design of the spillway dam which was adopted is of the same general type as the one at Gatun, the crest piers and the gates being exactly the same. It is straight in plan, however, and the profile is of slightly different form on account of the difference in height. The discharging capacity at maximum lake level was estimated to be about 92,000 sec-ft. (2600 cu. m-sec.), which will probably be sufficient. Should there be need of disposing of a greater quantity than this, the lock-filling culverts can be utilized to afford an additional capacity of about 25,000 sec-ft. (708 cu. m-sec.). (Plates IV and V.)

A part-tide dam across the Rio Grande at Corozal, a few miles below Miraflores, prevents the water above it from fluctuating with the tides in the Pacific, the range in the pool below the dam being only about 4 feet (1.2 m.) and the depth of water at the toe varying from about 21 to 25 feet (6.4 to 7 m.). With such a depth of water, extending across the entire front of the dam and for some distance down stream, to check the velocity and absorb the energy of the overfalling water, it was not considered necessary to use baffle piers like those adopted at Gatun, nor to pave the surface of the rock below the toe of the dam. (Fig. 3.) The maximum discharge for which the structure was designed will occur very seldom, perhaps never, and protective devices can be installed, if the ordinary use of the dam for regulating Miraflores Lake results in any appreciable erosion of the rock.

The drainage area tributary to Miraflores Lake is only 66.1 sq. miles (171 sq. km.) and the maximum run-off will seldom exceed 7650 sec-ft. (216 cu. m-sec.). This is cared for by opening a single spillway crest gate for such lengths of time as are necessary, a method deemed better than providing special culverts with additional gates and machinery, as it requires the

Fig. 3.   Miraflores Spillway.   Completed Dam.

attendants to be familiar with the operation of the large gates and affords frequent opportunities for examining them.

The gate-operating machines at Miraflores spillway, as at Gatun, are located in a tunnel extending throughout the length of the dam. As the inflow of water from Gatun Lake, in the event of the breaking down of a lock at Pedro Miguel, would cause Miraflores Lake to rise at the rate of 0.6 feet (0.18 m.) a minute, and as the earth esplanade about the locks is only 4 feet (1.2 m.) above the ordinary lake level, the spillway gates must be opened promptly after that accident happens. Automatic self-starters, actuated in a float switch in a well, connected directly with the lake, are therefore provided in addition to the manual control of the motors, so that a rise of the lake above a certain point automatically causes the spillway gates to open.

The crest gates at both spillways can be painted or more extensive work on them can be executed at any time by using the caisson (Plate VI) which permits the unwatering of any gate. The caisson is a rectangular steel box, having timber sills and keels to fit against the seats provided for it at all gate openings, which can be floated into place at the gate to be repaired and sunk upon its seat by admitting water into the interior compartments in proper amount.

Fixed ballast, of concrete, causes the caisson to float upright in the water, and swash bulkheads assist in maintaining its longitudinal stability when it is partly filled with water and is being towed. Two caissons are provided, one of which is kept near each of the spillways.

Paper No. 16

DESIGN OF THE LOCK WALLS AND VALVES OF THE PANAMA CANAL.

By

L. D. CORNISH, M. Am. Soc. C. E.
Formerly Designing Engineer for Isthmian Canal Commission
Office of Division Engineer, War Dept.
Cincinnati, Ohio, U. S. A.

———

In Paper No. 14, by Brig. General Hodges, is described how the designing force of the Assistant Chief Engineer was divided into six subdivisions. Cooperation among these subdivisions was essential, as the designs and plans prepared by each were more or less affected by those of others; and the plans as a whole had to be in agreement, to avoid errors in construction. Divided responsibility as to the errors in plans could not be tolerated and the system adopted was so successful that a brief description of it is worthy of record.

The tracings originating in one subdivision were submitted for review to every other subdivision whose plans might be affected, and there such affected portions were checked and the tracing signed by those in charge. Subsequent alterations or additions to plans had to be conspicuously shown and the revised tracing dated and initialed by all concerned. A record was kept of all blue prints sent to the construction divisions, together with the acknowledgment of their receipt. By this system the responsibility for mistakes in plans or construction could be ascertained in a few moments, and the result was that serious or costly errors did not occur during the entire construction of the locks and spillways.

CONDITIONS IMPOSED TO GOVERN DESIGNS.

Limiting unit pressure on plain concrete or foundation rock 300 lbs. per in² (21.1 kg per cm²).

All reinforced concrete structures to be designed in accordance with the last report and recommendations of the American Engineering Societies' Joint Committee on Concrete and Reinforced Concrete, with the following additional limitations taken from I. C. C. Standard Specifications for Reinforced Concrete design.

LIMITATIONS.

Protection Against Salt-Water Corrosion. For structures subjected to salt water, salt air, or spray the surface of slab reinforcement shall be protected by at least 1½″ (3.81 cm), beam reinforcement 2″ (5.8 cm), and girder and column reinforcement 2½″ (6.35 cm) of concrete.

Allowable Stress in Steel. The allowable stress in steel under working loads shall not exceed 16,000 pounds per square inch (1125 kg/cm²), and no less value shall be used unless economical or constructional reasons therefor can be shown, or as hereinafter specified. (See par. 6, note 3.)

Composition. The composition of concrete for reinforced concrete construction, unless by special authority of the Chairman and Chief Engineer, shall consist of Portland cement, clean gravel or crushed rock, and clean sand mixed in the proper proportions.

(a) Concrete composed of run of bank gravel mixed with cement shall not be used in any reinforced concrete structures, the plans of which do not specifically state that the use of such material is permitted by authority of the Chairman and Chief Engineer.

(b) The coarse aggregate of crushed stone or gravel shall be of a size which shall pass through a 1½″ (3.81 cm) ring, but not a ¼″ (0.635 cm) ring or horizontal screens having holes of these diameters.

(c) Run of bank gravel. All material which will not pass a 1½″ (3.81 cm) ring shall be rejected.

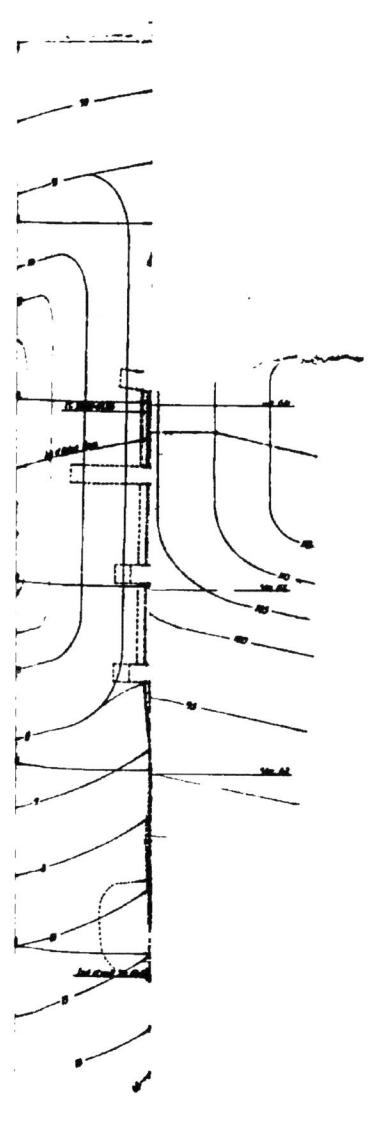

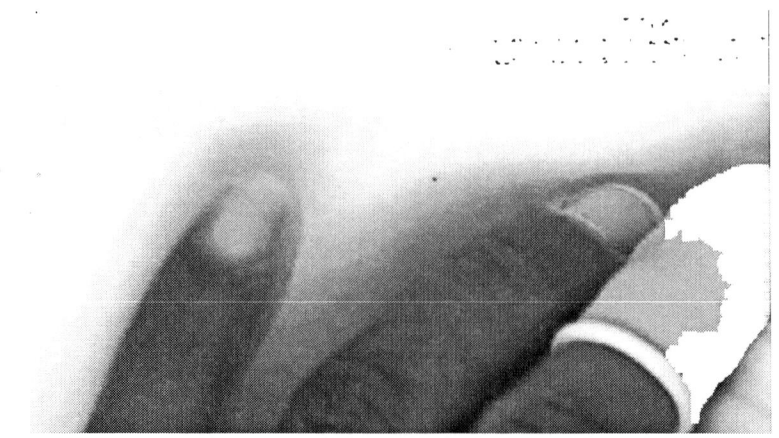

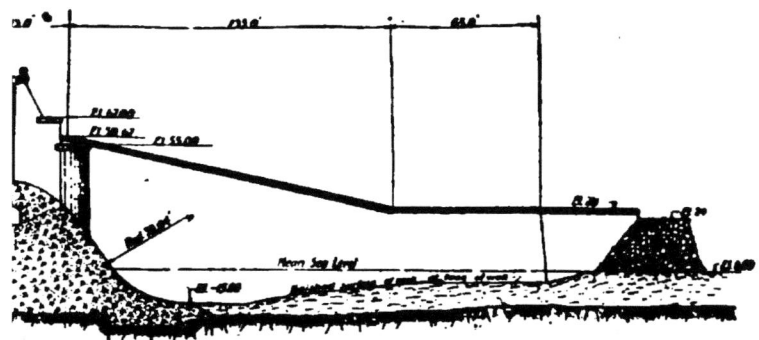

SECTION B-B

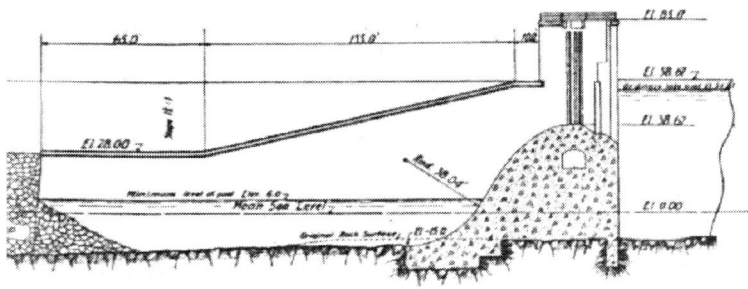

SECTION A-A

Assumed Compressive Strength of Concrete (in pounds per square inch).

Composition	1:1:2	1:1½:3	1:2:4	1:2½:5	1:3:6
Porto Bello or Ancon rock*......	3,300	2,800	2,200	1,800	1,400
Porto Bello or Ancon rock†......	2,800	2,400	1,850	1,500	1,150
Porto Bello or Ancon rock‡......	2,300	1,950	1,500	1,250	1,000
Proportion of cement to aggregate	1-2	1-3	1-4	1-5	1-6
Run of bank gravel§...................	1,800	1,500	1,200	1,000	800

In Kilograms per square Centimeter.

Composition	1:1:2	1:1½:3	1:2:4	1:2½:5	1:3:6
Porto Bello or Ancon rock*......	232	197	155	127	98
Porto Bello or Ancon rock†......	197	169	130	105	81
Porto Bello or Ancon rock‡......	162	137	105	88	70
Proportion of cement to aggregate	1-2	1-3	1-4	1-5	1-6
Run of bank gravel§...................	127	105	84	70	56

Bond Stress. The unit bond stress for deformed bars shall not exceed 7 percent of the assumed compressive strength of concrete.

Plans. On all plans shall be noted:

(a) The quality of concrete to be used.

(b) The designing live load.

(c) The maximum compressive fiber stress in the concrete.

(d) The maximum fiber stress in the steel.

(e) The class of inspection necessary.

---

* To be used only when the construction is to be subjected to careful engineering inspection.

† To be used when construction is to be subjected only to foreman inspection or for proportioned gravel concrete with engineering inspection.

‡ To be used for structures which will be permanently submerged, in which case the steel reinforcement shall not be stressed above 14,000 pounds per square inch (9843 kg/cm²).

§ To be used when the gravel and sand are not to be separated and proportioned.

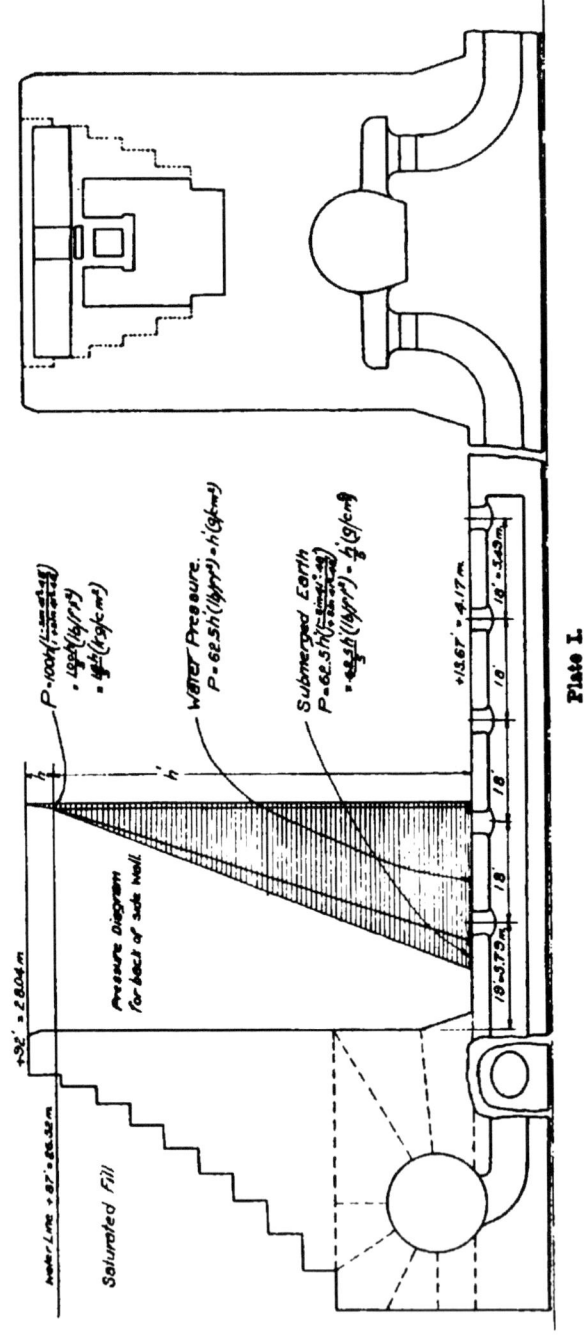

Plate I.

Weight of plain concrete 144 lbs. per ft³ (2.3 g per cm³).

Weight of reinforced concrete 150 lbs. per ft³ (2.4 g/cm³).

The weight of back fill for all walls was assumed to be 100 lbs. per ft³ (1.6 g per cm³) with 40% voids, which gives a saturated weight of 125 lbs per ft³ (2 g per cm³) and a submerged weight of 62.5 lbs per ft³ (1 g per cm³). The angle of internal friction was assumed to be thirty degrees for dry and saturated back-fill of all walls, except the side walls of upper Gatun lock, where the fill was carefully selected and placed and an angle of 41° 48′ assumed. The horizontal unit pressure resulting from these assumptions and using the formula $P = w\,h\left(\dfrac{1 - \sin\theta}{1 + \sin\theta}\right)$ are shown graphically in Plate I.

MAIN WALLS.

Plate I shows a typical cross section of the side and middle walls and the culvert system for emptying and filling the locks.

The main culverts in the walls have the same area, but the middle wall culvert was so designed as to facilitate the examination and replacing of cylindrical valves.

The lateral culverts were made elliptical in shape to decrease the depth of excavation, and the openings from the culverts into the lock chamber were rounded on both sides to eliminate contraction in the jet of water flowing through them.

The sectional area of the main culverts was fixed at 255 sq. ft. (23.68 m²) as the area which would govern the time of filling or emptying the locks. Wherever possible, without incurring too great an expense, the area was increased, in order to reduce the losses of head, and all openings to the main or branch culverts were shaped to fit the *vena contracta* curve. See Plate No. III, Paper No. 14, by Brig. Gen. Hodges, for areas of entire culvert system.

In designing the side walls of the upper locks of the Gatun flight it was assumed that the back-fill was saturated to lake level, 5 ft. (1.524 m) below the coping of the walls, because of its character as part of the Gatun dam. For side walls at all other places the ground-water level was assumed to be that of the adjacent country below, the back-fill being permeable material.

This resulted in the walls for Gatun upper locks being 5 ft. (1.524 m) wider than at other places.

The limiting dimensions of the toe on the lock faces of the wall were fixed by the clearance requirements of naval vessels.

Dry back-fill was assumed for the middle wall, drainage culverts being provided through the solid masonry at the gates and Stoney valves.

With the foregoing assumptions, the problem of the design of these walls consisted mainly in finding the best location for the main culverts, the lock chamber being assumed as unwatered for side-wall design and one lock chamber full and one empty for the middle-wall design.

The walls above the horizontal plane shown in the figure were designed as retaining walls, the resultant pressure being kept within the middle third. The portion below the plane was divided into voussoirs and various tentative designs analyzed by the graphic method to find a satisfactory line of thrust which could be passed through all the joints, and also checked by the algebraic method.

Plate II, Figure 1, shows a section of the middle wall of the lower Miraflores locks taken between the lateral culverts, and is typical of all the other middle walls. This wall is higher by 3 ft. (.914 m) than the middle wall of any other lock, is subjected to pressure from brackish water assumed to weigh 63.5 lbs. per cu. ft. (1.016 g/cm²), and is therefore exposed to greater stresses. For analysis, the wall about the culvert is divided into blocks by imaginary joints. Joints a-b, c-d, k-l, and m-n are of equal width. The external forces acting on the wall, as shown on the figure, are expressed in tons of 2000 lbs., and in metric tons (1000 kg.). The resulting stresses are given in the following table, the first column giving the initial stresses due to the weight of the concrete and back-fill, allowance having been made for voids and the weight of machinery; the second column gives stresses due to water pressure; the third column the algebraic sum of the preceding columns; and columns 4, 5, and 6 give the same data expressed in the metric system:

Stress	Initial	Water	Resultant	Initial	Water	Resultant
	lbs. per sq. inch.			kg. per cm²		
at a	+52.8	−17.6	+35.2	+3.71	−1.25	+2.46
b	+69.7	−4.9	+64.8	+4.90	−0.34	+4.56
c	+69.7	+16.3	+86.0	+4.90	+1.15	+6.05
d	+52.8	+6.4	+59.2	+3.71	+0.45	+4.16
k	+73.5	−67.3	+6.2	+5.17	−4.73	+0.44
l	+73.5	+44.6	+118.1	+5.17	+3.14	+8.31
m	+73.5	−44.6	+28.9	+5.17	−3.14	+2.03
n	+73.5	+67.3	+140.8	+5.17	+4.73	+9.90
u	+11.0	−21.8	−10.8	+0.77	−1.53	−0.76
u¹	−7.6	+54.0	+46.4	−0.54	+3.80	+3.26
t	+11.0	+58.3	+69.3	+0.77	+4.10	+4.87
t¹	−7.6	−3.4	−11.0	−0.54	−0.23	−0.77
r	−6.8	+28.5	+21.7	−0.48	+2.00	+1.52
q	−6.8	+24.6	+17.8	−0.48	+1.73	+1.25

Horizontal force in	Initial	Water	Resultant	Initial	Water	Resultant
	Tons of 2000 lbs.			Metric Tons		
a-b	−3.18	+23.28	+20.10	−2.88	+21.08	+18.20
c-d	+3.18	+28.62	+31.80	+2.88	+26.00	+28.88
k-l	−3.18	+35.98	+32.80	−2.88	+32.63	+29.75
m-n	+3.18	+28.62	+31.80	+2.88	+26.00	+28.88
r-q	−7.40	+28.62	+21.22	−6.75	+26.00	+19.25
Vertical force in						
r-q	0.00	18.69	18.69	0.00	16.95	16.95

The stresses given in the foregoing table were derived by Brig. Gen. H. F. Hodges, from a rigorous algebraic analysis made by him while he was Assistant Chief Engineer, and the figures obtained from a careful graphic analysis made by the writer agree with these within the allowable errors of the graphic method and slide rule computations.

If the middle culvert be in communication with the lock chamber, which is filled with water, other assumptions being as before, a small amount of tension will be produced near the inner surface of the culvert, and therefore it is reinforced, although it is not intended to fill the middle culvert when one of the locks is dry.

Plate II, Figure 2, shows a plan of the middle wall at the gate recess and buttress, all details being omitted. The wall for the distance shown is massive, except for the voids due to

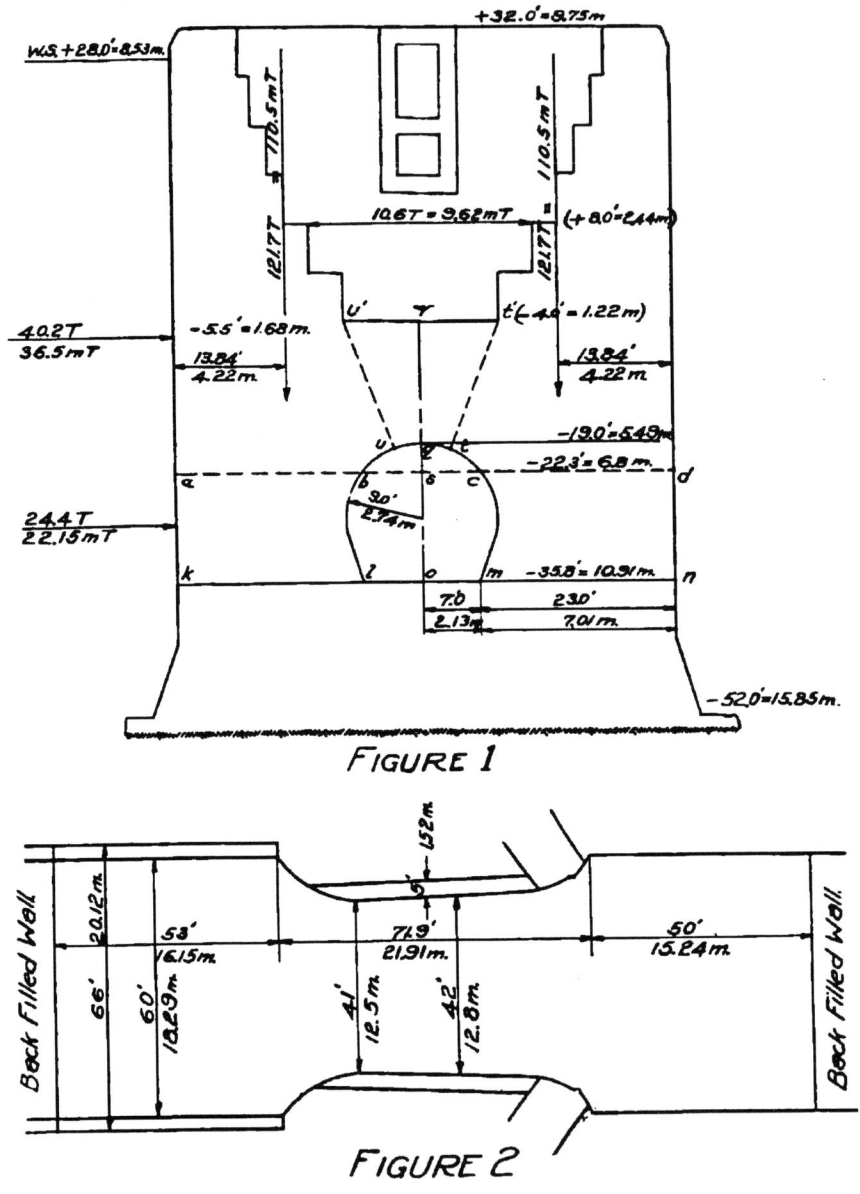

FIGURE 1

FIGURE 2

Plate II.

machinery rooms, operating and drainage tunnels and the main culvert. The design of this wall was based on a method of construction such that the narrow and weaker portion could transfer some of its load to the wider portion by arch or beam action. At Pedro Miguel and Miraflores locks the concrete was placed in 6-ft. (1.83 m) tiers of blocks with broken vertical joints; and at Gatun locks the monoliths with continuous vertical joints were keyed together, and the monolith at the recess given oblique joints, such that the blocks would act as voussoirs of a horizontal arch against pressure on either side.

By analysis it was found that the masonry in the narrow part of the recess, acting as a beam or arch, was strong enough to transfer all of its load to its abutments, and it is evident, therefore, that it is safe to consider that the entire 175 ft. (53.3 m) of wall, shown by the figure, will act as a unit. The mean thickness of this portion of wall is 53.5 ft. (16.3 m), and a section of this thickness and the full height of the wall was analyzed under the worst operating conditions. Under certain improbable, if not impossible, conditions of water pressure under the wall, a small amount of tension was indicated, and therefore the wall, at the gate recess, was tied to the foundation rock by old rails.

It may be noted in Plate II, Figure 2, that the back of the recess tapers, so that the clearance, when the miter gates are in the recesses, increases uniformly toward the miter end. With such large gates, analysis showed that this taper and an unusual length of recess were necessary in order to facilitate the flow of the displaced water without creating objectionable heads.

LOCK FLOORS.

In general, the floors of the locks did not require special designs, as the foundation rock was practically impervious and unfissured. The floor consisted of a layer of concrete from one to three feet (0.3 to 0.91 m) thick, and at places where some seepage or fissure might exist, weep holes were left through the concrete.

The rock under the upper end of Gatun upper lock was quite porous in character, and an attempt was made to cut off

the underflow, as described elsewhere, in Paper No. 11, by Brig.
Gen. Sibert, but floors to resist a hydrostatic head due to Gatun
Lake were thought necessary for the upper or southern part of
the lock-flight. From the emergency dam sill to the upper miter
gate sills was the most vulnerable section, and for it a flat floor
of concrete 20 ft. (6.1 m) thick was adopted, which, when
analyzed as a flat arch, would safely resist the possible 83-ft.
(25.3 m) head under it. From the upper miter gate sill to the
intermediate gates a design was adopted, as shown in Plate III,
which consists of 13 ft. (3.96 m) of concrete anchored to the rock
foundation by old rails grouted into holes drilled in the rock.
The rails are of varying length, those at the middle reaching to
33 ft. (10.06 m) below the floor level. The assumed pressure on
the under surface of the concrete was due to an 87-ft. (26.5 m)
head, and the analysis was made on the assumption that the concrete and rock above the bottom of the rails would together withstand the head, by their combined weight and action as an
inverted arch.

APPROACH WALLS.

The rock on which the Gatun Locks are founded dips
abruptly both north and south, and under both approach walls
is from zero to 100 ft. (30.48 m) below the desired grade; and
being overlaid with very soft material, it was necessary to give
special attention to the design of the approach walls.

The surface at the site of the south middle-approach wall was
lower than the desired grade. Test piles showed that the soil
was too soft to develop the desired friction, except in a stratum
about ten feet thick and twenty feet below the ground surface,
which was 10 ft. (3.05 m) above sea-level. To go to rock, piles
from seventy to one hundred feet would be required, which was
impracticable. It was finally decided to make a fill 100 ft. (30.48
m) wide and about 25 ft. (7.62 m) deep, and, after it had been
consolidated, to drive reinforced concrete piles through the fill
and into the hard stratum previously noted. The wall design for
the pile foundation consisted of a reinforced concrete slab, which
embraced the pile heads, to support a cellular reinforced concrete wall of as light weight as possible. To stiffen the structure

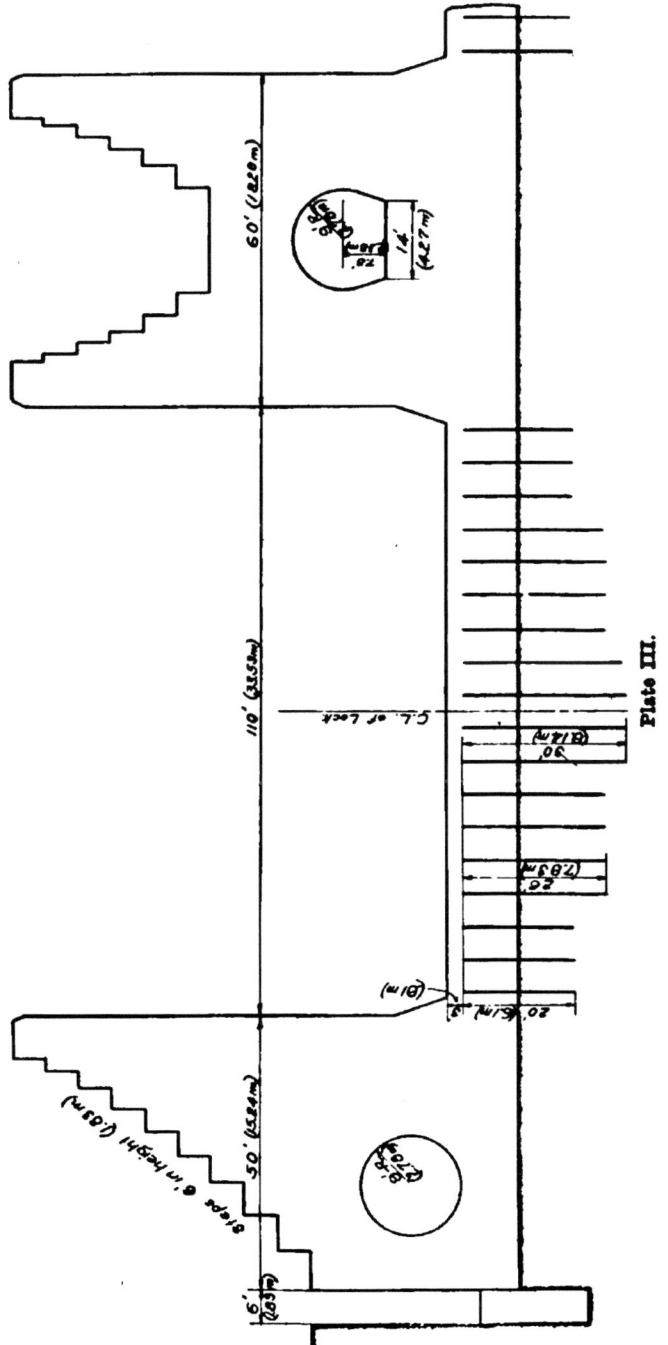

Plate III.

against the impact of ships, three longitudinal rows of cells were adopted, each cell being about 13 by 18 ft. (3.96 by 5.49 m) in the clear and both face and partition walls heavily reinforced. During construction, the wall settled about two feet (0.61 m), and at one time was settling faster on one side than the other. An outside longitudinal row of cells was filled with water in an attempt to make the structure settle evenly, and the attempt proved successful. This wall continued to settle after the lake was filled, and the construction of the decking, tracks, etc., had to be deferred for some time.

All approach walls had two rows of timber fenders placed near the top and were supported by chains, as shown in Plate IV. The impact of a ship was transmitted by the buffer timber to nests of coil springs placed in the wall at five-foot (1.52 m) intervals.

The side approach or flare walls at the south entrance to Gatun locks consist of concrete piers supporting bridges composed of steel girders embedded in concrete. The walls project into Gatun Lake, and therefore there is a considerable area of open water behind them, which is in direct communication with the water of the forebay proper through the openings in the flare walls. This type of wall was necessary in order to prevent the piling up of water in the forebay during storms on the lake which would cause the waves to run toward the lock entrance.

The north middle-approach wall of Gatun locks also required special consideration, on account of the great depth to rock and the soft material overlying it. The earth was excavated as low as practicable, in spite of many difficulties (for a description of which see Paper No. 11, by Brig. Gen. Sibert), and wooden piles were driven to rock. A thick concrete slab was constructed embedding the tops of the piles, and upon the slab was constructed the wall. See Fig. 1. The design consisted of transverse arched piers on 50-ft. (15.24 m) centers. A pier consisted of two small rectangular piers 10 ft. by 18 ft. (3.05 by 5.49 m), joined at the top of a circular arch transverse to the axis of the approach wall. These transverse piers were bridged at the top by steel plate-girders, embedded in concrete for protection and strength. The steel girders were designed with light compression flanges sufficient in area to take safely the compressive stress due

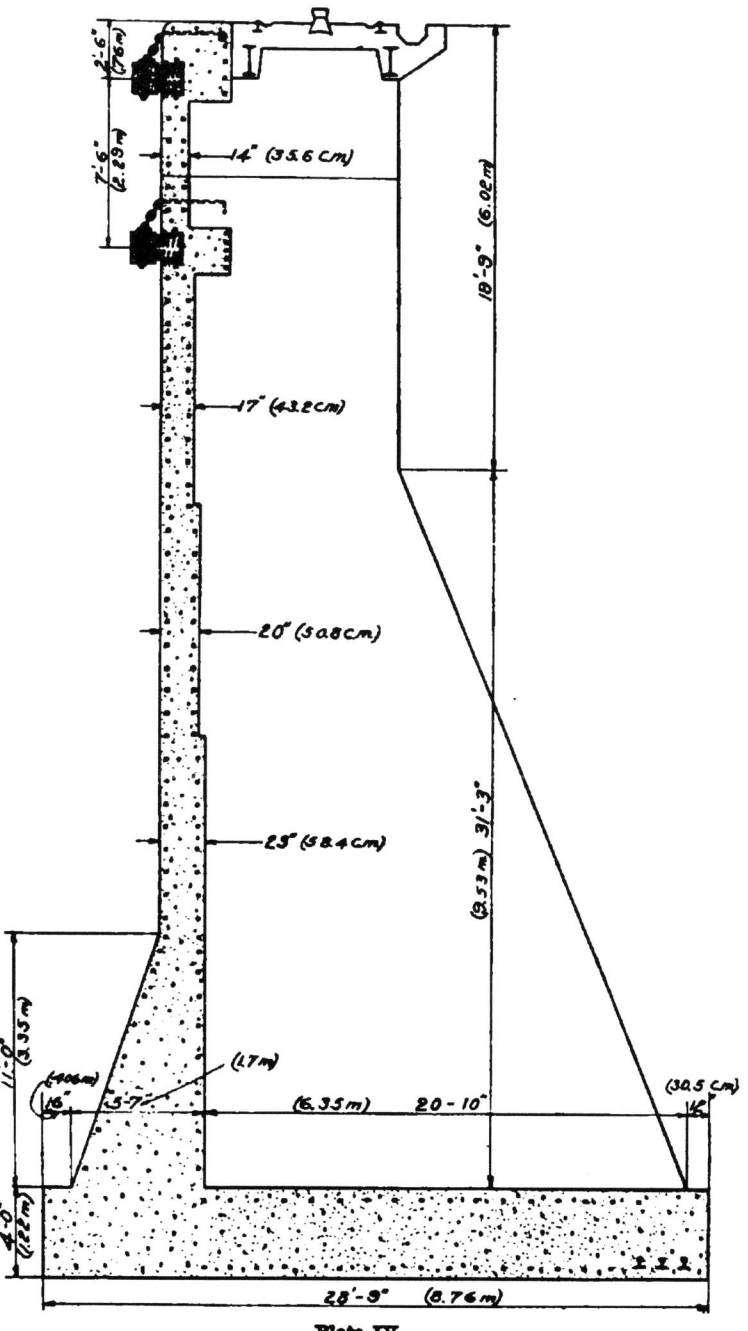

Plate IV.

to the dead load of the wet concrete and the construction equipment, and with heavy tension flanges for the added tensile stress due to live loads, which would not occur until the concrete had properly aged.

In the picture of the north middle-approach wall, Fig. 1, the end of the wall for a short distance is seen to be pointed and considerably lower than the remainder of the wall. This part of the wall is the base, or support, for a superstructure, which consists of a timber crib, the outside of which is of solid timber five feet thick. The timber structure is provided as a buffer against

Fig. 1. North Entrance of Gatun Lower Locks, Showing Completed Approach Wall.
June, 1913.

which carelessly handled ships will strike, instead of hitting solid masonry, with possibly disastrous results to the ship.

It is believed that the damage to the crib and a ship colliding therewith will be materially less than the damage due to a collision with a solid concrete wall. These timber cribs are provided at the ends of all middle-approach walls; and where the water level may vary considerably, they are floating structures tied to piles.

The north flare walls are of massive concrete founded on rock.

The north middle-approach walls of the Pedro Miguel and Miraflores locks are of similar design. They are of cellular reinforced concrete, but as they were to be filled, no longitudinal interior walls were necessary, as the filling would provide the resistance to impact. The transverse walls forming the pockets or cells are 2 ft. 6 in. (0.76 m) thick, on 15-ft. (4.57 m) centers, with reinforcing rods which tie the face walls together and take the stress due to the pressure of the fill. The face walls are designed as continuous beams of indefinite number of spans and are doubly reinforced. The locomotive tracks on the decking are supported by I-beams, which have their bearing on the transverse walls. The wall for Pedro Miguel is founded on rock at the desired grade; but at Miraflores the rock is at a considerable depth below grade and the foundation consists of cylindrical reinforced concrete caissons sunk to rock and filled with concrete. The tops of the caissons are connected by a system of reinforced concrete girders, which support the cellular superstructure.

The greater part of the south middle-approach wall of Pedro Miguel locks and the entire south-approach wall of the Miraflores locks are of massive gravity type, consisting of two retaining walls stepped on the back until they meet near the bottom of the wall. It was intended that the two walls should be back-filled with ordinary excavation, consisting mainly of broken rock, which would have a large angle of internal friction with correspondingly low lateral pressures. This resulted in a design in which the ratio of base to height was smaller than any other walls of the locks. A few drains were provided, so that, after construction and before water was admitted into the canal, water could not accumulate and subject the walls to hydrostatic pressure. On the supposition that the walls might be back-filled with earthy material and the drains choked up, as actually occurred, the wall was so designed that, under this condition and with water pressure in all joints, the resultant unit pressure would not be excessive. Part of the backfill of these walls was dropped from a considerable height, and the wedge action induced by the impact, combined with the normal lateral pressure, produced a deflection of about one inch (25 m) at the top of the wall.

Plate IV shows a section of the reinforced concrete retaining wall adopted for certain side-approach and flare walls. At Pedro Miguel locks this type of wall rested on a rock foundation, whereas at the north approach to Miraflores locks a considerable length of it rested on a pile foundation. The thickness of the vertical slab diminished at intervals, from the bottom to the top, to minimize the changes in spacing and size of the horizontal reinforcement. The counterforts were spaced on 15-ft. (4.57 m) centers and were 2 ft. 6 in. (0.76 m) thick, heavily reinforced, and served as supports for the towing-track beams. Owing to the possibility of the back-fill arching between some of the counterforts, the vertical slab was designed as a continuous beam of indefinite number of spans, under the worst possible condition of loading, and therefore is double reinforced, as shown. Strong reinforced beams were designed to support the spring buffers located on 5-ft. (1.52 m) centers. All approach walls were equipped with buffer timbers, the location of which below the coping of the wall was similar, and as shown in the section.

RISING-STEM GATE VALVES.

The main valves for controlling the filling and emptying system of the locks were a modified type of the well-known Stoney sluice-gate. The maximum head to which the valves would be subjected varied a great deal according to their location, but study developed that there would be little economy in modifying the structural members in accordance therewith. One design was therefore adopted for all operating valves of this type.

The ordinary counterweighted type of gate with flexible connection to operating machinery was considered but rejected, partly on account of complications in masonry design caused by the counterweight, but mainly because of the lack of a stiff connection to the operating mechanism to permit the application of force in closing the valves.

The valve as adopted has a rising stem connected to the gate near its center, the stem passing through a water-tight bulkhead into the machinery chamber and being connected to the operating mechanism, as described in paper No. 14, by Mr. Schildhauer. The stems were of steel pipe approximately 6¾ in. (17.1 cm) inside diameter, and finished to 8 in. (20.3 cm) outside diameter for passing through a stuffing box in the bulkhead. The principal members of the valve are of nickel steel. There are, in all, 118 such rising stem valves installed.

Each valve is approximately 19 ft. (5.79 m) high by 10 ft. (3.05 m) wide and is built up of six horizontal beams spaced 3 ft. 6 in. (1.07 m) apart, the five upper beams being 20-in., 80-lb. (50.8 cm, 36 kg) I-beams, and the lower beam an L-shaped steel casting 20 in. (50.8 cm) deep. The upstream leg of this casting projects 12 in. (30 cm) below the web, the latter having seven open-cored holes through it, the object of the projecting leg and holes being to facilitate the flow of water and the operation of the gate when opened under high heads. (See detail of bottom seal, Plate V.) With this design of bottom member, no difficulty has been experienced in starting the valve to rise under pressure, such as has been noted in certain other cases, and attributed to the development of a vacuum under the lower edge of the valve when the seal is first broken. The skin is placed on the upstream face of the gate and consists of buckle-plates with the convexity downstream. Each buckle is supported on four sides. The stem is connected to the web of the I-beams by a steel casting, and the back flanges of all beams are cross-connected by tie plates, to distribute the pull of the stem.

Plate V shows a horizontal section through a pair of valves in their chambers, and sectional details of the seals. The pier is reinforced by two plate girders, to take the reaction of the gates, and the point is protected by an iron casting. For a short distance above and several feet below the gate, the sides, top and bottom of the valve chamber are protected by cast-iron wearing surfaces.

Motion of the valve is limited to one-fourth inch (6.4 mm) laterally by the clearance of the side rollers, and to the same amount upstream by the clearance between the bearing strip and the casting shown bolted to the wall casting. The former casting is built in short sections and is removable, to provide space for moving the gate if it should become necessary.

After the valves were completed in the shop they were placed on a planer, and the faces of the roller tracks surfaced to the same plane, and the bearing straps also surfaced to a plane parallel to the plane of the faces of the roller tracks, thus removing any warp in the gates.

The bottom seal is clearly shown in the detail, the finished under surface of the lowest casting resting on babbitt-metal. The top seal, as shown, consists of an adjustable casting bolted to the valve, having in the jaw of the casting a strip of rubber which comes in contact with the casting bolted to the roof of the valve chamber, as the valve comes to a seat on the bottom seal.

To prevent excessive leakage at the sides of the valve, so common to Stoney gates, a new seal was devised, as shown in the detail of the vertical side seal. This seal consists of a thin phosphor-bronze spring, bent to a radius, to which is attached a bronze point to form the line of contact with the wall casting. The spring is fastened to the valve between a bronze strap and the skin plate, and another bronze strap provided so that the water pressure cannot cause excessive deflection in the spring. The joint between the spring parts and the gate is made tight by a canvas gasket soaked in red lead and oil. The location of the curved spring is so arranged that there is initial stress in the spring sufficient to keep the point in contact, and any additional pressure from the water serves to press the point more firmly against its seat. The leakage through this seal is, in many cases, imperceptible. Valves in the lower locks which are exposed to salt water have zinc strips fastened in contact with the bronze, so as to confine the electrolytic action to the zinc and bronze, and thus preserve the steel and iron.

The so-called guard valves, 18 in number, located in the three branches of the culvert entrance in the side walls, are identical in structural design with the valves previously described, but are not of the rising-stem type. The elevation of the intake was such that there was insufficient height above the valve for the rising-stem machinery; therefore, these valves are equipped with counterweights connected to the valves by chains and have a special type of operating machine, as described in Paper No. 20, by Mr. Schildhauer.

The first order for valves consisted of four, for testing purposes. The tests and further study developed the advisability of making certain minor modifications, not only in the valves but also in the castings which form the valve chamber.*

In July and August, 1914, seven tests among four different sets of valves, including ten different valves, under a 52-ft.

---

* For a description of these tests see Annual Report of Isthmian Canal Commission, 1912, page 72.

(15.85 m) head at the center of pressure on valve, gave a mean leakage per gate of 1.23 c.f.s. (0.035 cu. m. per sec.). The maximum was 2.06 (0.057 cu. m. per sec.) and the minimum 0.78 c.f.s. (0.022 cu. m. per sec.). Under average operating conditions this indicates a total leakage at Gatun locks of 6.8 c.f.s. (0.192 cu. m. per sec.) and at Pedro Miguel of 5.6 c.f.s. (0.158 cu. m. per sec.) or a total of 12.4 c.f.s. (0.35 cu. m. per sec.) from Gatun Lake.

CYLINDRICAL VALVES.

Plate VI shows a section of a cylindrical valve and valve chamber, and certain details.

No satisfactory data could be obtained as to the discharge efficiency of valves of this type, and in the design an attempt was made to proportion and shape the various parts so that the coefficient C in the filling formula for the locks would be reasonably large, when using the middle-wall culverts.

Results thus far, as shown by tests and in operation, indicate that C for middle-wall culverts is only 0.59, whereas it is 0.88 for side-wall culverts.

The valve seat is made of ordinary gray cast iron and so shaped as to minimize contraction of the flowing jet. The moving part of the valve and the valve body are made of a special grade of cast iron, or so-called semi-steel. The valve cover, which is anchored in the walls, is of gray cast iron.

The valve seats were carefully set and concreted in, and subsequently the remainder of the valve was completely assembled in place, inside the forms for the valve chamber, and the placing of the concrete continued. The well for the valve stem was formed by lap-welded pipe incased in the concrete. The valve body is bolted to the cover and also supported by four pedestals, which in turn are bolted to and supported by the valve seat. The pedestals form the guides for the moving valve body, and at top and bottom are tapered to facilitate their removal. With the valve stem and pedestals removed, the valve bodies may be collapsed and taken from the chamber for repairs or renewal. The bottom seal is made by contact of the metal parts, and the top seal by leather gaskets, which lap over the joint. These valves take pressure from either direction, necessitating a double set of leather seals, as shown in detail. When tested under a 60-ft. (18.29 m) head the average leakage per valve was about 0.1

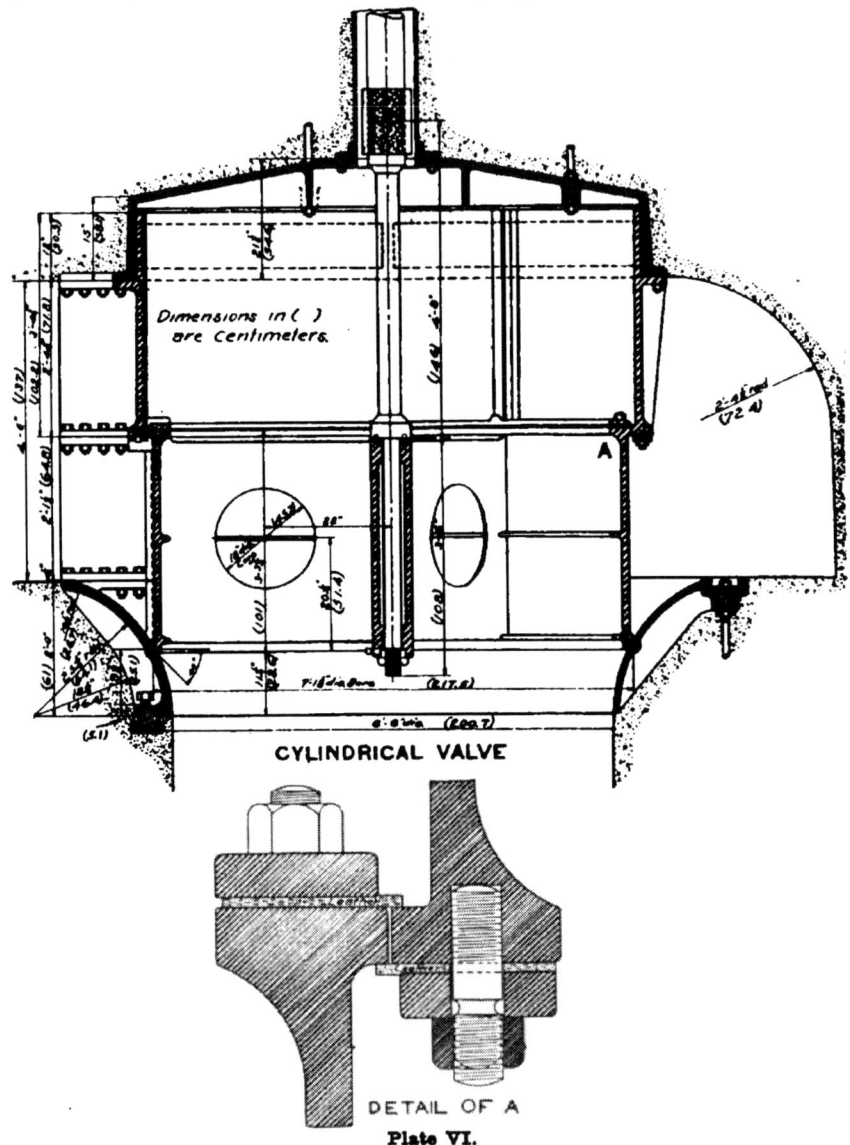

CYLINDRICAL VALVE

DETAIL OF A

Plate VI.

c.f.s. (2800 cu. cm. per sec.). Examination indicated that the leather seal was sufficiently rigid to support the moving portion of the valve and prevent its seating properly at the bottom.

Thereafter, the segments which clamp the leather seal were beveled slightly on the edge, to permit an easier bending of the gasket. Further tests were made, and the leakage found to be about 0.01 c.f.s. (280 cu. cm. per sec.) or one-tenth of that previously measured.

At the top of the valve-stem casing a vent pipe is provided with check valve on its end. This valve prevents water under pressure from flowing into the machinery room, and permits the access of air to the casing when the valves are in action and the flowing water would tend to produce a vacuum in the casing and thus reduce the flow.

LOCK GATES, CHAIN FENDERS AND LOCK ENTRANCE CAISSON.

By

HENRY GOLDMARK, M. Am. Soc. C. E., M. Inst. C. E.
Consulting Engineer
Late Designing Engineer, Isthmian Canal Commission
New York, N. Y., U. S. A.

LOCK GATES.

The Lock Gates on the Panama Canal excel any previous work of the kind in the number and size of the gates, and the total tonnage. There are in all forty-six gates of two leaves, the weight of which, including the anchorages and other parts embedded in the concrete, amounts to 68,000 tons of 2000 pounds. Their cost was over $7,000,000. The leaves are 65 feet wide and vary in height from 47 to 82 feet, and in weight from 400 to 750 tons, not counting the fixed parts. The largest gate is 50 per cent higher than any previously built, and weighs fully three times as much. Even the smallest is much larger than any of the same type elsewhere. Though the Panama gates are wider as well as higher than any other miter gates, the increase in width over previous gates is only moderate, as locks 100 feet wide have been in use for nearly 60 years. The pressures that are sustained by the gates are unusually heavy, even for such high gates, as the locks are arranged in flights, so that the maximum head, in ordinary service, may amount to twice the single lift.

The positions of the several gates and their heights are shown on the general plan of the locks (Plate I), while the reasons governing their arrangement have been discussed in the paper dealing with the locks as a whole.

Such large gates presented unusual difficulties, so that their feasibility had been seriously questioned by critics of the lock type of canal, while the magnitude of the work made a satisfactory and still economical design a matter of great importance. A thorough investigation of all the main features of the gates was, therefore, made before proceeding with the final plans. In this paper certain of these preliminary studies are first summarized, and the conclusions drawn from them are given. A general description of the gates follows, with an account of the most important details, and the requirements as to materials and workmanship. The stresses are next discussed, and the methods used in the field erection described in some detail. The last section gives the weights and costs of the gates.

Choice of Type.

The first question to be decided was the type of construction, the choice lying between the mitering gate with two leaves and some form of single-leaf gate. The latter type, in the shape of floating and rolling caissons, is common in dry docks and other harbor works, but has rarely been used in canal locks. For canals, mitering gates have long been the standard form and have given excellent satisfaction, even in locks as wide as 100 feet.

Under the circumstances, the presumption was in favor of the mitering gate. It was thought, however, that in view of the very great dimensions and pressures at Panama, it would be wise to make a detailed comparison of the two types.

Of the different forms of single-leaf gates, the rolling gate which opens by sliding into a recess in one of the walls was the only one seriously considered, as there are various practical objections to all other varieties of single-leaf gates.

Thus, the swinging gate turning on a vertical pivot at one end presents serious difficulties in the case of the Panama locks, as it would be very hard in practice to suspend such huge leaves from anchorages at the top of the walls and to support their weight without using rollers on the lock floor, which are objectionable for various reasons. Swinging gates also shorten the available length of the lock chamber more than miter gates do, at least in the case of lower gates.

Plunging gates, which descend into pits, require deep recesses in the floor, which would be inaccessible and likely to fill up with silt and debris. Part of the moving mechanism would also probably be under water and inaccessible. Another form which has sometimes been used on a small scale, viz., the tumbling gate, which revolves about a horizontal axis on the bottom, is objectionable for similar reasons. No form of the single-leaf gate, except the rolling gate, has ever been used on a large scale, although all of them have been tried—some varieties on very large gates. It was not thought wise at Panama to use any form of construction which had not proved its reliability by a long term of successful service on works of considerable magnitude and importance.

The comparative plans and estimates were, therefore, confined to rolling gates and mitering gates of the usual form. Several designs were made of rolling gates, differing in their details. A height of 77 feet was used in all the designs. The two types are compared in Table I. The rolling gate, the weights and cost of which are given, was of the form common in harbor works—a rectangular caisson, with several plate and open decks, which rests on wheeled trucks and opens by moving endwise into a recess in the lock walls. Nickel steel was used to reduce the weight. The miter gate was practically identical in design with the gate as built, but some minor parts were not included in the estimate.

TABLE I.

Single-Leaf Type.

Rolling Gate	110 ft. Lock			77 ft. High
Structural nickel-steel	2,405,000 lbs. @		6.25c	$150,300.00
Structural carbon-steel	300,000 "	"	4.50c	13,500.00
Carbon-steel castings	212,000 "	"	8.00c	16,940.00
Miscellaneous parts	20,000 "	"	20.00c	4,000.00
Total	2,937,000 "	"	6.29c	$184,740.00

Double-Leaf Type.

Mitering Gate	110 ft. Lock			77 ft. High
Structural carbon-steel	2,430,000 lbs. @		3.785c	$ 91,975.50
Carbon-steel castings	186,000 "	"	7.86c	14,619.60
Miscellaneous parts	104,000 "	"	14.7c	15,286.90
Total	2,720,000 "	"	4.48c	$121,882.00

The table shows that the rolling gate would be somewhat heavier than the miter gate, and very much more expensive. Taking into account the additional masonry required, its cost would be nearly double. Besides being cheaper than the rolling gate, the miter gate is also lighter and less complicated. None of the moving parts are under water, except the pintle and its bearings, which are well protected and have proved very durable in practice. Its operation requires less time and effort, while its reliability in service has been tested on a much more extended scale and fully proven.

The rolling gate has many complicated and inaccessible parts, while the trucks and rails are liable to injury and obstruction. The deep recesses in the walls are not only expensive, but are also objectionable on other grounds, and the operation of the gate is slower and requires more power.

It has been maintained that the stresses in single-leaf gates can be determined with more accuracy than in miter gates, but this point, though true to some extent, has little practical value, as miter gates can be built of ample strength, without making them unduly heavy. Greater resistance as barriers in case of accidental collision is another advantage claimed for single-leaf gates. This claim is hardly based on actual experience, but is probably true to some degree, and for this reason rolling gates were seriously considered for the "safety" gates in the Panama locks, which duplicate the operating gates at the lower end of the upper locks. Even for these, as well as for all other gates, it was finally decided to use the well-tried and simpler mitering type.

Shape of Leaf and Angle of Sill.

The next point to be settled, after the adoption of the mitering type, was the form of leaf. The relative merits of curved or "arched" leaves and those having a straight downstream flange have long been debated. In the former, the curve of pressure —i. e., the curve which gives the position of the resultant force acting on each cross section—coincides closely with the centre line of the leaf, eliminating most of the transverse stress and reducing the weights of the horizontal frames. In ordinary cases the saving in weight is small, so that straight gates, having many practical advantages, are generally used. At Panama, the large dimensions and heavy pressures made the theoretical saving more important. It was feared, also, that, unless spaced very closely, straight girders might require unduly heavy upstream chord sections.

An extended series of estimates was therefore made, covering a number of different shapes and two different angles of the sill. The results are summarized in Tables II and III. The straight shapes used in the comparative estimates had the same general form as the adopted design (Plate II), but varied in thickness from 5 to 9 feet. The parallel sides of the girders simplify the construction, while the curved ends, which were made in the actual construction of the gates without much difficulty and without heating the angles, look better than sharp bends and avoid concentrated stresses. The curved gates were of crescent shape, and 32 inches wide at the quoin and miter ends, while they were 5 feet and 6 feet thick at the center. The straight girder 7 ft. wide with a rise of sill equal to 1/4 of the lock width was taken as the standard.

The relative weights given in Table II are in each case the average derived from six separate designs, corresponding to six different hydrostatic loads. 72 girders were computed in all.

TABLE II.

Weights of Horizontal Girders.

	Straight Girders					Curved Girders	
Thickness	5 ft.	6 ft.	7 ft.	8 ft.	9 ft.	5 ft.	6 ft.
Rise of Sill, ¼ Lock Width..	1.21	1.08	1.00	1.02	1.02	0.78	0.79
Rise of Sill, ⅛ Lock Width..	......	0.97	0.93	0.95	......	0.83	0.85

TABLE III.

Weights of Complete Gates.

	Rise of Sill, ¼ Width		Rise of Sill, ⅛ Width	
	Straight Leaf 7 ft. Thick	Curved Leaf 6 ft. Thick	Straight Leaf 7 ft. Thick	Curved Leaf 6 ft. Thick
77 ft. Gate	1.00	0.92	0.97	0.94
45 ft. Gate	1.00	0.95	0.98	0.95
All gates on canal	1.00	0.93	0.97	0.95

The tables show that the smaller rise of sill would give a slight saving in weight for the straight type. It would, however, require much thicker masonry walls, as the pressure exerted by the gates at right angles to the wall would be 40 percent greater. The larger rise of 1/4 was, therefore, adopted. It has the further advantage of reducing the arc through which the leaves swing. The tables show, further, that the saving in favor of the curved type, though it is over 20 percent for the individual girders, is much less when the entire gate is considered, the average for all the gates on the canal being only 7 percent. It was found that this small saving in weight would be outweighed by the greater cost of constructing curved gates. Estimates submitted by experienced contractors indicated an increase in the unit prices of fully 15 percent, making the cost of the arched type 7 percent higher. The experience gained in building the gates shows that this was a decided under-estimate. It is believed that straight gates would have been preferable, even if they had cost somewhat more than curved gates. Among their advantages, perhaps the most important is the shallower recess in the lock walls. For the shapes used in Table III, the depths of the recesses were 8 ft. 6 in. for the straight, and 12 ft. 6 in. for the curved leaf, so that in order to avoid excessive stresses in the masonry it would have been necessary to increase the thickness of the entire middle wall considerably if curved gates had been used. The saving in masonry would, of itself, have justified the adoption of the straight leaf.

Further advantages are the greater width of the straight gate, which adds to the rigidity and renders the interior more accessible, and the more favorable position of the centre of gravity, which is entirely inside of the leaf, so that the stresses, when it is swinging clear, are very moderate. Besides this, the straight shape has some practical advantages during construction. The girders are much easier to handle, so that railroad and steamship companies readily agreed to ship them fully riveted from the contractors' works in the United States to the lock sites, while curved girders could only be handled in several sections, requiring a large amount of field splicing. There was also little doubt that the simpler shape would assure more accurate workmanship and reduce the liability to errors.

From the computations given above and the other considerations mentioned, the straight leaf 7 ft. thick appeared, on the whole, to be preferable to any other form. However, before making a final decision it was necessary to make sure that a leaf of this form would have the requisite stiffness. This question was extremely important, especially in such high gates. Mathematical analysis was of little assistance. From a comparison with large gates previously built, it was thought that the 7-ft. leaf would prove entirely satisfactory as far as rigidity is concerned. It was, therefore, decided to adopt the form shown

Fig. 1.   Middle Level, Gatun Locks.   East and West Chambers, Looking toward Atlantic Entrance.

on Plate II for all gates. As a matter of fact, the gates, in actual operation, have proved to have ample stiffness.

General Description of the Gates.

The structural arrangement of the gates is shown on Plate III, the general plan of the 82-ft. leaf. The other gates differ mainly in the number and spacing of the horizontal girders and the thickness of the sheathing and cover plates. The distances between girders were made as nearly uniform as possible, only three different panel heights—3 ft. 8 in., 4 ft. 2 in.

and 5 ft. 0 in. being used in all the gates. This helped to make the girders and other parts interchangeable, not only in any one leaf, but in all the gates on the canal. The rather close spacing was found necessary in order to avoid excessive loads on the girders. Near the bottom, a still smaller panel height would have been more economical, but would have made access to the interior too difficult. The vertical system of gate-framing with only two horizontal girders and numerous vertical beams was con-

Fig. 2. Leaves 124 and 125 Miraflores Locks. Lower Guard Gates.

sidered, but found uneconomical and, in fact, not practicable for such large and high leaves.

The frame or skeleton of the gate consists essentially of the horizontal girders, the vertical bracing, the intercostals which stiffen the sheathing plates at intervals of about two feet, and two vertical diaphragms in each panel, built in between the girders, which transfer the thrust of the leaves along the quoin and miter posts to the web plates in the horizontals. Sheathing, doubling and cover plates are riveted to the upstream and downstream sides of the main frame, while the ends of the leaf are closed by flat vertical plates connected to the girders by continuous bent plates. The details of the sheathing plates are shown on Plates IV and V. They are from 7/16 in. to 1 in. thick, and were built in three lengths on the upstream, and two lengths on the downstream side. The width of the sheathing plates corresponds to the panel height. The cover plates on the girders outside of the sheathing were built in single lengths. Where two covers were necessary, the shorter was made 6 or 7 inches narrower than the other to allow easy caulking along all

Fig. 3. Leaves 25 and 26, Gatun Locks.

edges. Typical girder sections are given on Plates II and IV. The flange consists in almost all cases of 8-in. by 8-in. angles on the upstream, and 6-in. by 6-in. angles on the downstream sides. The web plates are from 1/2 in. to 15/16 in. thick and have angle or I-beam stiffeners at intervals of about two feet. Towards the ends, the webs are strongly reinforced to transmit the heavy thrust.

The vertical bracing, end diaphragms and the intercostals are shown on Plates II and IV. There are seven lines of vertical bracing, consisting of plate-and-angle frames built in between the horizontals and forming practically continuous girders from the top to the bottom of the gates. The intercostals consist of 8-in. ship channels, except in the panels having little or no strain, where they are replaced by 6-in. by 3½-in. angles.

The lower part of the leaf forms an air or flotation chamber, subdivided into four water-tight compartments, while the upper part is arranged to permit the water to flow in and out freely as the level in the lock rises and falls. Flotation chambers are rather undesirable, and can generally be avoided in smaller gates. At Panama a single-skin design was practically out of the question, as it would have made the size of the pintle on which the leaf rests and the hinge pin, at the top, unduly large, besides requiring an undesirable arrangement of the sill to avoid excessive uplift, when the gates are closed. The air chambers reduce the weight of the leaf to 1/3 to 1/4 of the total weight in the dry. They are accessible at the bottom by manholes when the locks are pumped out, and at all times by a manshaft and ladders extending to the top of the leaf. As shown in Plate VI, there is in each leaf a centrifugal pump driven by an electric motor and controlled by a float switch on the top deck. The rivet spacing and other structural details in the gates followed the rules for high-grade ship and structural work, and do not need special comment. Some important parts should, however, be described more fully, which presented special difficulties and required somewhat novel details.

These are, first, the anchorages and their connections, and the pintle and other members supporting the weight of the gates; second, the quoin and miter bearings, and the sills; and third, the foot-walks and hand-railings.

Anchorages and Gate Supports.

The general arrangement of the anchorage is given on Plate VII, while the connecting parts in the leaf are shown in the structural plans. The longitudinal and transverse anchors extend about 30 feet into the concrete. The former, which is always in tension, has the usual eyebar form. The transverse anchor, departing from previous practice, is a stiff-riveted frame. It sustains reversing stresses—an outward pull and inward thrust for different positions of the leaf—without depending on the strength of the concrete near the top. The anchor frames were shipped from the United States completely riveted up and were erected without difficulty. A heavy steel casting at the

Fig. 4. Gates in Upper Lock, Gatun.

top of the wall is fastened to both anchors, the details providing a small adjustment to allow for errors. The yoke, a smaller casting of vanadium steel, is connected to the larger casting by an adjustable system of wedges. It carries the bronze bushing, in which the main pin turns, and transmits the pull of the gate, due to its own weight, to the anchors. Sample yokes tested to destruction sustained a pull of over 3,000,000 pounds, or nearly six times the greatest working load. The pin is 10 in. in diameter and of wrought nickel-steel. It acts in double shear, being fastened to the web plate of the top girder and also to a special jaw plate, which is securely bolted to the top girder and the sheathing.

In the design of the pintle, and the other parts supporting the weight at the bottom, existing practice was followed quite closely. They are shown in the general plans and on Plate VIII. The pintle is 16 inches in diameter, hemispherical in shape and made of hammered nickel steel. It is secured in a vanadium-steel casting, the weight being distributed by a larger casting of carbon steel that rests directly on the concrete. A cast shoe, also of vanadium steel, is fastened to the gate, and carries the bushing which turns on the pintle. The bushings are carbon-steel castings in the gates that are always in salt water, and manganese-bronze in the others. Zinc rings were used in certain of the gates to protect the bronze from electrolytic corrosion.

Quoin and Miter-Post Bearings and Sills.

The bearings along the quoin and miter posts in almost all existing lock gates, are of timber. At Panama the high pressures made it difficult, if not impossible, to use wood without making the bearing of excessive width or increasing the stresses beyond safe limits. Timber is also rather short-lived in tropical waters. Metallic bearings were, therefore, adopted for the quoin and miter posts, but the clapping sills attached to the bottom of the leaf and the sill timbers in the masonry are of greenheart timber.

The metallic bearings are required to have great compressive strength, as the thrust exerted by the leaves against each other and against the fixed quoins amounts, in some places, to fully 300,000 pounds per vertical foot. The joints must also be practically water-tight, as separate timber cushions are not used to prevent leakage as in most other gates with metallic bearings. It was by no means easy to find a satisfactory method for obtaining such perfect contact on surfaces nearly 80 feet in height. As the total length of the bearing pieces in all the gates is very great, in fact almost three miles in all, the importance is appar-

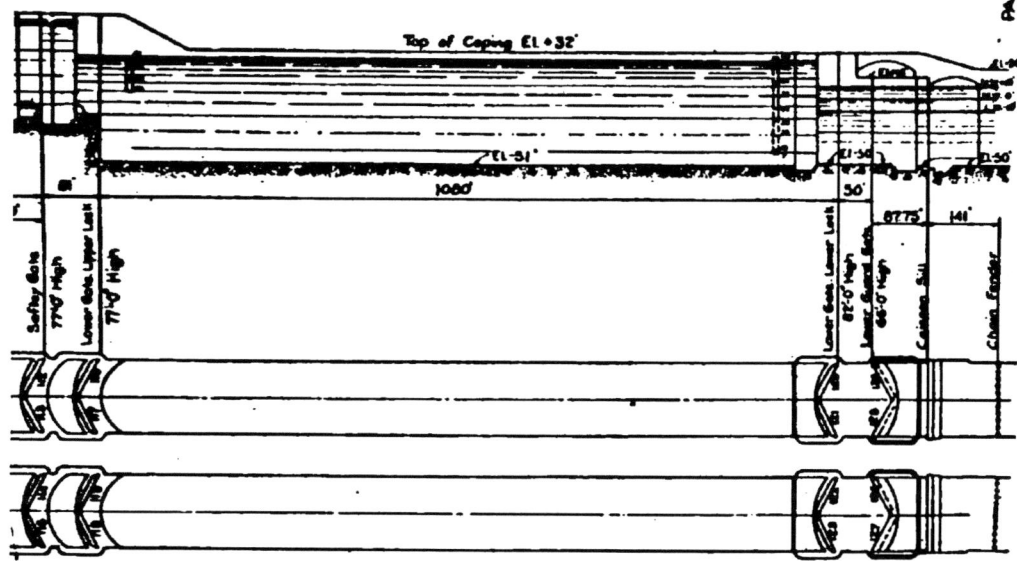

PACIFIC OCEAN

Top of Coping El +32'

1080'

Safety Gate 77'-6" High
Lower Gate Upper Lock 77'-0" High
Lower Gate Lower Lock 82'-0" High
Lower Guard Gate 66'-0" High
Caisson Sill
Chain Fender

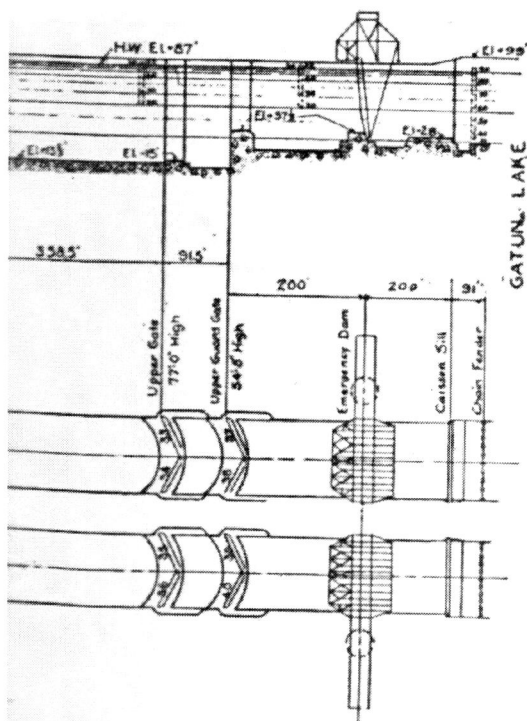

H.W. El +87'
El +99'

GATUN LAKE

358.5'
91.5'
200'
209'
91'

Upper Gate 77'-0" High
Upper Guard Gate 54'-0" High
Emergency Dam
Caisson Sill
Chain Fender

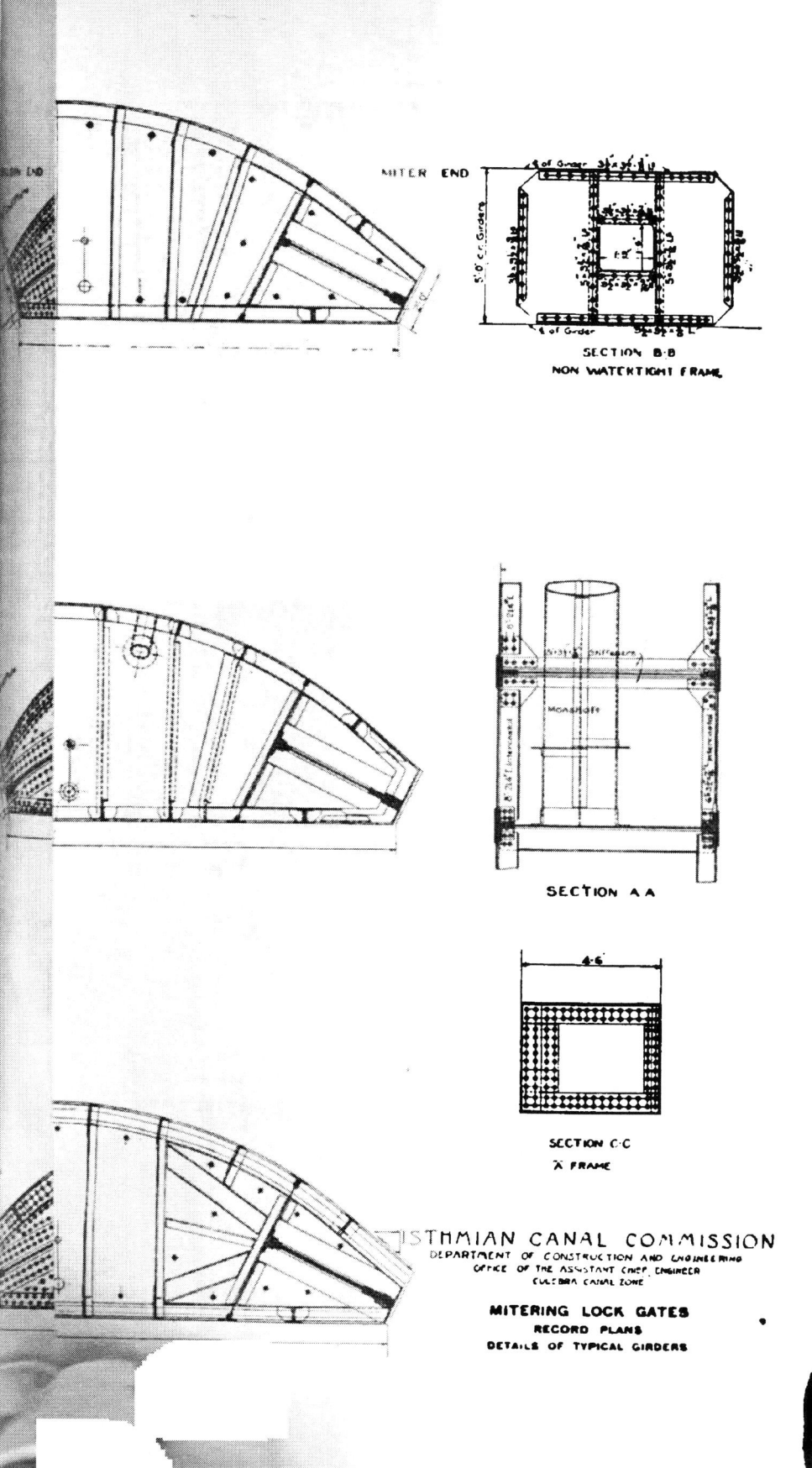

MITER END

SECTION B-B
NON WATERTIGHT FRAME

SECTION A A

SECTION C-C
"A" FRAME

ISTHMIAN CANAL COMMISSION
DEPARTMENT OF CONSTRUCTION AND ENGINEERING
OFFICE OF THE ASSISTANT CHIEF ENGINEER
CULEBRA CANAL ZONE

MITERING LOCK GATES
RECORD PLANS
DETAILS OF TYPICAL GIRDERS

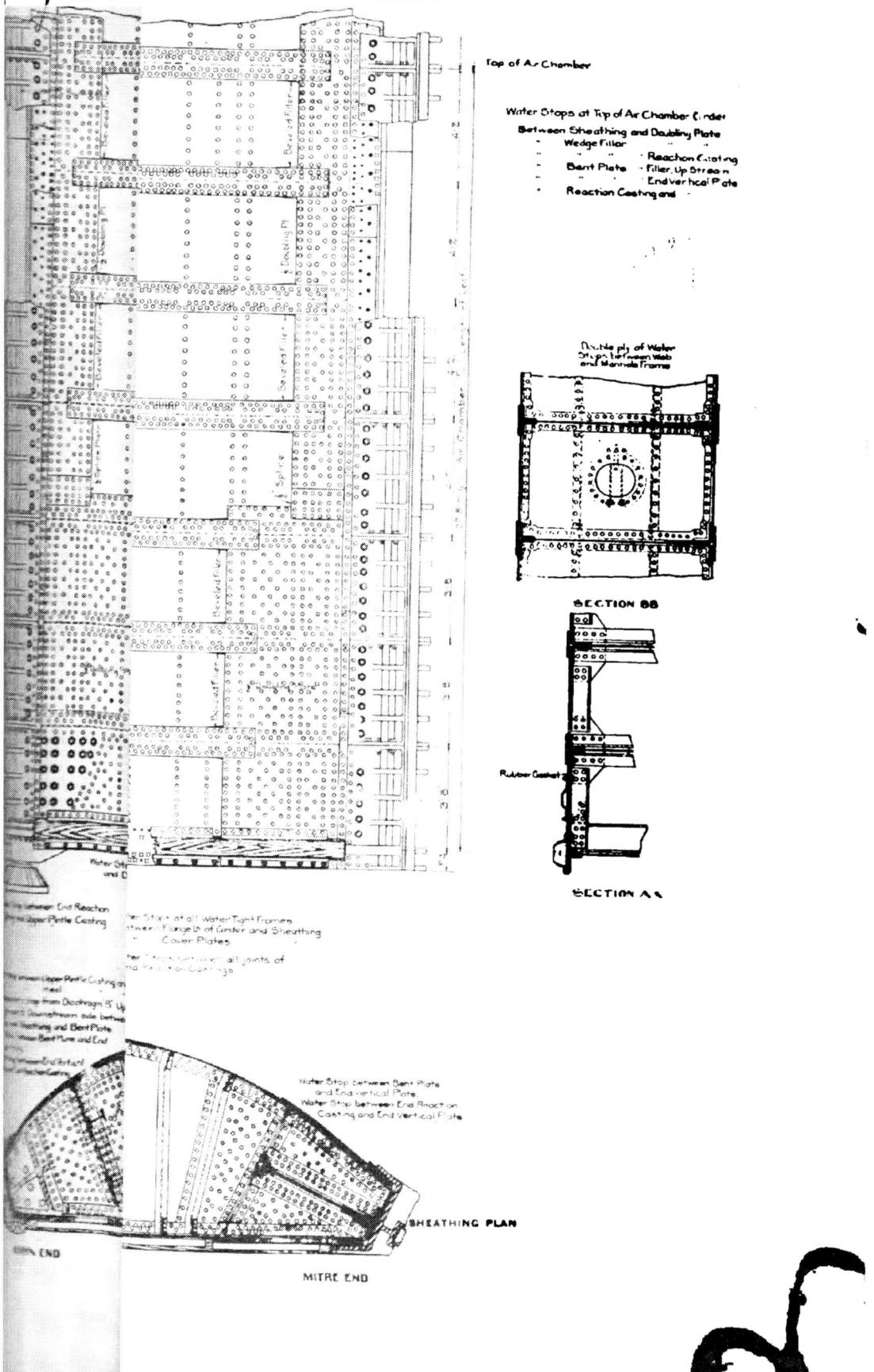

Beveled Filler   Beveled Filler

Top of Air Chamber

Water Stops at Top of Air Chamber Girder
Between Sheathing and Doubling Plate
"   Wedge Filler
"   " Reaction Casting
"   Bent Plate   " Filler, Up Stream
"   " End Vertical Plate
"   Reaction Casting and

Double ply of Water
Stops between Web
and Manhole Frame

SECTION BB

Rubber Gasket

SECTION AA

Water Stops at all Water Tight Frames
Between Flanges of Girder and Sheathing
Cover Plates

Lower End Reaction
Upper Plate Casting

Water Stop between Bent Plate
and End Vertical Plate
Water Stop between End Reaction
Casting and End Vertical Plate

SHEATHING PLAN

MITRE END

ent of making the adjustment in an inexpensive and still exact manner. Machining the plates after erection was very undesirable, as the rapid changes in temperature would have made it difficult to obtain accurate results, while the method would, in any event, be slow and very expensive.

The scheme finally adopted is shown on Plate IX, Figs. 8 and 9. Heavy steel castings were embedded in the lock walls at the hollow quoins when the concrete was poured. These castings vary in width at different elevations, to keep the pressure on the concrete constant. Similar castings were attached to both ends of the gates by rivets and bolts, in sections corresponding to the panel heights. The bearing pieces are smoothly finished plates of rolled nickel steel about 3 in. thick, secured to the castings in machined recesses provided for the purpose. They are secured by small bolts placed about 18 inches apart. After the bearing pieces were accurately aligned, melted babbitt metal was poured into the spaces between the castings and the plates. On the miter posts, the bearing pieces are slightly convex, having a radius of 16 feet, so that the surface of contact, which is very narrow, cannot depart far from the center of the plate. At the quoin end, the plate attached to the gate is convex, and bears against a concave surface in the hollow quoin. The radii are $10\frac{1}{2}$ in. and 12 in., respectively, so that the difference in curvature is about the same as at the miter bearings. The strength of the bearings was demonstrated by numerous special tests made prior to the adoption of the design, which have been corroborated by the action of the gates in service. Theoretical investigation proved of little value in ascertaining the stresses.

The shapes and clearances of the masonry and gate leaf at the quoin end were carefully arranged to facilitate the adjusting of the bearing plates, and the pouring of the babbitt. The pintle has an eccentricity of $3\frac{1}{2}$ in., with reference to the center of pressure, which insures the easy opening and closing of the leaf. The method used in adjusting the plates will be described in detail when the erection of the gates is discussed. This type of bearing is believed to be entirely novel. It has so far proved very satisfactory, as there are practically no deformations at the bearings and no leakage through the joints. The design has been followed in several large locks built subsequently.

The details of the sills are shown on Plate X. The fixed sill consists of 12-in. by 14-in. timbers, bolted to a continuous steel casting, and set in cement mortar to give a better bearing and facilitate adjustment. The sill is strengthened by inclined and vertical rods imbedded in the masonry, which are held in position by light angle-iron frames which keep the rods in position while the concrete is being placed. The clapping sill fastened to the leaf differs from common practice by the addition of a rubber seal to prevent leakage. This consists of a narrow strip of pure rubber secured to a 3-in. by 2-in. angle-iron bolted to the leaf. This seal seems to fulfill its purpose in a satisfactory manner. It is shown on Plate X.

Foot-walks.

The foot-walks consist of removable concrete slabs with a cast iron curbing. In the lower guard-gates the walk is 8 ft. wide, and has a fixed gas-pipe railing. In all other leaves, its width is about 2 ft. 9 in., and a collapsible railing is provided, which is lowered when necessary to avoid interference with the tow lines. A simple screw mechanism operated by an electric motor on the top of the gates is used. It works automatically as the leaves open and close, but can also be operated by a push-plate on the lock wall. The arrangement is shown on the general gate plans and in greater detail on Plate XI.

Material and Workmanship.

As far as possible, steel made in accordance with the usual bridge or ship standards was used; special alloy steels and bronzes being confined to a few parts. All steel was made by the open-hearth process. The specified requirements for the different grades were as given on the following page.

The usual bending and drifting tests were also required. Some difficulty was encountered in securing nickel steel agreeing exactly with the specifications. As this material is used only in compression, a moderate increase in hardness and reduction in ductility were permitted. All other grades met the requirements fully.

The babbitt metal used for backing up the bearing plates on the quoin and miter posts contains about 90 percent of lead, 8 percent of antimony and small quantities of tin and copper.

When tested in samples 4 in. square it withstood a compres-

Grade of steel	Ultimate tensile strength ($TS.$)	Yield point Min.	% of Elongation Min.	Miscellaneous
Rolled carbon-steel	60,000 ± 4,000	55% of $TS.$	$\dfrac{1,500,000}{TS.}$ in 8"	and $\dfrac{150,000}{TS.} - (t - 6)$ in 8" for material over ¾" thick if t = thickness in eighths of inches.
Rivet-steel	50,000 ± 4,000	55% of $TS.$	$\dfrac{1,500,000}{TS.}$ in 8"	
Rolled nickel-steel	85,000 to 100,000	55% of $TS.$	$\dfrac{1,750,000}{TS.}$ in 2"	Must contain not less than 3.25% of nickel.
Carbon-steel castings	70,000 min.	31,500	18 in 2"	
Vanadium-steel castings	70,000 min.	40,000	20 in 2"	Must contain at least 0.16% of vanadium.
Machinery steel	80,000 min.	40,000	20 in 2"	
Manganese bronze	75,000 min.	40,000	25 in 2"	

sive stress of 25,000 lbs. per square inch without permanent deformation.

A high grade of workmanship was necessary in order to obtain accurate dimensions and a proper distribution of the stresses. The requirements usual in the highest grade of bridge and tank work were, therefore, specified, and great care was taken to secure accurate work. Steel templates were used for laying out all important parts; and the ends of the horizontal

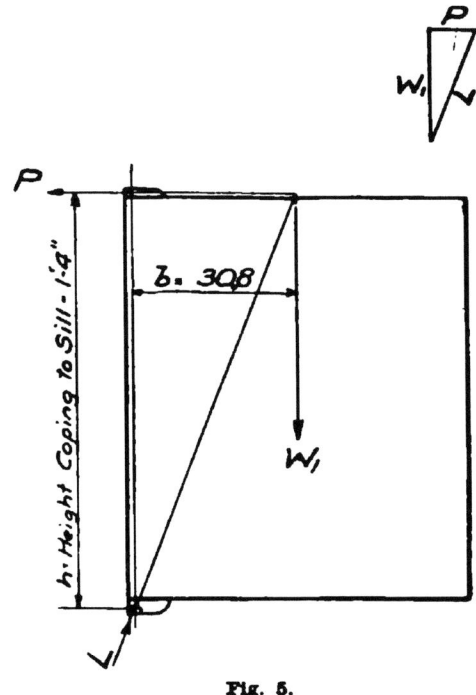

Fig. 5.

girders, end diaphragms and castings were "finished" to secure correct angles and lengths.

All sheared edges, except in a few minor details, were planed, as well as all rolled edges that were to be caulked. Seven-eighths- and one-inch rivets were used in almost all cases. In metal over ¾ in. thick, the holes were first drilled from the solid, while sub-punching was used in thinner material. The diameter of these sub-punched or drilled holes was specified to be ⅛ in. smaller than the nominal rivet diameter, but a diameter of 1 1/8 in. was actually used for most of the rivets. After assembly in the shop or field, all these holes were enlarged by reaming. All bolt holes were also reamed out in the shop or field, a driving fit being required in all important cases.

Further requirements as to workmanship are referred to under "Erection."

Stresses.

The stresses in the gates fall under two heads: those due to their weight and those due to water pressure.

The former govern the design of the anchorages and their connections, also of the pintles and castings that support

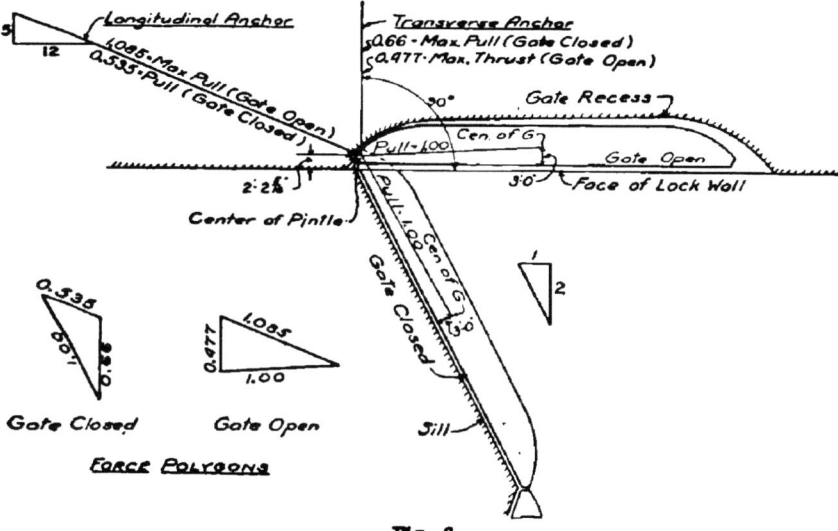

Fig. 6.

the weight of the leaves at the bottom and of some adjacent parts of the gates themselves. These stresses have maximum values when the leaf is swinging in the dry, which are reduced by buoyancy when the locks are in service. All parts were proportioned to be of ample strength under the maximum stresses in the dry, but the bearing areas in the pintles and hinge pins, on which the leaves turn, were based on the working loads with water in the locks. The inclined reaction at the bottom varies with the weight of the gate, while the horizontal pull at the top is nearly constant for all leaves in the dry, varying only from 276 to 289 tons. (See Fig. 5.)

The arrangement of the longitudinal and transverse anchors

is shown on Fig. 6. The former is always in tension, the pull being greatest when the leaf is wide open, while the transverse anchor is subjected to reversing stresses, the maximum outward pull corresponding to the closed and the greatest thrust to the open position. The diagram gives the forces acting on the anchors for a gate pull of unity. From these the values for the several gates can readily be found. The maximum unit stress is 17,000 lbs. per sq. in. in the eyebars and from 8000 to 14,000 lbs. per sq. in. in the transverse frames. The working stresses, with

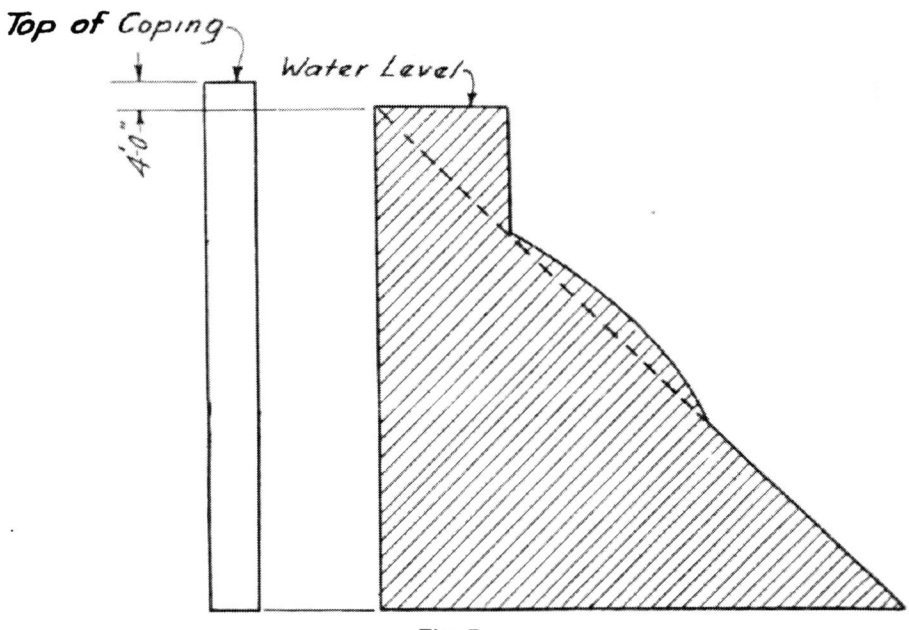

Fig. 7.

forty-one feet of water on the sills are from 22 to 33 percent of the above values.

The pressures on the pintle are from 1600 to 2400 lbs. per square inch for the different gates when the locks are in service. In the dry they vary from 7300 lbs. to 9000 lbs. per sq. in. On the hinge pin at the top the pressures are 5700 lbs. under extreme, and from 1200 to 1800 lbs. per sq. in. under working conditions. The loading on the concrete below the foundation casting never exceeds 400 lbs. per square inch. When the gates are closed, with a full head on the upstream and none on the downstream side, the weight on the pintle varies from 56 to 100 tons for different gates. This gives perfect safety against uplift. A further reduction was not feasible, as the air chambers could not be made any higher.

The stresses in the gates when they are supporting water pressure can not be found with great accuracy. The uncertainty arises mainly from the varying pressure against the sill, but also from the complex construction, which makes the stresses indeterminate, even when all external forces are known. It is possible, however, to find values which will not be exceeded in actual service. The gates, as a whole, are under their highest stress when supporting a full head, with no water on the downstream side, and to secure uniformity, this extreme condition was assumed throughout, though in some of the gates it will rarely, if ever, occur.

The principal parts carrying stress are the sheathing, the intercostals and the main horizontal girders. Besides this, the vertical diaphragms which transmit the end thrust and the vertical bracing must be considered. The sheathing was computed as a flat plate, though it also acts as a part of the horizontal girder flange. Bach's formula was used, with coefficients for "supported" edges, viz.:

$$t = 0.4b \sqrt{\frac{1}{1 + \frac{b^2}{a^2}} \frac{H}{s}}$$

in which t is the thickness of the plate in inches, a and b the height and width of the panel, H the head in feet, and s the stress in the steel in pounds per square inch. The permitted stress, s, was 8000 lbs. for the downstream face, where the local stress is greatest when the gates as a whole carry no load. For the upstream sheathing, it was reduced to 5000 lbs., as the plates on this side, besides supporting the direct water pressure, also act as part of the girder flange when the gate is resisting an hydrostatic head.

The intercostals were computed as beams on two supports, with maximum stresses of 12,000 lbs. per square inch. The load carried by an intercostal was taken as $\frac{a^4}{a^4 + b^4} W$, a and b being the height and width of the panel and W its total load.

The horizontal girders act as arches for transferring the hydrostatic load to the side walls, though in most cases, owing to the vertical stiffness of the leaf, a part of the load is carried to the sills. The sill pressure is uncertain, as it depends upon the length of the leaves, and varies with the temperature and with changes in the quoin and miter bearings and the sill timbers. In proportioning the girders, it was necessary, in each case, to assume the most unfavorable case of sill contact. The typical loading used is shown on Fig. 7. Towards the bottom the full hydrostatic load corresponding to "no contact" was assumed, while for the girders within about 20 feet from the top a mini-

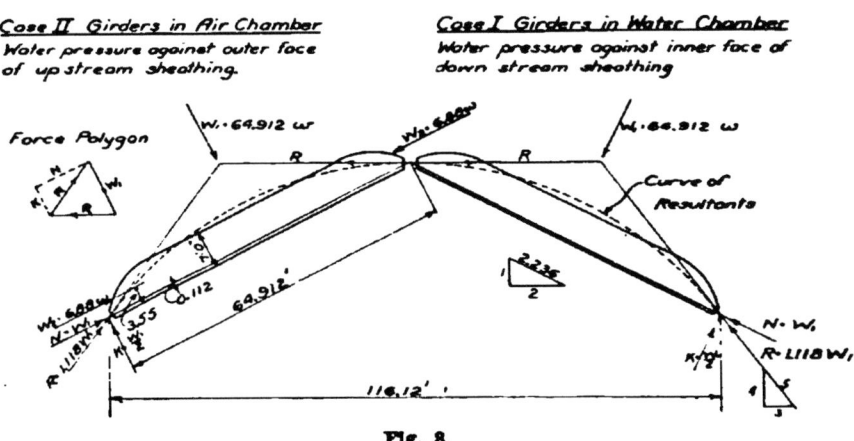

Fig. 8.

mum head of 20 feet was adopted to avoid unduly light construction. The girders near the middle of the height were shown by an extended analysis which can not be given here, to carry somewhat heavier loads than those due to water pressure, at least in gates over 54 ft. 8 in. high. A small percentage was, therefore, added to the hydrostatic loads which act on these girders.

For convenience, the computations were based on a typical girder supporting 100 feet of head on a horizontal strip a foot high, corresponding to a load of 6250 lbs. per linear foot of girder flange. The coefficient C of this girder was taken as 1, so that the different girders have coefficients $C = \dfrac{bd}{100}$, d being the hydrostatic head at the elevation of the girder and b the height of sheathing supported by it. The cross sections of horizontals are directly proportional to their coefficients.

The external forces acting on girders in the water and air chambers, respectively, are shown in Fig. 8. In the former case the water pressure acts on the inner face of the downstream sheathing, while in Case II, corresponding to the air chambers, the pressure is directed against the outside of the upper face.

The stress at each cross section may be considered as due to a single resultant, which, as a rule, does not act at right angles to the section nor at its center of gravity. Near the ends, the pressure is taken mainly by the reinforced web, as the resultant acts close to the centre of gravity. At other points, the assumption, usual in plate girder design, was made that the shear is resisted entirely by the web and the normal force by the chords.

Case I Waterchamber

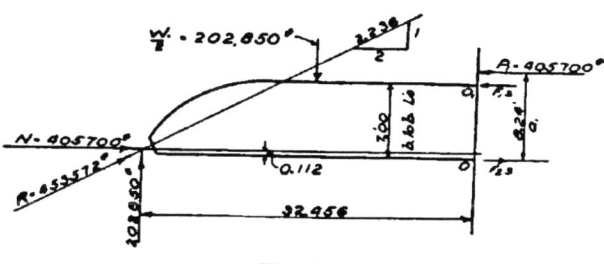

Fig. 9.

In addition to the angles and cover plates, one-sixth of the web and a strip of sheathing from $4\frac{1}{2}$ in. to 6 in. wider than the widest cover plate were included in the chord sections. The results obtained under the above assumptions, agreed within reasonably close limits with those obtained by more complex methods, in which the web was assumed to take a part of the bending stress. The permissible unit stress was fixed at 14,000 lbs. per square inch. If, as is probable, the whole sheathing acts as part of the girder flange, the stresses would be from 1500 to 4000 lbs. less.

The flange sections were determined at the center of the leaf and at a point in the downstream face 26 feet from the center line, also where necessary at the ends of cover plates. The governing stresses were compressive, the tensile stresses at the middle of the downstream face being quite small. The method used will be readily understood from the following example. Let Fig. 9 represent a girder in the water chamber having a coefficient $C = 1$. If P_1 is the resultant thrust on the central section, a_1, its distance from the downstream face, and F_1 and F_2 the required cross sections, we have by moments about 0,

$$P_1 a_1 = 0.112\,N + 32.456\,K - 16.228\,\frac{W_1}{2}.$$

For a coefficient $C = 1$ we have

$$N = P_1 = 405700 \text{ lbs. and } \frac{W_1}{2} = K = 202850 \text{ lbs.}$$

so that

$$A_1 = \frac{405700 \times 0.112 + 202850 \times 32.456 - 202850 \times 16.228}{405700} = 8.24 \text{ ft.}$$

Increasing a_1 by 3 in. to allow for incorrect mitering, change of temperature, etc., and assuming the centre of gravity of each flange at the back of its chord angles, we obtain by moments about 0 and 0_1,

$$F_1 = \frac{405700 \times (8.24 + .25)}{7\,s} = \frac{492050}{s}$$

and

$$F_2 = \frac{405700 \times (8.24 + .25 - 7)}{7\,s} = \frac{86355}{s}.$$

For a unit stress of 14,000 lbs. per square inch, these equations give $F_1 = 35.10$ square inches, and $F_2 = 6.16$ square inches, F_2 being in tension. The results for all cross sections are given in the following table:

Required Girder Sections in sq. in. for coefficient $C = 1$

	Water Chamber	Air Chamber
Upstream flange at center line	35.10	36.76
Downstream flange at center line	6.16	4.71
Upstream flange 15 ft. from center line	27.97	29.58
Downstream flange 26 ft. from center line	15.30	16.75

For other girders the required sectional area is obtained by multiplying the above values by the coefficient C of the girder.

The web plates are ½ in., ⅝ in. and ¾ in. thick, except in the bottom girders, which have $1\frac{1}{8}$-in. webs in all gates over 54 ft. 8 in. high to resist direct water pressure. The maximum shear occurs at a point 24 feet from the center line, where the depth of the leaf is 78.6 inches. If $t =$ the web thickness, the total shear for $C = 1$ will be 24 by 6250 $= 150,000$ lbs. and the

$$\text{unit stress} = \frac{150000}{78.6t} = \frac{1906}{t} \text{ lbs. per square inch.}$$

Computed on this basis, the shearing stresses for the web plates in the different gates vary from 4500 to 7000 per square inch.

The end diaphragms withstand a thrust which is equal to $R = 72.572 \times 6250 \ C. = 453575 \ C$, if $C =$ the mean coefficient of adjacent girders. The dimensions of the diaphragms depended largely on the rivet connections. A unit stress of 10,000 lbs. was used.

The vertical bracing was designed to be of ample strength to transfer to the sill a load of 50,000 lbs. per linear ft., but the design of the details was governed mainly by practical considerations.

Erection.

The erection of the gates at the lock sites formed a part of the lock gate contract. The methods to be used were left to the contractors, though their plans were subject to approval by the Chief Engineer of the Commission. The scheme proposed in the beginning proved entirely satisfactory and was modified but slightly during the progress of the work. The erection was a work of much difficulty, owing in part to the large size and number of the gates and the high degree of accuracy required, and in part to the remote location, the climatic conditions and the character of the labor available.

The plant installed at each lock site included a power house with electrically-driven air compressors and motor-generator sets, several erection bridges, numerous locomotive cranes and falsework frames, besides a large quantity of smaller machines and accessories. The necessary electric current, water and coal and the locomotives for switching service, were furnished free of charge by the Commission, but all supplies, the complete erecting plant and all labor were paid for by the contractors.

All material was received at the lock sites by rail, the storage yards being situated on one side only of each lock, and quite close to the lock walls.

Little difficulty was met with in delivering the steel work in excellent condition, although the girders, some 1500 in all, were 65 ft. long and weighed as much as 18 tons each. These girders and also the vertical frames and diaphragms, and some minor parts, were riveted up complete in the United States. The arrangement of the service tracks is shown on Plate IX, Fig. 1. The two tracks extended as a rule the entire length of the lock, and in some cases additional tracks were provided so as to enlarge the area available for storage. As shown in the plan, the track nearest the lock was connected by a curve to the rails on the erection bridges which span the lock chambers and the middle walls. These bridges and their positions when in use are shown in Figs. 2, 3 and 4, Plate IX, and in some of the photographs. They were moved forward on the lock walls from gate to gate, being supported on the temporary extension pieces shown in Fig. 3, Plate IX.

Practically all handling was done by locomotive cranes which first unloaded the material in the storage yards and subsequently served for placing the separate parts on flat cars, towing the cars on to the erection bridges, and finally lowering the members into their permanent positions in the gates.

The work of erection was divided into three parts: first, the erection proper, that is, putting of the material in place and fastening it by temporary bolts; second, the bolting up and reaming out of the rivet holes, the driving of the field rivets, and the caulking; third, the finishing—which included the attachment and adjusting of the reaction castings and bearing plates, the moving of the leaves into position on the pintles and their connection to the anchorages; finally, the testing for water tightness, the adjusting of the sill timbers, the erection of the foot walks and other minor parts, and the painting.

Erection proper began for each leaf with the placing of the bottom girder to which the castings at the pintle end and the reaction frame at the miter end had been permanently fastened in the storage yard. Two cranes were used for handling this girder, which weighed 24 tons. One crane was sufficient for all other gate parts. The girder was lowered on to a platform of I beams which rested on the sill walls and on small temporary pedestals of concrete. This blocking was just high enough to permit the leaf to clear the pintle when it was being rolled into its final position. As shown in Fig. 2, Plate IX, the leaf was placed about 4 ft. from its final position, and at an angle of 45° with the lock walls. The rest of the skeleton was then built up, the vertical frames being attached in each panel before the successive horizontals were lowered into place. The intercostals were usually placed later. Great care was taken to keep the ends of the gate as straight as possible, and the entire leaf was carefully plumbed before any rivets were driven in the sheathing. During the entire erection guy lines were kept attached to the leaves at the top and at a point half way up. The ends were rarely out of plumb more than $\frac{1}{8}$ in. in the height of the gate. The total height was kept within $\frac{1}{4}$ in. of the nominal dimension by using adjustable fillers at every fourth panel when necessary.

The rivets in the skeleton, that is, those connecting the vertical frames, diaphragms and intercostals to the girders, were next driven. The holes for these rivets had been reamed to their full size in the shop, using special templates. The erection proper was completed by attaching the sheathing, cover and doubling plates. Only a small number of bolts was inserted at this time so as to release the erection bridges as soon as possible for use elsewhere.

The second step in the erection process was the bolting up, reaming and riveting. The reaming was done in part by small pneumatic or electric reamers, but mainly by larger machines similar to those used in shops, which were carried on heavy platforms suspended from the top of the gates.

The riveting was done mainly from small platforms attached to the leaves by brackets. Towards the end of the work complete scaffolds were built on both sides of the gates. Standard pneumatic machines were used for all rivets, except the countersunk rivets in the end plates, which were driven by hand in order to distort these plates as little as possible. The riveters were mainly West Indian negroes without any previous experience in mechanical work, with white gang-leaders. The total number of field driven rivets was nearly 6,000,000, and 660,000 were driven in a single calendar month without working over eight hours per day or on Sundays. After the riveting was practically done, the entire downstream face of the gate and the upstream

face of the air chamber were caulked to water tightness. St
dard pneumatic machines were used.

The third step in the erection process—the finishing—
begun by attaching the reaction castings along the quoin
miter posts to which the bearing plates are secured. These ?
ings have been fully described in a previous section of
paper.

In order to insure good contact between the reaction cas
ings on the gates and the structural frames, the end plates in

Fig. 10. Upper Guard Gates, Pedro Miguel Locks. East Chamber Forebay and
Construction of Approach Wall.

the latter were carefully ground with emery wheels, though no
attempt was made to obtain an absolutely true surface for the
whole height of the leaf. As the castings are only one panel high,
it was deemed sufficient to secure a good bearing for each casting separately, especially along the outer edges of the casting
and opposite the reaction diaphragms. Small depressions were
not considered objectionable. The final exact alignment of the
bearings was obtained by adjusting the bearing plates which are
fastened in the recesses of the castings. To insure water tight-

ness a sheet of canvas, soaked in red lead, was placed between these end plates and the castings, while wedge-shaped plates were used in the space between the flanges on the castings and the gate sheathing plates. All edges were fully caulked where necessary.

The nickel-steel bearing plates were next attached to the castings, but were not finally adjusted until the leaf had been moved onto the pintle and attached to the anchorage.

The leaves, while they were being moved into place, were supported by two steel false-work frames, one on each side of the leaf, which are illustrated on Figs. 5 and 6 of Plate IX. They were put in place by locomotive cranes standing on the lock walls, after practically all the rivets had been driven and were attached to the gates by numerous temporary bolts. These frames stood on pedestals which rested on rollers, as shown in Fig. 7 of Plate IX. A wedge in these pedestals permitted the frames to be raised slightly so that the leaf hung suspended between them. The frames were then moved on their rollers by means of hydraulic jacks until the leaf was in its proper position, when it was lowered onto the pintle and the top hinge connected to the anchorage.

The steel bearing-plates at the quoin and miter ends were a novel feature of the design, and their erection and accurate adjustment required great care. The details of these bearings are shown in Figs. 8 and 9 of Plate IX.

The castings embedded in the fixed quoins were put in place by the Commission's forces when the concrete was poured, but the adjusting of the bearing plates in these castings formed a part of the gate contract. Many of the castings were set somewhat out of line, but the adjustment of the plates provided for in the plans proved ample in almost all cases. The plates were attached to these castings by permanent 1-in. bolts spaced about 17 in. apart. Their exact adjustment was made by these bolts and by temporary stud bolts placed at intervals of about 2 feet along the center line of the plates. A fine steel wire was fastened at the top and the bottom of the quoin so as to pass exactly through the center, to which the curved surfaces of the bearing plates were to be set, a metallic template of proper shape being used. It is believed that the deviation in the surface does not exceed 4/1000 to 5/1000 of an inch from a correct position, except where the machining was defective. Melted babbitt metal was next poured into the spaces between the plates and the castings through some of the bolt holes at intervals of about 4 feet. Little difficulty was experienced in pouring the metal successfully, though a rather large melting pot and a high temperature were found to be desirable. In order to avoid explosions from dampness, it proved necessary to blow hot compressed air into the spaces to be filled just before pouring. The joints between the bearing plates and the castings were caulked.

The bearing plates in the leaves themselves were adjusted in a similar manner. They were loosely bolted to the castings before the leaves were placed on their pintles. For the accurate adjustment at the miter ends, the following method was used: The leaves were revolved to a closed position and the bearing pieces at the miter end at the top and bottom were so placed as to divide the available distance as equally as possible so that the average thickness of babbitt metal should be the same in both leaves, and the nickel steel pieces should project beyond the castings an equal amount. This work was done at about 6:30 A. M. when the leaves have their minimum length. The gates were then partly opened and a wire stretched on one of the leaves from the top to the bottom. All plates in that leaf were brought to this straight line by screw adjustment and at once babbitted. After the plates in one leaf were thus secured, the leaves at the same hour on a succeeding morning were again closed to exactly the same position as shown by a mark on the sill. The bearing plate at the bottom of the second leaf was then, by means of the screw bolts, forced into close contact with the corresponding plate of the leaf first babbitted. The plate at the top was not brought into direct contact with the bearing on the first leaf, but a small piece of steel $\frac{1}{32}$ inch thick was interposed while the plate was being adjusted. This was done so that a small opening might remain between the leaves, as it is desirable, in operation, to have the leaves meet first at the bottom.

After again opening the leaves a wire was tightly stretched on the second leaf so as to touch the top and bottom bearings. The bearings were accurately adjusted to this wire and babbitted. The two leaves were subsequently closed, again in the early morning, to test their exact fitting, and slight inaccuracies removed by emery wheels. As a result of the process described there should be a space between the leaves in the early morning, varying uniformly from 0 at the bottom to $\frac{1}{32}$ in. at the top. It was found that during the day the leaves do not elongate at the bottom, while at the top they gradually expand until about 2 P. M., at least in sunny weather; the maximum extension was found to be as high as $\frac{3}{16}$ in., or even $\frac{1}{4}$ in. At such times a straight line drawn from the top to the bottom of a leaf would not touch the metal at all points, as the surface is slightly concave. The deviations were found to be very small, not over a few thousandths of an inch in any case. These conditions will change somewhat after the gates have been in service longer, as the pins will wear, allowing the leaves to sag slightly. So far the bearings have remained absolutely water tight.

For the plates at the quoin ends of the leaf, a simpler method was used. With the leaves accurately closed against the sill, the several bearing plates were forced against the fixed plates in the hollow quoins so as to secure very perfect contact for their whole height. With the plates firmly held, the leaf was then revolved to an open position and the babbitt metal poured through holes in the face of the plates. The adjustments of the plates in both quoin and miter ends was made by the permanent bolts which fastened the plates to the castings, and small temporary bolts or jacks pressing against the ends of the permanent bolts. The adjustment at the quoin ends almost always preceded the miter post adjustment.

The adjustment of the timbers at the sill was made after the miter and quoin bearings were completely finished. These timbers rest in castings. A space about 1 in. wide was left on the bottom and back of the timbers for grouting. The timbers were adjusted by pressing them against the gate leaves when the latter were closed.

All leaves were carefully tested for water tightness. In order to do this the leaf was blocked up securely and the entire. air chamber filled with water, the manshaft being also filled to the very top of the leaf so that the hydrostatic head at the bottom was equal to the full height of the gates. Any leaks along the caulked seams or at the rivets were at once corrected by caulking. The tightness of the bulkheads subdividing the air chambers was afterwards tested by successively emptying the several compartments, thus exposing the bulkheads to pressure on one side. The leaves in the tests showed but few and unimportant leaks so that as a rule a leaf was made absolutely water tight in a few hours.

Painting.

The protection of the gates from corrosion is very difficult at Panama, as the atmosphere is always humid and the water in the locks contains considerable percentages of sulphuretted hydrogen, carbonic acid and other impurities owing to the large amount of decaying vegetation. Repainting is difficult and expensive, and may also cause a serious delay in the traffic, as the locks have to be operated continuously through all seasons of the year. It was therefore thought justifiable, even at a somewhat increased expense, to use the very best available means of protecting the gates. All material in the shops was thoroughly cleaned by sand blasting or pickling, priming coats being applied immediately after this cleaning. For the entire interior, bitumastic enamel was selected, a proprietory compound which is applied hot and has been used on shipboard for a long time with excellent results. These surfaces were given a priming coat of "bitumastic solution" which was applied cold in the shop, and the enamel was applied after the gates were fully erected. Coatings of this kind are very much more expensive than ordinary paints and require great care in application. The interior surfaces coated in this way have so far remained in perfect condition in both the air and water chambers of the gates.

On the outside of the gates several different kinds of paint were applied in order to find out by actual trial that which is on the whole most suitable. At Gatun two coats of red lead and two coats of a paint containing about equal parts of red lead and graphite were used, while at Pedro Miguel three coats of a damp-proof paint, and at Miraflores two coats of a proprietory carbon paint were applied. Some of the gates that are always in salt water were given one coat of United States Navy anti-corrosive and one coat of anti-fouling over priming coats of red lead. None of these paints has proved satisfactory for the portions of the gates permanently submerged. Surfaces that are always above the high water level, and even those which are at times under water, have remained in good condition in all the locks, that is, all the paints have proved satisfactory, except in parts permanently submerged.

Since the summer of 1914, the gates have been largely repainted, using the guard gates as cofferdams, where feasible. Since the floating caissons reached the Isthmus in October, 1914, those surfaces in the lower locks not previously accessible have also been recoated.

Weights and Costs.

There are, in all, 46 gates of two leaves each, of which 20 are in the Gatun, 12 in the Pedro Miguel and 14 in the Miraflores Locks. Their locations in the lock chambers are shown on Plate I. Six of the gates are 47 ft. 4 in. high from the top of the walls to the sill; four, 54 ft. 8 in.; two, 66 ft. 0 in.; twenty, 77 ft. 0 in.; four, 77 ft. 10 in.; eight, 79 ft. 0 in.; and two, 82 ft. 0 in. high.

The shipping weight of the metal work in all the gates was 58,582 tons of 2000 pounds. The total costs of the completed gates, not counting the fixed steel embedded in the concrete, nor the pumps, motors and electric wiring, are shown in the following table:

Cost of Gates.

	Total	Per ton	Per lb.
Contract payments	$5,510,846.05	$ 94.07	4.70 cents
Miscellaneous expenses	484,525.91	8.27	0.41 "
Inspection in United States	129,241.45	2.21	0.11 "
Inspection on Isthmus	70,232.76	1.20	0.06 "
	$6,194,846.17	$105.75	5.28 "

The cost of the inspection amounted to 3.32 percent of the total cost exclusive of inspection, of which 2.15 percent covered the shop and 1.17 percent the field inspection.

The weight of the fixed parts, i. e., the anchorages, reaction castings, sill reinforcements, and foundation castings, was approximately 8322 tons, or about 14 per cent of the weight of the gate leaves. The cost of the fixed parts delivered on the Isthmus was $576,974.30. The average weights and contract costs of the several gates were as follows, the figures being given for one <u>leaf</u> in each case:

	Heights	Weight in tons	Contract costs
Upper guard gate	47′ 4″	395	$38,861.00
Lower guard gate	47′ 4″	402	39,459.00
Gate	54′ 8″	465	45,261.00
Lower guard gate	66′ 0″	574	54,830.00
Gate	77′ 0″	692	64,952.00
Gate	77′ 10″	693	65,111.00
Gate	79′ 0″	722	67,525.00
Gate	82′ 0″	745	69,656.00

The weights of the several leaves when in use are from 18 to 27 tons greater than the figures given in the last table, as the concrete foot walks, the cement filling in the bottom panel, the mitering machines, the pumps, motors and electric wiring, and some minor accessories were not included.

The principal contract prices, per unit, for the erected material, were as follows: Riveted structural work, including rivets, 3.785c. per lb.; turned steel bolts and nuts, 7.3c. per lb.; carbon-steel castings, 7.86c. per lb.; vanadium-steel yokes and lower pintle castings, 12.3c. per lb.; other vanadium-steel castings, 11.2c. per lb.; forged or rolled nickel steel, 11.7c. per lb.; manhole covers (cast steel), 22.2c. per lb.; bronze bushings, 41.0c. per lb.; hand-railing, including mechanism, 32.1c. per lb.; valves and stuffing boxes in pumping system, 67.4c. per lb.; piping in same, 12.8c. per lb.; babbitt metal back of bearing plates, 12.26c. per lb.; greenheart timbers in sills and fenders, $132.00 per M. ft. B. M. The enamel in the interior and two coats of paint on the outside of the gates are included in the above prices.

The lock gates were built under a contract with the McClintic-Marshall Construction Company, of Pittsburgh, Pa., dated June 21, 1910. The field erection began about June 1, 1911, and was entirely completed in January, 1914, although the gates were sufficiently advanced to permit the lockage of vessels from ocean to ocean by October 1, 1913, through one of the twin flights.

CHAIN FENDERS.

The chain fenders serve for protecting certain of the lock-gates against injury from collision. As shown on the general plan of the locks, Plate I, the gates thus guarded are those in the upper and lower approaches to each lock, as well as the intermediate and lower operating gates at Pedro Miguel and in the upper chambers at Gatun and Miraflores.

These gates are more likely to be struck than any others, as vessels are more frequently out of control in these parts of the locks and the destruction of these gates might also be especially disastrous to the canal as a whole.

The fenders consist essentially of heavy chains, which normally remain stretched across the locks near the surface of the

Fig. 11.   Chain Fender in Upper Approach to Pedro Miguel Lock, Middle Wall.

water, being lowered to the bottom of the chamber when vessels under proper control are ready to pass the gates. When accidentally struck, the chains pay out against a resistance, so as to stop the vessels gradually with as little injury as possible.

Chain fenders similar to those used at Panama have been employed in Great Britain for the last fifteen or twenty years. In these English fenders the resistance to paying out is obtained by the friction of two or more turns of the chain about a fixed horizontal drum or bollard placed on one of the lock walls. The chain, usually a 1⅝-in. chain, is lowered and raised by an hydraulic engine on the other wall. This mechanism appears to work well as far as raising and lowering the chains are concerned, but the method used for producing the resistance in an emergency appears to be somewhat crude and likely to be uncertain in its action.

An extended study was made to arrive at a more satisfactory design. The use of a heavy chain arranged for raising and lowering was adhered to in all the preliminary designs. It was thought best, however, to install the machinery for raising and lowering the chain, as well as the mechanism for furnishing the resistance in an emergency, on both of the lock walls. It was thought that if the chain were lowered from both sides it could not fail to rest on the bottom for the entire width of the lock, while in the English fenders it had proved necessary to install small additional chains for pulling the large chains into the corners at the bottom of the lock, so as to avoid fouling vessels. This trouble was not met with in the operation of the Panama fenders, so that the symmetrical arrangement seems justified. It also greatly increases the capacity of the fender in stopping vessels.

Various designs were considered, differing in the mechanism for lowering and raising, as well as in the emergency resistance.

Three forms of resistance were studied: First, the raising of heavy weights; second, the friction of metallic surfaces; third, the friction of a fluid flowing through a small orifice.

Winding engines moved by electric motors were adopted for raising and lowering the chains in the first two types, while in the plan using a fluid resistance, the chain is raised and lowered by hydraulic machinery.

The principal objection to the use of weights for checking the travel of the chain is the enormous mass required when large vessels are to be stopped. Very large recesses in the masonry would be necessary, while the length of chain available, and hence the total capacity of the fender, proved to be less than with other types. This type of fender was made the subject of preliminary study only.

Designs, using metallic and hydraulic friction, respectively, were quite fully developed. In the first case, the machine proposed resembled quite closely the anchor windlasses with wild-cat sprocket wheels used on ship board. A post brake with metallic surfaces was to be connected to the main shaft of the winding engine. In case of emergency the brake would be brought into action automatically by a tripping device for lowering a heavy counterweight.

The machine promised to be thoroughly efficient when in good working order, but had some serious drawbacks inherent in its type. These are: First, variability of the coefficient of friction, which would be especially great in the Isthmian climate; second, the complicated device necessary for lowering the counterweight; third, the use of wildcat sprocket wheels at rather high speeds. For this and other reasons the hydraulic type was finally chosen.

The adopted design is shown on Plate XII, which represents the machinery installed in all the pits, except in the lower approaches to Miraflores Lock, where the great range of the tide made it necessary to modify the design slightly.

The mechanism for raising and lowering the chain consists of a system of hydraulic cylinders operated by an electrically driven centrifugal pump, and the necessary sheaves, bearings and connections for attaching and supporting the chain. There are two fixed cylinders, one at the top and the other at the bottom of the pit, and a moving intermediate cylinder to which the two lower chain sheaves are connected by eyebars. Two similar fixed sheaves at right angles to the lower sheaves are supported on riveted girders spanning the pit at the top. The weight of the upper cylinder is also suspended from the girders. The chain passes through a heavy hawse-pipe casting of steel in the lock wall, being supported on an idler. The hawse-pipe is secured to riveted steel anchors deeply embedded in the concrete. The chain makes a quarter turn around one of the upper sheaves, then passes down and makes a half-turn around one of the lower movable sheaves, coming up, it next makes a half-turn around the second sheave at the top and then goes down on the other side of the machine. It then makes a half-turn around the second movable sheave, and passing up is securely fastened to one of the beams at the top.

The vertical forces resulting from the upward pressure of

the cylinder and the downward pull of the chain on the upper sheaves, are practically balanced, as the cylinder and bearings are attached to opposite sides of the same girders. The tension in the horizontal portion of the chain, leading from the first fixed sheave to the hawse-pipe is balanced by the compressive force in the riveted strut connecting the horizontal beams to the hawse-pipe casting. In this way the total horizontal pull exerted by the chain in the emergency case, as well as in daily service, is transferred to the anchorage. The dimensions and strength of the cylinders, as well as of the riveted parts and of all the details were based on a pull of 600,000 lbs. on the chain, which is somewhat in excess of the ultimate strength of the chains.

The upper cylinder is of cast steel, with an internal diameter of 40 in. and metal 2 in. thick. It is built up of two sections and a cover, connected by male and female flanges and steel bolts. Bronze bushings are provided at the bottom of the cylinder and at a point about half-way up, as guides for the moving cylinder.

The interior of the large cylinder is machined only where the bushings are inserted. The intermediate or moving cylinders are made of cast iron in two sections, connected by interior flanges and bolts. The metal is $2\frac{1}{2}$ in. thick with closely spaced horizontal ribs to withstand the heavy collapsing pressure acting on the outside in emergency service. The cover is of cast steel. The outside of this cylinder was turned to a uniform diameter of 38 in.

The lower cylinder is a cast iron plunger 25 in. in diameter cast in one section and connected to a heavy base casting securely anchored to the concrete at the bottom of the pit.

The joints between the intermediate and upper cylinders and between the intermediate and lower cylinders are kept tight by stuffing boxes and glands with hemp packing. They may be tightened without removing any part or interfering with the operation of the machine. Any leakage at the stuffing boxes may be readily observed on the outside. In this respect, a system of plungers is better than a cylinder and piston, besides being cheaper and avoiding the great difficulty of boring out such large cylinders smoothly, especially if made of cast steel.

The sheaves are steel castings; they are grooved wheels without sprockets. The peripheral surfaces on either side of the grooves are not cylindrical, but slightly conical, the diameter at the faces of the wheels being a little smaller than close to the grooves. This somewhat novel form results in a closer contact between the chain link and the sheave, and reduces the bending moment on the links. The arrangement of the sheaves gives a four-fold reduction. The maximum stroke of the moving cylinder is 21 ft. 3 in., so that the chain pays out 85 feet from each wall, a length which is sufficient for lowering it to the bottom of the deepest lock and gives ample travel to the chain when stopping vessels.

The arrangement of the pump, the valves and the piping is shown on the general plans and the small diagram of Plate XII. The chain is lowered and raised by introducing water under pressure into the bottom and top cylinders respectively. The pressure required in the first case, mainly for lifting the heavy moving parts, is about 160 lbs. per square inch, while on the downward stroke, little power is required, except at the very end of the travel, where the tension in the chain rises rapidly.

It may be noted that the pipe leading from the pump to the bottom of the pit is fitted with a check valve which closes against upward flow, while a by-pass in the same line has an ordinary gate valve. By keeping the latter almost entirely closed, the rate of flow is kept very small on the downward stroke, so that a vacuum is avoided in the upper cylinder without increasing the size of the pump unreasonably. When raising the cylinder the flow is, of course, through the main pipe. The open tank receives the extra volume of water displaced from the upper cylinder on the upward stroke. It is placed high enough to keep all parts of the piping flooded, so as to avoid a possible vacuum. All the pipes and fittings are of steel, excepting in the suction line from the tank. The pump has a 6-inch suction and a 5-inch discharge. It is of two-stage design, the first being of the volute, and the second of the turbine type, and is direct connected to a 70-hp. induction motor, making 460 to 500 revolutions per minute.

The operating valve for changing the direction of flow is of special design. It is a double piston valve operated by a small motor.

The travel of the cylinder is controlled by a limit switch mechanism connected to the upper sheaves. This is also arranged to automatically start the pump, when through leakage the cylinder has moved a predetermined distance from its upper or lower position.

The operating valve and pump motors in normal service are started simultaneously from the central control house. At the end of the stroke, the pump is stopped by the limit switch, the valve remaining unchanged. Local control is also provided. The time required for raising or lowering the chain in the deepest lockchamber is about one minute.

The chains were made from soft wrought iron bars 3 in. in diameter, the links being about 10 in. by 17 in. in size. The section spanning the lock is a stud-link chain, while the parts that pass over the sheaves have open links. The breaking strength of the stud-link chain is about 500,000 lbs., and of the open-link chain about 450,000 lbs. The proof tests to which all the lengths of chain were subjected are 300,000 lbs. and 275,000 lbs., for the stud- and open-link sections respectively.

As the function of the fender is the stopping of vessels in case of impact, the most important feature of the design is the means provided for this purpose.

The total resistance to the travel of the chain is produced in part by the weights of the intermediate cylinder and other moving parts, in part by the internal friction of the machinery, and the friction of the chain along the hawse-pipe casting, in part by the resistance produced by the flow of water through special valves, inserted in the piping system.

The position of the operating valve, when the chain is in place across the top of the lock, is shown on the piping diagram. If the chain is struck by a vessel the pressure in the upper cylinder rises, but cannot exceed a maximum fixed by the setting of the resistance valve. It is maintained at this maximum as the chain pays out under strain and the water from the cylinder is discharged through one or both of the valves.

The resistance valve was selected from several designs by full size shop and field tests.

In the former, water under varying pressure, up to 750 lbs. per square inch, was supplied by a pump and accumulator, and the pressure maintained at the valve was continuously recorded by steam engine indicators. In the field tests, one of the fender machines was fully assembled in its pit, but the central portion of the chain, which spans the lock chamber, was disconnected. A pull was then exerted on the chain that remained connected to the machinery by the winding engine of a Lidgerwood unloader, placed on the other wall. The pressure in the cylinder was gradually raised, by changing the setting of the resistance valve, to a maximum of 630 lbs. per square inch. Numerous indicator cards were taken for various valve settings. Very uniform pressures were shown on the cards obtained from both of the valves tested, indicating that under actual working conditions a very constant resistance can be counted upon.

As the result of these tests, a valve made by the Ross Valve Manufacturing Company, of Troy, N. Y., was selected. It is a differential piston-valve of 6 in. diameter, the main valve being regulated by a small auxiliary valve, which is directly connected to the upper cylinder of the fender, so that the pressure in the cylinder itself is regulated, eliminating the variable friction loss in the piping between the cylinder and the valve.

A final series of tests was afterwards made to determine the resistance to the paying out of the chain resulting from the weight of the moving cylinder and other parts and the frictional resistances in the machine and hawse-pipe. For this purpose an hydrodynamometer was inserted in the cable close to the winding engine and the rope pull determined from indicator cards taken at the dynamometer. By taking cards simultaneously in the main cylinder of the fender machine and at the dynamometer, the total friction was readily found.

As the result of these tests, it was decided to set the resistance valves for a pressure of 360 lbs. per square inch. For this pressure, the frictional resistance proved to be about equal to the resistance due to the pressure in the cylinder. Under these conditions the working load on the chain would be about 220,000 lbs. or from 40% to 50% of its breaking strength.

As the friction is likely to be somewhat less in actual service, it is believed that the stress used is proper for emergency conditions.

The stopping power of the fender depends on its distance

from the gate it protects, as well as the working stress on the chain. The minimum distance is 70 feet from hollow quoin to chain. With a pull of 220,000 lbs. a vessel of 5000 tons displacement and moving at 5.5 knots should be checked without injury to the gate, assuming that its propelling machinery is at rest when it strikes the chain. For vessels of 10,000 and 60,000 tons, the corresponding speeds are 3.9 and 1.5 knots. The vessel in each case is supposed to be moving along the axis of the lock, so that the chain pays out equally from both lock walls.

In the lower approaches to Miraflores locks, the great tidal range made a modified design necessary, which is shown on Plate XIII. In this plan, the same system of cylinders is used as in the other fenders, and the pumps, piping, electric equipments, etc., are also practically the same. The chain is stretched across the lock for stopping vessels at either of two different levels. according to the stage of the tide. The chain itself is endless, and there are two separate hawse-pipes, idlers and recesses in the walls and floor. By a simple chain-stop mechanism, the part of the chain that passes through either hawse-pipe may be connected with the operating machinery and raised and lowered, the part which passes through the other hawse-pipe remaining at rest, with its central portion lying across the bottom of the lock.

The chain fender machines were built by the United Engineering & Foundry Company of Pittsburgh, Pa., the pumps by the Cameron Pump Works, of Phillipsburg, N. J., and the electric equipment by the General Electric Company. The erection was done by the Commission's forces.

LOCK-ENTRANCE CAISSON.

This caisson serves to close the head and tail bays of the lock flights, so as to permit the lower and upper guard gates to be examined, repainted and repaired. It also contains a pumping plant of large capacity for unwatering the locks.

The caisson is of ship form, with curved surfaces and vertical ends. The extreme length is 113 ft. 10 in., the moulded breadth 36 feet, the width of the top deck is 18 feet, and the depth at the side 65 feet.

The stability is insured by some 850 tons of concrete and iron ballast and by subdividing the interior by a continuous longitudinal bulkhead and numerous transverse bulkheads.

Fig. 12. Lock Entrance Caisson.

With fixed ballast only, the caisson floats at a draft of 32 feet, which is increased to a maximum of 61 feet by flooding when it is in place on the deepest sills. To assist in keeping the caisson on an even keel, trimming tanks are provided at each end.

The longitudinal elevation and section and typical cross sections of the caisson are shown on Plates XIV and XV.

There are five decks in all, the one next to the top being an open truss, the others of solid plate construction. To avoid all danger of accidentally scuttling the caisson, the deck which carries the operating machinery is made water-tight. The freeboard is 1 foot, with the water inside up to this deck. The transverse bulkheads are spaced at intervals of 12 feet, with smaller intercostal frames spaced 2 feet apart. The hydrostatic pressure is carried to the ends by the decks and by intermediate breast hooks. The cushion timbers are of green heart.

Fig. 13. Lock Entrance Caisson on Way to Canal Zone.

The total weight of each caisson, exclusive of ballast, is estimated at 1570 tons, of which 140 is the weight of the pumping equipment.

The pumping system includes four centrifugal pumps of the volute type, with a 20-inch discharge, besides a small auxiliary pump. The average capacity of each of the large pumps, when pumping out the locks, was specified to be at least 13,000 gallons per minute.

The arrangement of the pumps and piping permits drawing the water from either side of the caisson and discharging it through the opposite side. This allows the caisson to be cleaned and painted on both sides, when in place at the lock entrances, without special docking. After the level in the lock has been lowered to about 3 feet of the lock floor through the regular suction pipe, the remaining water is pumped out through a removable auxiliary inlet pipe, temporarily connected to the caisson at a lower elevation.

The flooding of the caisson is done through special flooding valves, while two of the four large pumps are arranged for pumping it out.

The pumps and ventilating fan are driven by electric motors, while the cranes and windlasses are operated by hand. Three-phase alternating current at 25 cycles is used, the voltage being 2200 for the main pumps, 220 for the smaller pump and fan, and 110 for the lighting.

The current is carried from the lock walls by removable cables, leading to outlets at both sides at either end of the caisson.

The caisson was built by the Union Iron Works at San Francisco and towed to the Isthmus. The pumps are Worthington pumps driven by General Electric motors. The caisson and the pumping equipment have proved satisfactory in service.

The writer's principal assistants in the work of designing were the following: Gates, Mr. J. M. Hammer, M. Am. Soc. C. E., and Mr. F. E. Sterns; chain fenders, Mr. F. E. Sterns, Mr. J. Soderberg and Mr. E. H. Baughman; lock-entrance caisson, Mr. L. A. Mason.

Mr. Hammer also had charge in the U. S. of the approval of the detail plans and the shop inspection for the lock-gates and the greater part of the chain-fender work.

Mr. George F. Guynn was chief inspector for the lock-gate erection, and Mr. Mason for the construction of the caisson.

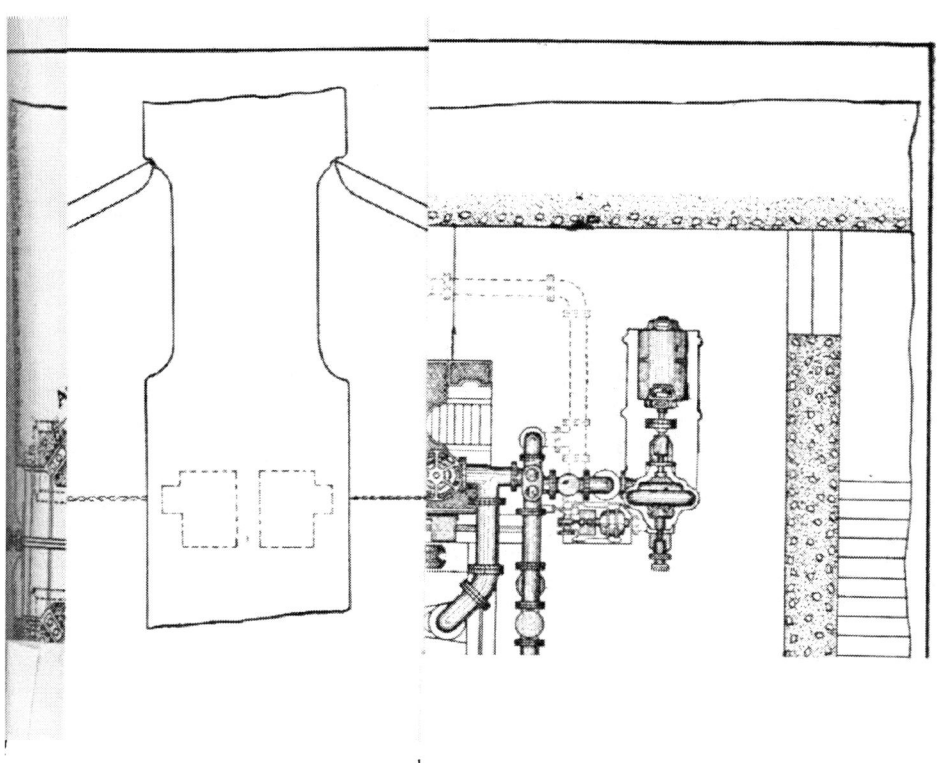

EMERGENCY DAMS ABOVE LOCKS OF THE PANAMA CANAL.

By

T. B. MÖNNICHE, M. Am. Soc. C. E.
Engineer of Docks, Panama R. R.
Cristobal, Canal Zone, Panama

NECESSITY FOR EMERGENCY DAMS.

When it was decided to build a lock canal through the Isthmus of Panama, one of the important problems to be dealt with was safeguarding against the danger to which such a canal is exposed. It was necessary, in case of accident to the lock gates, to provide means for preventing a serious injury or total destruction of the locks. In view thereof, the Isthmian Canal Commission has provided for various safety devices. No ships, excepting small motor boats and other light craft, will be allowed to pass through the locks under their own power, but will be towed through by electric locomotives.

At the entrance to the locks, and at the lower end of the upper lock of each flight, double pairs of mitering lock gates have been installed. As a still further precaution, fender chains are to be placed on the upstream side of the double gates and intermediate gates of the upper locks, and on the down stream side of the double gates at the lower end of each flight of locks. These devices are a strong guarantee to the safe operation of the lock gates, and the possibility of destruction of these gates is, therefore, very remote. If, however, the gates should be carried away through faulty operation, accident, malice, or through any other cause, the locks would form a raceway for the water of Gatun Lake or Miraflores Lake, and no repairs could be made to the lock gates before this flow should be stopped. It was therefore decided that the locks should be provided with emergency dams. It may be thought that excessive precautions have been taken for the safety of the canal, but, as is pointed out in "Engineering," in its issue of July 18, 1913, numerous accidents have occurred to date on lock canals, and therefore great precautions are necessary.

Various schemes were considered by the Commission for checking this flow of water, and from these the emergency dam of the swing-bridge type was selected.

STRUCTURAL DETAILS OF DAMS.

The design, as shown on Plates Nos. 1a, 1b and 1c, consists of two vertical cantilever trusses with unequal arms, pivoted on the sidewalls of the locks, and capable of being turned from a position parallel to the locks until the long arm spans the channel. The length of the long arm is 164 ft. 3 in. and of the short arm 98 ft. 0 in. The distance from center to center of vertical trusses is 32 ft. 0 in. The long arm carries the wicket girders, rolling gates, and horizontal truss. These may be said to form the dam proper. A framing of heavy girders transfers the load from the vertical trusses to the center pivot, which consists of a circular base casting, imbedded in the masonry, upon which rests a bronze disk 43 in. in diameter between two hardened steel ones. The diameter of the base casting is 9 ft. 0 in., and its weight is 34,000 lbs. On top of the disk another casting is placed, which is fastened securely to the cross girders between the vertical trusses. Six trailing wheels, adjusted to clear their circular track slightly, when the bridge is balanced, are provided to take the overturning effect of a wind pressure from any direction. The balancing of the whole superstructure about its transverse axis is accomplished by means of a large block of concrete placed on the short arm. The turning is done by means of pinions and rack, driven by electric motors, as in ordinary swing-bridges. The wicket girders are pivoted at one end to the supporting superstructure on pins, about which they are revolved from their original horizontal position until their lower ends come in contact with the bottom sill of the lock. The reactions produced by the moving water, and later by the static pressure on the gates, are taken at the upper ends of these girders, through a horizontal truss system, to the lock walls, and, at their lower ends, directly into the masonry sill. The gates are lowered in horizontal tiers, closing the canal across its entire width by the depth of each succeeding set, thereby gradually converting the dynamic pressure to a static head.

On account of the great depth and velocity of current, the following special features, different from similar designs, have been found necessary. The horizontal truss is placed on the downstream side of the two vertical trusses, in order to counteract the overturning moment of the long wicket girders, hung in a horizontal position when the bridge is balanced and swinging. A system of booms and sway frames was provided to support these girders and the horizontal truss. The first horizontal tier of gates to be lowered is stored on the wicket girders; the remaining gates are hung vertically between the main trusses and immediately below the floor, and are used in adjusting the equilibrium of the whole structure about its longitudinal axis.

Studies showed that the length of the wicket girders determines the depth of the horizontal truss, which forms part of the counterweight of the dam about its longitudinal axis. The longer the wicket girders are made, the greater the depth of the horizontal truss will be, and thereby the distance from the edge of the lock wall to the center pivot of the dam, which in turn will increase the length of both arms of the dam. It is desirable, therefore, that the elevation of the horizontal truss, to which the wicket girders are pivoted at their upper ends, be kept as low as possible. As far as this point is concerned, it is evident that a swing-bridge of the center-pivot type is to be preferred to one of the rim-bearing type, as the bottom chord of the vertical trusses for a center-pivot swing-bridge may be low enough to clear the top of the lock walls, whereas the bottom chord of these trusses for a drawbridge of the rim-bearing type must be at an elevation above the top of the large rim-bearing girder.

Up to the time when these studies were being made, the heaviest drawbridge of the center-pivot type weighed 2,200,000 lbs., whereas the heaviest drawbridge of the rim-bearing type weighed 5,500,000 lbs. In view of the great advantages offered by a swing-bridge of the center-pivot type, only this type of swing-bridge was taken into consideration, although its estimated weight was 6,700,000 lbs., or practically three times heavier than any swing-bridge of this type ever constructed. In connection herewith, I desire to call attention to Mr. C. C. Schneider's valuable paper on Movable Bridges, published in the American Society of Civil Engineers' Transactions, Vol. LX, which has been of great assistance to the writer in the design of the emergency dams. As stated in this paper, it appears that the consensus of opinion is in favor of the center-bearing type of swing-bridges, which has partially been proved by the building of new bridges of this type weighing up to 6,600,000 lbs. The only limiting feature in this type of swing-bridge seems to be the size of the two center cross girders, each of which, in case of the emergency dams, is 55 ft. 3 in. long and 11 ft. 0 in. deep, weighing 64,000 lbs.

The emergency dams are located on the side walls, 200 feet upstream of the upper guard gates. There are two at each set of locks, one being a right-hand dam and the other a left-hand dam. The dams at Gatun and Pedro Miguel are of equal size, whereas the dams at Miraflores are of smaller size, due to less depth of water above the lock floor.

Figures 1 to 4 give an idea of how the dams are to be operated. Figure 1 shows the west emergency dam at rest on the side wall of the lock, and the east dam swung across the lock chamber. Figure 2 shows the dam swung across the lock chamber, and the lowering of the wicket girders, all wicket girders being lowered simultaneously. Figure 3 illustrates the method of lowering the gates, viz., in horizontal tiers. Figure 4 shows the dam placed in its final position. Although these photos illustrate clearly the general method of operating the dams, they do not convey any idea of the enormous force and great flow of water which the dams are intended to check, in case they should be called into service.

The only time an emergency dam of this type has been called into service was on June 9, 1909, when the gates of the Sault Ste. Marie canal were wrecked. The width of the forebay of the Sault Ste. Marie canal was 150 ft., and the depth of water was 22 ft. The measured velocity of flow after the wrecking of the lock gates was 7 feet per second in the forebay and 15 ft. per second in the lock chamber. The "Engineering News" and the "Engineering Record" describe this accident in their issues for the month of June, 1909, illustrating it by various photographs.

Fig. 1. Gatun Upper Locks. Looking North From Deck of Steamship on Lake.

Fig. 2. Final Test of West Emergency Dam, Pedro Miguel Locks. Dam Swung
Across Lock and Wicket Girders Being Raised.

Fig. 3. Final Test of East Emergency Dam, Gatun Upper Locks. Dam Swung
Across Lock and Fourth Horizontal Tier of Gates Being Lowered.

Fig. 4. Final Test of West Emergency Dam, Pedro Miguel Locks. Dam Swung
Across Lock and All Gates Lowered.

The width of the forebay at Gatun is 110 ft., the maximum depth of water is 49 1/3 ft., and the maximum elevation of water above sea-level is 87 ft. In case the lock gates for one flight of locks at Gatun should be carried away, the calculated velocity of the current at the emergency dams would be 24 feet per second, the depth of water 36 feet and the discharge through the locks would be 95,000 cubic feet per second, or nearly one half of the amount of water passing over the Horseshoe Falls at Niagara. Comparing these figures with the corresponding figures for the Sault Ste. Marie canal and the photographs of this accident, one may form an idea of what the situation would be in case the emergency dams for the Panama Canal should be brought into action.

Vertical Trusses.

The general outline of the truss on the long arm is determined by the requirements of the parts which it supports. The elevation of the floor is fixed by the clearance required for storing the gates in a vertical position between the floor beams and wicket girders. The proper slope of the ties which support the booms gives a minimum height of the top chord above the floor, and, as this provides sufficient depth of truss for the portion which spans the locks, the chord is made horizontal over that distance, and a variable depth of truss is obtained by sloping the bottom chord, beginning at a point immediately beneath the floor at the extremity of the long arm. The panel lengths for this part of the span being determined by the spacing of the wicket girders, sub-panels are introduced, and the Warren system of bracing, with riveted members and connections, is used. The vertical posts of this system are sub-members, and their cross-sections can therefore be made alike, simplifying all members connecting to the same. Eye-bars are used for all tension members of the short arm, also for the inclined top chord on the long arm, and the diagonal tension member connecting to this chord. It will be noted on Plate No. 1-a that the vertical truss at each side of the center post is formed by a quadrilateral system. Equilibrium in this truss system, while the dam is swinging, can be obtained only when the stresses in the two center diagonals are equal, and hence, also, the vertical components of these members, which are carried by the center cross-girders. The slopes of the top-chord eye-bars, on either side of the center post, are therefore different, and so chosen that the reaction on the two center cross-girders will be equal while the dam is swinging.

The bottom chord, the end posts, and all diagonals of stiff construction are built up of plates and angles, forming double-channel sections with flanges turned out, the only exception being the first diagonal on the short arm, for which the flanges have been turned in. The channel sections of the bottom chord and of the two diagonals at the center are laced together by 6-in. by 3½-in. by ⅜-in. angles. The end posts and the three diagonals near the end of the long arm, also the first diagonal near the end of the short arm, are laced together by 2½-in. lacing-bars, the remaining diagonals being laced by 3½-in. by 2½-in. by ⅜-in. angles.

The top chord on the long arm is also built up of plates and angles of double-channel sections, but with flanges turned in, each channel section being laced by two ½-in. bars.

The vertical posts on the long arm, directly above the wicket girders, are built up of plates and angles, forming double-channel sections with the flanges turned in. The sections are laced by single lacing, consisting of 2½-in. by ⅜-in. bars. The webs of the posts are placed perpendicular to the plane of the vertical truss, due to the bending to which they are subjected on account of the eccentric load imposed upon them by the wicket girders.

The center posts are built up of plates and angles in the same manner as the center diagonals, and are also laced by 6-in. by 3½-in. by ⅜-in. angles. The balance of the posts are built up of two 15-in. channels laced together by 2½-in. lacing-bars, their webs placed parallel to the plane of the vertical truss. All sub-members are built up of four 6-in. by 4-in. by ⅜-in. angles, forming an I section. These angles are laced by double lacing, consisting of 2½-in. by ⅜-in. bars.

Floor Beams.

The floor beams are built up of plates and angles forming double-channel sections with flanges turned out; they are laced by double lacing consisting of 2½-in. by ⅜-in. bars. The reason for adopting double-channel sections for the floor beams is that they, besides being subjected to bending, are also subjected to considerable compression transferred from the upstream booms.

Horizontal Truss.

The horizontal truss is of the Warren type with subdivided panels and riveted joints throughout. It is supported at short intervals by hangers attached to the overhanging booms, and carries no load until the dam is in place. At each panel point of the compression chord are brackets, braced in horizontal and vertical planes, in which the upper ends of the wicket girders fit and are pivoted on horizontal pins.

The compression chord is built up of plates and angles, forming double-channel sections with their flanges turned out, and their webs are placed in a horizontal plane. The sections are laced by means of large tie-plates. All other members of the horizontal truss are built up of plates and angles, forming H-sections, with their webs placed in a vertical plane, the only exception being the small diagonals of the center panel, which are built up of two angles, the vertical legs of which are laced together by single lacing consisting of 2½-in. bars.

Wicket Girders and Sills.

The wicket girders are designed to resist torsion, side forces, or rough usage of any character to which they may be subjected while being lowered into a swift current. They are of box section, their length being 64 ft. out to out, and their depth being 7 ft. 0 in. One 150-lb. crane rail, riveted to the top or upstream flange of each wicket girder, forms the track on which the gate wheels roll. The two webs are rigidly connected by channel stiffeners, and present a smooth outside surface to the water, with a minimum exposed area. Large holes in both webs provide drainage and access for painting the interior surfaces. The girders are connected in pairs by a system of lateral bracing in the plane of the top flange. This bracing presents only a small area to the current, and is omitted in the lower panel.

Each pair of wicket girders is provided with a shallow cross-frame at the first panel point from its upper end. The lower ends of the wicket girders permit, therefore, considerable vertical motion relative to each other, caused by the unequal action of the lowering tackle attached to each girder. The cross-frames are of sufficient strength, however, to prevent this motion when the wicket girders are approaching their final position against the bottom sill, while being operated in still water. The reason for this is that the horizontal component of the weight of each wicket girder while in this position is only 1/20th of the weight of the wicket girder, and that this force is counteracted by the horizontal component of the ropes and tackle, so that the resultant force pressing the wicket girders against the sill is very small. If large obstructions should have settled in any of the pockets provided for the wicket girders on the lock floor, and the dam were to be operated in still water for training purposes, there would, due to the strength of the cross frames, be no danger of one girder of a pair entering its pocket ahead of the other, and thereby unduly warping the lateral system out of shape.

During the accident of the Sault Ste. Marie, one of the wicket girders was warped entirely out of shape and rendered useless on account of finding obstructions on the sill. The sill for this emergency dam was constructed above the lock floor. Any material carried out by the current along the bottom of the canal could, therefore, easily become lodged against the sill. The wicket girders for the emergency dam at Sault Ste. Marie canal were constructed as single-web plate girders. Each pair of wicket girders was braced at its lower ends by a strong cross-frame having a solid web. Any obstruction on the sill that would cause one of the wicket girders of a pair to seat ahead of the other would, by the aid of the kinetic energy of the current, introduce torsion in the frame system of this pair of wicket girders. If the cross-frames were so constructed that they could resist the stresses to which they thus would be subjected better than the lateral system, the latter would deflect and warp the wicket girders out of shape.

Special precautions have been taken for the emergency dams of the Panama Canal to prevent material from lodging against the bottom sill. At the Pacific Locks the upstream side of the sill has been provided with a large sump, spanning the entire width of the canal. Heavy material carried downstream by the force of the current will collect in this sump, leaving the sill free from obstructions. The width of these sumps at Pedro Miguel and Miraflores is 32 ft., and their depth at Pedro Miguel is 14 ft. and at Miraflores 11 1/3 ft. At Gatun the elevation of the sill is 23 1/3 ft. above the floor of the forebay. No special precautions in this respect are therefore needed at Gatun. The sills for all dams are also provided with a pocket for each individual wicket girder. These pockets are shown on Plates Nos. 1-b and 6. They are 16 in. wide, the clearance between the wicket girders and the sides of the pockets being $\frac{3}{4}$ in. The upstream sides of the pockets are flaring, so that the force of the current might, if necessary, force the wicket girders laterally to their proper place for entering the pockets. When the wicket girders have entered the pockets, they rest against steel castings imbedded in the masonry. The faces of these castings have a slope of about 1 to 3 from the vertical. Any material that might have settled in these pockets, in still water, can easily be washed out by the current that would arise in case of accident. It is, therefore, hardly conceivable that any material can collect in the pockets provided for the wicket girders, unless the large sump spanning the canal, upstream of the sill, has first been filled by such material. It might be possible for material of about the same weight as water, such as water-soaked logs, to be caught between the sill and wicket girders just as the latter are entering their pockets, but the possibility of this is very remote. Provision has been made against this possibility, however, by providing sufficient power for hoisting the wicket girders against the current, thus allowing such obstructions to pass downstream. In case of an accident, the current created through the forebay might not in all places run parallel to the center line of the forebay. In lowering the wicket girders in this current they might, therefore, be subjected to large lateral forces. The point of application for these forces would be approximately at the center of gravity of the area of the web of each wicket girder. Since each pair is provided with a top lateral system only, and the point of application of the lateral forces is below the plane of the top lateral system, each individual girder would be subjected to torsion. This is an added reason for adopting a box section instead of a single-web section for the wicket girders, as in the latter case it would be necessary to provide each pair also with a bottom lateral system, which, besides increasing the resistance offered to the current, would also tend to warp each girder out of shape if improperly seated.

Each wicket girder is designed to resist the torsion caused

by a current of 24 ft. per second, striking it under an angle of 30° to the longitudinal center line of the forebay, and the top lateral system for each pair of girders has been proportioned accordingly.

As previously explained, the danger of material lodging in the pocket provided for each wicket girder is very remote. Even if this should occur, there is no danger of warping the wicket girders, as the cross-frames at their lower ends have been omitted, also the bottom lateral system. Each wicket girder would, in such an event, remain in its original plane; the top lateral system would warp, and the connections between the shallow cross-frame and the wicket girder would be torn loose, but the strength of each wicket girder would not be seriously impaired thereby. If the obstructions in the pockets were very large, it might be doubtful if the gates could be lowered, although the gates are so constructed that they allow of warping to some extent.

Gates.

As shown on Plate No. 4, the gates are structural frames covered with buckle-plates and supported by flanged wheels turning on roller bearings. The convex sides of the buckle-plates for the two upper gates have been turned upstream, in order to provide sufficient room for the wheels. For the three lower gates, the convex sides of the buckle-plates have been turned downstream, as thereby greater strength of the buckle-plates is obtained without interfering with the desired size of the wheels.

All gates have the same width, 18 ft., whereas their heights range from 9 ft. to 11 ft. Each gate is carried by 12 wheels, six of which bear on each of the two wicket girders supporting the gate. The wheels are held in journal castings of L-shape. These castings are bolted to the structural frame of the gate, and each forms the support for the roller bearings of two wheels. Due to the flexibility of the connections of these castings, the load upon each wheel is a statically determinate factor which would not be affected by the deflection of the wicket girders, nor by the warping of the gates. When these wheels are brought into position on the top flange of the wicket girders, Z-bar guides engage under the outer side of the head of each rail and prevent uplift of the gates, while the flanges of the wheels prevent lateral displacement. The upper and lower edges of each gate are wedge-shaped and interlock with the edges of the gates above and below (see Plate No. 6). These "noses" are formed by a bent plate filled with concrete. They are arranged to allow the gates to be brought into close contact and yet to give room for the fastenings of the hoisting lines.

It is evident that the first horizontal tier to be lowered is subjected to the greatest kinetic pressure from the water, this pressure diminishing as succeeding tiers are lowered, until it is finally checked by the lowering of the fifth tier. The static pressure, however, increases according to the number of gates lowered, due to the increasing difference in elevation of the water on the two sides of the gates. Calculations show that the greatest combined pressure, while the gates are being lowered, occurs on the third tier, and that this pressure is very nearly as great as the static pressure to which this tier is subjected when all the gates have been lowered.

The average water pressure upon each tier of gates while being lowered in the current, as shown on Plate No. 10, is as follows:

Gates No. 1 .... 1260 lbs. per sq. ft.
  "   "   2 .... 1500 "   "   "   "
  "   "   3 .... 1560 "   "   "   "
  "   "   4 .... 900 "   "   "   "
  "   "   5 .... 360 "   "   "   "

The maximum wheel loads, while in motion, occur on the lowest wheels of gates No. 3, which are each subjected to 38,300 lbs. The maximum static wheel loads, while at rest, occur on the lowest wheels of gates No. 1, which are each subjected to 65,470 lbs. The equivalent total load on this gate is illustrated on Figure 5, taken during the shop tests described later.

In order to simplify the shop work on the gates, the wheels and roller-bearings for gates Nos. 1, 2 and 3 were made alike (see Plate No. 5). Each roller bearing for these wheels consists of 20 rollers of ½-in. diameter and 3⅞-in. length. Each roller-bearing for gates No. 4 consists of 18 rollers of ½-in. diameter and 2⅝-in. length, and for gates No. 5, 18 rollers of ¼-in. diameter and 2¼-in. length.

The axles of the wheels for all gates have also been provided with end-thrust ball-bearings, in addition to the roller-bearings, and each roller-bearing has been provided with a ball-bearing at both ends. The roller-bearings and the ball-bearings are completely filled with grease, and provided with felt washers at both ends to prevent water from entering the bearings.

As can be seen from the above, great care has been taken to reduce the friction on the wheels and to prevent the gates from binding or sticking while being lowered under water pressure.

Fig. 5. Test Load on Gate No. 1.

Tests made in the shop to determine the frictional resistance and strength of the bearings are described in detail later. The very favorable results obtained are confirmed by the fact that during the tests of the East Dam at Gatun, described at the end of this paper, observations showed that the entire set of gates, while subjected to the full static head, moved down, relatively to the wicket girders, as these were forced upward.

In view of these tests, there is little danger of inability to lower the gates on account of the water pressure imposed upon them while being lowered in a current. If, however, the gates should stick from unforeseen causes, it is thought that a pressure brought to bear on the upper edge of the topmost gate, with the aid of the interlocking "noses" previously mentioned, would be more effective than any device for pulling them down. The weight of one gate would always be available for this purpose, and moderate blows or weights on the upper edge should be effec-

Fig. 6.   Gatun Locks.   East Emergency Dam Subjected to a Head of 20 Ft. of Water.

tive. The vertical apertures of four inches between each set of gates, which were provided for clearance while handling them, can be closed by forcing drive pipes down into the grooved edges of adjacent gates, as shown on Plate No. 6 and Figures 6 and 7.

Turning and Wedging Machinery.

The general plans of the turning and wedging machinery are shown on Plates Nos. 2 and 3.

Before any attempt can be made to turn the dam, it must be balanced about its center pivot while swinging. Balance of the structure about its longitudinal axis was carefully investigated during the design of the dams, and it was thought that any unbalance of the dams, caused by slight variations in the weight of the completed structure, could be adjusted by shifting the gates on the floor beams. The final calculations of the balancing of the dams, made from the shop drawings, showed, however, that there was only a small margin left for shifting the gates downstream on the floor beams. It was therefore decided to fill the downstream chord of the horizontal truss with concrete. On

Fig. 7. Vertical Apertures Between Gates and Drive Pipe in Place. Gates Subjected to Full Static Head.

the completed dams, the gates are located midway between the two extremities to which they can be shifted. A large concrete block at the extreme end of the short arm gives transverse balance. This block is provided with pockets, and the final adjustment was made by placing a proper amount of pig iron in these pockets. In order to reduce the size of the concrete block and the load on the center pivot, the turning machinery is located at the extreme end of the short arm, thus forming a part of the counterweight.

The whole structure is turned about its center pivot by means of two main pinions that are geared with a rack quadrant. These pinions are connected to two motors by two separate trains of spur gears and one equalizer gear, the latter being directly in mesh with the motor pinions. (See Plate No. 2.)

The radius of the rack quadrant has been made as large as conditions will allow, in order to reduce the force required for turning the dam and, also, the size of the two main pinions.

The two main pinions are shrouded on their upper sides, and the teeth of the rack, with which they are in mesh, are of special design, in order to allow for expansion. The equalizer gear serves the purpose of equalizing the tooth pressures of the main pinions upon the rack, due to imperfection in size of the teeth of the rack.

The two motors for turning the dam have each a capacity of 112 horsepower. They are reversible and are furnished with solenoid brakes. Each motor can be operated by its own controller, and is so connected that either controller can be used in turning the dam, but each will be of sufficient capacity to turn the dam independently. A limit switch is connected to the motors, to cut off the current when the end of the long arm of the dam is near the closed position. The exact position of the dam while turning is shown on an indicator located in the operating house. An air buffer has been bolted to the horizontal truss at the extreme end of the long arm to take any shock as the structure is brought to rest after turning.

In order to secure solid bearings for the structure while at rest, and while operating wicket girders and gates, provision has been made for one pair of wedges at the center and at each end. All wedges are driven simultaneously by one 25-horsepower motor, located at the center directly under the floor. This motor is controlled from the operating house, where also the wedge indicator is located.

The separate machines for driving each pair of wedges are located at the center and at both ends, respectively. Each machine consists of one worm and one worm gear, the latter connected to two separate trains of spur gears, each driving one wedge by means of a double toggle-joint. The machines at both ends are connected to the motor by a line-shaft and by one reduction of spur gears.

For the purpose of centering and of locking the dam while in closed or in open position, the dam has been provided with an end latch at the long arm. This latch is operated, in accordance with ordinary drawbridge practice, simultaneously with driving or releasing wedges.

A semaphore connected to the end latch, as shown on Plate No. 1-a, indicates the position of wedges drawn, end latch raised, and dam ready for turning. This semaphore indicates also the position of latch in place, dam centered, and wedges ready for driving.

Electric current will ordinarily be used to operate all machinery located on the dam, and will be obtained from underground cables coming to the surface near the center casting, as shown on Plate No. 3; but in all cases provision is made for hand power. All motors and electrical equipment have been designed for alternating current, 25-cycle, 3-phase, and 220 volts, delivered at the switchboard.

The main switchboard is located in a small house on the long arm of the dam near its center, as shown on Plate No. 1-a.

Wicket-Girder Hoisting Machine.

Each pair of wicket girders is raised and lowered by means of two 7-part lines of one-inch diameter plough-steel wire rope with a hemp center. The lead lines pass over sheaves at the end of the booms and are carried back to the hoisting drums. The machinery for each pair of girders is composed of two worm-driven hoisting units and one motor unit. Each hoisting unit consists of a drum with its gearing. Both worms are driven by silent sprocket chains from the motor unit. All gearing and the sprocket chains are inclosed in oil-tight cases to afford complete protection against the weather. Each machine is controlled separately from the operating platform directly in the rear. The operation of lowering the wicket takes place at high speed, while lower speed is used for raising the wicket. By turning the handle of the controller to the lowering position, the motor is started, and, at the same time, a solenoid is energized, which draws the jaw clutch on the motor shaft into mesh with the high-speed gearing. The girder is lowered at a uniform rate of speed to its seat in the floor of the lock, the time for lowering being 4 minutes and 40 seconds. In case of failure of the electric current, the girder can be lowered into place by means of a hand-operated capstan. Should it be found necessary to raise the girder against the current to allow an obstruction to be washed out of the girder seat, this can be done by bringing the controller handle to the hoisting position. This movement engages the clutch with the slow-speed gearing, and the girder is hoisted back to its original position, the time of hoisting being 18 minutes. A limit switch stops the movement in either direction at the proper time.

Gate-Hoisting Machines.

There is one machine for hoisting and lowering each vertical set of gates. It consists essentially of ten hoisting drums, two for each gate, on a common shaft. This shaft is motor driven through spur gears and a worm and worm gear. The worm gearing is self-locking and will hold a gate in any position when the motor is at rest. Each gate is operated by two drums, from each of which it is suspended by a crucible cast-steel flat wire rope $\frac{3}{8}$ in. by 2 in., nominal size. Each pair of drums can be thrown in or out of service by jaw clutches. While handling a gate, all drums not attached to this gate are out of service. They are held from moving by detent levers, which engage automatically whenever the jaw clutches are withdrawn.

Normally, all gates except those of the lower tier are hung up under the floor system. (See Figure 2, and Plate No. 1-b.) The gates of the lowest tier, or gates No. 1, are kept habitually on the wicket girders when the latter are in their raised position. Gates No. 2 are held in position by a hanging rod, whereas gates Nos. 3, 4 and 5 are hooked to trolleys, which run on rails fastened to the floor beams. To lower gates No. 1, it is necessary, first, to release the hooks holding the gates on to the wicket girders. These hooks are pivoted to the wicket girders, and they release the gates automatically when the gates are hoisted a few inches. After the gates have been hoisted, thus releasing the hooks, the machines are reversed and the gates are lowered. To lower the next tier, the jaw clutches for gates No. 2 are thrown in, and these gates are first hoisted until limit switches stop the motors of the hoisting machines. The hanging rods, which supported the gates, are then turned up and out of the way of these gates by means of a lever located on the floor, the machines are reversed, and the gates are lowered. While lowering, the gates are guided by structural frames until the wheels bear on the rails of the wicket girders and the Z-bar guides engage under the railheads. These frames are placed above and in line with the top flange of the wicket girders as shown on Plate No. 1-c and Figure 7. To lower the third tier, the jaw clutches for gates No. 3 are thrown in and the gates are hauled along the rails on the floor beams until they hang under the drums of the hoisting machines with their wheels against the guides mentioned for gates No. 2. The gates are then hoisted until they are automatically unhooked from the trolleys, this operation being controlled by the limit switch. They are then lowered into place. Gates No. 4 and No. 5 are lowered in the same manner as gates No. 3. To hoist the gates, the operations are reversed. The trolley track has sufficient slope toward the middle of the dam to cause the gates to run to their proper position for storage. The operation of placing the gates can, if necessary, be effected by hand, a capstan being provided, which is geared to the motor shaft. The wicket girder and gate-hoisting machinery was designed in the electrical and mechanical subdivision of the Assistant Chief Engineer's Office.

Miscellaneous.

As shown on Plates Nos. 1-a and 1-b, one foot-walk has been provided from the operating house to the end of the dam and another on top of the horizontal truss for its whole length. Two ladders are located at the end of the short arm and one at the end of the long arm. On the upstream side of the short arm a stairway leads to the upper foot-walk, and on the downstream side of the long arm, near the center, a stairway connects the two foot-walks. A 3-ton trolley and chain-hoist in the operating house and a 5-ton one on the long arm will serve the purpose of handling machinery parts, when required, for repairs.

The most important parts of the dam, and all places over which a man might be required to pass, are illuminated by 40-watt incandescent lamps.

STRESSES AND SYSTEM OF FRAMING.

For determining the sizes of the various members, the following conditions of loading were considered:

Case   I   Dam swinging.

Case II   Wedges driven, wicket girders being lowered in current and about to touch sill.

Case III   Wedges driven, wicket girders resting on sill, no current.

Case IV   Wedges driven, wicket girders and all gates lowered, and total static water pressure upon gates.

For each of the above cases, with the exception of case I, the total panel loading of the upstream vertical truss is different from that of the downstream vertical truss. It should be noted, that, considering each of the three latter causes of loading by itself, the magnitude and also the points of application of the panel loadings vary for each panel. This is caused by the sway frames transferring the loads acting upon the dam to the vertical trusses, as is shown on Plate No. 8, where the stresses in the sway frames for the various conditions of loading are given, and on Plate No. 9, where the panel loadings are given for that one of the two trusses which is subjected to maximum stresses for each case of loading.

The stresses for the vertical trusses have been calculated for the same four conditions of loading as for the sway frames.

For case I, the vertical trusses act as cantilever girders, and for cases II, III and IV as continuous girders with end supports lowered. The latter condition is caused by the wedges, which have been designed for raising the ends of the dam only a fractional part of the deflection of the vertical trusses, while the dam is swinging.

The stresses in the vertical trusses for cases II, III and IV were determined in the following manner. For each of these cases the reaction at the end of the long arm, panel point A_o, was considered as the redundant force. The stresses S', produced in the trusses due to a load of 1,000,000 lbs. at A_o, as well as the stresses S_o, produced by the actual loading for each specific case, could therefore be determined in the same manner as for an ordinary cantilever span. After determining these stresses and those for case I, the deflection ΔA_0 of panel point A_0 was calculated for each case of loading by Otto Mohr's work equation:

$$\Delta A_o = \frac{S_o \times S' \times l}{E \times A}$$

"l" being the length of each member in question, "A" its sectional area, and "E" the modulus of elasticity. The deflection at A_o for case I was then substracted from the deflection calculated for each case of loading, to which were added the vertical lifts of the wedges. This result, when divided by the deflection due to 1,000,000 lbs. and multiplied by the load of 1,000,000 lbs. is the actual reaction at A_o for each case of loading. Having thus found the reaction at A_o for each case, the two other reactions can easily be determined and all stresses derived by simple statics.

This method is especially adapted to the above case, offering a quick solution and taking full account of the deflection of all web members, also of pin clearances. The various methods ordinarily used for continuous bridges dealing with movable loads would be very laborious and not exact.

In regard to the purpose of the various systems of trusses and bracing composing the dam, it is evident that the vertical trusses resist the vertical loads, the horizontal truss resists the horizontal loads produced by the water pressure, and the sway frames transfer the torsional moments acting upon the dam to the vertical trusses and the horizontal truss. The sway frames also form an important part of the dam, by bracing the inclined portion of the bottom chord of the upstream truss; this portion of the downstream truss, in addition to being braced by the sway frames, is also braced by the horizontal truss. No other bracing can be provided for these chords, as the bottom lateral system cannot be extended over the whole length of the long arm, due to the interference which would be caused with the lowering of the gates. As far as the top lateral system is concerned, it might, at first glance, appear to be unnecessary to extend it over the whole top chord, instead of over the horizontal part of the long arm only. This is correct for the conditions of loading, case II, III and IV, but not for case I, as the reaction conditions for case I are entirely different from those of cases II, III and IV. If the top lateral system were not to be extended over the whole length of the top chord, the inclined portion of the bottom chord of both vertical trusses would be unbraced for case I, as each sway frame would be at liberty to revolve in its own plane and the horizontal truss would be hinged at one end only, viz., the end towards the center of the dam.

In order to have the bottom chords of the vertical trusses braced for case I, it is necessary to extend the top lateral system over the whole length of the top chord. By making this extension, the short arm and the two first panel points on the long arm are entirely enclosed by six truss systems, viz., two vertical trusses, two lateral systems and two portals, so that an entirely stiff structure for this portion of the dam is secured. An analysis will show that the stiffening of this part of the dam will prevent the cross frames from revolving, and thereby cause the desired result of stiffening the bottom chord of the vertical trusses.

MATERIALS.

All steel work entering into the construction of the dams was thoroughly cleaned of all mill scale, rust, etc., before painting was allowed. The structural work was pickled or sand blasted, depending upon the size of the pieces, before assembling into the various members.

The structural material used for the gates, sway frames, lateral systems, floor, and machinery supports is carbon steel of the quality commonly used for steel railway bridges. The rivets throughout the dam are of carbon rivet-steel of ordinary composition.

For the vertical trusses, horizontal trusses, wicket girders and longitudinal and transverse girders at center, nickel steel is used. The chemical and physical requirements of the unannealed rolled specimens of this material are as follows: Ni, 3% minimum; P, 0.04% maximum; S, 0.05% maximum; ultimate strength, 80,000 lbs. to 100,000 lbs.; yield point, 50,000 lbs. minimum; elongation in 8 in. for plates and shapes up to and including $\frac{3}{4}$ in., 16% minimum; and over $\frac{3}{4}$ in., 15% minimum; cold bending for material $\frac{3}{4}$ in. and under, 180 degrees around pin with diameter 2 x t, and for material over $\frac{3}{4}$ in., 180 degrees around pin with diameter 3 x t, t being thickness of material. For the nickel-steel eye-bars the following tests are given as typical. For the specimen tests, yield point, 58,500 lbs., ultimate strength 100,000 lbs.; elongation in 8 in., 15%; reduced area, 27%; fracture, $\frac{1}{2}$ cup. For the full size tests, yield point 57,000 lbs.; ultimate strength 95,000 lbs.; elongation in 12 in., 33%;

reduced area, 34%; fracture, silky. The specimen tests were taken before annealing, and the full size tests, in which the bar is tested to destruction, were taken after annealing. The annealing of the eye-bars was performed with great care, and the satisfactory results, as shown by the above tests, are, in a large measure, due to the annealing treatment. The chemical properties of the nickel-steel eye-bars are as follows: C, 0.33; P, 0.015; Si, 0.09; S, 0.03; Mn, 0.59; Ni, 3.3.

Important castings, such as trolley yokes supporting the gates and the castings forming the supports for the roller bearings in the gates, are of vanadium steel, specially heat treated. These castings have the following average physical properties: yield point 46,000 lbs.; ultimate strength 76,000 lbs.; elongation in 2 in., 25%; reduced area, 36%. The average chemical properties of these castings are as follows: C, 0.280; P, 0.033; Si, 0.300; S, 0.040; Mn, 0.620; V, 0.180.

The upper and lower disks of the center pivot are made of forged chrome vanadium steel. The physical properties of this steel are as follows: Elastic limit, 175,000 lbs.; ultimate strength, 200,000 lbs.; elongation in 2 in., 8%. This steel has average chemical properties as follows: C, 0.350; Mn, 0.850; S, 0.027; P, 0.025; Si, 0.140; Cr, 0.990; V, 0.220. These disks are 43 in. in diameter and 5 in. in thickness through the center; the approximate area of each is 1452 sq. inches; the total load upon the disk is 6,700,000 lbs.; therefore, the minimum unit pressure is 6,700,000 divided by 1452, or 4620 lbs. per sq. inch. This is the highest unit pressure that has ever been used in a similar location. Blanks for these disks were cut from a sand-cast ingot. After forging it into shape, the disks were carbonized for about six days at a temperature of 1850 degrees F. and then air annealed. After the air annealing, the disks were machined to a true radial surface. They were then reheated to a temperature of 1600 degrees F. and quenched in water. The disks were turned within one thirty-second of an inch of the final size, then shipped to the point of assembling, where the concave surfaces of each were ground and polished to gauge.

Between the upper and lower steel disks there is placed, as noted before, a forged manganese-bronze center disk. This disk is also 43 in. in diameter, but is 7 in. thick through the center. For testing purposes, three test pieces were cut from each disk. One piece was cut radially to the disk, one tangentially and the third was cut by a hollow drill through the center of the disk. The material of this disk is of exceptionally high quality, as evidenced by the following average physical properties, it being added that the results obtained from each set of test specimens did not vary more than 5%; yield point, 90,000 lbs.; ultimate strength, 120,000 lbs.; elongation in 2 in., 18%; reduced area, 15%. The following is the average chemical composition of this metal: Cu, 66.84; Z, 20.43; Mn, 3.17; Al, 6.22; Fe, 2.14; Si, trace; undetermined, 1.20.

The bronze was first made by regular crucible process, and, after a sufficient quantity had been melted, it was poured into a chilled iron mold approximately cubical in shape. Sufficient excess was cast in the ingot (about 20% of the weight of the ingot) to allow turning off the head and thereby securing solid metal. The piece was then heated to a forging temperature, about 1600 degrees F., and forged into the approximate shape of the center disk. After forging the disk, the test specimens were cut from the blank in the manner given above, and, if the tests proved satisfactory, the disk was rough-turned prior to shipment to the point of assembling. The disks were then turned and polished to gauge and grooves cut on each convex surface for grease.

Chemical and physical tests were made, by the commission, of 20 different brands of grease in order to determine a suitable grease for lubricating the surfaces of the disks. All of these tests showed that the three different brands of Whitmore grease which were tested were, for the desired purpose, far superior to any of the other brands. The physical tests were made on three small disks of 4 in. diameter, the upper and lower disks being made of case-hardened steel, and the middle disk of manganese bronze of the same quality as used for the dam. The tests were carried out by revolving the center disk by means of a lever and by varying the load upon the disk. In examining the disk, after the test, it was found that when the pressure reached 5000 lbs. per sq. inch, all brands of grease except Whitmore's escaped under the pressure, leaving the metal bare in spots. For some of the lighter brands, the bare spots were found when the pressure reached 3000 lbs. per sq. inch. For the lightest brand of Whitmore grease, bare spots were found at a pressure of 8000 lbs. per sq. inch, whereas for the two other brands of Whitmore grease, no bare spots could be detected at as high a pressure as 12,000 lbs. per sq. inch. No tests were made for higher pressures, as the machine did not have the capacity. In view of the results of these tests, the heavy grade of Whitmore's grease was adopted for the center disks and the wedges, and the light grade for all roller bearings.

After erection, tests were made on the West Emergency dam at Pedro Miguel. The excess counter-weight on the short arm was removed, so that the dam was balanced and the trailing wheels were not touching their tracks, also the main pinions were taken out of mesh with the rack. The dam was turned by pulling on a chain hoist, and the pull was recorded by a dynamometer. Attempts were made to pull the dam around at a uniform speed, and to note maximum and minimum readings. Although the dynamometer had been checked and found to be correct, it was further checked during these tests by fastening it at two different places on the long arm of the dam. It was at first fastened at the inner end of the horizontal truss and then at the outer end. The calculated turning moments obtained from the recorded pulls on the dynamometer and the measured lever arms at which the dynamometer was fastened, agreed very closely with each other, the average turning moment being 630,000 ft. lbs. As the total load on the center disk is 7,600,000 lbs. and the radius of the disk is 21.5 inches, the coefficient of friction, f, acting at the circumference of the disk will be:

$$f = \frac{630,000 \times 12}{21.5 \times 6,700,000} = 0.0525.$$

In view of the excellent results of the tests on the center pivot, it was decided to make tests of lubricants for the journals of the trailing wheels at the end of the short arm, as it had been found to be advisable to increase the load on these wheels from 20,000 lbs. on each to 43,000 lbs. on each. A certain grease had been placed in these journals during erection. After the pockets provided in the concrete counter-balance had been filled with the additional desired amount of pig iron, the tests were repeated in the same manner as had been done for the center pivot. The recorded average turning moment showed an increase during this test of 226,000 ft. lbs., making the total turning moment equal to 856,000 ft. lbs. The radius of the trailing wheels is 1.12 ft., the radius of the axles, 0.21 ft. and the lengths of the axles at each side of the wheels are 5⅜ in. The unit pressure, upon the projected area of the axle, due to the load of 43,000 lbs. is 805 lbs. per sq. inch. The force F_1, applied at the rack to overcome the total friction of the trailing wheels is:

$$F_1 = \frac{856,000 - 630,000}{92.25} = 2,450 \text{ lbs.}$$

Assuming the coefficient of rolling friction = 0.001 ft., the force F_2, applied at the center of the wheels, to overcome the rolling friction is

$$F_2 = \frac{86,000 \text{ lbs.} \times 0.001}{1.12} = 77 \text{ lbs.}$$

The force, F, applied at the rack, to overcome the journal friction of the trailing wheels is: $F = F_1 - F_2 = 23,373$ lbs. After these tests were made, all grease was removed from the journals, then Whitmore grease was applied and new tests were made. The recorded average turning moment for these tests was 650,000 ft. lbs. The force, F_1, applied at the rack to overcome the total friction of the trailing wheels was:

$$F_1 = \frac{650,000 - 630,000}{92.25} = 217 \text{ lbs.}$$

and the force, F, to overcome the journal friction was $F = F_1 - 77 = 140$ lbs., as compared with 2373 lbs. for the grease first tried.

The amounts the wedges had to be driven were arbitrarily chosen for the long arm as 1½ in., and for the short arm, ⅞ in. The calculations of the wedging machinery were based upon a coefficient of friction of 10%, applied at upper and at lower surfaces of wedge. As the contractor for the dams doubted that the wedging machinery could drive the wedges the full amount, and, as this amount was an arbitrary one, he was allowed, for the first dam which was built, to adjust the wedges in such a manner that they raised the dam only one half of the amount originally decided upon. The wedging machinery performed this work so well that, for the second dam which was built, the wedges were adjusted for three quarters of the original amount, and, as this work was also performed with ease, the wedges for the third dam were adjusted to raise the dam the full amount. It is difficult to determine accurately the coefficient of friction for the wedges, but it is safe to assume that this coefficient is well below 10%.

The maximum load on one roller-bearing of the gate wheels will be 32,750 lbs. This, distributed over three rollers of a bearing, would give about 10,900 lbs. per roller. The rollers are made of chrome steel of the following properties, viz.: C, 1.05; Mn, 0.23; S, 0.034; P, 0.017; Si, 0.26; Cr, 1.20. This material has a yield point of 163,300 lbs. No permanent set was found on rollers tested under a load of 63,000 lbs. The tool-steel sleeves, in which the rollers are carried, have the following properties: C, 1.05; Mn, 0.28; S, 0.035; P, 0.019; Si, 0.193. The wheels for the gates are of case-hardened chrome-vanadium steel of the following properties: C, 0.24; P, 0.012; Si, 0.14; S, 0.025; Mn, 0.5; Cr, 0.9; V, 0.21. This material has a yield point of 76,000 lbs., an ultimate strength of 96,000 lbs., with an elongation of 20% in 2 in., and reduction of area of 60%.

After the gates were assembled, friction tests were made at the contractor's shops. Figure 5 shows gate No. 1 subjected to a load equivalent to the full static head of 467,000 lbs., the load placed upon the gate being 450,040 lbs. and the weight of the gate itself being 17,610 lbs.

The tests for each gate were divided into three parts. The first part consisted in loading the gate to an amount equal to the sum of the kinetic and the static water pressures while lowering the gate in a current, and in measuring the force required to move the gate horizontally. The second part consisted in loading the gate to an amount equal to the maximum static water pressure to which the gate might be subjected. The third part consisted in a repetition of the first part. This test was made to ascertain if the force required for moving the gate horizontally had changed, due to overstraining the roller-bearings during the second part of the tests. The forces recorded during the first and third parts of the tests may be expressed in percentages of the weight of each gate; they are as follows: for gate No. 1, 4.2% and 2.6%; for gate No. 2, 3.4% and 3.4%; and for gate No. 3, 4.2% and 3.5%; for gate No. 4, 4.3% and 3.4%; for gate No.

5, 1.6% and 1.5%,—the first mentioned percentages being for the first part of the tests, and the second mentioned for the third part. The excellent results of these tests may be due as much to the splendid work done on the roller-bearings as to the grease used for these bearings.

ERECTION.

The dams were erected in the position parallel to the lock walls. Three tracks were used, one on the center line and one on each side. The track nearest the lock wall was carried on wooden bents over the pit into which the wicket girders swing. The other two tracks were carried over this pit on the wicket girders, which had been placed in a temporary position on heavy cribbing.

Erection began with the placing of the center pivot-casting and cross girders, and proceeded simultaneously towards the outer ends of both arms. The vertical trusses were erected on blocking slightly above the calculated camber elevations. Over the pit under the long arm the blocking was supported by the wicket girders. The short arm was lowered to its camber elevations before the long arm was completed. Great care was taken in maintaining the calculated camber elevations and in riveting the members of the vertical trusses immediately after assembling.

After completion of the vertical trusses and their bracing, the horizontal truss was erected, starting at the outer end. It was supported by blocking along the tension chord and by bolts at the lower chord of the vertical truss. The booms and framing supporting the horizontal truss were erected as the erection of this truss progressed. Each wicket-girder boom was bolted to its framing on the ground and then assembled into the structure.

The floor system was next put in place and the erection of the hoisting machinery begun. The pin ends of the wicket girders were raised by means of block and tackle, secured to the floor beams, and the pins placed. The outer ends were temporarily supported while the gates were lifted into storage position.

The installation of machinery went on during almost the entire erection period. The houses for the motors and switchboards were begun immediately after the concrete counter-weight block was completed, and, in the removal of the house forms, work on the motors and switchboards was commenced and was completed simultaneously with that on the houses.

INSPECTION.

For inspection of materials and erection, the same plan was followed for the emergency dams as for the lock gates and other

Fig. 8.   East Emergency Dam, Gatun Locks, Subjected to a Head of 50 ft. of Water.

important work coming under the jurisdiction of the Assistant Chief Engineer, viz., the placing of the designing engineer of each particular work in charge of inspection. As comparatively few data were at hand for obtaining the best results from the various materials composing the structure, considerable experimental work was necessary. This work required a closer cooperation with the contractor than usually is the case. This was especially so in regard to the vanadium case-hardened gate wheels and the chrome-vanadium steel disks, in connection with which credit is due to Mr. R. F. Wysor, Inspector for the I. C. C. and Mr. Bowman of the Carnegie Steel Company.

FINAL TESTS.

The acceptance test for each dam included placing it in position across the lock chamber in the dry, and then restoring it to its original position parallel to the lock walls. See Figs. Nos. 1, 2, 3 and 4. The time recorded for the actual operation of the various parts of the East Emergency Dam at Gatun during this test was as follows:

	Mins.	Secs.
Drawing wedges		19
Turning dam	1	44
Driving wedges		20
Lowering wicket girders	4	40
Lowering gates No. 1	3	02
Throwing clutches for gates No. 2		49
Lowering gates No. 2	3	25
Throwing clutches for gates No. 3		49
Lowering gates No. 3	3	03
Throwing clutches for gates No. 4		49
Lowering gates No. 4	2	32
Throwing clutches for gates No. 5		49
Lowering gates No. 5	2	02
Total	24	23

The total time required for bringing the dam into position was 42 minutes and 17 seconds, and the time lost between the various operations was 17 minutes and 54 seconds. This lost time will probably be reduced by the employment of skilled workmen in operating the dam.

The minimum time in which the dam was brought back to its original position was 1 hour, 27 minutes and 59 seconds.

On the 5th and 6th of May, 1914, this dam was subjected to its full static head as shown on Figures 6, 7 and 8. The dam was brought into place in still water, after which the culverts leading from the upper lock were opened, thus letting out and lowering the water below the dam. Figure 6 gives a rear view of the dam, while subjected to a head of 20 ft. of water, or

approximately the same head to which the dam at Sault St
Marie was subjected, during the accident previously mentione
As can be seen from Figure 6 and Figure 8, there is ve
little leakage in alternate panels of the dam, thus showing t
comparatively tight joint obtained by the bent plates provid
for the upper and lower edges of each gate. As shown on Pla
No. 4, these plates have not been extended over the who
width of the gate, as this would necessitate making an oblo
cut in these plates to provide clearance for the drive pipes. T
openings which thus remain unclosed at the lower corner of ea
gate are shown on Plate No. 6. The larger leakages, whi
also occur in alternate panels, are due to these uncovered ope
ings, although it may appear as if the leakage occurred betwe
the horizontal joints of the gates. A considerable amount
leakage also takes place at the sill, where a ¾-in. clearance
provided at each side of the wicket girders. The total leaka
of this dam while subjected to the full static head of 50 ft.
measured, was 950 cu. ft. per second, or, in other words, 1 ⁊
the total calculated discharge in case the gates were carried aw
and before the Emergency Dam should be brought into action.

While lowering the water below the dam, measurements we
taken of the elevation of the compression chord of the horizon
truss. These measurements showed that the elevation of t
chord increased with the static head produced on the dam, a
that this increase in elevation was $1\frac{1}{4}$ in. for the full static he
The elevation of the top of the upmost gate remained, howev
the same during the whole test, which shows that a relative m
tion took place between the gates and wicket girders, althou
the gates were subjected to their full static head, which is grea
than the head to which they will be subjected while being lo
ered in a current, as previously pointed out. The change
elevation of the horizontal truss is caused by the water pressu
producing an upward force, due to the inclined bottom flange
the wicket girders.

CONTRACTORS AND COST.

The contract for the manufacture, delivery, and erection
all dams was let to U. S. Steel Export Company, which sub
the structural-steel work and the turning and wedging machine

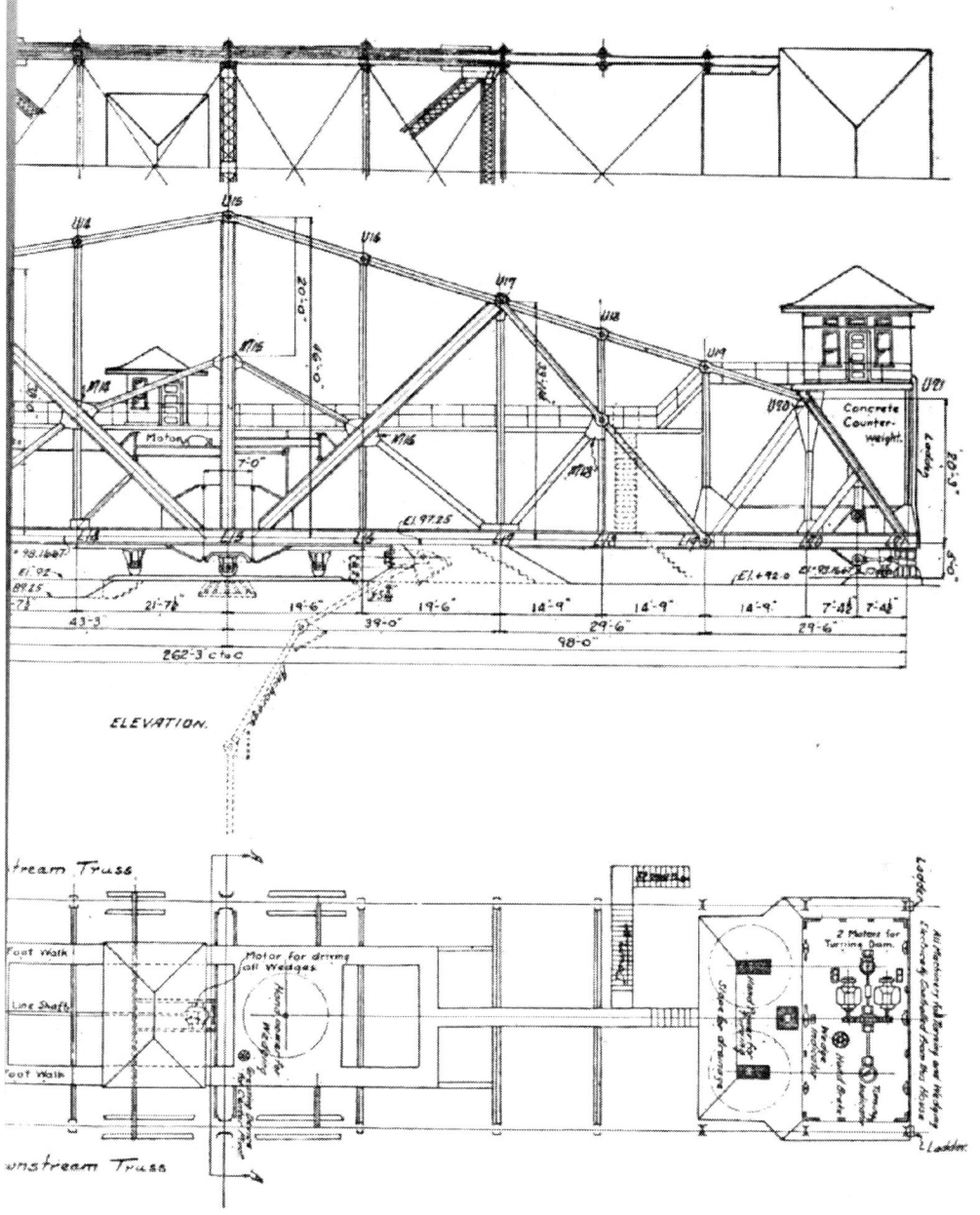

ELEVATION.

PLAN OF FLOOR.

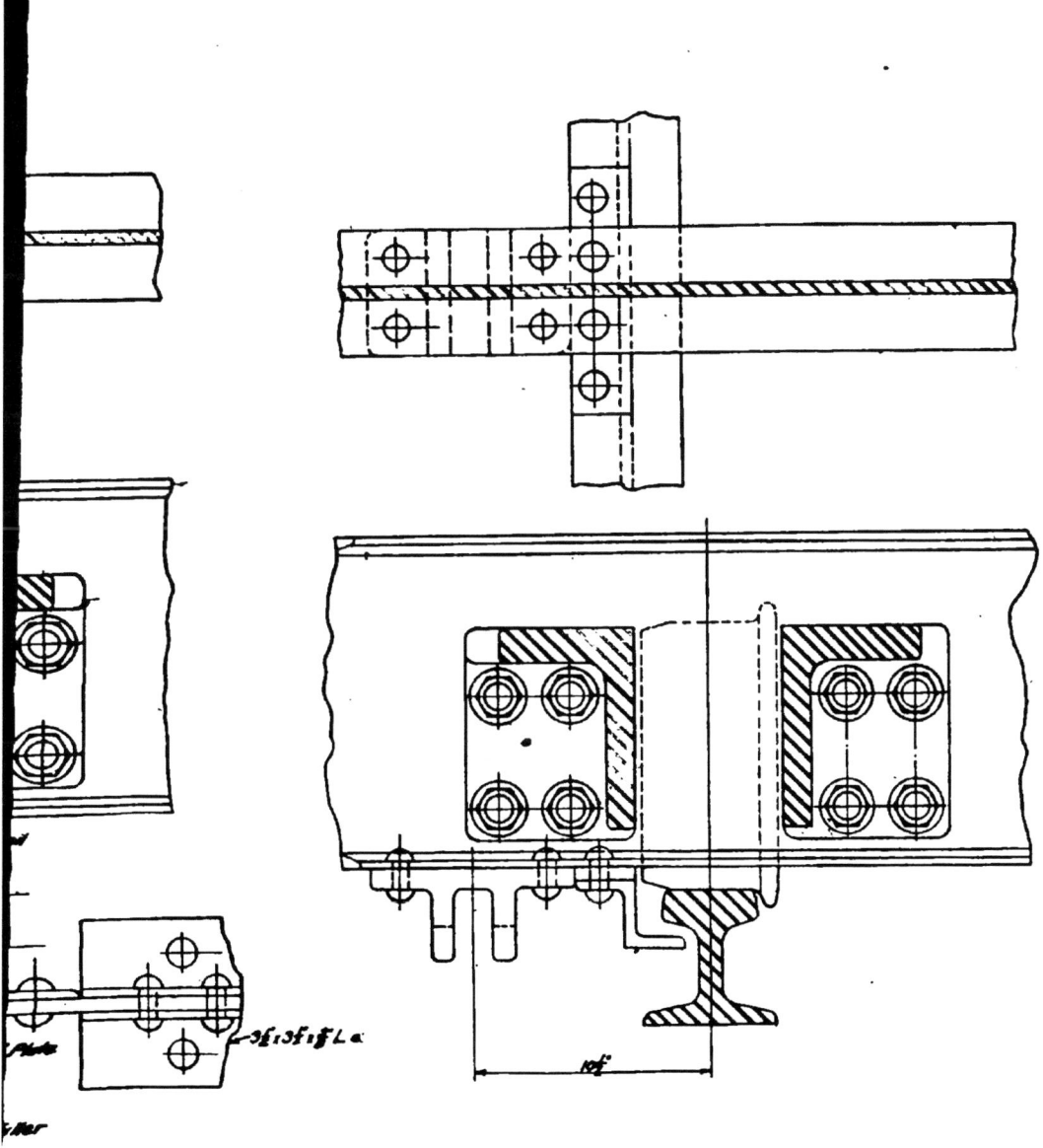

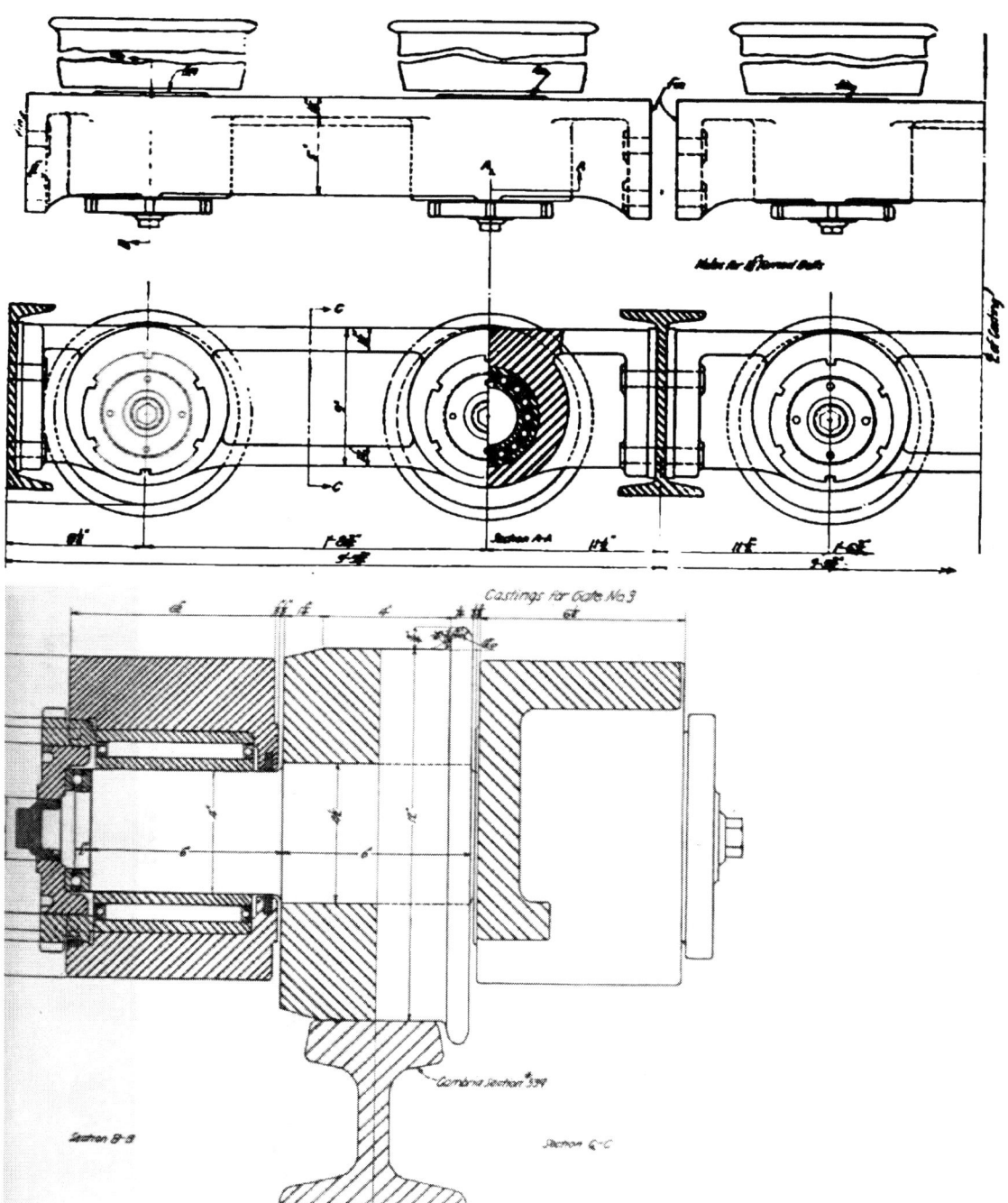

Plate No. 5.   Roller Bearings for Gates.

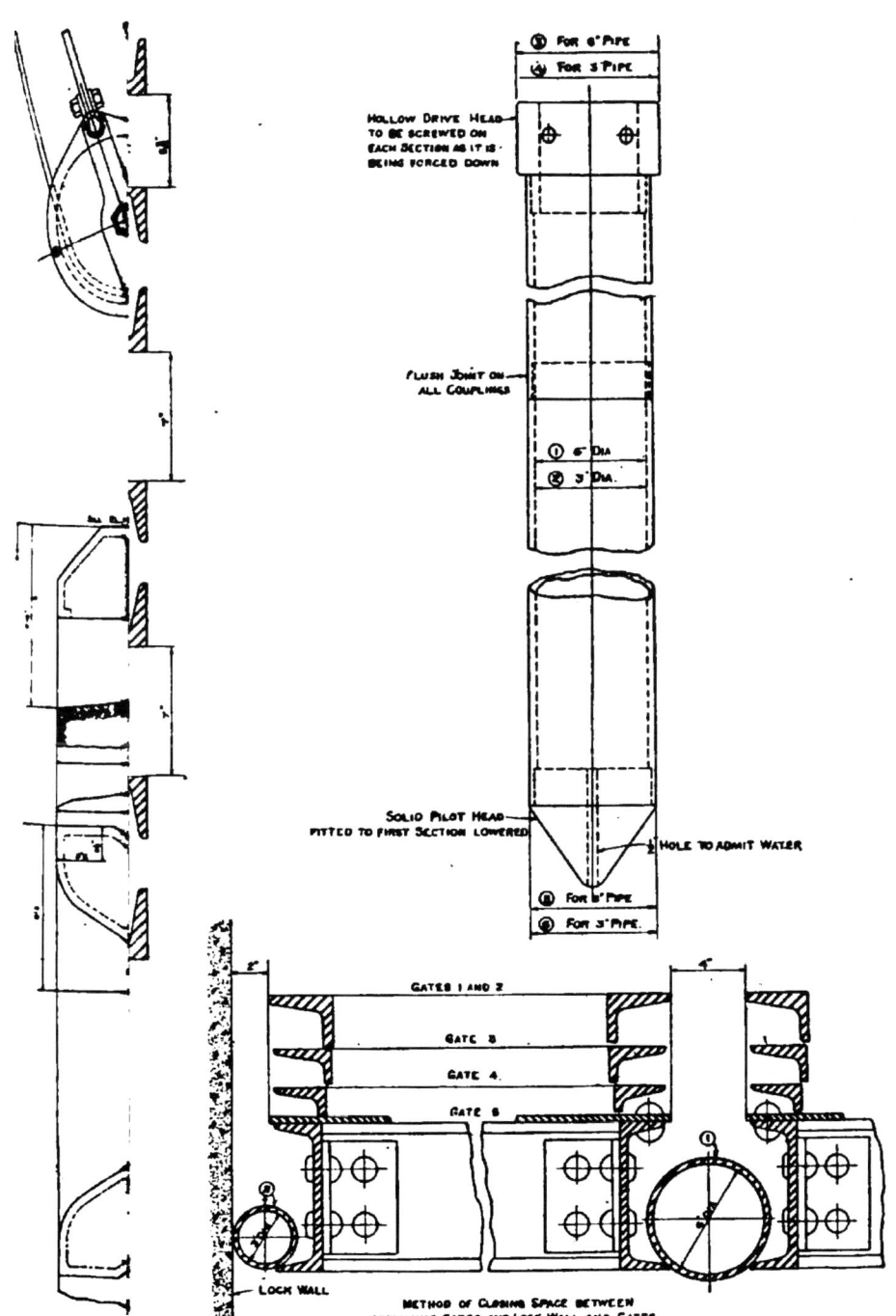

FOR 6" PIPE

FOR 3" PIPE

HOLLOW DRIVE HEAD
TO BE SCREWED ON
EACH SECTION AS IT IS
BEING FORCED DOWN

FLUSH JOINT ON
ALL COUPLINGS

① 6" DIA.

② 3" DIA.

SOLID PILOT HEAD
FITTED TO FIRST SECTION LOWERED

HOLE TO ADMIT WATER

FOR 6" PIPE

FOR 3" PIPE.

GATES 1 AND 2

GATE 3

GATE 4.

GATE 5

LOCK WALL

METHOD OF CLOSING SPACE BETWEEN
ADJOINING GATES AND LOCK WALL AND GATES.

to the American Bridge Company, the roller bearings to the Standard Machinery Co., the girder and gate hoisting machinery to the Otis Elevator Company, and the electrical equipment to the General Electric Company.

The total cost of the dams at Gatun and Pedro Miguel, including inspection, is $1,729,900.40, making the average cost of each of these dams $432,475.10. The dams at Miraflores cost $726,402.60, making the cost of each dam $363,201.30.

FINIS.

In the task of designing the emergency dams, valuable assistance was rendered by Mr. C. Derrick and Mr. Frank H. Moore, Assistant Engineers of the I. C. C., to whom the writer is indebted, also to Mr. O. E. Hovey, Assistant Chief Engineer of the American Bridge Company and his former Assistant Engineer, the late Mr. Blythe.

HYDRAULICS OF THE LOCKS OF THE PANAMA CANAL.

By

R. H. WHITEHEAD, Assoc. M. Am. Soc. M. E., M. Am. Inst. E. E.
Ass't Superintendent, Pacific Locks, The Panama Canal
Pedro Miguel, Canal Zone, Panama

———

The purpose of this paper is to give mathematical expression to the hydraulics of the locks of the Panama Canal. Many unexpected phenomena have been observed since the locks have been put into operation, some of which are very helpful and others disadvantageous. Their analyses are presented with the hope that they may assist designers of locks; accordingly the subject is treated from this viewpoint, and recommendations are made showing how to secure desirable results.

A correlation of this paper has not been possible with the Panama Canal papers presented before this Congress because of the limited amount of time and the extent of the subject covered.

The arrangement of valves and culverts is described and the object and expectations of the design given. The observed characteristics of the system are first mentioned briefly. It is shown that the safe rate of changing levels while locking a vessel is dependent on the distribution of water, and that in the locks of the Panama Canal a maximum rate of 7.5 ft. (2.29 m.) per minute with a good distribution is preferable to a rate of 4.5 ft. (1.37 m.) per minute with an inferior distribution. It is shown that the distribution for filling is more important than for emptying the chambers.

An analysis is made of the present distribution through the openings of the lateral culverts on the basis of negligible friction in the lateral. The unlike discharges through the openings are explained, and recommendations are made showing how to obtain correct distribution.

The coefficient of friction f is determined from observations taken during full discharge through the lock culverts, and it is shown that the main culvert valves when fully opened offer a negligible resistance to the flow of water. The coefficient f for the lateral culverts is obtained by deduction.

An arithmetical analysis is then made for the flow through the lateral culverts and openings, making all allowances for friction. The distribution for the main culvert and the individual laterals is also determined, making all allowances for friction. The total initial energy of the water is entirely accounted for and the lock coefficient C is determined. The analysis is proven by the actual value of C obtained from the filling curves and the observed distribution. Recommendations for uniform distribution for the system follow.

The filling and emptying curves for Pedro Miguel locks for all conditions of operation are next discussed. It is shown that the over-travel of the water in the locks is due to a head previously neglected and called the dynamic head. The true equation of flow is determined. It is shown that the dynamic head causes greater values of C by use of the ordinary equation of flow than the actual value, and it results in a large saving of time for the change of levels. The actual value of C is determined for all conditions of operation for the 900-ft. (275 m.) Pedro Miguel lock.

The value of the dynamic head is determined for locks having complex culvert systems and is calculated for the side-wall culvert. It is shown that its value depends on the location taken and that this explains the back-pressure on the lower safety gates in addition to that on the upper gates.

The rising stem valves are briefly described and an analysis is made of all friction losses, the coefficient of roller train friction is determined in particular, and the operating characteristics of the valves under various heads are stated.

The miter-gate moving machine is described and the duty cycle determined. It is shown that the principal resistive force to movement of a miter-gate leaf is due to lowering of the water level on one side of the leaf caused by its displacement. The effect of simultaneous and non-simultaneous operation of the leaves of a gate on the duty cycle is explained. The effect of difference of salinity of the water on the two sides of the gate, the immersion, and the area of the chamber or the contracted section controlled by the gate are given. The beneficial effect of the dynamic head on the operation of the gates is discussed.

The currents which occur on opening a gate with a difference of salinity of water on the two sides are first illustrated by diagrams obtained with pole floats. The theoretical value of these currents and certain characteristics are compared with actual observations. The handling of vessels in these currents is discussed in conclusion.

ARRANGEMENT OF VALVES AND CULVERTS AND EXPECTATIONS OF THE DESIGN.

The arrangement of valves and culverts is the same in principle for all locks of the Panama Canal. Fig. 1 is a general view of the Pedro Miguel single-lift locks.* The locks are in duplicate sets, with a common center wall. The water is distributed over the area of the lock through a large number of openings in the lock floor. These openings are connected in transverse rows to lateral culverts, which alternately connect to the main longitudinal culverts in the side and center walls. The main culverts extend the length of the locks, connecting to the forebay at the upper end and tail bay at the lower. The flow of water is controlled by rising-stem valves, which also sectionalize the main culverts and thereby cause proper diversion. The side-wall laterals connect freely to the main culvert, and those to the center wall are equipped with cylindrical valves at the entrance point. The center-wall culvert may be used for either lock by opening the cylindrical valves to that lock and closing them to the opposite lock. Cross-filling is frequently resorted to by opening the laterals to both locks.

All main-culvert valves control an opening 8 ft. (2.44 m.) wide and 18 ft. (5.49 m.) high, or 144 sq. ft. (13.39 sq. m.) in

---

* See Plate of ''General Design of the Locks, Dams and Regulating Works of the Panama Canal'', by Brig. Gen. H. F. Hodges, for a general plan of Pedro Miguel Locks.

area. The side culvert draws through three of these valves from
the forebay, making a total intake area of 432 sq. ft. (40.2 sq. m.).
A pair of valves forming the second set for filling is placed 320
ft. (97.6 m.) from the intake and control an opening of 288 sq. ft.
(26.8 sq. m.). Between the two sets of valves the main culvert
has an area of 432 sq. ft. (40.2 sq. m.) for about the first 50 ft.
(15.25 m.), and an area of 333 sq. ft. (30.9 sq. m.) for the remaining distance. From the second set of filling valves to the tailbay the main culvert has an area of 255 sq. ft. (23.7 sq. m.), and
is controlled by a set of valves placed opposite the intermediate
gate and two lower sets for emptying, each consisting of a pair
of valves having a total opening of 288 sq. ft. (26.8 sq. m.). The
main culvert communicates with the lock chamber through twelve
laterals and an opening for inspection purposes. The entrances
to the laterals have an area of 55 sq. ft. (5.11 sq. m.), and the
opening has an area of 20 sq. ft. (1.86 sq. m.). Eleven of the
laterals connect to the main chamber and one to the space between the two lower gates. This last lateral is controlled by a
non-operating valve set so that the water rises and falls at the
same rate between the gates as in the main chamber. Each of
the laterals to the main chamber has a cross-sectional area of
40.9 sq. ft. (3.8 sq. m.), or a combined area of 450 sq. ft. (41.8
sq. m.). Each of the laterals opens into the lock through five
circular openings each 12.23 sq. ft. (1.137 sq. m.) in area, or a
total of 673 sq. ft. (62.6 sq. m.) for the eleven laterals. The
most contracted area therefore is that of the main culvert, 255
sq. ft. (23.7 sq. m.).

In the center culvert conditions are similar except that the
two upper sets of filling valves are exactly the same and the large
culvert extends to the upper set. Two entrances are provided,
each having an area of 360 sq. ft. (33.4 sq. m.). There are but
ten laterals provided to each chamber, and the entrance to each
has an area of 33.2 sq. ft. (3.08 sq. m.). The various total areas
are therefore 360 sq. ft. (33.4 sq. m.) intake, 333 sq. ft. (30.9
sq. m.) to upper set of valves, 288 sq. ft. (26.8 sq. m.) for valves,
255 sq. ft. (23.7 sq. m.) main culvert, 332 sq. ft. (30.8 sq. m.)
entrances to lateral culverts, 409 sq. ft. (38 sq. m.) total area of
lateral culverts, and 612 sq. ft. (56.8 sq. m.) for lateral culvert
openings.

Fig. 1. General View of Pedro Miguel Locks from Luisa Hill.

The system was designed with the expectation of obtain[ing]
practically uniform water distribution. With such a dist[ribu-]
tion it was expected to change the water levels at a maxi[mum]
rate of 3 ft. (0.915 m.) per minute. The side-wall culvert[s]
designed to give this rate for the major part of the operati[on]
regulating valve openings, and the center-wall culvert w[as in-]
tended as an auxiliary which might be used to accelerat[e the]
last few feet of flow, and in this manner perform the [entire]
change of levels in 15 minutes.

OBSERVED CHARACTERISTICS OF THE SYSTEM AND IM[POR-] TANCE OF GOOD DISTRIBUTION.

The maximum rate when filling the 900-ft. (275 m.)[lock]
with the side-wall culvert is 4.5 ft. (1.37 m.) per minute[;]
with both culverts fully opened for the entire period of [fill]
the maximum rate is about 7.5 ft. (2.29 m.) per minute.[The]
distribution for filling with both culverts is good, but for on[e cul-]
vert alone it is not what was expected. In locking vessels [it]
is preferable to use both culverts with the 7.5-ft. (2.29 m.)[rate]
than one with the lower 4.5-ft. (1.37 m.) rate. It thus hap[pens]
that on account of its effect on the total distribution, the c[enter-]
wall culvert, while originally intended as an auxiliary, has p[roved]
a very important factor in the safe and rapid handling of v[essels.]

The distribution for filling the chamber is of a gr[eater]
importance than for emptying. In filling, the maximum [rate]
occurs with the smallest opportunity for adjustment, an[d the]
vessel is subject to action of jets discharging at high velo[city]
from the openings in the floor of the lock. These jets a[t]
the surface of the water and with uneven distribution caus[e the]
water to pile up on one side of the vessel, thereby tendi[ng to]
force the vessel out of position and against the lock wall, [unless]
securely held. In emptying, the opportunity for adjustme[nt is]
in proportion to the flow, and the energy of the flowing wa[ter is]
dissipated in the culverts and in the lock below or in the tai[lbay.]
The water is drawn into the openings from all direction[s and]
the surface remains perfectly placid.

No trouble whatever has been experienced in the han[dling]
of vessels in down lockages with the use of one or both cul[verts.]

although it is known that the distribution is not uniform. There-fore in the operation of the locks, vessels on up lockages are given preference for double culvert operation, and the center-wall culvert is used on down lockages only for saving time. The remote-control system makes it possible to change the center-wall culvert from one lock chamber to its twin in 30 seconds. With light traffic, such as at present, two culverts are generally used on all lockages.

With a perfectly uniform distribution, or, better yet, a dis-tribution that will automatically center the vessel in the locks so that it will not drift against the walls and so that there will be no tendency for motion along the axis of the lock, the safe rate of change of levels need only be limited by economy of lock design. It is believed that with both culverts the locks of the Panama Canal are a distinct step in this direction, as they safely handle large vessels through a lift of 32 ft. (9.76 m.) in eight minutes. The analysis of the present distribution and recommendation for perfect distribution follow.

DISCHARGE THROUGH LATERAL CULVERT OPENINGS WHEN FILLING LOCKS, NEGLECTING FRICTION.

Fig. 2 shows the design of the horizontal lateral culverts and their openings in the lock floor. An approximately equal dis-charge was expected from the five like openings of any lateral, the calculated friction losses in the lateral having a small effect. As the total kinetic and potential energy of any particle of water must be constant, neglecting friction, for all positions of the par-ticle during the passage through the lateral and openings, the velocity of discharge for all openings must be the same, even with different size openings.

In the operation of the locks the discharge is not the same for all the openings. The maximum discharge occurs through the opening farthest from the culvert entrance, and the dis-charge decreases with increasing increments through the suc-cessive openings with approach to the lateral entrance. Only a very small part of the total discharge takes place through the opening nearest the lateral entrance. The discharge does not take place perpendicularly from the openings, but has a drift in the direction of flow through the lateral; this drift becomes greater through the successive openings with approach to the throat of the lateral. Fig. 3 illustrates these facts.

The explanation is that the velocity of approach causes the drift of the jet from the normal and thereby causes a contracted section, elliptical in the case of circular openings. The rate of discharge equals the product of this contracted section and the jet velocity. The jet velocity being the same for all openings, the discharge is in proportion to the cross-sectional area of the jet.

If the area of the openings is taken as F, the cross-sectional area of the jet issuing at an angle from the normal is approximately $F \cos a$ where a is the angle of the jet. This neglects natural contraction. Natural contraction with rounded edges, if any, is small; all designers consequently use rounded edges. If the flow takes place at an angle through an orifice with rounded edges, neglecting contraction, the area of the jet will be somewhat greater than $F \cos a$. The author assumes that the natural additional contraction due to the angular flow is compensated for by the increase of area. The drift of the jet at the entrance to the orifice is taken as a. If the orifice has a thickness or approaches a short tube, the drift from it will be smaller than a, as the sides of the orifice or short tube tend to straighten the jet with the normal.

$$\sin a = \frac{\text{velocity of approach}}{\text{velocity of the jet}}$$

The quantity of water discharged from like openings in a horizontal culvert of uniform cross-section is obtained as follows:

Let $q =$ quantity discharged through any opening
Let $Q =$ quantity flowing past opening in lateral
Let $v =$ jet velocity, the same for all openings

$F =$ area openings $A =$ area lateral $K = \dfrac{F}{A}$

Then

$$v^2 = \frac{q^2}{F^2} + \frac{(Q + q)^2}{A^2}$$

solving

$$q = \frac{-K^2 Q + \sqrt{(1 + K^2)\, F^2 v^2 - K^2 Q^2}}{1 + K^2}$$

Fig. 3. East Chamber of Pedro Miguel Lock Looking North. All Valves in East Wall Fully Open.

For the last opening furthermost from entrance of lateral

$$q_1 = \frac{\sqrt{F^3 v^2 (1 + K^2)}}{1 + K^2}$$

substituting

$$q = \frac{-K^2 Q + \sqrt{(1 + K^2)^2 q_1^2 - K^2 Q^2}}{1 + K^2}$$

Using this formula and calling q_1 equal to 100 per cent, the relative discharge can be easily calculated for any number of openings by taking the successive openings, beginning at number one having the discharge of q_1.

Fig. 4 shows the relative discharge through a number of like openings in a horizontal culvert for various values of K. It will be noted that for $K = 0.1$ water will flow through only 17 end openings and will pass by any additional number of openings between opening 17 and the entrance of the lateral. For $K = 0.2$ water will flow through only 10 openings.

In other words, when the velocity in the lateral equals the jet velocity v there is no normal velocity component to cause a discharge through the opening, also when the total cross-sectional area of the jets equals the cross-sectional area of the lateral, flow will not take place through additional openings.

For the laterals and openings as shown on Fig. 2, the value of $K = 0.3$. Consequently, neglecting friction, the discharges from Fig. 4 are as follows:

1st opening	....	100 per cent.
2nd "	....	89 " "
3rd "	....	73 " "
2nd "	....	51 " "
1st "	....	29 " "

By reference to Fig. 4 it will be seen that the presence of additional openings of like size would result in a very small increase in total lateral discharge.

Experiments on short brass tubes with various numbers and sizes of openings confirm the theory advanced.

This unequal discharge makes it difficult to keep a vessel central in the locks when using one culvert for filling, the vessel being forced over towards the wall or culvert from which the filling is taking place. It is frequently necessary to close the filling valves part way to prevent possible damage to the vessel.

If there is a quantity of salt water in the chamber when filling begins, the tendency to force the vessel toward the wall, the culvert of which is being used for the filling, is especially great.

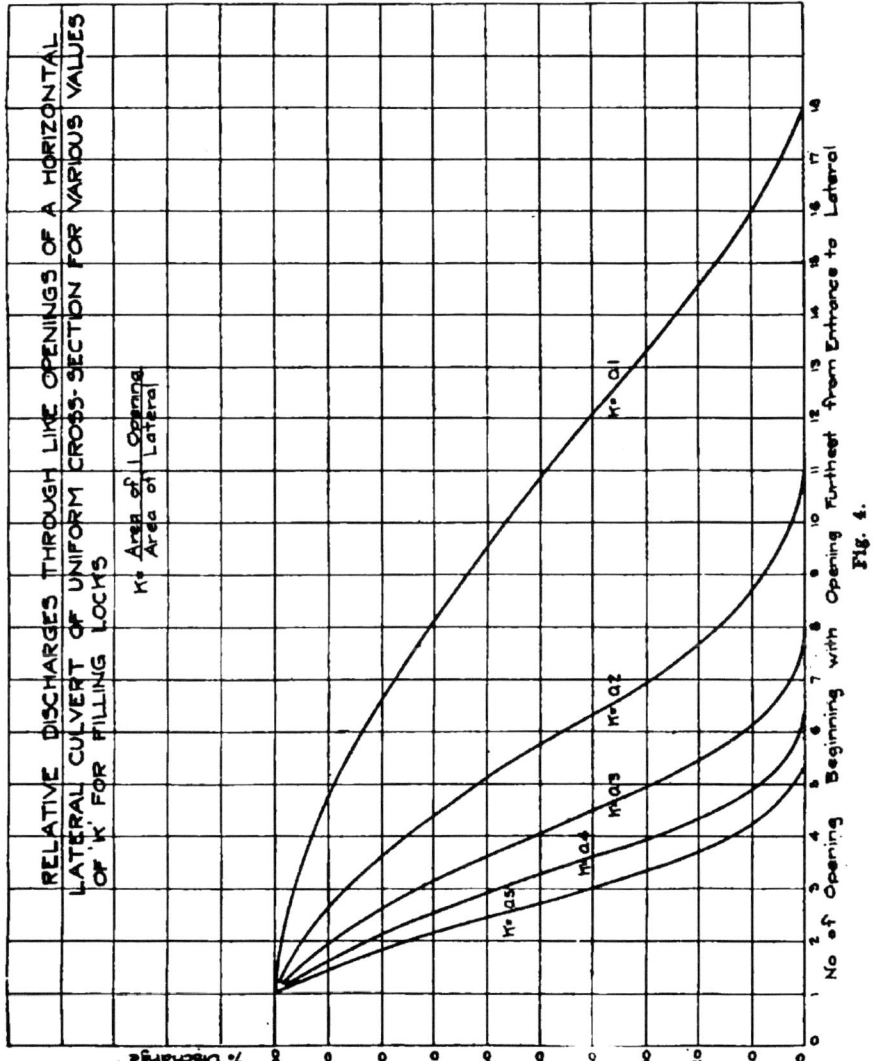

Fig. 4.

This reason is that, in addition to the normally more rapid rise along the opposite wall, the fresh water is forced to the top with augmented velocity by the pressure of the denser salt water.

This tendency was distinctly demonstrated during the up-lockage of the "Santa Clara" through the Pacific locks on June 18th. In the lower chamber at Miraflores, when the side-wall culvert was being used, the towing locomotives could not hold the vessel away from the side wall. In the upper chamber, where the water was comparatively fresh, this trouble was not experienced to such a great extent, and the locomotives were able to keep the vessel central in the lock. At Pedro Miguel, both culverts were used and the vessel remained in the center of the chamber with hardly any effort. All merchant vessels are required to have their sides clear before passage through the Canal, so that they can rub against the lock walls without injury.

RECOMMENDATIONS FOR DESIGN OF LATERAL CULVERTS AND THEIR OPENINGS.

When emptying a lock the water is drawn into the openings from all directions, and there is no contraction at the openings as in the case of filling the locks. Any contraction in the lateral caused by the impact with the inflow from the openings acts the same as friction in the lateral, and the tendency is therefore for maximum discharge through the openings nearest the culvert entrance. An attempt therefore to obtain uniform distribution for filling by varying the size of openings would result in a worse distribution for emptying, and the method is therefore undesirable.

The distribution for filling could be made uniform by having a tapering culvert, so as to have a like velocity of approach for like openings. This probably would not have any serious effect on the distribution for emptying.

If, from a construction standpoint, it is thought advisable to make the laterals of uniform cross-sectional area, and to have them connect to the culvert in a similar manner to those of the Panama Canal, the value of K should be chosen small enough to obtain a reasonably good distribution, or a small number of openings used. For the Panama Canal locks, and using five openings, K should be no greater than 0.1.

The ideal design, and the one that would automatically center vessels in either up or down-lockages, is to connect the main culvert to the middle of the lateral culvert instead of to one end, so that the water flowing into the lateral would branch off in both directions. When filling the locks, the maximum discharge would then occur through both end openings, and would decrease through successive openings with approach to the center line of the locks. The inclination of the jets would likely be beneficial rather than harmful, and, when emptying, the water would be drawn at the maximum rate through the openings nearest the center line of the lock, which would also tend to hold the vessel central.

FRICTION LOSSES.

In order to determine friction losses in the valves and culverts, the valves in the east culvert of Pedro Miguel lock were opened wide, allowing full discharge through the culvert from Gaillard Cut, with the surface of water at 84.8 ft. (25.85 m.), to Miraflores Lake, then at elevation 52 ft. (15.85 m.). The rate of discharge through the culvert was found to be 7660 cu. ft. (217 cu. m.) per second.

The elevation of the water after equilibrium was reached as obtained at several points was as follows: (See Fig. 5.)

			Feet	Meters
Point	(1)	Elevation Gatun Lake at Gamboa	84.8	(25.85)
"	(2)	Elevation Gatun Lake at lock forebay..	83.9	(25.59)
"	(3)	In guard valve shaft	76.6	(23.35)
"	(4)	In culvert shaft under dam	72.1	(21.98)
"	(5)	In 350-ft. lock	63.5	(19.36)
"	(6)	In 550-ft. lock	57.6	(17.56)
"	(7)	In Miraflores Lake	52.0	(15.85)

The potential heads, or heads above datum 52 are as follows:

Point	(1)	Gatun Lake at Gamboa	32.8	(10.00)
"	(2)	Gatun Lake at lock	31.9	(9.74)
"	(3)	In guard valve shaft	24.6	(7.50)
"	(4)	In culvert shaft under dam	20.1	(6.13)
"	(5)	In 350-ft. lock	11.5	(3.51)
"	(6)	In 550-ft. lock	5.6	(1.71)

Neglecting currents in the lock sections, the velocities through the culvert at different points obtained by dividing the full discharge by the various cross-sectional areas are as follows:

	Feet Per Sec.	Meters Per Sec.
Through guard valve and screens	17.7	(5.41)
Through upper culvert	23.0	(7.02)
Through rising-stem valves	26.6	(8.11)
Through main culvert	30.0	(9.15)

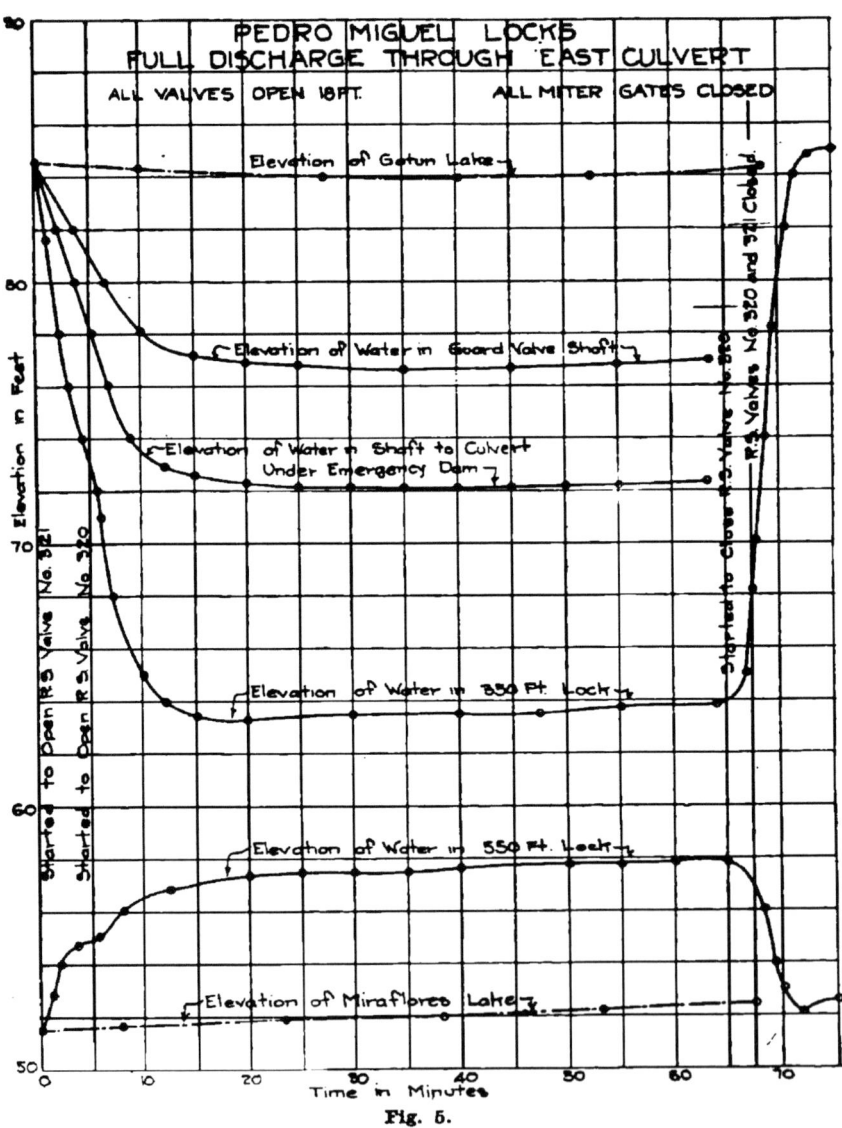

Fig. 5.

The corresponding velocity heads found from the formula $\frac{v^2}{2g}$ are as follows:

	Feet	Meters
Through guard valves	4.9	(1.49)
Through upper culvert	8.2	(2.50)
Through rising-stem valves	11.0	(3.36)
Through main culvert	14.0	(4.27)

The total heads or potential plus velocity heads as obtained by addition are:

		Feet	Meters
Point (1)	Gatun initial lake-level head at Gamboa	32.8	(10.00)
" (2)	Gatun Lake at locks	31.9	(9.73)
" (3)	At guard valves and screens	29.5	(8.99)
" (4)	At culvert shaft	28.3	(8.63)
" (5)	At culvert for 350-ft. lock	25.5	(7.78)
" (6)	At culvert for 550-ft. lock	19.6	(5.98)
" (7)	Outlet	14.0	(4.27)

The friction losses for the various culvert sections are obtained by subtraction between the above and are as follows:

	Loss Head Feet	Loss Head Met.	Per-cent Total
Between (1) and (2). Thru channel in Gaillard Cut	0.9	(0.27)	2.7
Between (2) and (3). Thru screens, intake and guard valves	2.4	(0.73)	7.3
Between (3) and (4). Thru upper culvert	1.2	(0.36)	3.6
Between (4) and (5). Thru rising-stem valves No. 314 and No. 315 and connecting culvert	2.8	(0.86)	8.6
Between (5) and (6). Thru rising-stem valve No. 320 and No. 321 and connecting culvert	5.9	(1.80)	18.0
Between (6) and (7). Thru rising-stem valves No. 326 and No. 327 and No. 332 and No. 333 and connecting culvert	5.6	(1.71)	17.1
Lost in discharge	14.0	(4.27)	42.7

These values are plotted in Fig. 6, and it is shown that the total-head curve is practically a straight line which changes its slope only with change of culvert cross-sectional area, excepting a sudden drop due to the intake. The presence or number of valves had no effect on the friction losses, showing that the friction in the valves is a negligible amount when the valves are fully opened.

$$H = \frac{fl}{4r}\frac{v^2}{2g}$$

Using the formula

l is the length of culvert

r is the hydraulic radius and is equal to $\dfrac{\text{cross-sectional area}}{\text{perimeter}}$

f is the coefficient of friction

$\dfrac{v^2}{2g}$ is the velocity head

and H is the head loss due to skin friction.

Fig. 6 shows that in 1000 ft. (304.8 m.) of culvert having an area of 255 sq. ft. (23.7 sq. m.), and diameter of 18 ft. (5.49 m.), the friction loss H was 10 ft. (3.05 m.) for a velocity of 30 ft. (9.15 m.) per second. $\therefore f = 0.0128$.

For 250 ft. (76.2 m.) of upper culvert, having an area of 333 sq. ft. (30.9 sq. ft.) the friction loss H was 1.1 feet (0.336 m.) for a velocity of 23 ft. (7.02 m.) per second. $\therefore f = 0.011$.

Mr. Mansfield Merriman, in his treatise on hydraulics, gives a very complete tabulation of the value of f for velocities up to 15 ft. per second for clean iron pipes up to 6 ft. in diameter, with which the coefficients determined compare very favorably. This is not surprising, as the walls of the culverts are made smooth by the action of the water. From the tabulation, the value of f decreases with increase of velocity and diameter; the variation of f is however small for large-size pipes with large velocities. For the lateral culverts having an area of 40.9 sq. ft. (3.8 sq. m.), it appears that a coefficient of $f = 0.015$ is about correct, the value being obtained by deduction, using the principle of variation shown in the tables mentioned.

Figs. 7 and 8 show the design of the intakes for the side and center walls. The intake losses for the side walls form 7.3 percent of the total head. Special tests were made to determine the intake losses for the center wall, observations being taken while filling the chamber at the manhole between valves Nos. 312 and 313 and Nos. 316 and 317. These observations are as follows:

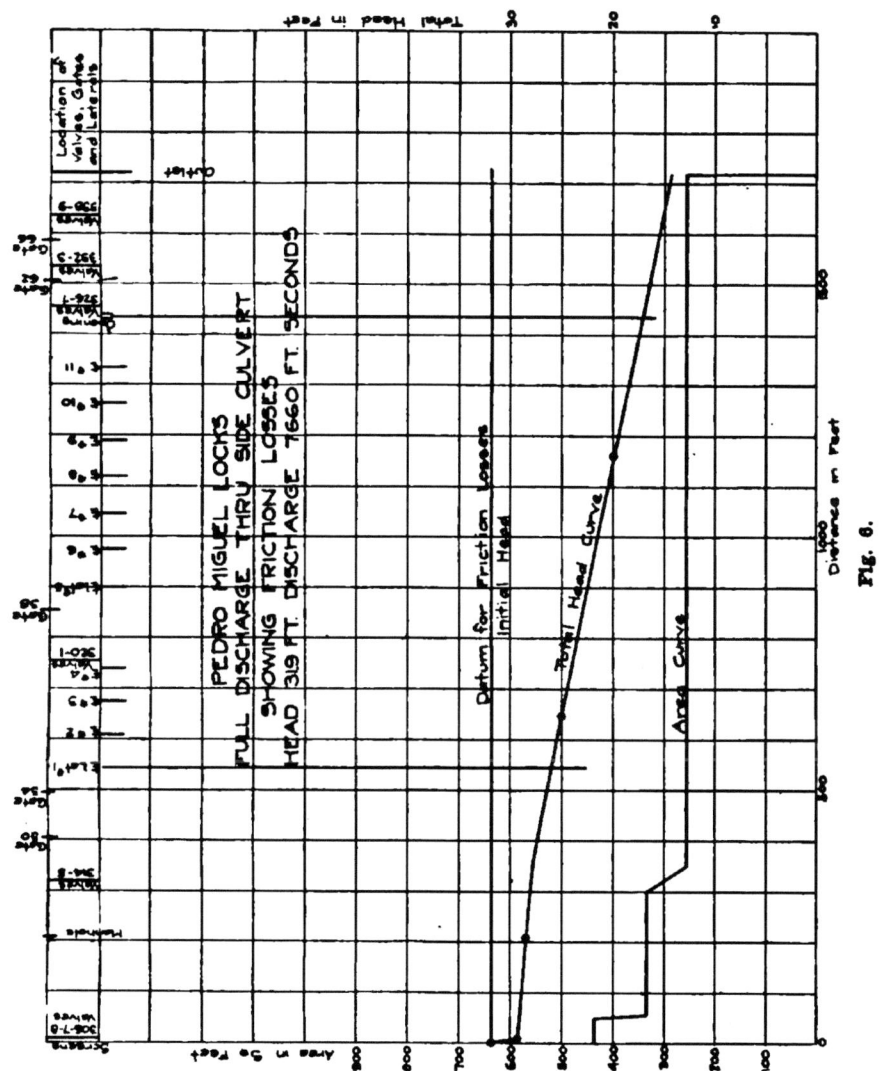

Fig. 6.

Time from Opening	Observed Pressure Head		Velocity		Velocity Head		Total Head	
	Ft.	Meters	Ft. per Sec.	Met. per Sec.	Ft.	Meters	Ft.	Meters
4 minutes	26.0	(7.93)	19.85	(6.05)	6.15	(1.86)	32.15	(9.79)
5 "	26.7	(8.15)	18.60	(5.67)	5.4	(1.63)	32.1	(9.78)
6 "	27.4	(8.36)	17.05	(5.20)	4.5	(1.38)	31.9	(9.74)
7 "	28.0	(8.54)	15.90	(4.85)	3.9	(1.20)	31.9	(9.74)
8 "	28.6	(8.73)	14.60	(4.45)	3.3	(1.01)	31.9	(9.74)
9 "	28.9	(8.82)	13.88	(4.23)	3.0	(0.92)	31.9	(9.74)

The total head without friction should be 32.7 ft. (9.98 m.). The friction losses for maximum flow are therefore about 0.8 ft. (0.25 m.), or approximately 2.5 percent. The loss is less than for the side-culvert intake, as it was measured while drawing in water from both sides of the center wall, there being no regulating valves installed.

DISCHARGE THROUGH OPENINGS OF LATERAL CULVERTS CORRECTED FOR FRICTION LOSSES.

The perimeter of the lateral culverts at the 40.9 sq. ft. (3.8 sq. m.) area section is 22.86 ft. (6.98 m.). The hydraulic radius is therefore 1.79 ft. (0.545 m.). The coefficient of skin friction is taken as 0.015. The loss of head for a length l of culvert and a velocity v is formulated.

$$H_1 = \frac{0.015}{4 \times 1.79} l \frac{v^2}{2g} \text{ for English system.}$$

$$= \frac{0.015}{4 \times 0.545} l \frac{v^2}{2g} \text{ for metric system.}$$

The discharge through any particular opening results in a change of velocity in the lateral and a consequent loss of head as expressed by Borda's formula

$$H_2 = \frac{(v_a - v_b)^2}{2g}$$

in which v_a is velocity before reaching opening and v_b is velocity past opening. If the discharge through the opening is q cu. ft. or meters per second, then

$$H_2 = \left(\frac{q}{A}\right)^2 \frac{1}{2g}$$

In calculating this loss in the following, it has been found that a negligible error results in assuming q equal to its theoretical value without friction as previously determined.

A considerable loss must result due to deflection of the water through the openings. This loss is assumed as 25 percent of the jet velocity head, in absence of data on the subject. Any reasonable assumed loss from 20 percent to 30 percent has no appreciable effect on the relative amount of discharge through the openings of the lateral culvert in question.

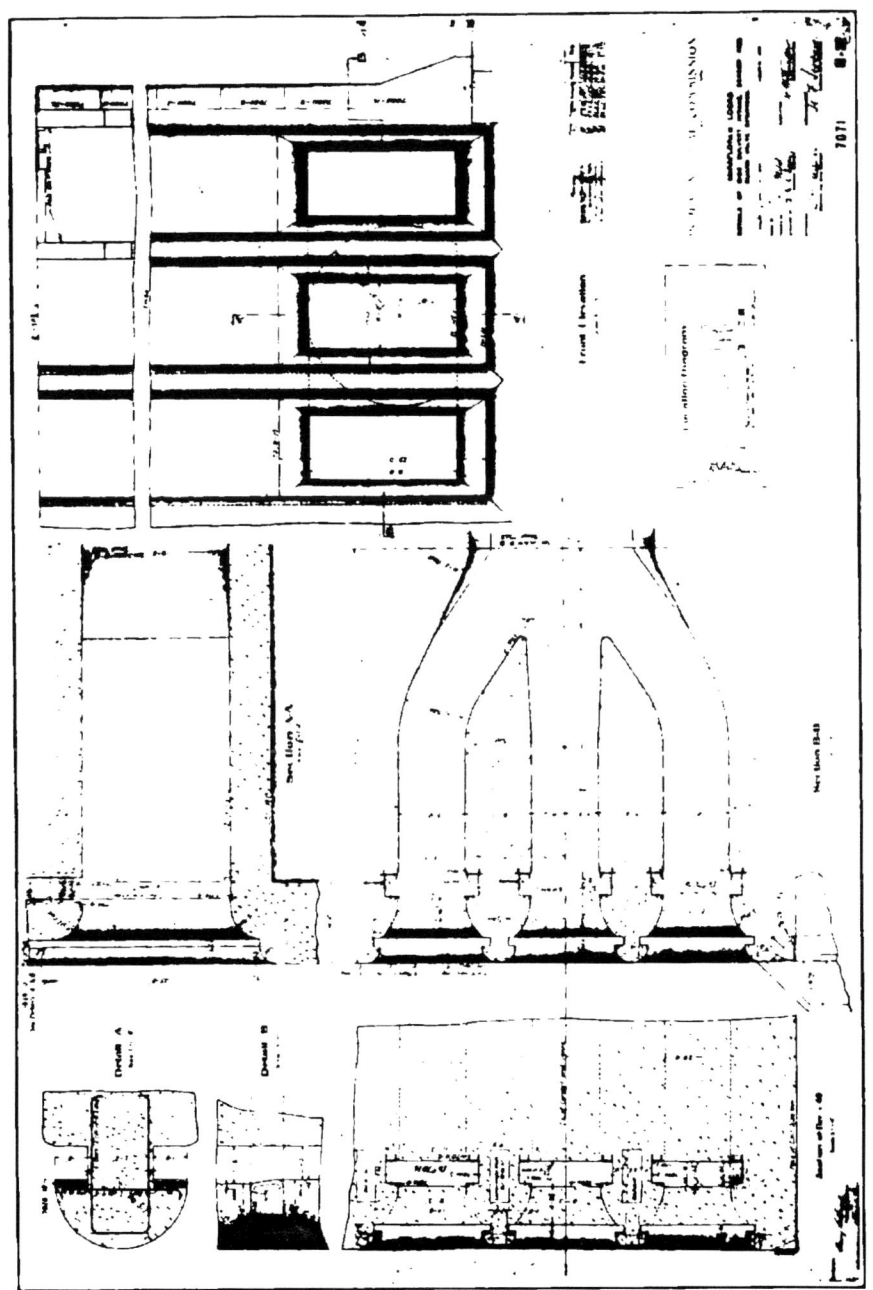

Fig. 7.

The relation between the quantity q discharged through any opening, the quantity Q flowing past the opening in the lateral, and the jet velocity is expressed by the formula previously derived:

$$q = \frac{\sqrt{(1 + K^2)\, F^2 v^2 - K^2 Q^2} - K^2 Q}{1 + K^2}$$

in which $K = 0.3$ and $F = 12.23$ sq. ft. (1.137 sq. m.).

Numbering the openings from 1 to 5, as before, commencing with opening No. 1 most distant from the entrance to the lateral—

Let $q_1 = 250$ cu. ft. (7.08 cu. m.) per second

Then $v_1 = 21.3$ ft. (6.50 m.) per second

$\dfrac{v_1^2}{2g} = 7.07$ ft. (2.155 m.)

$H_s = 1.77$ ft. (0.541 m.) loss at opening

$H_1 = 0.02$ ft. (0.0061 m.) loss account skin friction between openings 1 and 2

$H_2 = 0.46$ ft. (0.1402 m.) loss due to change of velocity account discharge at opening No. 2

Total head at 2nd opening—9.32 ft. (2.84 m.)

$\dfrac{v_2^2}{2g} = 7.45$ ft. (2.27 m.)

$v_2 = 21.9$ ft. (6.68 m.) per second

$q_2 = 226$ cu. ft. (6.40 cu. m.) per second, or 90.5% of q_1

$H_1 = 0.08$ ft. (0.0244 m.) loss account skin friction between openings 2 and 3

$H_2 = 0.31$ ft. (0.0947 m.) loss due to change of velocity account discharge at opening No. 3

Total head at 3rd opening—9.71 ft. (2.96 m.)

$\dfrac{v_3^2}{2g} = 7.77$ ft. (2.37 m.)

$v_3 = 22.3$ ft. (6.81 m.) per second

$q_3 = 189$ cu. ft. (5.35 cu. m.) per second, or 76% of q_1

$H_1 = 0.16$ ft. (0.0488 m.) loss account skin friction between openings 3 and 4

$H_2 = 0.15$ ft. (0.0458 m.) loss due to change of velocity at opening No. 4

Total head at 4th opening—10.02 ft. (3.055 m.)

$\dfrac{v_4^2}{2g} = 8.04$ ft. (2.45 m.)

$v_4 = 22.7$ ft. (6.94 m.) per second

$q_4 = 140$ cu. ft. (3.96 cu. m.) per second, or 56% of q_1

$H_1 = 0.23$ ft. (0.0702 m.) loss account skin friction between openings 3 and 5

$H_2 = 0.05$ ft. (0.0152 m.) loss due to change of velocity account of discharge at opening No. 5

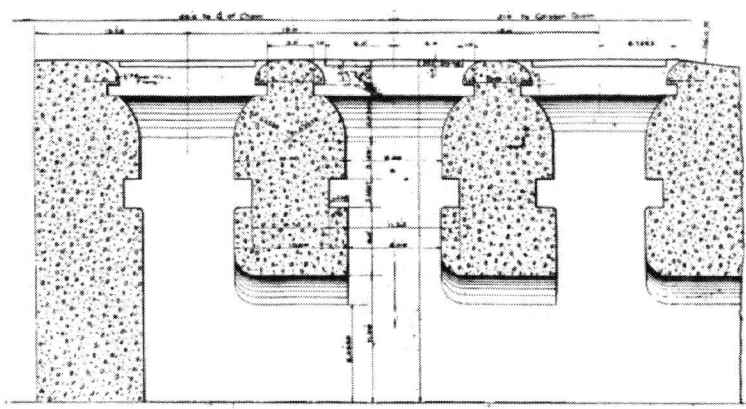

HORIZONTAL SECTION THROUGH INTAKE
scale ⅜" = 1'-0"

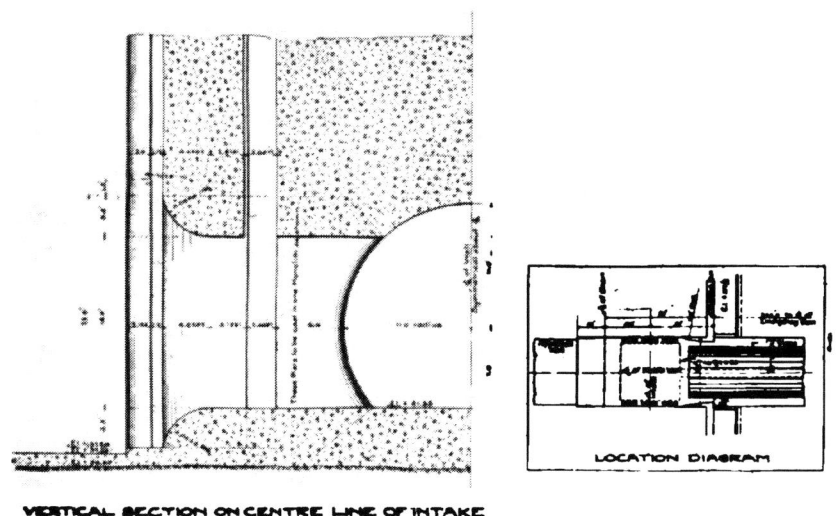

VERTICAL SECTION ON CENTRE LINE OF INTAKE
scale ⅜" = 1'-0"

LOCATION DIAGRAM

Fig. 8. Centre Culvert Intake.

Total head at 5th opening—10.30 ft. (3.14 m.)

$$\frac{v_5^2}{2g} = 8.25 \text{ ft. } (2.52 \text{ m.})$$

$v_5 = 23.0$ ft. (7.02 m.) per second

$q_5 = 88$ cu. ft. (2.59 cu. m.) per second, or 35% of q_1

Friction losses between opening No. 5 and main
culvert, skin friction.. 0.78 ft.   (0.238 m.)

*Estimated losses due to 90° turn, 16%................ 1.18 ft.   (0.360 m.)

Total head on lateral without entrance losses...... 12.26 ft.   (3.74 m.)

Total discharge through lateral.......................... 893 cu. ft. (25.38 cu. m.)

The total head on lateral without entrance losses is called the effective head, in the absence of a better name; where h is this head the total discharge, called q, is formulated

$$q = C A \sqrt{2g h}$$

in which, from above

$$C = 77.7\%$$

The discharge through the openings, allowing for friction, compared to those obtained without such allowance are—

	With Friction	Assuming no Friction
Opening No. 1............................100%	100%	
" " 2.................... 90.5%	89%	
" " 3.................... 76%	73%	
" " 4.................... 56%	51%	
" " 5.................... 35%	29%	

The total effective area of the five openings is 40.1 sq. ft. (3.72 sq. m.), which is slightly less than the area of the lateral, or 40.9 sq. ft. (3.80 sq. m.).

TOTAL DISCHARGE THROUGH LATERAL CULVERTS WHILE FILLING LOCKS.

With a negligible velocity of approach, the coefficient of contraction for a sharp-edged circular orifice is 0.61. If a tube of the same cross-sectional area is substituted for the orifice, and the length of the tube is sufficient for the contracted section to expand and fill it, the coefficient of discharge for the tube is 0.82. The coefficient of contraction at the entrance to the tube is, however, the same as for an orifice, or 0.61. The increased discharge

---

* See Church's Mechanics, page 728, 1904 edition, Bends in pipes of circular section, friction losses.

of the tube over the orifice is due to the presence of a partial vacuum at the section of contraction. With no losses, the coefficient for the tube would be unity. There is, however, an entrance loss and a loss when the contracted-section velocity changes to the velocity for the full tube. This latter loss is expressed by Borda's formula and is

$$H = \frac{(v_a - v_b)^2}{2\,g}$$

in which H is the head loss, v_a velocity at section of contraction, and v_b velocity for full tube.

In filling the locks with the side-wall culvert, the lateral farthest upstream discharges first, the discharge being noticeable about 30 seconds after the first motion of the valves. The laterals progressing down the lock discharge one after another with very short intervals, the lateral at the lower end of the lock discharging last of all. After flow is established through all laterals, the discharge through the last four downstream laterals is noticeably greater than through the remaining laterals, which show decreasing discharges with approach to the filling valves. At some instant during the filling, one of the downstream laterals may appear to give a slightly greater discharge than the others, but it will not always be the same lateral.

With culvert friction the only consideration, the discharge through the laterals nearest the filling valves should be greater than through the laterals downstream.

If the discharge through the last lateral downstream is taken as 900 cu. ft. (25.5 cu. m.) per second, and the head at the lateral entrance as 13.2 ft. (4.02 m.), and this discharge is assumed with an initial 32 ft. (9.76 m.) head, the head at the entrance to the lateral nearest the filling valve will be greater than 20 ft. (6.1 m.), which would cause a much greater discharge through this lateral if there were no other factors involved.

The comparison between the tube and the orifice gives the explanation of the results obtained. Contraction occurs at the entrance to the laterals due to the angular flow into their entrances caused by the velocity of approach. A loss of head occurs when the velocity is changed from that at the section of contraction to where the lateral entrance is fully filled. If the area of the contracted section is assumed the same for the lateral culverts as for their openings, then the loss of head is

$$H = \frac{v^2}{2g}\left(\frac{1}{\cos a} - 1\right)^2$$

where v is the velocity for full lateral flow and a is the angle of drift.

If $q =$ total discharge through the lateral
$Q =$ quantity flowing past lateral in main culvert
$F =$ area lateral entrance
$A =$ area of main culvert
$a =$ angle of drift

Then $\tan a = \frac{F}{A}\left(\frac{Q+q}{q}\right)$

Also $v = \frac{q}{F}$

This loss tends to make the discharge through the downstream laterals greatest, while friction losses in the main culvert tend to make the discharge through the upstream laterals greatest. Due to the large magnitude of these two factors, results, to be of any value, must take cognizance of both.

An arithmetical analysis is made in the following, in which the discharge through the various lateral culverts is computed, and all friction losses allowed for according to the formulae given, for the side-wall culvert. The analysis of the lateral culverts and openings is used as a basis; as in the case of the lateral-culvert openings, the friction due to the deflection of the water into the lateral is taken as 25% of the velocity head at the section of greatest contraction, or $\frac{0.25\,v^2}{2g\cos^2 a}$.

The area of the lateral-culvert entrance, F, is 55 sq. ft. (5.11 sq. m.). It is assumed that full expansion takes place in the length of lateral having this area. The area of the main culvert, A, is 255 sq. ft. (23.7 sq. m.).

If q is the discharge through any lateral, then the loss of head due to change of velocity in the main culvert is $\left(\frac{q}{A}\right)^2\frac{1}{2g}$.

The loss due to skin friction for a length l of culvert of diameter d, as previously determined, is $H = \frac{fl}{d}\frac{v^2}{2g}$ in which $f = 0.013$ for the main culvert.

In making the following analysis for the side-wall culvert,

the "cut and try" method has been used, it having been found that the value of the discharge can be easily determined in about two trials.

The laterals have been numbered from 1 to 11 inclusive, progressing downstream. On the downstream side of the 11th lateral, as previously mentioned, there is an opening leading from the chamber to the culvert, having an area of about 20 sq. ft. (1.86 sq. m.). There is also a separate lateral feeding the 11,000 sq. ft. (1023 sq. m.) space between the lower safety and operating gates. The quantity flowing past the 11th lateral for the purpose of caring for these has been taken as 1300 cu. ft. (36.8 cu. m.) per second. The calculations are based on a total discharge of 900 cu. ft. (25.5 cu. m.) per second through lateral No. 11.

Lateral No. 11

> Quantity flowing past lateral in main culvert = 1300 cu. ft. (36.8 cu. m.) per sec.
>
> Take discharge through lateral as 900 cu. ft. (25.5 cu. m.) per sec.
>
> $$\tan a = 0.527 \qquad a = 27° \; 47' \qquad \cos a = 0.885$$
>
> $\left(\dfrac{1}{\cos a} - 1\right)^2$ is negligible; hence no loss occurs due to sudden expansion.
>
> Velocity in section of contraction = 18.5 feet (5.64 m.) per second.
>
> 25% entrance-velocity head loss = 1.33 ft. (0.406 m.)
>
> Effective head on lateral = 12.4 ft. (3.78 m.), from data previously given.
>
> Total head in main culvert at lateral No. 11 = 13.73 ft. (4.19 m.)

Lateral No. 10

> Quantity flowing past lateral in main culvert = 2200 cu. ft. (62.3 cu. m.) per sec.
>
> Skin friction between laterals 10 and 11 = 0.06 ft. (.0183 m.)
>
> Loss due to change of velocity at lateral 10 = 0.190 ft. (0.058 m.)
>
> [Assume q_{10} = 890 cu. ft. (25.2 cu. m.) per sec.]
>
> Total head at lateral 11 = 13.73 ft. (4.19 m.)
>
> Total head at lateral 10 = 13.980 ft. (4.266 m.)
>
> $$\tan a = 0.747 \qquad a = 36° \; 46' \qquad \cos a = 0.801$$
>
> $\left(\dfrac{1}{\cos a} - 1\right)^2 = 6.1\%$
>
> 25% entrance-velocity head loss = 1.590 ft. (0.485 m.)
>
> Loss due to expansion 6.1% = 0.249 ft. (0.076 m.)
>
> Effective head on lateral = 12.14 ft. (3.705 m.)
>
> Discharge = 890 cu. ft. (25.2 cu. m.) per sec., or 99% of q_{11}.

Lateral No. 9

> Quantity flowing past lateral in main culvert = 3090 cu. ft. (87.5 cu. m.) per sec.

Skin friction between laterals 9 and 10 = 0.119 ft. (0.0363 m.)

Loss due to change of velocity at lateral 9 = 0.184 ft. (0.0562 m.)

[Assume q_9 = 875 cu. ft. (24.75 cu. m.) per sec.]

Total head at lateral 10 = 13.980 ft. (4.266 m.)

Total head at lateral 9 = 14.283 ft. (4.358 m.)

$\tan a = 0.975$ $a = 44°\ 17'$ $\cos a = 0.7159$

$$\left(\frac{1}{\cos a} - 1\right) = 15.6\%$$

25% entrance-velocity head loss = 1.92 ft. (0.586 m.)

Loss due to expansion 15.6% = 0.615 ft. (0.1875 m.)

Effective head on lateral = 11.748 ft. (3.585 m.)

q_9 = 875 cu. ft. per sec. (24.75 cu. m.), or 97.2% of q_{11}.

Lateral No. 8

Quantity flowing past lateral in main culvert = 3965 cu. ft. (112.25 cu. m.) per sec.

Skin friction between laterals 8 and 9 = 0.196 ft. (0.0598 m.)

Loss due to change of velocity at lateral 8 = 0.173 ft. (0.0528 m.)

[Assume q_8 = 850 cu. ft. (24.05 cu. m.) per sec.]

Total head at lateral 9 = 14.283 ft. (4.358 m.)

Total head at lateral 8 = 14.652 ft. (4.470 m.)

$\tan a = 1.218$ $a = 50°\ 37'$ $\cos a = 0.6345$

$$\left(\frac{1}{\cos a} - 1\right)^2 = 33\%$$

25% entrance-velocity head loss = 2.32 ft. (0.708 m.)

Loss due to expansion 33% = 1.226 ft. (0.374 m.)

Effective head on lateral = 11.106 ft. (3.388 m.)

q_8 = 850 cu. ft. (24.05 cu. m.) per second, or 94.5% of q_{11}.

Lateral No. 7

Quantity flowing past lateral in main culvert = 4815 cu. ft. (136.3 cu. m.) per sec.

Skin friction between laterals 7 and 8 = 0.289 ft. (0.088 m.)

Loss due to change of velocity at lateral 7 = 0.159 ft. (0.0485 m.)

[Assume q_7 = 815 cu. ft. (23.1 cu. m.) per sec.]

Total head at lateral 8 = 14.652 ft. (4.470 m.)

Total head at lateral 7 = 15.100 ft. (4.606 m.)

$\tan a = 1.485$ $a = 56°\ 3'$ $\cos a = 0.5585$

$$\left(\frac{1}{\cos a} - 1\right)^2 = 62.5\%$$

25% entrance-velocity head loss = 2.76 ft. (0.842 m.)

Loss due to expansion 62.5% = 2.13 ft. (0.650 m.)

Effective head on lateral = 10.21 ft. (3.114 m.)

q_7 = 815 cu. ft. (23.1 cu. m.) per sec., or 90.6% of q_{11}.

Lateral No. 6

Quantity flowing past lateral in main culvert = 5630 cu. ft. (159.4 cu. m.) per sec.

Skin friction between laterals 6 and 7 = 0.395 ft. (0.1205 m.)

Loss due to change of velocity at lateral 6 = 0.142 ft. (0.0433 m.)
    [Assume q_6 = 770 cu. ft. (21.8 cu. m.) per sec.]
Total head at lateral 7 = 15.100 ft. (4.606 m.)
Total head at lateral 6 = 15.637 ft. (4.770 m.)
$\quad$ tan a = 1.788 $\qquad$ a = 60° 47′ $\qquad$ cos a = 0.4881

$$\left(\frac{1}{\cos a} - 1\right)^2 = 110\%$$

25% entrance-velocity head loss = 3.21 ft. (0.979 m.)
Loss due to expansion 110% = 3.36 ft. (1.025 m.)
Effective head on lateral = 9.067 ft. (2.766 m.)
q_6 = 769, approx. 770 cu. ft. (21.8 cu. m.) per sec., or 85.5% of q_{11}.

Lateral No. 5

Quantity flowing past lateral in main culvert = 6400 cu. ft. (181.2 cu. m.) per sec.
Skin friction between laterals 5 and 6 = 0.511 ft. (0.156 m.)
Loss due to change of velocity at lateral 5 = 0.119 ft. (0.0363 m.)
    [Assume q_5 = 705 cu. ft. (19.9 cu. m.) per sec.]
Total head at lateral 6 = 15.637 ft. (4.770 m.)
Total head at lateral 5 = 16.267 ft. (4.962 m.)
$\quad$ tan a = 2.17 $\qquad$ a = 65° 16′ $\qquad$ cos a = 0.4184

$$\left(\frac{1}{\cos a} - 1\right)^2 = 194\%$$

25% entrance-velocity head loss = 3.67 ft. (1.119 m.)
Loss due to expansion 194% = 4.96 ft. (1.513 m.)
Effective head on lateral = 7.637 ft. (2.330 m.)
$\quad$ q_5 = 705 cu. ft. (19.9 cu. m.) per sec., or 78.4% of q_{11}.

Lateral No. 4

Quantity flowing past lateral in main culvert = 7105 cu. ft. (201.1 cu. m.) per sec.
Skin friction between laterals 4 and 5 = 1.40 ft. (0.427 m.)
Loss due to change of velocity at lateral 4 = 0.109 ft. (0.0332 m.)
    [Assume q_4 = 675 cu. ft. (19.1 cu. m.) per sec.]
Total head at lateral 5 = 16.267 ft. (4.962 m.)
Total head at lateral 4 = 17.776 ft. (5.422 m.)
$\quad$ tan a = 2.48 $\qquad$ a = 68° 2′ $\qquad$ cos a = 0.3741

$$\left(\frac{1}{\cos a} - 1\right)^2 = 282\%$$

25% entrance-velocity head loss = 4.21 ft. (1.284 m.)
Loss due to expansion 282% = 6.62 ft. (2.019 m.)
Effective head on lateral = 6.946 ft. (2.119 m.)
q_4 = 672, approx. 675 cu. ft. (19.1 cu. m.) per sec., or 74.6% of q_{11}.

Lateral No. 3

Quantity flowing past lateral in main culvert = 7780 cu. ft. (220.2 cu. m.) per sec.
Skin friction between laterals 3 and 4 = 0.681 ft. (0.208 m.)

Loss due to change of velocity at lateral 3 = 0.078 ft. (0.0238 m.)
    [Assume q_3 = 570 cu. ft. (16.1 cu. m.) per sec.]
Total head at lateral 4 = 17.776 ft. (5.422 m.)
Total head at lateral 3 = 18.535 ft. (5.654 m.)
        tan a = 3.15 a = 72° 23'   cos a = 0.3026

$$\left(\frac{1}{\cos a} - 1\right)^2 = 534\%$$

25% entrance-velocity head loss = 4.60 ft. (1.403 m.)
Loss due to expansion 534% = 8.94 ft. (2.727 m.)
Effective head on lateral = 4.995 ft. (1.524 m.)
        q_3 = 570 cu. ft. (16.1 cu. m.) per sec., or 63.3% of q_{11}.

Lateral No. 2

Quantity flowing past lateral in main culvert = 8350 cu. ft. (236.3 cu. m.) per sec.

Skin friction between laterals 2 and 3 = 0.785 ft. (0.240 m.)
Loss due to change of velocity at lateral 2 = 0.046 ft. (0.014 m.)
        [Assume q_2 = 440 cu. ft. (12.4 cu. m.) per sec.]
Total head at lateral 3 = 18.535 ft. (5.654 m.)
Total head at lateral 2 = 19.366 ft. (5.908 m.)
        tan a = 4.29 a = 76° 53'   cos a = 0.2269

$$\left(\frac{1}{\cos a} - 1\right)^2 = 1160\%$$

25% entrance-velocity head loss = 4.84 ft. (1.476 m.)
Loss due to expansion 1160% = 11.58 ft. (3.322 m.)
Effective head on lateral = 2.946 ft. (0.910 m.)
q_2 = 438, approx. 440 cu. ft. (12.4 cu. m.) per sec., or 49% of q_{11}.

Lateral No. 1

Quantity flowing past lateral in main culvert = 8790 cu. ft. (248.7 cu. m.) per sec.

Skin friction between laterals 1 and 2 = 0.87 ft. (0.265 m.)
Loss due to change of velocity at lateral 1 = 0.00 ft. (0.000 m.)
        (Assume q_1 is negligible.)
Total head at lateral 2 = 19.366 ft. (5.908 m.)
Total head at lateral 1 = 20.236 ft. (6.173 m.)

In this case, regardless of the value assumed for q_1, the entrance losses plus the expansion losses based on that value are so large that when they are subtracted from the total head there is not a sufficient value of the effective head remaining to cause the assumed amount of flow. For small assumed values of q_1, the losses exceed the total head at the lateral. Theoretically, therefore, a steady discharge through the lateral is impossible. From actual observations, at times the water surface shows no sign of discharge, and again a very small discharge from one or two of the openings (the observations being taken after flow is established through all laterals). The discharge through the lateral is therefore assumed as zero. Under abnormal conditions, with about a foot of water in the lock and the leakage from the upper valves flowing into the chamber, a suction has been noted in this lateral, while a discharge occurred from the remaining laterals.

Totals

Total discharge, all laterals = 8790 cu. ft. (248.7 cu. m.) per second.

Total head at lateral 1 = 20.236 ft. (6.173 m.)

Observed friction losses between intake and first lateral with 7660 cu. ft. (217 cu. m.) per sec. discharge, approximately 6 ft. (1.83 m.) (See Fig. 7)

These losses, with above discharge = 7.88 ft. (2.403 m.)

Total head for above flow = 28.116 ft., or approximately 28.1 ft. (8.58 m.)

A total discharge of 8790 cu. ft. (248.7 cu. m.) per second would cause a change of levels in the 900-ft. (274 m.) lock at the rate of approximately 4.3 ft. (1.31 m.) per minute, which checks with actual observations for this head. Repeated observations of the action of the water indicate the correctness of the distribution shown after flow is established.

RECOMMENDATION FOR TOTAL LATERAL CULVERT DISTRIBUTION.

The analysis for the total discharge through the lateral culverts gives the explanation for the water discharging at maximum rate through the downstream laterals. This unequal discharge results in a tendency for the vessel to drift towards the upper gates when filling. This tendency to date has been very small, but it will undoubtedly become an important factor when handling ships approaching the full capacity of the locks, as there will be a smaller opportunity for adjustment of the flow. On emptying the locks the vessels tend to drift downstream, showing that the laterals downstream discharge more than the upstream laterals under this condition. This was also determined experimentally as follows:

The intermediate gates were closed and the chamber emptied through the center-wall culvert, seven laterals being connected to the 550-ft. (168 m.) lock, and three to the 350-ft. (107 m.)

lock. A large positive head was observed on the intermediate gates. One of the seven laterals was then closed and observations were repeated with the same result. It was finally found that with four valves open to the 82,500-sq. ft. (7670 sq. m.) section, and three to the 40,500-sq. ft. (3760 sq. m.) section, that the water levels in both sections remained the same. In other words, the three valves upstream discharged only 66 percent as much water, on the average, as the four downstream valves.

Tests were made in the same manner for filling with the center-wall culvert, and it was found that with three laterals connected to the 350-ft. (107 m.) lock section, and five laterals open to the 550-ft. (168 m.) lock section, that the water levels remained the same in both lock sections during the entire period while filling. This shows that the three upstream valves discharged on the average of 82 percent of the average amount discharged by the five downstream laterals. Using the calculation shown for the side-wall culvert, the figure obtained for the above condition is 86.5 percent. This, however, is only an approximate check, as there are losses in the cylindrical valves which also affect the distribution.

With the system of distribution used, it is evident that the distribution can be improved for both filling and emptying by throttling the downstream laterals. Throttling the downstream laterals would decrease the total quantity flowing past the upper laterals, and would thereby also increase the discharge through these laterals when filling the locks. It might therefore be wise, under certain conditions, to provide a non-operating valve for the entrance to each lateral and to make a setting of these valves by trial to obtain the distribution desired. If intermediate gates were not used, the discharge through the farthest upstream and downstream laterals could be made a maximum, and all tendency to drift along the axis of the locks would be eliminated.

The culvert system could be designed so that the losses due to angular flow into the laterals would be balanced by the friction losses in the main culvert, and a uniform distribution thereby obtained for filling, but this would result in a worse distribution for emptying.

The best method, where possible, would be to have the intake and discharge connect to the middle of the longitudinal culvert;

this would give an ideal distribution for both filling and emptying of the locks, as, when filling, the maximum discharge would
take place through both end laterals, and would decrease with

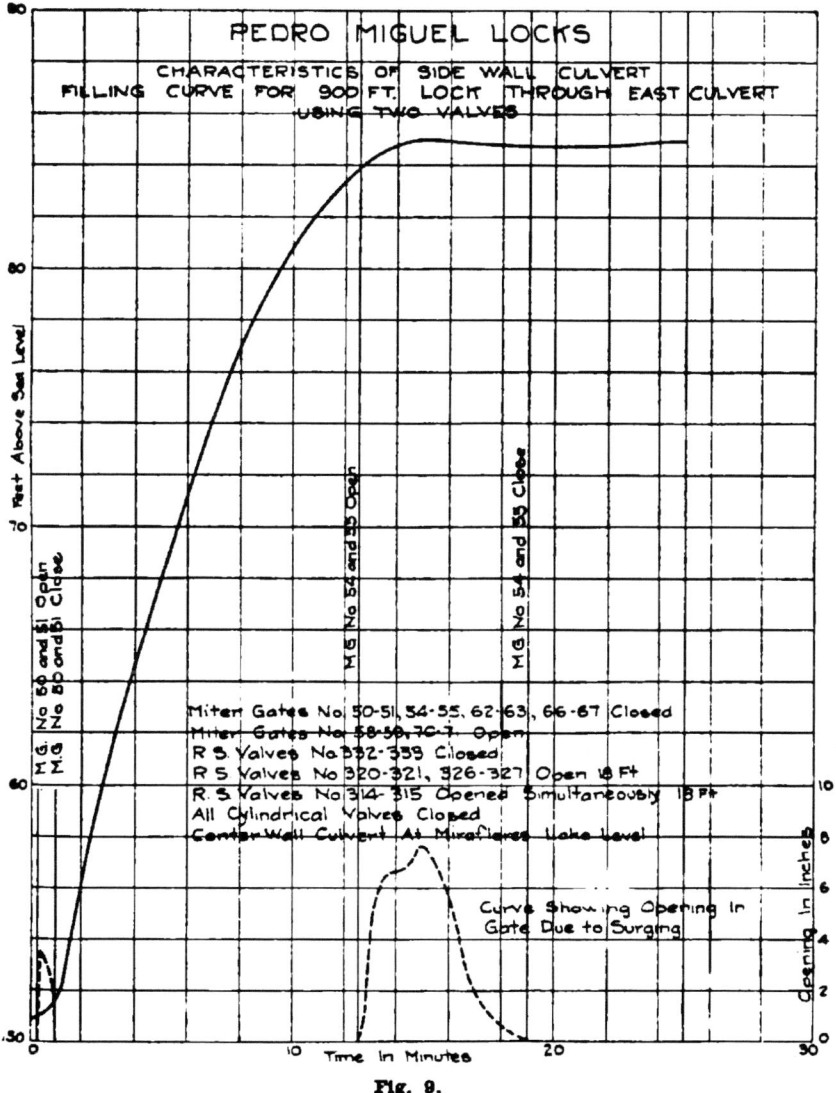

Fig. 9.

approach to the middle laterals. When emptying, the middle
laterals would discharge the maximum amount, and the end laterals the minimum. This would eliminate all tendency for
motion along the axis of the locks and would keep the vessel

central longitudinally. This is based on locking one vessel at a time, but for two small ships locked through together any tendency to drift would not be serious.

DETERMINATION OF TRUE EQUATION OF FLOW.

When filling or emptying a chamber having an area A through an opening of cross-sectional area F, where C is the coefficient of discharge for the opening, the time t for change of levels is formulated

$$t = \frac{2\,A\,(\sqrt{h_1} - \sqrt{h_2})}{C\,F\,\sqrt{2g}}$$

where h_1 and h_2 are the initial and final heads for the period taken.

Figs. 9 and 10 show the filling and emptying curves for the Pedro Miguel 900-ft. (275 m.) lock, using the side-wall culvert. The curves do not follow the above formula. Due to the dynamic effect of the water in the lock culverts, a retardation of the flow takes place at the beginning and an acceleration at the end of the operation, which results in an overtravel of the levels and in a back-pressure on the miter gates.

Assuming a lock full of water being discharged into a reservoir of large capacity, as in Fig. 10, the velocity is constantly changing, the expression $\frac{dv}{dt}$, or the acceleration due to this change of velocity, is of considerable importance for long culverts. If l is the length of the culvert, or in the case of the locks of the Panama Canal, the equivalent length of the main culvert, then the force P exerted due to this acceleration is

$$P = -\frac{w}{g}\,F l\,\frac{dv}{dt} \qquad \begin{array}{l} w = \text{weight of unit quantity water} \\ g = \text{acceleration due to gravity} \end{array}$$

The increase or decrease of pressure Δh expressed in terms of equivalent water column is

$$\Delta h = -\frac{l}{g}\,\frac{dv}{dt}$$

Consequently the equation for filling becomes

$$\frac{v^2}{2c^2 g} = h - \frac{l}{g}\,\frac{dv}{dt}$$

or

$$2\,g\,h = \frac{A^2}{F^2\,C^2}\left(\frac{dh}{dt}\right)^2 - \frac{2\,l\,A}{F}\,\frac{d^2 h}{dt^2}$$

a differential equation of the second order between h and t.

The correctness of this equation was tested by actual application of the curves for emptying Pedro Miguel locks shown in Fig. 11. The first and second differentials were obtained graph-

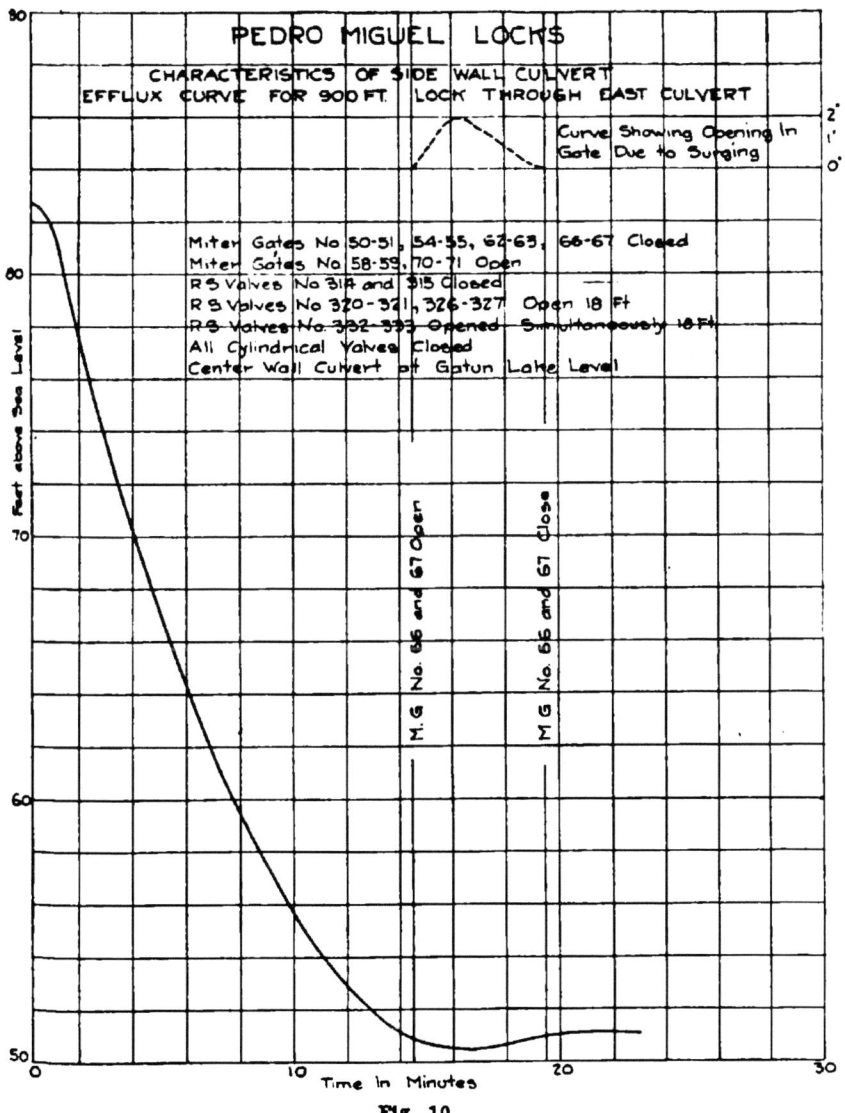

Fig. 10.

ically, the first was squared and multiplied by a constant, so that its value was equal to h when $\dfrac{d^2 h}{d t^2}$ was equal to zero, and similarly for the curve for the second differential. They were then superimposed on the original curve shown in Fig. 10. Fig. 11 shows that the curves nearly follow the derived equation.

The curves clearly illustrate the action of the flow which becomes established about 1½ minutes after the filling valves

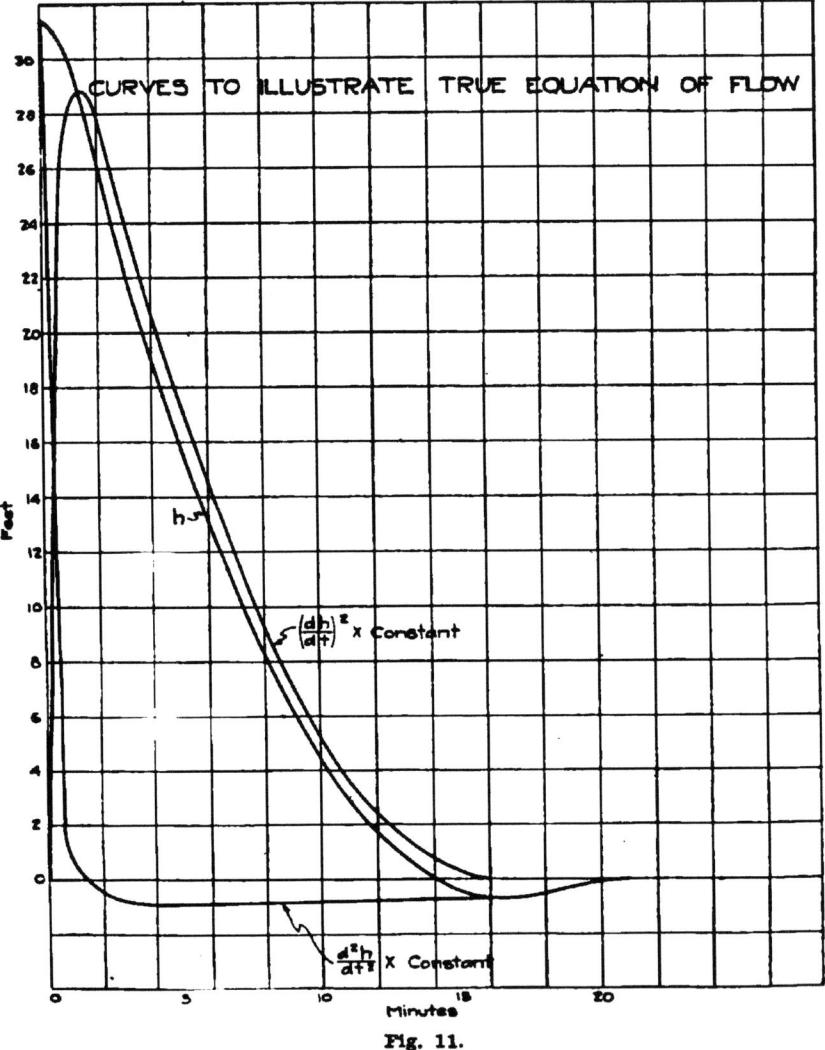

Fig. 11.

are started open. As it requires one minute to open these valves, it can be safely said that no appreciable loss of time results from the initial storage of energy in the lock culverts. After the flow becomes established the stored energy is returned at such a rate that the second differential term has a constant value. This value is called the dynamic head, and it results in the negative value of h at the end of the emptying operation.

Major Pillsbury, in the March-April, 1915, number of Professional Memoirs, Corps of Engineers, U. S. A., presented a paper on "Excess Head in Large Locks". He derived the differential equation shown in a different manner, by use of the equation of energy. He also obtained a first integration of this equation as follows:

$$\left(\frac{dh}{dt}\right)^2 = \frac{2\,g\,F^2\,C^2}{A^2}\left[h + D - (h_0 + D)\,\epsilon^{\frac{h-h_0}{D}}\right] \qquad \begin{aligned} h_0 &= \text{initial head} \\ h &= \text{head at any time } t \end{aligned}$$

where D is the dynamic head. An analysis of this equation shows that the expression $(h_0 + D)\,\epsilon^{\frac{h-h_0}{D}}$ becomes negligible as soon as the flow is established and confirms the graphical analysis presented. After the flow becomes established and D is a constant, the equation becomes

$$2\,g\,h = \frac{A^2}{F^2\,C^2}\left(\frac{dh}{dt}\right)^2 - 2\,g\,D;$$

the equivalent linear equation obtained by integration is

$$t = \frac{2\,A}{C\,F\,\sqrt{2g}}\left[\sqrt{h_1 + D} - \sqrt{h_2 + D}\right].$$

Also, as $\frac{d^2h}{dt^2} = \frac{C^2\,F^2}{A^2}\,g$ when constant and $D = \frac{2\,l\,A}{2F\,g}\frac{d^2h}{dt^2}$ when $\frac{d^2h}{dt^2}$ is constant $D = C^2\frac{l\,F}{A}$, and the true equation for change of levels after flow is established is

$$t = \frac{2\,A}{C\,F\,\sqrt{2g}}\left[\sqrt{h_1 + C^2\frac{l\,F}{A}} - \sqrt{h_2 + C^2\frac{l\,F}{A}}\right]$$

As the levels overtravel by an amount equal to the dynamic head, the overtravel of the water is directly proportional to the area and length of culvert feeding the lock and inversely proportional to the area of the lock chamber.

The overtravel as determined is independent of the initial head, as long as there is a small allowance for initial storage of energy. Tests, made by filling locks with various initial heads, have demonstrated this to be correct, the same overtravel being observed in all cases.

The application of the derived equations to the curve in Fig. 10 shows that the value of C is practically constant for all parts of the curve and equal to 0.73. The overtravel, or value of D, shown is 0.7 ft. (0.213 m.). The length of culvert, as obtained from formula

$$D = C^2 \frac{l F}{A},$$

gives a value for l of 638 ft. (194.6 m.)

In the case of the locks of the Panama Canal this is the equivalent length of main culvert. The determination of D from designing data for complex culvert systems is discussed separately.

The overtravel also shortens the filling operation, as the water travels at its slowest rate after actual equalization. Taking time for emptying lock from any head h to o, the equation becomes

$$t = \frac{2 A}{C F \sqrt{2 g}} \left(\sqrt{h + D} - \sqrt{D} \right).$$

The time saved by the dynamic head is therefore

$$T = \frac{2 A}{C F \sqrt{2 g}} \left(\sqrt{h} + \sqrt{D} - \sqrt{h + D} \right).$$

Applying this equation for emptying the locks, a saving of 129 seconds is effected due to the dynamic head—a remarkable saving of time.

GENERAL DISCUSSION OF FILLING AND EMPTYING CURVES FOR PEDRO MIGUEL LOCK.

The coefficient C as determined by use of the true equation of flow for Pedro Miguel locks for all conditions of operation is as follows: The values are practically constant for all limits after flow is established.

Filling chamber with two culverts................................... 0.65
Emptying chamber with two culverts.............................. 0.67
Filling chamber with side culvert.................................... 0.82
Emptying chamber with side culvert............................... 0.73
Filling chamber with center wall culvert......................... 0.52
Emptying chamber with center wall culvert.................. 0.66

The distribution for filling with the center-wall culvert is about the same as for the side-wall, due to its low coefficient of 0.52 as compared with the side-wall coefficient,

0.82; with both the culverts wide open the side-wall culvert overbalances the center-wall and causes vessels to drift toward the side-wall. This is easily overcome by only opening the side-wall filling valves part way. The center-wall culvert has only ten laterals, whereas the side-wall culvert has twelve. Using the analysis of the side-wall previously given, the coefficient therefrom is 81%. By calculation, the omission of one lateral would make the coefficient 81%, of the two laterals 78.8%, and of three laterals 74.8%. The fact that the center-wall culvert has only ten laterals does not therefore explain the low coefficient; neither is it due to the intake losses, main-culvert losses, or to lateral-culvert losses, as these are practically the same for the center-wall as for the side-wall. The only explanation is that there must be very large losses in the cylindrical valves due to the angular flow into them when filling the locks.

The coefficient for emptying through the side-wall culverts is less than for filling. Skin friction does not explain this. It would be expected that the maximum losses would occur in filling due to the heavy losses at the entrances to the upstream laterals and the fact that, in general, the water has farther to travel when filling than emptying, due to the distribution in the two cases.

It is evident therefore that other losses exist besides skin friction and the loss due to the normal change of velocity in the culverts. The writer's theory is that the impact of the inflowing water against the water flowing through the main culvert results in a contraction in the main culvert and subsequent expansion losses. On this assumption such losses would decrease with increase of the quantity flowing in the main culvert up to the lateral, and consequently the effect on the total distribution would be to cause increased discharge through the laterals nearest the emptying valves.

The expected value of C was 0.65. This value has been obtained or exceeded in all cases except in filling with the center-wall culvert. It should be remembered, however, that this culvert was originally intended as an auxiliary, and that under this condition the losses in the cylindrical valves would not be important.

CALCULATION OF VALUE OF DYNAMIC HEAD FOR COMPLEX CULVERT SYSTEMS.

As the dynamic head depends on the rate of change of velocity and the length of culvert through which the flow takes place, it is evident that its value depends on the location taken for the complex culvert system of the locks of the Panama Canal. Considering, first, the main longitudinal culvert,—the value of the dynamic head when filling the locks at the first lateral is dependent on the length of culvert to the first lateral and the rate of change of velocity of the total flow. Between the first and second laterals the velocity is decreased, due to the discharge through the first lateral; the rate of change of the decreased velocity and the length of culvert between the first and second laterals result in a dynamic head which, added to the dynamic head for the first lateral, gives the dynamic head for the second lateral. It is thus easily shown that the dynamic head increases in value for the different laterals when progressing downstream. This accounts for the back pressure on the lower safety gates in addition to the back pressure on the upper gates at the end of the filling operation.

The value of the dynamic head for the entire system is obtained by a summation of the individual dynamic heads multiplied by the percentage of total flow affected.

It will be noted that the dynamic head as shown by Figs. 9 and 10 is 1.0 ft. (0.305 m.) for filling, whereas it is only 0.7 (0.214 m.) for emptying the locks, using the side-wall culvert. This is mainly due to the distribution, as the laterals farthest from the filling valves discharge the largest amounts when filling and those nearest the emptying valves discharge the maximum when emptying. Consequently, the water, on an average, travels a greater distance when filling than when emptying the locks.

The value of the dynamic head d for a length of culvert l of cross-sectional area a carrying p percent of the total flow is

$$d = -\frac{l}{g} \frac{p F}{a} \frac{dv}{dt},$$

where F is cross-sectional area of portion of culvert carrying total flow, and where v is the velocity at this section.

TABLE I.

Calculated Values of Dynamic Head for Side Wall Culvert.

Coefficient $C = 82\%$ for 255 sq. ft. (23.7 sq. m.) section. Area lock = 123,000 sq. ft. (11,420 sq. m.)

PORTION OF CULVERT	Part of Total Flow	AREA sq. ft.	AREA sq. m.	LENGTH ft.	LENGTH m.	DYNAMIC HEAD ft.	DYNAMIC HEAD m.	TOTALS ft.	TOTALS m.
Intakes	1.00000	432	(40.1)	50	(15.25)	.0413	(.0126)	.0413	(.0126)
Upper culvert to valves 414-415	1.00000	333	(30.9)	270	(82.5)	.2890	(.0883)	.3303	(.1009)
Valves 414-415 to Lat. No. 1	1.00000	255	(23.7)	225	(68.6)	.3140	(.0958)	.6443	(.1967)
Laterals No. 1 to No. 2	1.00000	255	(23.7)	65	(19.8)	.0908	(.0276)	.7351	(.2243)
Laterals No. 2 to No. 3	0.9499	255	(23.7)	65	(19.8)	.0862	(.0263)	.8213	(.2506)
Laterals No. 3 to No. 4	0.8850	255	(23.7)	65	(19.8)	.0803	(.0245)	.9016	(.2751)
Laterals No. 4 to No. 5	0.8082	255	(23.7)	160	(48.8)	.1810	(.0551)	1.0826	(.3302)
Laterals No. 5 to No. 6	0.7280	255	(23.7)	72	(21.95)	.0732	(.0223)	1.1558	(.3525)
Laterals No. 6 to No. 7	0.6403	255	(23.7)	72	(21.95)	.0645	(.0197)	1.2203	(.3722)
Laterals No. 7 to No. 8	0.5476	255	(23.7)	72	(21.95)	.0551	(.0168)	1.2754	(.3890)
Laterals No. 8 to No. 9	0.4509	255	(23.7)	72	(21.95)	.0453	(.0138)	1.3207	(.4028)
Laterals No. 9 to No. 10	0.3513	255	(23.7)	72	(21.95)	.0353	(.0108)	1.3560	(.4136)
Laterals No. 10 to No. 11	0.2501	255	(23.7)	72	(21.95)	.0252	(.0077)	1.3812	(.4213)
Laterals No. 11 to No. 12	0.1478	255	(23.7)	100	(30.5)	.0222	(.0068)	1.4033	(.4281)
Lateral No. 12 to opening	0.0455	255	(23.7)	20	(6.1)	.0013	(.0004)	1.4046	(.4285)

As $\frac{dv}{dt} = -C^2 \frac{F}{A} g$ when flow is fully established, where C is the lock coefficient and A is the area of the chamber, by substitution

$$d = C^2 \frac{F}{A} \left(\frac{l \, p \, F}{a} \right).$$

The value of the dynamic head up to any point is equal to a summation of all the values of d for the culvert sections carrying the flow to that point. The dynamic head for the system is the summation of the individual dynamic heads multiplied by their percentage p of total flow, or

$$D = C^2 \frac{F^2}{A} \Sigma \frac{l p^2}{a} \, ;$$

for a simple culvert carrying the total flow, this reduces to the formula previously given,

$$D = C^2 \frac{l \, F}{A}.$$

The equivalent length of culvert, L, for a complex system is therefore

$$L = F \Sigma \frac{l \, p^2}{a}.$$

The values of the dynamic head at the entrances to the lateral culverts are calculated in Table I for the side-wall culvert, the values of p being obtained from the distribution previously given.

The total value of D for the main culvert as obtained from the formula, using the figures given,

$$D = \Sigma \, p \, d = 1.2021 \text{ ft. } (0.367 \text{ m.})$$

The lateral culverts will cause a slight increase of D for the total system, for instance, for the distribution calculated for the various openings and a maximum discharge of 900 cu. ft. (25.45 cu. m.) per second, the calculations are as given in Table II.

For the entire lateral culvert, $D = 0.0722$ ft. (0.0220 m.). By calculation, the increase of dynamic head for the system due to the laterals is 0.0605 ft. (0.0184 m.), making the value of D for the entire system 1.263 ft. (0.385 m.). The observed value of D is 1.0 ft. (0.305 m.); however, considerable leakage occurs from the chamber due to the "cracking" open of the miter gates from back pressure. The area created for efflux on this account is about 60 sq. ft. (5.58 sq. m.). Assuming an average head of 0.5

TABLE II.

Calculated Values of Dynamic Heads for Lateral Culverts.

FROM—	Part Total Flow	AREAS		LENGTH		DYNAMIC HEAD		TOTALS	
		sq. ft.	sq. m.	ft.	m.	ft.	m.	ft.	m.
Main culvert to Opening No. 5	.1023	40.9	(3.8)	50	(15.25)	.0445	(.0136)	.0445	(.0136)
Openings No. 5 to No. 4	.0923	40.9	(3.8)	18	(5.48)	.0145	(.0044)	.0590	(.0180)
Openings No. 4 to No. 3	.0763	40.9	(3.8)	18	(5.48)	.0120	(.0036)	.0710	(.0216)
Openings No. 3 to No. 2	.0546	40.9	(3.8)	18	(5.48)	.0085	(.0026)	.0795	(.0242)
Openings No. 2 to No. 1	.0287	40.9	(3.8)	18	(5.48)	.0045	(.0014)	.0840	(.0256)

ft. (0.153 m.), for two minutes the efflux would theoretically amount to about 41,000 cu. ft. (1160 cu. m.), which would result in a decrease of the overtravel of 0.33 ft. (0.10 m.). The calculated value of the dynamic head is therefore in close agreement with the actual value.

A comparison of the calculated values of the dynamic head for the various laterals and for the openings of the laterals shows that the difference of values is so small that the effect on the total distribution is negligible.

THE RISING-STEM VALVES.

In all cases except cross-filling between adjacent locks of the same level, the flow of water is controlled by pairs of rising-stem valve machines.

This machine consists in a rising-stem passing through a stuffing box in a watertight bulkhead, connected to a gate valve at the lower end and to a guided cross-head at the upper end. The cross-head is moved vertically through a distance of 18 ft. (5.49 m.) by means of two vertical revolving screws, which transmit the force through two non-revolving nuts in the cross-head. Each screw is driven from the motor shaft by a gear and pinion reduction and two bevel gears. Two sub-bases carry the motor, limit switch, extended shaft bearings and thrust bearings. The two live roller trains, against which the gate travels when under pressure, are constrained to move at half the rate of the gate travel by chains actuated by the cross-head. The chains pass over pulleys and are fastened to rods which pass through the stuffing boxes in the watertight bulkheads. The lower ends of the rods are attached to the live roller trains. The two ends of the cross-head are slotted to allow the cross-head nuts to travel 6 in. (0.152 m.) after the valve has seated, and to allow the machinery to stop without shock.

Extensive tests have been made on the rising-stem valves to determine their performance under various heads, and especially to determine the losses resulting from water pressure and the coefficient of roller-train friction. Before the machines were put into operation their losses when operating in the dry were found to be as follows, all losses being reduced to equivalent forces at the valve stem:

Operation of the Valve in the Dry.

		Opening Valve		Closing Valve	
		Lbs.	Kg.	Lbs.	Kg.
1	Weight of valve and accessories, cross-head, and equivalent weight of roller train	31,500	(14,300)	31,500	(14,300)
2	Side-seal friction due to initial tension	1,000	(450)	1,000	(450)
3	Valve, steam and roller train friction	8,000	(3,630)	8,000	(3,630)
4	Equivalent wt. on cross-head [1±(2+3)]	40,500	(18,380)	22,500	(10,220)
5	Coefficient thrust-screw friction	.073		.083	
6	Thrust-screw sliding friction	23,900	(10,840)	14,700	(6,670)
7	Binding friction between nuts and screws	2,100	(960)	2,100	(960)
8	Losses in gearing between motors and screws	19,000	(8,620)	12,400	(5,630)
9	Total machine and valve friction (2+3+6+7+8)	54,000	(24,500)	38,200	(17,340)
10	Total force to move valve (9±1)	85,500	(38,800)	6,700	(3,040)

480 revolutions of motor give an 18-ft. (5.49 m.) movement of the valve. Motor synchronous speed is 500 r.p.m. It takes 63 seconds to open valve, and 58 seconds to close it.

The coefficient of roller-train friction was found from dynamometer tests at Gatun locks to be 0.025. Using this coefficient, the calculated losses for the most severe condition of operation follow :

Opening Valve Under 79-Ft. Head.

		Lbs.	Kg.
1	Friction of side seals due to water pressure	4,170	(1,890)
2	Water pressure against top seal (upward force)	5,420	(2,460)
3	Rolling friction of roller trains (coef. 0.0250)	16,250	(7,380)
4	Total added friction due to water pressure (1—2+3)	15,000	(6,810)
5	Total valve, roller-train, and seal friction in the dry	9,000	(4,090)
6	Weight of valve and accessories, cross-head and equivalent weight of roller trains	31,500	(14,300)
7	Equivalent weight on cross-head (4+5+6)	55,500	(25,200)
8	Coefficient of thrust-screw friction	0.064	
9	Thrust-screw sliding friction	28,000	(12,700)
10	Thrust-screw and nut-binding friction	2,100	(950)

11	Losses in gearing between motor and screws......	21,000	(9,540)
12	Total friction machine and valve friction, (4+5+9+10+11)	75,100	(34,090)
13	Total force required to break seals (6+12)........	106,600	(48,390)

The maximum equivalent weight on the cross-head is calculated above as 55,500 lbs. (25,200 kg.), including the weight of the cross-head and accessories—2900 lbs. (1320 kg.). The machines were designed to exert a lifting force of 60,000 lbs. (27,200 kg.) at the cross-head, and before the final contract was awarded the first two machines successfully stood a test with 60,000 lbs. (27,200 kg.) load in addition to the weight of the cross-head.

The force for closing the valve is the same for all conditions of operation, as an increase of roller-train friction is neutralized by the decrease of thrust-screw friction.

Tests made under operation give the calculated force shown and demonstrate the correctness of the coefficient of roller-train friction used. No increase of friction has been noted after two years' service.

The force while opening the valve is practically the same during the entire period, showing that the total pressure or head against the valve remains constant.

The valves have been closed repeatedly against high heads when equalizing between chambers, with no noticeable surging or shock. The leakage under a 30-ft. head (9.15 m.) is about 1.25 cu. ft. (0.035 cu. m.) per second per pair of valves.

The total discharge through the valves is not directly proportional to the opening; coefficients based on the area of the openings of the valves may greatly exceed unity due to the velocity of approach. In certain cases, such as equalizing between levels, it makes very little difference in the total flow whether one or both valves are open.

OPERATION OF THE MITER GATES.

Each set of miter gates was built to withstand full hydrostatic pressure, and at the time the locks were watered, this pressure was successively applied to each set. The main operating gates at Pedro Miguel are 79 ft. (24.1 m.) high, their sill is at elevation + 13 ft. (3.97 m.). The maximum elevation of Gatun Lake is + 87 ft. (26.54 m.). If a lock chamber were unwatered, the upper operating gates would be required to withstand a 74-ft. (22.57 m.) head of water. As each miter-gate leaf is 65 ft. (19.8 m.) in length, the full hydrostatic pressure per leaf would then be 5550 tons (5.04 x 10^6 kg.).

In normal operation, the maximum pressure on any set of gates occurs on the lower operating gates at Miraflores upper lock. The sill of these gates is at elevation — 18.3 ft. (5.58 m.). When the water in the lower lock is at low tide, or — 10 ft. (3.05 m.), and the upper lock at Miraflores Lake level, elevation + 55 ft. (16.78 m.), the net pressure per leaf is 5380 tons (4.89 x 10^6 kg.), practically equivalent to the maximum as calculated above.

The mechanism for the remote control of the lock gates is not equipped with an interlock to prevent the opening of a set of leaves before equalization of water levels. None is necessary, as the miter gate moving machines are just strong enough to operate the gate after equalization. For example, in the case of a difference of 2 ft. (0.61 m.) in levels on the two sides of the upper operating gates at Pedro Miguel, there would be 74 ft. (22.57 m.) of water against the upstream side, and 72 ft. (21.96 m.) against the downstream side. This difference would result in a net downstream pressure of 600,000 lbs. (272,000 kg.). With reference to the miter-gate moving machine, this pressure may be considered as applied perpendicularly at the center of the leaf, or a distance of 32½ ft. (9.91 m.) from the pintle. A perpendicular distance from the pintle to the center line of the strut of the moving machines is 11.5 ft. (3.51 m.), approximately, when the gate is closed. To open the leaf against a water pressure of 600,000 lbs. (272,000 kg.), the strut would have to exert a force of about 1,700,000 lbs. (772,000 kg.). The maximum force the strut can exert on opening a leaf is approximately 1,000,000 lbs. (454,000 kg.), and an attempt to open a leaf under these conditions would stall the motor after compressing the springs in the strut.

On filling or emptying a chamber, the water overtravels, after equalization, and back pressure on the gates results. This back pressure varies from 6 to 12 inches (0.152 to 0.305 m.), and causes the gates to open 8 inches (0.203 m.) between miter points, or to the full limit of strut spring compression. It requires 185,000 lbs. (84,000 kg.) to compress the springs solid, and a few inches is sufficient to do this. This helps to open the gates and also gives a positive signal that equalization has occurred.

In most cases there is a difference in density of the water on both sides of the operating gates, as with every lockage some salt water is locked up into the fresh water supply, as testified by the increasing salinity of Miraflores Lake. When conditions of equilibrium are established after opening the culvert connecting the chambers on the two sides of the gates the water levels are not always the same. For instance, at the 82-ft. (25 m.) gates at the lower end of Miraflores locks, which are generally kept closed while the culvert to the sea is kept open, the fresh water on the upstream side is from 4 to 8 inches (0.153 to 0.203 m.) higher than the sea water on the downstream side. This difference depends on the difference of densities and also on the position of the culvert outlet.

Assume the outlet at elevation of bottom of lock, and suppose the relative densities to be as 1.02 : 1.00. The sill of the gate is — 50 ft. (15.25 m.). High tide is — 10 ft. (3.05 m.). With 60 ft. (18.3 m.) of water on the downstream side of the gate, there would be 61.2 ft. (18.67 m.) on the upstream side, or a difference in levels of 1.2 ft. (0.37 m.). The total pressure on the gate depends on the density and the square of the head. Consequently the net total pressure per leaf would be 150,000 lbs. (68,000 kg.) more on the upstream side than on the downstream side. To avoid this large difference in pressure, a specially constructed culvert outlet was placed at elevation — 25 ft. (7.63 m.), or 25 ft. (7.63 m.) above the sill. This makes the resultant levels for the above conditions 60 ft. (18.3 m.) on the downstream side, and (60-25) 1.02 plus 25, or 60.7 ft. (18.5 m.) on the upstream side, and reduces the net pressure to about 24,000 lbs. (10,900 kg.) per leaf.

In making lockages at Miraflores, the levels on the two sides of the lower operating gates in the upper chamber differ at times by 1 ft. (0.305 m.) when equilibrium is reached between the upper and lower chambers. The net pressure per leaf tending to resist the opening of a leaf for this condition is approximately

100,000 lbs. (45,000 kg.). The gates are always opened when they "crack" from back pressure caused by the overtravel of the water before such a condition of equilibrium is reached; otherwise, it would put a severe duty on the miter gate moving machinery, and a heavy current would flow from the upper to the lower lock that would be undesirable, as soon as the gates were opened.

Another resistive force to the movement of a miter gate leaf is the difference in water levels on the two sides of a gate caused by the movement of the leaf, for instance, the area of the space between the upper guard gates and the upper operating gates is 11,000 sq. ft. (1020 sq. m.). If the upper guard gate is opened 2 ft. (0.61 m.), the area is enlarged by about 137 sq. ft. (12.7 sq. m.). As the minimum immersion of the guard gate is about 40 ft. (12.2 m.), the volume displaced by this movement amounts to 5480 cu. ft. (155 cu. m.). This lowers the water on the downstream side about 6 inches (0.152 m.) and creates a large resisting force to further outward, upstream movement of the guard gate until the difference in level is relieved by the influx of water through the opening between the leaves and through the auxiliary culvert. Similarly for opening the upper operating gates and using the 900-ft. (274 m.) lock. For a 4-ft. (1.22 m.) movement, assuming no influx, the water in the chamber would be lowered 2 inches (0.051 m.), and the resistive force would be 50,700 lbs. (23,000 kg.) per leaf. It has been found from the duty cycle of the moving machine that the maximum torque occurs, on opening the gate, about 20 seconds after the gate is opened, and on closing, about 20 seconds before gate is closed.

On account of the conditions just described, it has been found to be most satisfactory to open one of the leaves from 15 to 20 seconds before the other. This gives about the same opening between leaves as a simultaneous opening, as they join at an angle of 120 degrees, and gives a comparatively light duty to the motors, as only half the water is displaced. In opening four leaves, such as the upper guard and upper operating gates, one of the guard leaves is opened first; five seconds later, the operating leaf on the same side; 15 seconds after this, the other guard leaf; and five seconds after this, the second operating leaf. This method increases the normal time for opening the two gates by 25 seconds, but is much less severe on the operating machinery. For operating the gates in the dry, scarcely any power is required. The effect of eddy currents and backing-up of the water against the gate recess also tend to prevent movement of the gates, but these factors are small compared with those given.

When closing the gates the currents set up due to difference in salinity of water have a negligible effect on the operation of the gates. The currents caused by displacement of a vessel in motion or those resulting from use of the vessel's screw to date have had very little effect [the canal being open only to vessels of 30 ft. (9.15 m.) draft]. Surges, however, are set up in the chamber having a total amplitude as great as 1 ft. (0.305 m). These surges have a marked effect on the operation of the gates, resulting in positive or negative pressures, depending on the time the gate is closed with reference to the surge. The surges have in general a period of about one minute and a skilled operator can time the operation of the gates so as to avoid large positive pressures.

The displacement of the gate always tends to resist its motion, but the efflux rate for closing is greater than opening, due to the relative length of the strut in the two cases, the strut being elongated when opening and shortened when closing the gate by an amount equal to the compression of the strut springs. Where the areas controlled by the gate are large, it sometimes happens that the positive pressure caused by the surges mentioned is greater than the resistive pressure due to displacement, and the gates close with considerable violence. Consequently the operating gate leaves are operated simultaneously, so as to get the full cushion effect due to displacement.

DETERMINATION OF FORCE REQUIRED TO OPERATE MITER GATES.

The miter-gate moving machine consists of a miter-gate leaf which is opened and closed by a connecting rod or strut attached on one end to a pin on the leaf and on the other end to a pin on a large crank gear. The crank gear is driven through an arc of 197° by an induction motor through a train of gearing. Fig. 12 shows the position of the leaf, strut and crank gear at the start, when the leaf begins to open, and for an angle of the crank gear of 120° from closed position. The dimensions of the parts are shown, and the position of the crank gear is denoted by the

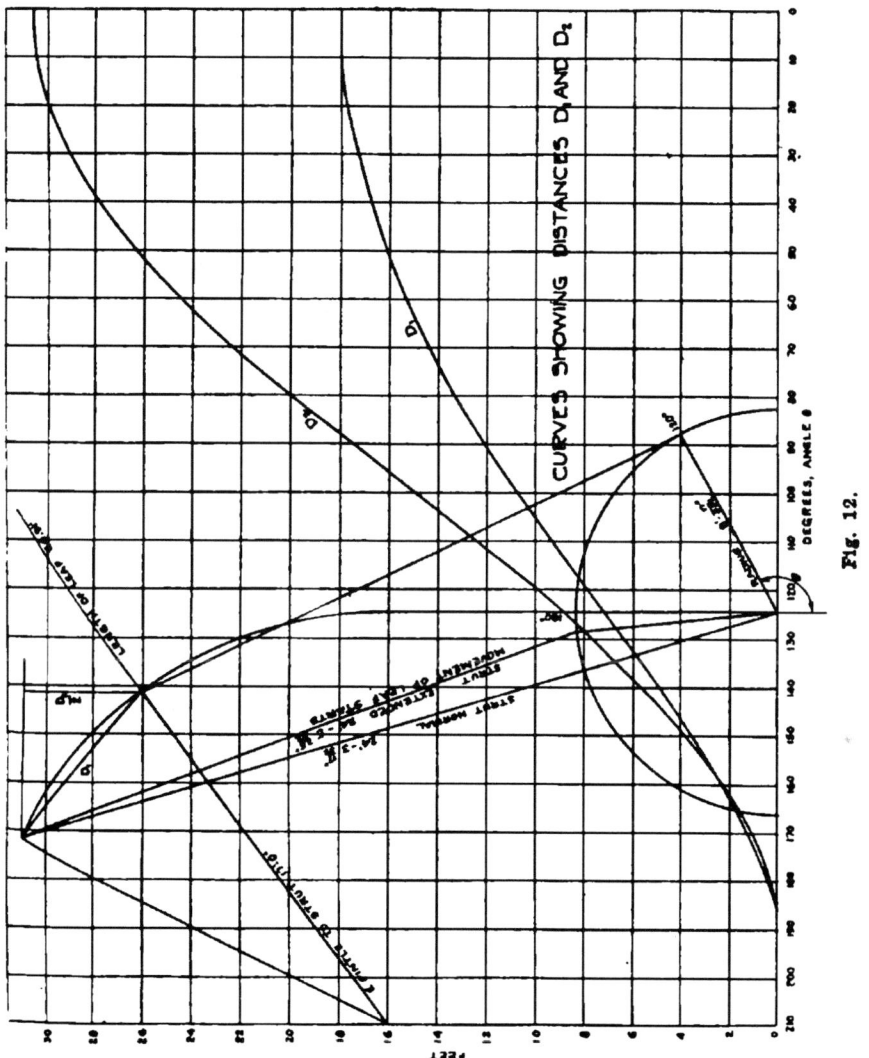

Fig. 12.

angle θ. The distances D_1 and D_2, as shown on the figure, were obtained graphically for all values of θ and plotted.

Fig. 13 shows the relative velocity of the leaf-strut pin to the crank-gear strut pin for all values of θ for opening the leaf. It is to be noted that the relative velocities at the extremities of travel are small, which is a very helpful factor. The graphical method used to obtain the values is indicated on the figure.

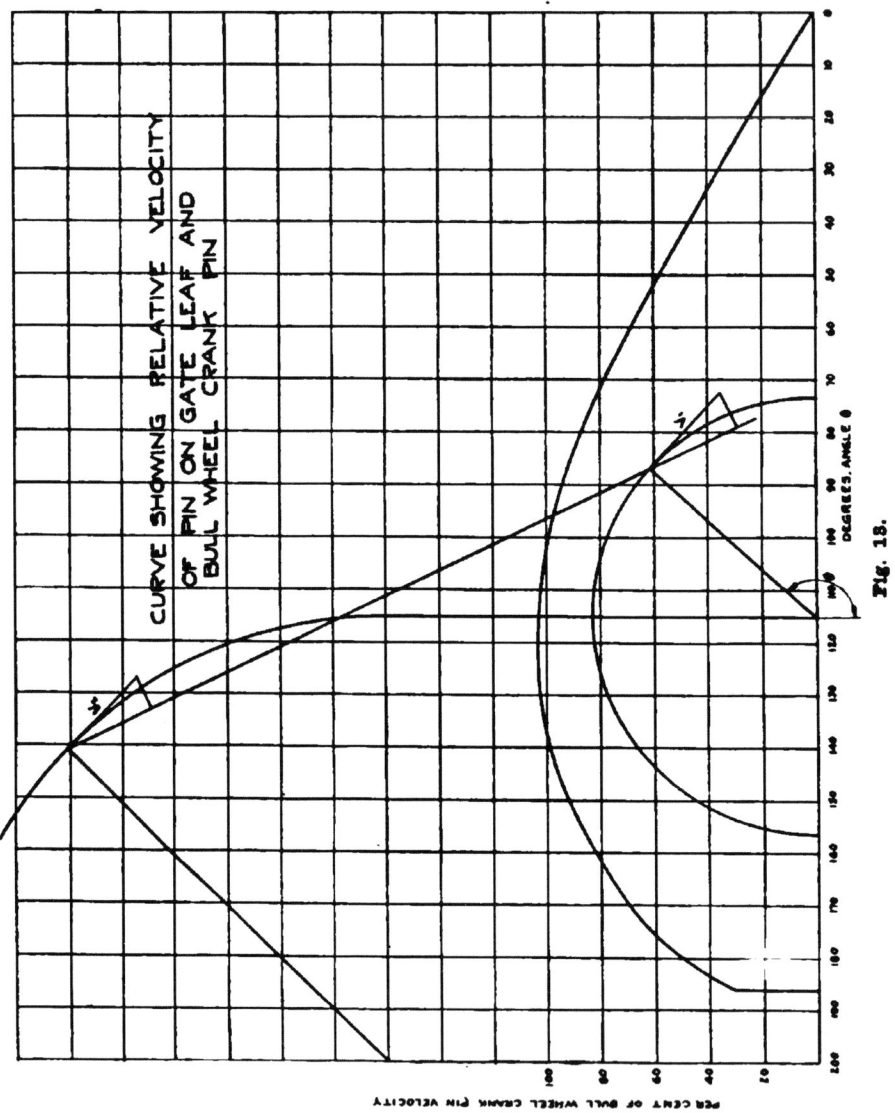

Fig. 18.

Fig. 14 shows the velocity of the miter end of the leaf, the distance between miter ends when opening two leaves simultaneously, and the distance between miter ends for opening one leaf, all plotted against time. The curves were obtained by use of the data on Figs. 12 and 13, and on the assumption that the crank gear travels at a constant speed and requires two minutes to open the leaf.

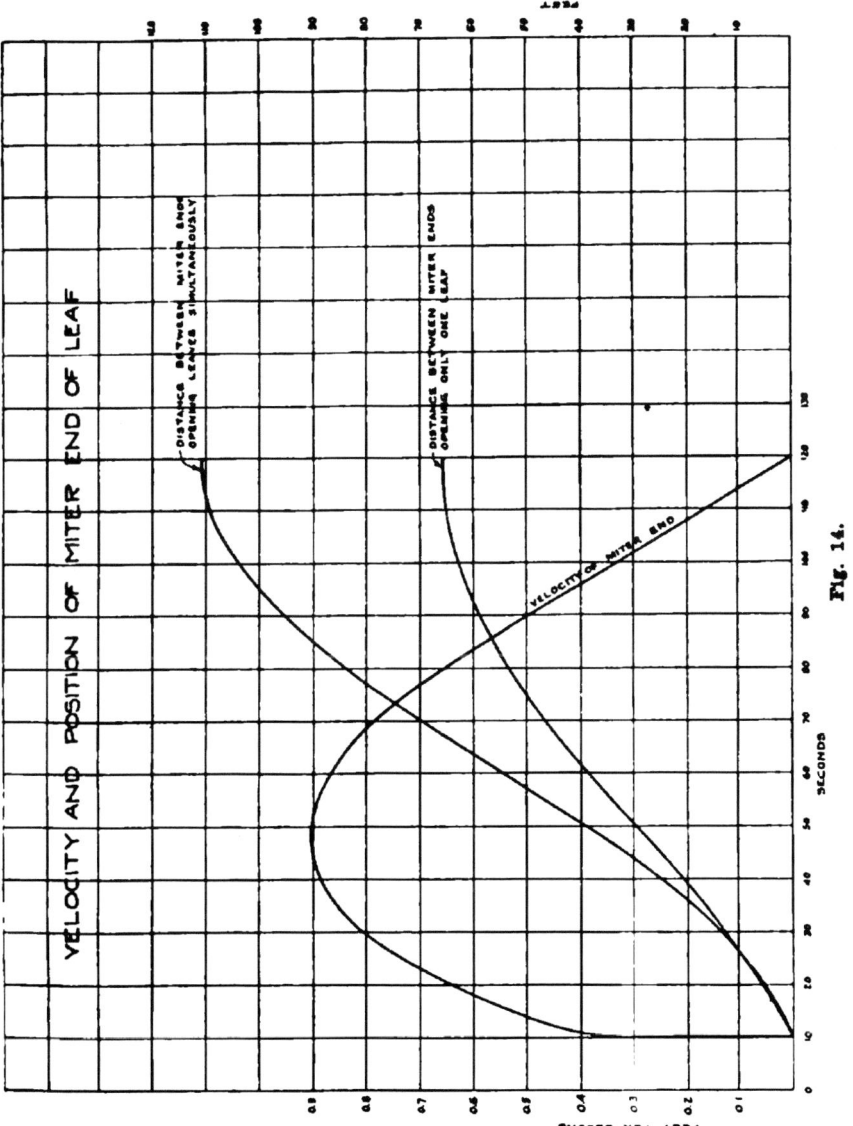

Fig. 14.

Fig. 15 shows the effect of opening two leaves of a gate simultaneously as against opening first one leaf and then the other. The case chosen is for a gate of 50 ft. (15.25 m.) immersion, controlling an area of 100,000 sq. ft. (9290 sq. m.). The displacement curve shown is calculated from the dimensions of

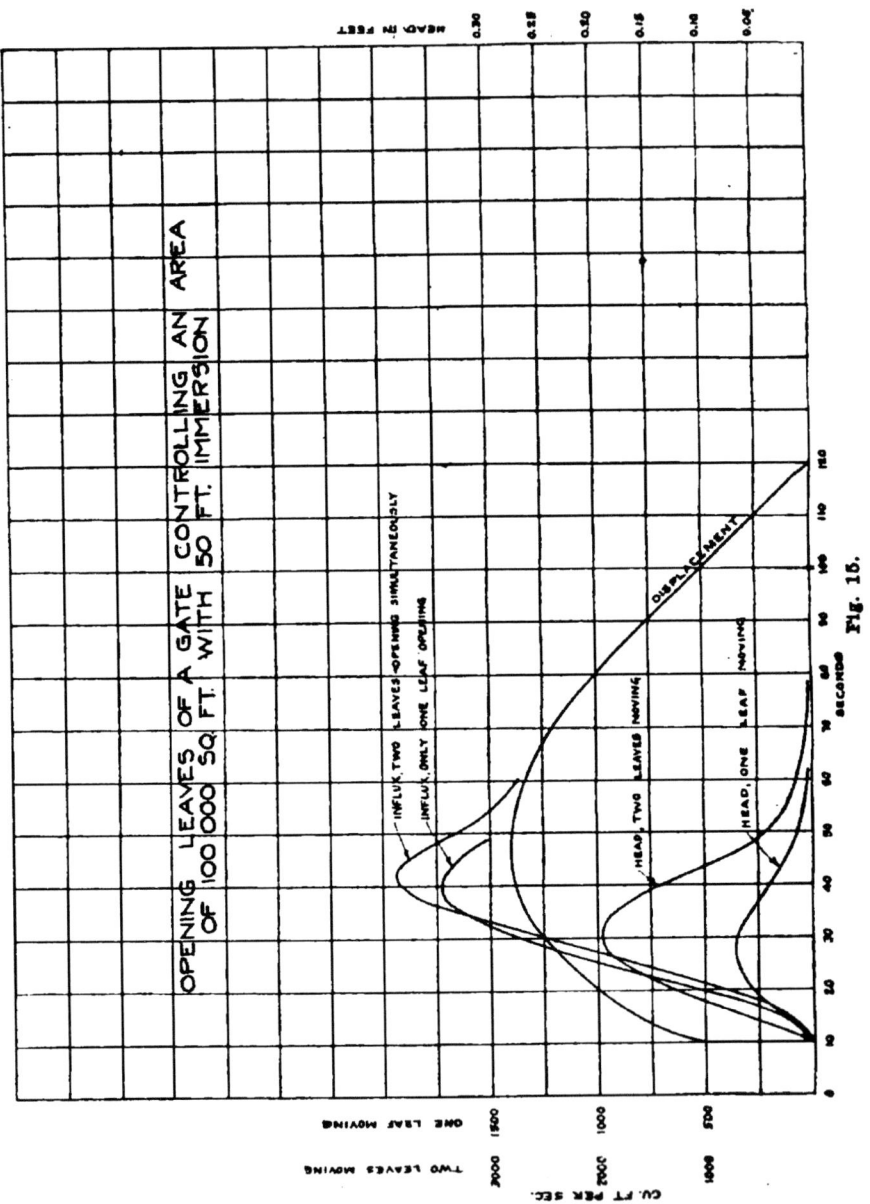

the gate and the immersion, and the use of curve in Fig. 14 showing velocity of miter end of gate. In the calculations it was assumed that no influx took place under the gate and the areas for influx were therefore the distances between miter ends shown in Fig. 14 multiplied by the immersion. The head curves shown were obtained by making calculations of displacement, influx, and resulting increment of head for each second. The maximum value for operating the leaves simultaneously is a head of 0.195 ft. (0.0595 m.) occurring 20 seconds after movement of leaf begins, and 0.075 ft. (0.0229 m.) for opening only one leaf occurring 18 seconds after. The beneficial effect of non-simultaneous operation of the leaves is clearly shown by the character of the curves.

Fig. 16 shows the total head curves for simultaneous operation of the leaves of a miter gate having a 50-ft. (15.25 m.) immersion and controlling various areas assumed constant. With the exceptions shown in the figure, it was assumed that no influx occurred under the leaves. The maximum values of head and time that maximum head occurs are as follows:

Area		Maximum Head		Time after Movement of Leaf starts
5,000 sq. ft.	(464 sq. m.)	1.25 ft.	(0.381 m.)	8.5 seconds
10,000 " "	(929 " ")	0.85 "	(0.259 ")	10.5 "
50,000 " "	(4645 " ")	0.31 "	(0.0945 ")	17.0 "
100,000 " "	(9290 " ")	0.195 "	(0.0594 ")	20.0 "

Fig. 16 also shows that on account of the actual influx occurring under the bottom of the gate the maximum head is 0.57 ft. (0.174 m.), instead of 0.85 ft. (0.259 m.) for the 10,000 sq. ft. (929 sq. m.) area curve, and that this head could be reduced to 0.39 ft. (0.119 m.) by having a clear sump without the present ledge obstructing the influx.

Figs. 17 and 18 show method of determination of duty cycle for opening Miraflores lower guard gates, assuming an immersion of 50 ft. (15.25 m.). These gates have the heaviest duty cycle of any of the gates of the Panama Canal, as they control a very small area, have a large immersion, and the smallest areas for the influx. Fig. 17 shows the displacement for simultaneous operation of the leaves, the area of the section, which increases with opening of the gate, the total area for influx, and the head and influx curves based on full theoretical influx. The maximum head shown is 0.595 ft. (0.181 m.). On Fig. 18 is shown the total pressure per leaf due to the heads obtained, the relative velocity of the leaf-strut pin and the crank-gear pin as obtained from Fig. 13, and the motor torque obtained from these data and

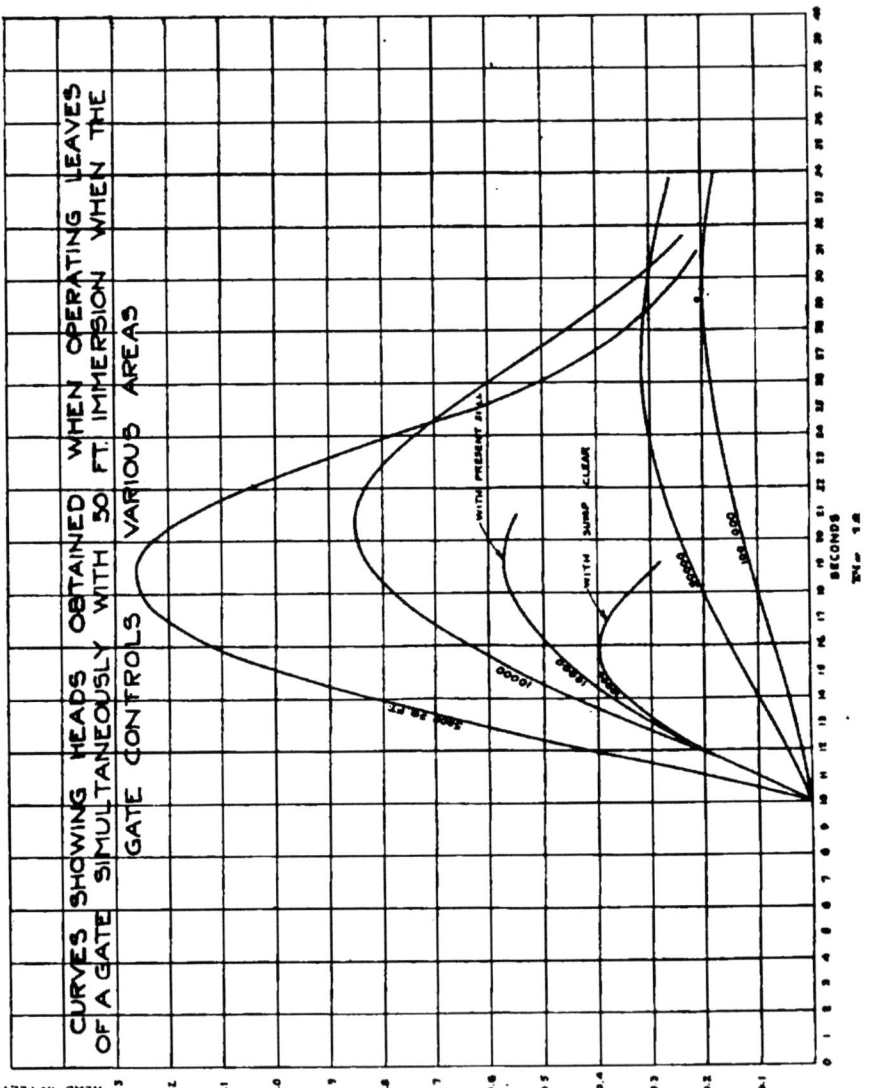

the gear ratio of 1660:1 between the motor and the crank gear. The total torque to move the leaf is obtained by adding this torque to the machine friction torque. The machine torque is taken as the motor torque obtained by test for operating the leaf

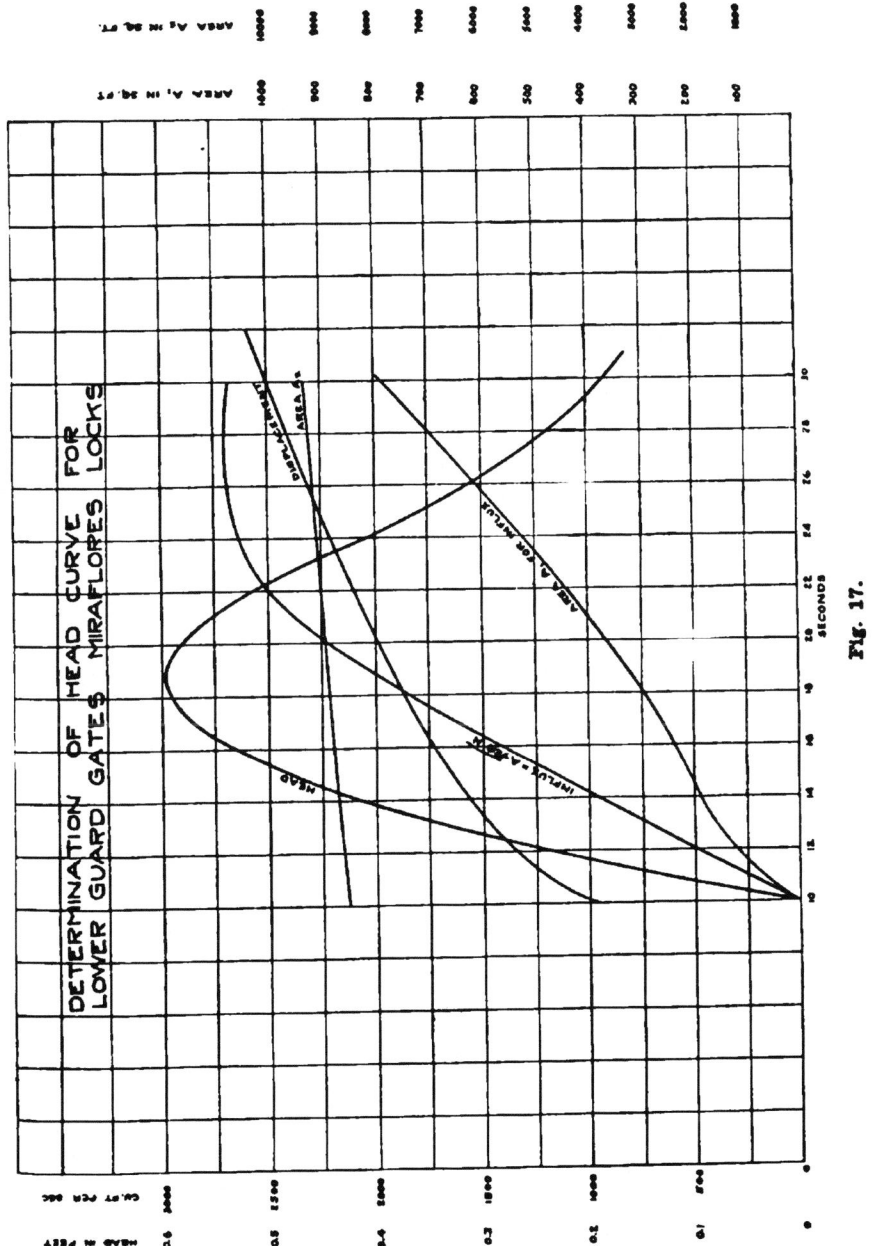

Fig. 17.

with the same immersion, with the companion leaf fully opened, so that there is ample area for influx; it therefore includes the

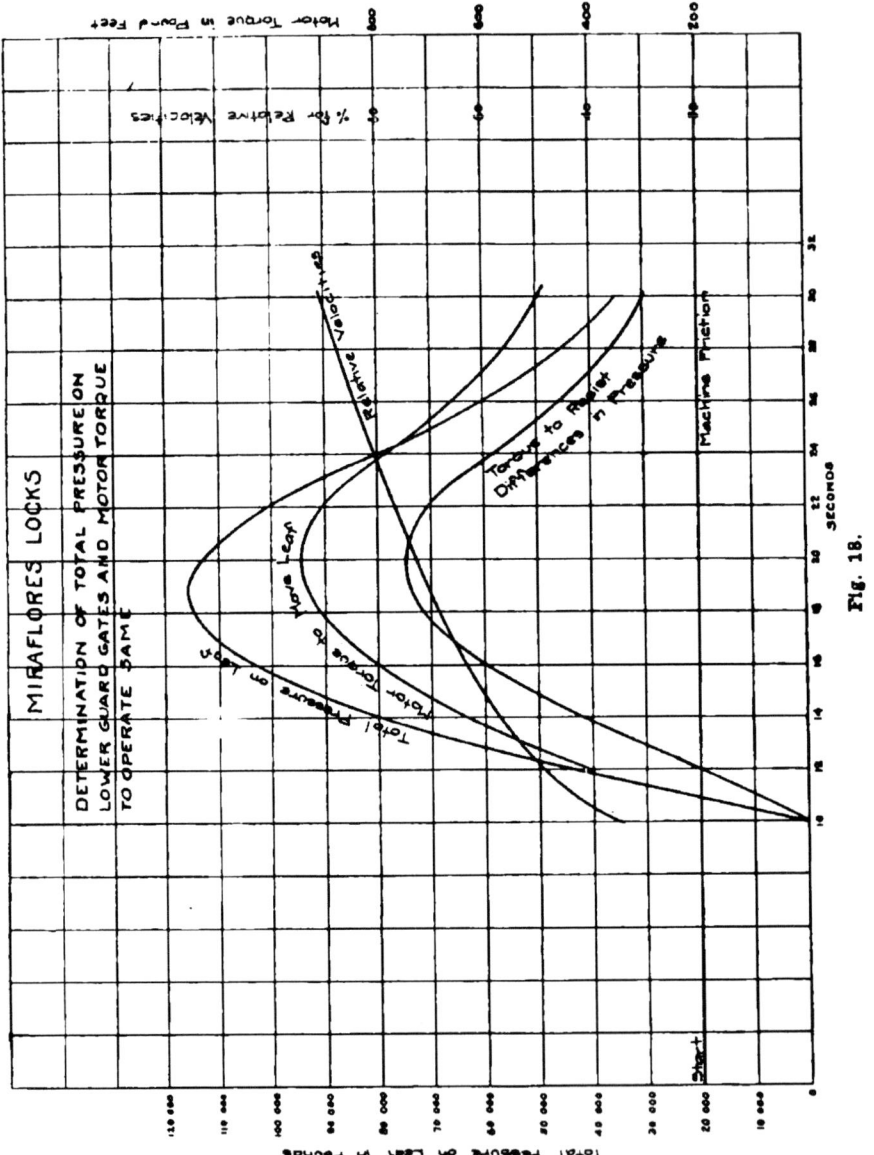

Fig. 18.

actual friction of the machine, leaf hydraulic friction, and the amount used for initial storage of energy. Its value is practically constant for the portion of the cycle shown, and then gradually decreases as the gate approaches the open position. The maximum net total pressure shown on the leaf is 116,000 pounds (52,700 kg.). This was calculated for fresh water weighing 62.4 pounds per cubic foot (1000 kg. per 1 cu. m.), and using a length of 63.4 ft. (19.33 m.) for the gate, the distance from center of hinge to miter end. The maximum motor torque occurs about one second after the maximum head, due to the increased velocity of the gate, and is 750 pound-feet (103.7 mkg.). Adding the machine friction makes the total motor torque 950 pound-feet (131.4 mkg.). The curves also show that the maximum torque occurs practically simultaneously with the maximum pressure on the leaf.

For salt water weighing 64.1 pounds per cubic foot (1027 kg. per cu. m.), the maximum pressure for the same difference in head is 119,000 pounds (54,000 kg.), and the corresponding total motor torque 970 pound-feet (134.4 mkg.).

Observations taken while opening the leaves simultaneously gave a maximum difference of levels, or drop in the contracted section, of 0.73 ft. (0.222 m.), and a motor torque, corresponding, of 1200 lb-ft. (166 mkg.). A head of 0.73 ft. (0.222 m.) results in a pressure on the gate of 154,000 lbs. (70,000 kg.). At the time of occurrence of this pressure, the velocity of the leaf-strut pin is 67% of the crank-gear pin, and the gearing reduction is 1660 to 1; the motor torque, to overcome this difference in pressure, is 960 lb-ft. (132.9 mkg.). Adding the allowance of 200 lb-ft. (27.7 mkg.), for machine friction makes the total torque 1160 lb-ft. (160.6 mkg.). The motor stalls when the torque exceeds about 1300 lb-ft. (180 mkg.), and slows down very perceptibly when this torque is approached; consequently the torque, assuming a uniform speed, would be higher than the observed torque.

The calculated duty cycle shown in Fig. 18 was based on a uniform speed and a unity coefficient for the influx. Experiments made on weirs indicate that the actual coefficient should be about 70%. By calculation, using a coefficient of 70% instead of unity, the maximum head would be 0.82 ft. (0.250 m.) occurring on the 21st second. The corresponding pressure on the gate leaves would be 164,000 lbs. (74,500 kg.), and the motor torque 1020 lb-ft. (141.3 mkg.). Adding the 200 lb-ft. (27.7

mkg.) torque for the various losses, the total torque figures 1220 lb-ft. (169 mkg.), which slightly exceeds the actual torque of 1200 lb-ft. (166 mkg.) on account of the slowing down of the motor and the resultant decrease in rate of displacement. The method given will enable therefore very close determination of the factors involved.

Acknowledgment is gratefully given to Mr. Maurice W. Fox for checking the calculations and preparing the figures given under this heading.

CURRENTS IN LOCKS DUE TO DIFFERENCE OF SALINITY.

It has been observed that in all cases where a gate is opened after equalization between water of differing salinity on its two sides, there is a heavy surface current from the fresh to the relatively salty water.

An investigation was made at Miraflores locks to determine the maximum average current velocity at various depths; in other words, to determine the current velocity for ships of various drafts. Seven telephone poles, of lengths from 5 ft. (1.5 m.) to 35 ft. (10.7 m.), were assembled in Miraflores Lake and weighted, so that they would float in a vertical position with only a foot or so protruding above the surface. These floats were locked through the west flight of Miraflores locks, from Miraflores Lake to the sea, and the effects of the currents noted by plotting the positions of the floats against time. In the figures referred to, the immersion of the floats in fresh water were as follows:

A	....	31.0 ft.	(9.45 m.)
B	....	27.5 "	(8.39 ")
C	....	19.5 "	(5.95 ")
D	....	13.5 "	(4.12 ")
E	....	10.0 "	(3.05 ")
F	....	7.5 "	(2.29 ")
G	....	4.0 "	(1.22 ")

In all cases, the gates were opened immediately after they cracked from back pressure, and the floats were released at the center of the chamber, on the north side of the opening gates, in a position as near the gates as a vessel would be allowed. The lockage was made when the Pacific was at low tide; the

depth of water over the sill of the upper lock and over the sill
of the lower lock was 41 ft. (12.5 m.), on equalization for the
respective openings of gates.

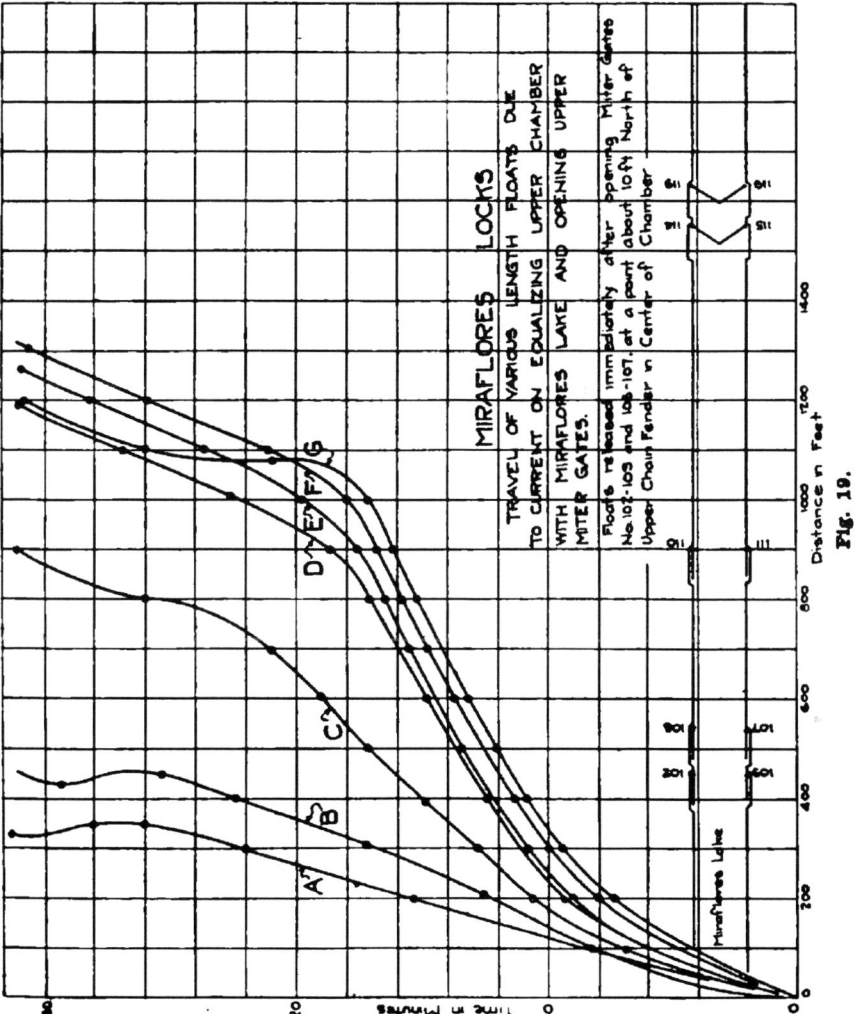

Observations were made of the currents set up on opening
the upper gates, between Miraflores Lake and the upper level;
on opening the operating gates between the upper and lower
levels; and on opening the lower gates between the lower level
and the Pacific channel.

On the opening of the upper gates (see Fig. 19), there was
plainly discernible a surface current toward the lower end of
the chamber. This current ran to the end of the chamber, when

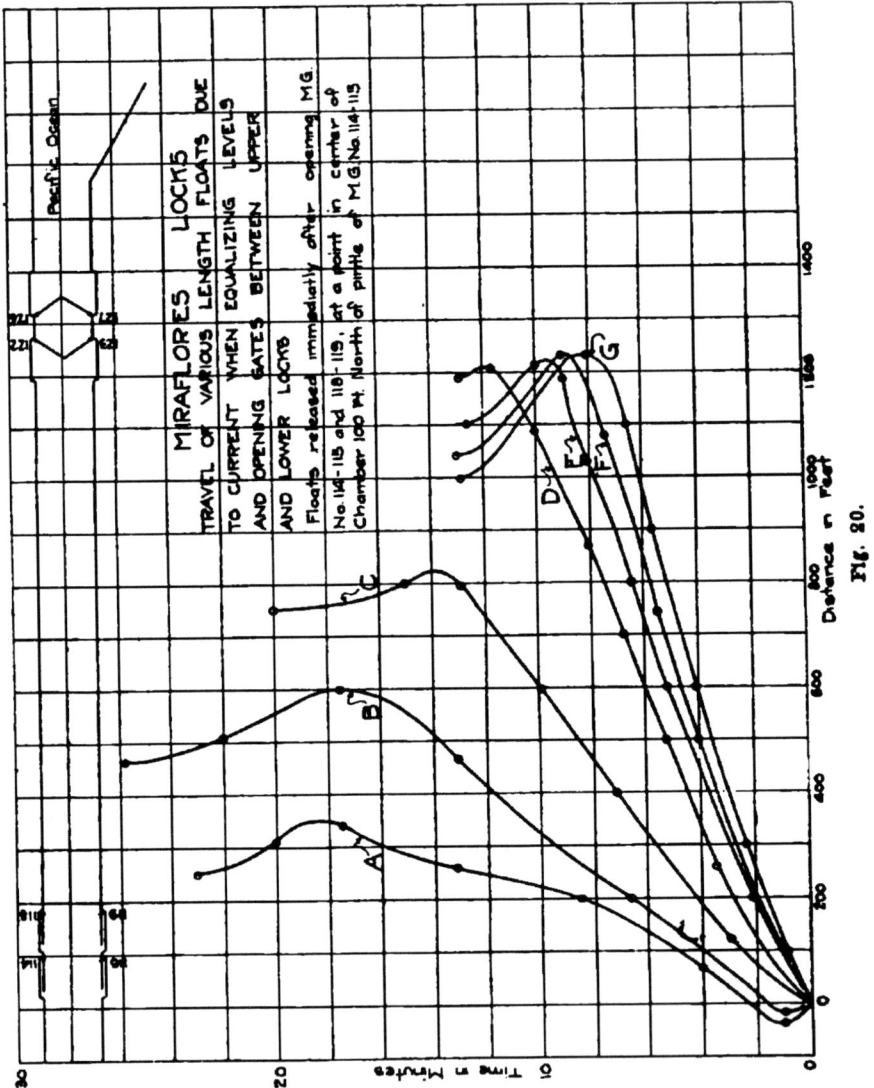

Fig. 20.

a reverse current was set up; the shorter floats traveled at the
rate of this current and reversed with it at the lower end of the
chamber. The shorter floats remained in a vertical position,
but the longer floats leaned as much as 30 degrees from the

vertical, and rose and fell a distance of about three feet (0.9 m.). This indicated that the longer floats were affected by a current below in a reverse direction from that of the top current. The

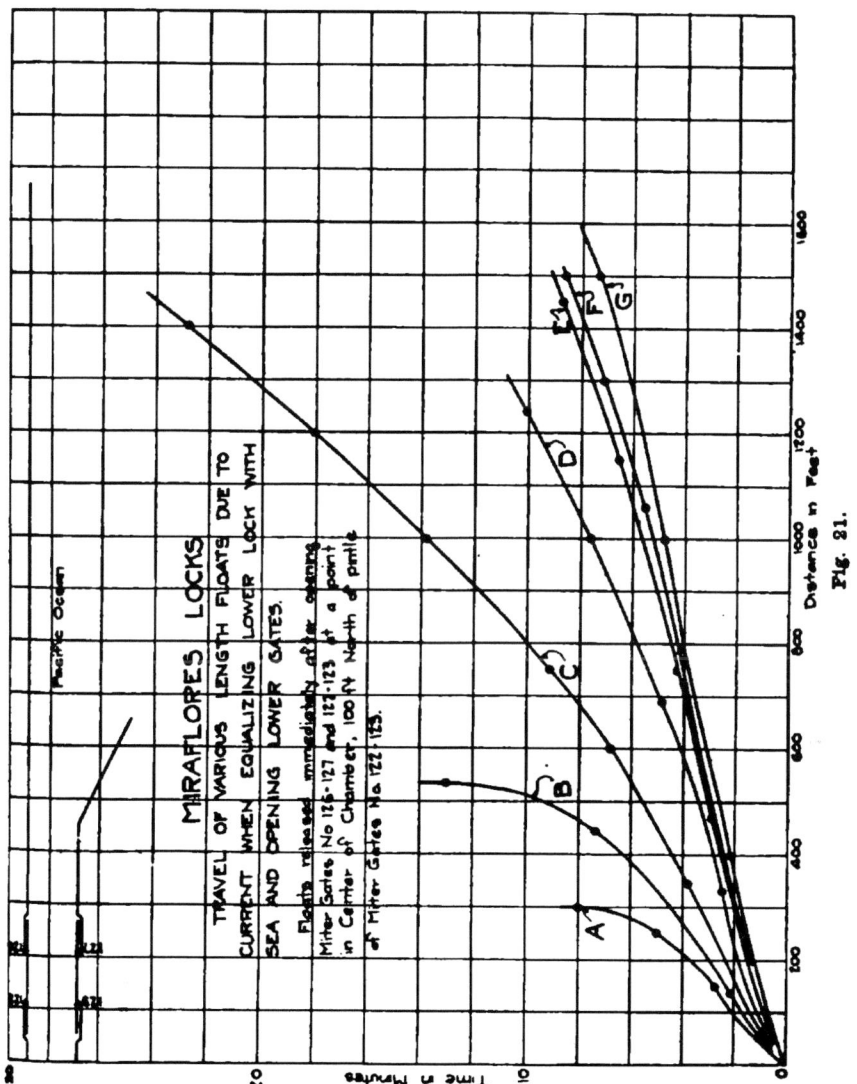

Fig. 21.

shorter floats remained in the center of the chamber until they reached its end, but the floats immersed to a depth greater than 20 ft. (6.1 m.) drifted toward one side or the other during the observations. The maximum velocity was attained by the sur-

face float and amounted to 1.76 ft. (0.537 m.) per second. The
31-ft. (9.45 m.) float had a maximum velocity of only 0.29 ft.
(0.089 m.) per second.

On opening the operating gate between the upper and the
lower level of the locks, with the water in the two chambers
equalized, the effect on the floats of respective lengths was practically the same as when the gate was opened between the lake
and the upper level (see Fig. 20), except that the floats traveled
at a faster rate. The maximum velocity was 3.37 ft. (1.027 m.)
per second for the surface float, and 0.59 ft. (0.180 m.) per
second for the 31-ft. (9.45 m.) float. This is ascribed to a
greater difference in density of water on the two sides of the
gate than was the case in locking the floats from the lake to the
upper level.

The strongest currents were obtained on opening the lower
gates, between the lower level and the sea (see Fig. 21). Since
there was no obstruction to the outward flow of the relatively
fresh water, there was no reverse surge on the surface. There
was, however, a steady decrease of speed as the forebay widened.
The maximum velocity was 4.1 ft. (1.25 m.) per second for the
surface float and 1.11 ft. (0.341 m.) per second for the 31-ft.
(9.45 m.) float.

In the test at the lower end of the locks, the shorter floats
floated down the center of the locks, turning to the west on leaving the forebay. The tendency to float to the west on leaving
Miraflores locks had been observed before in barges and other
vessels of light draft, and the path taken by such vessels when
allowed to drift free was the same as that of these floats. The
two shorter floats remained in a vertical position throughout the
operation, but the others had at times an inclination as great
as 30 degrees. At low tide the current values are much less
than for high tide; the observations presented therefore were
obtained under the most favorable conditions.

THEORETICAL VALUES OF CURRENTS DUE TO DIFFERENCE OF SALINITY.

Considering the condition at the lower end of Miraflores
locks, the water in the chamber on the upstream side of the
lower gate is relatively fresh to the salt water in the channel

below the gate. The chamber is kept in communication with the channel by the main culvert. For a state of equilibrium, the pressure on the plane of the culvert outlet due to the salt water in the channel must balance that due to the water in the chamber. The plane of balanced pressures is called the neutral plane. For all planes above the neutral the pressure due to the column of relatively fresh water exceeds that due to the column of salt water, and for all planes below the neutral the pressure due to the salt water is the greater. Consequently when a gate is opened having a difference of salinity of water on its two sides the relatively fresh water flows downstream above the neutral plane, and the salt water flows upstream into the chamber below the neutral plane. The velocities of the currents thus produced are formulated as follows:

Let K be the ratio of density of the salt to the relatively fresh water;

Let w be the unit weight of the relatively fresh water;

Let H_1 be the initial height of the salt water above the neutral plane;

Let H_2 be the initial depth of the salt water below the neutral plane;

Let a be any distance from the neutral plane between H_1 and H_2. Then KH_1 is the height of the relatively fresh water above the neutral plane, and $(H_1\text{-}a)\ Kw$ is the total pressure on a plane a distant from the neutral, due to the column of salt water above such a plane, and $(KH_1\text{-}a)\ w$ is the corresponding pressure due to the relatively fresh water, and $aw\ (K\text{-}1)$ is the difference in pressure tending to cause flow, and $a\ (K\text{-}1)$ is this pressure expressed in terms of equivalent water column.

The velocity v at a plane a distant from the neutral plane at the time of opening the gate is therefore

$$v = C \sqrt{2\,g\,a\,(K-1)}$$

The neutral plane is fixed at elevation — 25 ft. (7.62 m.) by means of the special culvert outlet previously referred to. At high tide, + 10 ft. (3.05 m.), the value of H_1 is 35 ft. (10.68 m.). The elevation of the gate sill is — 50 ft. (15.25 m.) and the corresponding value of H_2 is 25 ft. (7.62 m.). The maximum value of K from a number of observations taken of the initial difference in level on the two sides of the lower gates is 1.02. Fig. 22 shows the initial values of the fresh and salt water currents at all depths for the conditions mentioned as obtained from the formula given, using the maximum value of K and assuming the coefficient C as unity.

The total initial rate of influx or efflux is determined by integration of the velocity curve as follows:

$$Q = C \int_0^H \sqrt{2g(K-1)}\ W a^{\frac{1}{2}}\, da$$

in which W is the width of the locks, 110 ft. (33.55 m.).

$$Q \text{ Efflux} = \frac{2}{3} C H_1^{\frac{3}{2}}\ W \sqrt{2g(K-1)}$$

$$Q \text{ Influx} = \frac{2}{3} C H_2^{\frac{3}{2}}\ W \sqrt{2g(K-1)}$$

substituting the values for conditions shown in Fig. 22.

The initial rate of efflux of fresh water from the chamber is 17,300 cu. ft. (490 cu. m.) per second.

The initial rate of influx of salt water into the chamber is 10,400 cu. ft. (294 cu. m.) per second.

The efflux being 6900 cu. ft. (196 cu. m.) per second greater than the influx results in a lowering in the level of the fresh water in the chamber of 0.056 ft. (0.0171 m.) the first second and causes the neutral plane to move up, thereby decreasing the rate of efflux for the next second. In this manner the neutral plane very quickly assumes a midway position.

The importance of the special form of culvert outlet used is strongly emphasized, not only on account of it limiting the unbalanced pressures on the gates, but also that it establishes a neutral plane and in that manner reduces the initial velocities of the fresh salt water currents. As it is, the quantities of water set in motion by these currents equal those due to full culvert discharge into the tail bay.

COMPARISON OF THEORETICAL WITH ACTUAL CURRENTS AND EFFECTS ON VESSELS.

If a set of locks is used continuously for lockages in one direction and the fresh water is each time displaced by salt water in the lower chamber, the current values will be less than if an up lockage is followed by a down lockage, as the relative densities between the lower chamber and the sea will be greater in the latter case than in the former.   The maximum velocities

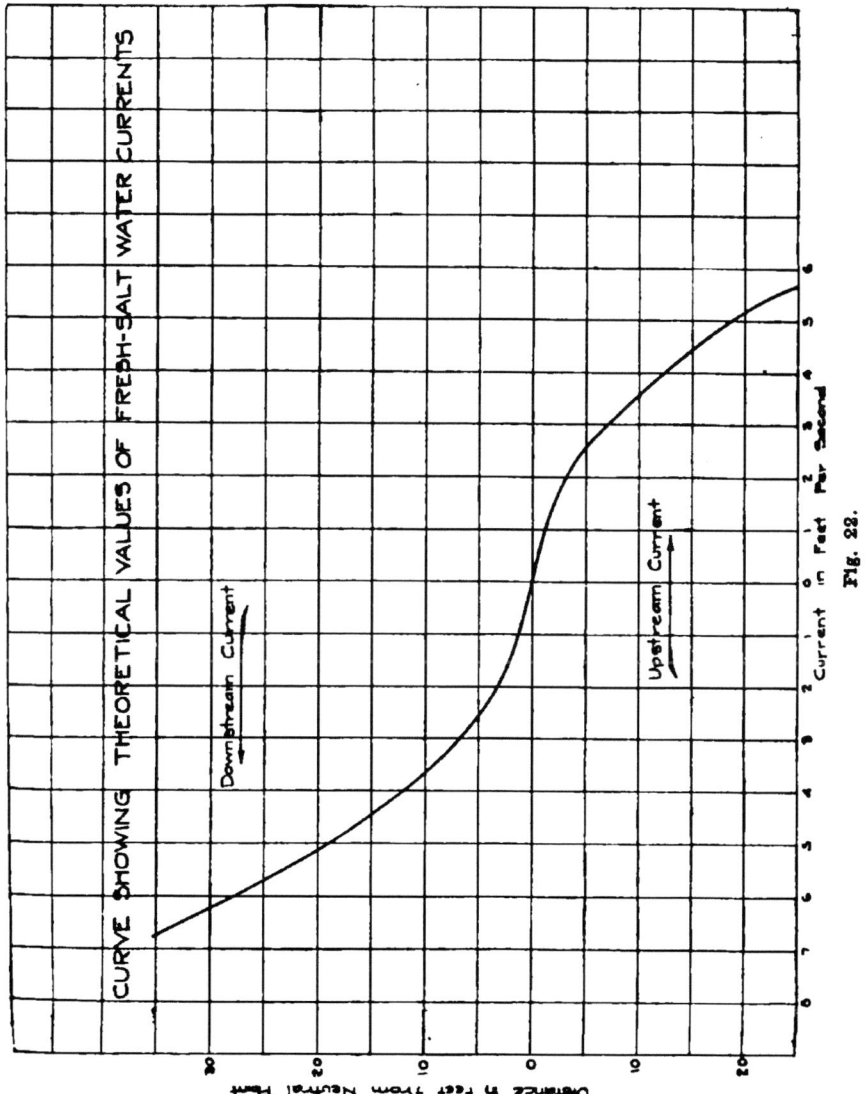

Fig. 22.

for low tide are less than for high tide, assuming the value of $K = 1.02$, and that the neutral plane shifts immediately to a midway position; the value for the initial maximum surface current for low tide is then 5.2 ft. (1.586 m.) per second, and for high tide 6.3 ft. (1.921 m.) per second (values obtained from Fig. 22).

Fig. 23 shows the values of the surface currents for a value of $K = 1.02$, as obtained from gaging, for a low tide of — 7 ft.

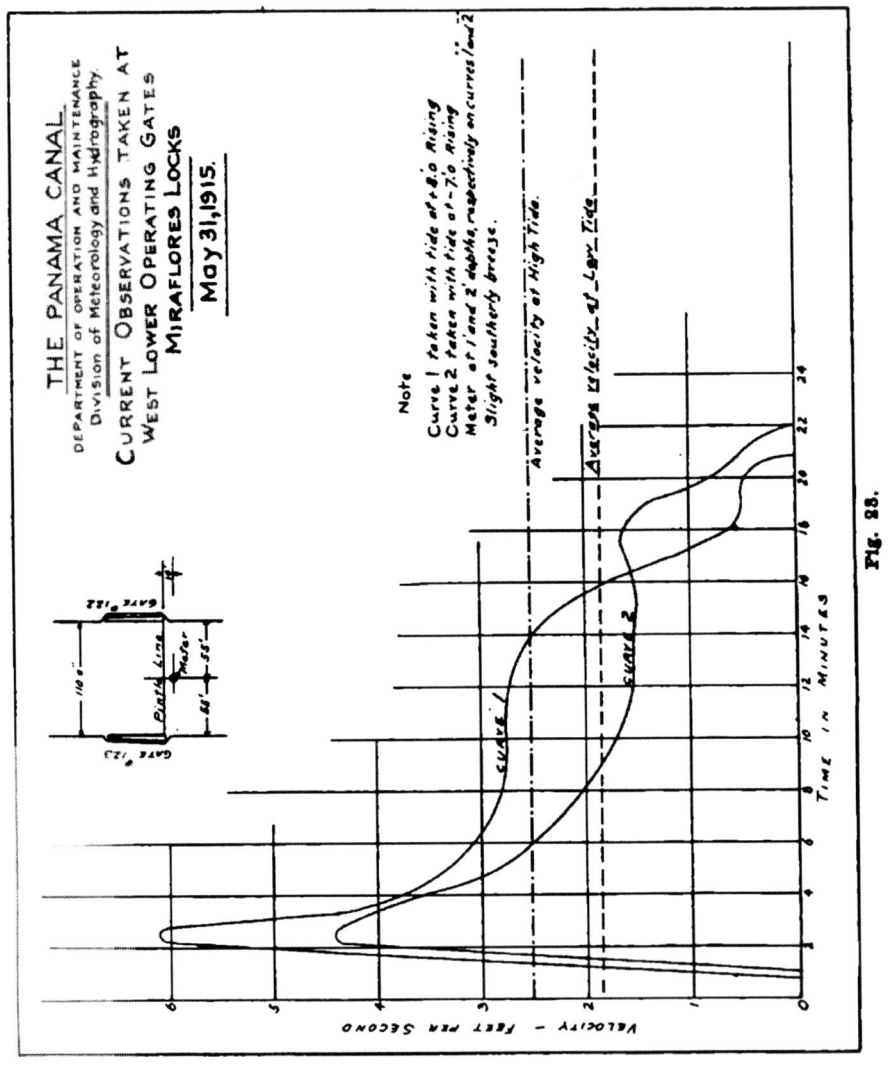

Fig. 23.

(2.135 m.) and high tide of + 8 ft. (2.44 m.). The maximum surface velocity for the low tide of — 7 ft. (2.135 m.) is 4.4 ft. (1.342 m.) per second, the theoretical value is 5.2 ft. (1.586 m.) per second; C is therefore 85%.

The maximum surface velocity for a tide of $+$ 8 ft. (2.44 m.) is 6.2 ft. (1.891 m.) per second, the theoretical value is the same, or C is 100%. Gagings were also made at a depth of 4.5 ft. (1.372 m.) below the surface, from the time of opening the gates until the flow ceased, for a falling tide of $-$ 3 ft. (0.915 m.). The maximum observed current was 4.65 ft. (1.418 m.) per second, and the theoretical current for this tide and depth of observation was 5.1 ft. (1.555 m.) per second; the value of C is therefore 91%.

The pole-float tests previously discussed were made at low tide. The value of K was not observed but is assumed as equal to 1.02. Comparing the values of current obtained from these tests to the theoretical values:

Immersion		Maximum Velocity		Theoretical Velocity		
Ft.	Meters	Ft. per sec.	M. per sec.	Ft. per sec.	M. per sec.	Values of C
0	(0)	4.40	(1.342)	5.2	(1.586)	85%
5	(1.525)	4.03	(1.229)	4.76	(1.451)	84%
10	(3.05)	3.3	(1.006)	4.39	(1.339)	75%
15	(4.575)	2.61	(0.784)	3.95	(1.205)	66%
20	(6.10)	1.88	(0.573)	3.38	(1.031)	55.5%
25	(7.625)	1.38	(0.421)	2.37	(0.723)	58%
30	(9.15)	1.11	(0.339)	1.46	(0.445)	76%

The above tests show the average maximum velocity for the immersion given; the theoretical velocity was obtained by integration of the velocity curve between the proper limits and then obtaining the average from this integration.

In the 1914 Annual Report of the Isthmian Canal Commission, and included under the report of the Engineer of Maintenance, are given the results of a number of tests made by the Chief Hydrographer to ascertain the value and direction of these currents at various depths. The tests were made at about mean tide and for the usual condition of operation, so that the value of K was less than 1.02. Unfortunately the value of K was not determined for the various tests; in fact the tests were made principally to determine the direction at various depths. The directions and relative velocities for various depths obtained practically agree with the theory presented for the initial current values. The average value of the surface current was found to be 2 ft. (0.61 m.) per second, and the average velocities at the various depths in theoretical proportion. These tests showed that the neutral plane remained at the same elevation during the entire flow and at a position of average depth.

Referring to Fig. 23, the average surface velocity for high tide of + 8 ft. (2.44 m.) is 2.51 ft. (0.766 m.) per second, and the average surface for low tide of — 7 ft. (2.135 m.) is 1.89 ft. (0.576 m.) per second. Assuming that the neutral plane remains at a position of average depth and that the average velocities are in proportion to the theoretical initial velocities as indicated by the tests mentioned, the duration of the currents can be calculated as in Table III.

The calculated time for high tide checks well with the actual time, but for low tide the calculated time is considerably in excess of the actual time. This difference may be due to a slight southerly breeze and the rising tide affecting meter readings. In the tests mentioned in the Annual Report, the duration of the currents was approximately 30 minutes, and the average surface velocity 2 ft. (0.61 m.) per second. The corresponding time obtained by calculation is 27.7 minutes.

Special equipment for the further measurement and study of these currents has been requisitioned. Unfortunately, however, it has not arrived on the Isthmus at the date of writing, and the subject must be gone into more extensively at some future date. The data presented however show that currents may be expected having a maximum value of 80% to 90% of the theoretical, and an average value of approximately 40% of the theoretical initial value, and that the duration of the currents can be computed by dividing the total initial volume of water in the chamber by the average efflux obtained by taking 40% of the theoretical initial efflux.

At the top of Fig. 21 is a single line sketch showing the relative positions of the lock gates, wing, and approach wall at the lower end of Miraflores locks. The wing wall is built at an angle of 30° to the axis of the locks. The fresh water currents from the locks spread out as soon as the wing wall is reached and tend to throw a vessel crosswise of the tail bay. This tendency is so strong that it is not safe to bring large vessels into the chamber under present conditions until the fresh salt water currents cease, which results in a delay of 20 to 30 minutes. Ships

TABLE III.

Duration of Currents, High and Low Tide.

	High Tide		Low Tide	
Theoretical initial efflux per sec.	12,950 cu. ft.	(367 cu. m.)	8,280 cu. ft.	(234 cu. m.)
Theoretical initial surface current per sec.	6.2 ft.	(1.891 m.)	5.2 ft.	(1.586 m.)
Average actual surface current per sec.	2.51 ft.	(0.766 m.)	1.89 ft.	(0.576 m.)
Corresponding average efflux per sec...	5,240 cu. ft.	(148.5 cu.m.)	3,010 cu. ft.	(85.2 cu.m.)
Depth of water in chamber........	58 ft.	(17.69 m.)	43 ft.	(. 13.11 m.)
Area chamber	121,000 sq. ft.	(11,220 sq. m.)	121,000 sq. ft.	(11,220 sq. m.)
Initial volume of water........	7,020,000 cu. ft.	(198,300 cu. m.)	5,200,000 cu. ft.	(147,000 cu. m.)
Time to replace with salt water........	22.3 min.		28.8 min.	
Actual duration of currents Fig. 23....	20.0 min.		21.1 min.	

of 450 ft. (137.2 m.) and under can be safely handled as the locomotives are powerful enough to resist the tendency mentioned. It is found advisable, however, to also use the vessel's power in addition. The main danger in bringing a vessel in is the possibility of its side striking the corner of the wing wall and of the bow colliding with the gate leaves. To make such a position impossible the authorities are considering the installation of dolphins or other device placed in the tail bay in such a manner that should a vessel start to assume a crosswise position the dolphins will arrest the motion and no harm can result. There is some question if it would not have been advisable to build the wing wall in such a manner that a vessel could be brought up close enough to the gates so that when the gates are opened the fresh-water current from the lock would not spread until after passing the stern of the ship.

At Gatun locks the depth of water in the tail bay is practically constant, the tidal fluctuations being less than 2 ft. (0.61 m.). The side-culvert outlet is placed at elevation — 20 ft. (— 6.10 m.), the mid-depth position. For like relative densities the currents would be the same as for the best condition of operation at Miraflores locks or extreme low tide. The relative densities between the lower chamber and the sea are less at Gatun than at Miraflores, as the fresh water is locked down three flights at Gatun and only two at Miraflores. In addition, the approach wall is not a solid wall, as is the case at Miraflores, but is made up of a series of arches. This enables the current to spread in both directions and greatly lessens the tendency mentioned, so that the conditions do not assume the seriousness of those at Miraflores.

The current from the lower locks to sea also makes it somewhat difficult for a vessel to leave the locks in it, as there is a very strong tendency to carry the vessel over toward the wing wall and the bank of the canal. The vessel can be held until the current subsides in the lock chamber, but this means the delay of 20 to 30 minutes. Accordingly, the plan adopted is to bring the vessel up to speed with the locomotives and cast off the lines in the chamber. The vessel can then pick up sufficient steerage way before leaving the locks to care for itself.

ELECTRICAL AND MECHANICAL INSTALLATIONS OF THE PANAMA CANAL.

By

EDWARD SCHILDHAUER, Fel. A. I. E. E., M. Am. Soc. C. E.
Mem. Am. Soc. M. E.
Formerly Electrical and Mechanical Engineer, Panama Canal Commission
New York, N. Y., U. S. A.

The study of the electrical and mechanical requirements for the Panama Canal was unhampered by previous installations which might affect the selection of the type of apparatus, or of the system for transmission of energy. The preliminary studies indicated that the electrical system of transmitting power to the apparatus required for the locks and spillways had decided advantages over the hydraulic or air systems hitherto used extensively. The conservation of water was considered an important item and it led to the adoption of the Construction Power Plants, with the idea of making them available as reserve stations. Thus in 1907-8, when the Construction Power Plants were purchased, the electrical system with a frequency of 25 cycles per second was the starting point of the present installation.

DISTRIBUTION OF POWER.

Hydro-Electric Station.

The principal power station is located at the Gatun spillway and consists of three 2000-kilowatt, 3-phase, 25-cycle, 2200-volt generating units direct connected to hydraulic turbines, operating at 250 revolutions per minute. The water is drawn from the forebay in Gatun Lake and discharged into the spillway channel at about eight feet above sea-level. Due to the fluctuations of Gatun Lake, the average yearly head will be approximately 77 feet. The design of the installation is such as to provide for three turbine units, and an extension of three additional units may be made in the future. The buildings with the machinery and electrical equipment are laid out on the unit principle. Each unit consists of a headgate, penstock, turbine, generator, governor, exciter, oil switch and control panel.

The alignment of the penstock is such that it is entirely covered by the fill of Gatun Dam. The penstocks are constructed of riveted steel plates covered with concrete, for protection against external corrosion and to strengthen them against the superimposed earth pressures.

The turbo-generator units are of the vertical type, the entire weight of the rotating element being supported by the top shield of the generator, by means of an overhung roller

Fig. 1. Gatun Hydro-Electric Station.

The station is on the east side of the spillway channel. The forebay is to the east of the spillway abutment where the gate house is located.

thrust bearing. The turbine is of the spiral-casing, one-runner, Francis type. The generator is separated from the turbine by a circular distance ring of sufficient height to permit the mounting of a direct-connected exciter between the two elements. This arrangement was adopted in lieu of separate turbo-exciters. In addition to the three direct-connected exciters, two motor-driven units of 100 kilowatts each have been provided. The exciters operate normally at 125 volts.

The main control switchboard is located on the second gallery, from which the operator may view the entire main apparatus. The switchboard operator controls all switching operations remotely, including the high-tension switches, exciter buses, governors, rheostats, field circuit-breakers and the head gates. For further details refer to Figs. 1 to 5, inclusive.

Reserve Station.

In the event of a total shut down of the transmission system between the Atlantic and Pacific ends of the Canal, or in the event of a water shortage, the Construction Power Plant erected in 1908 at Miraflores locks will be used as a reserve

Fig. 2.   Gatun Hydro-Electric Station.

The turbo-generators are of the vertical self-contained type of 2000 kw. capacity, 2200 volts, 25 cycles, operating at 250 revolutions per minute.

station. This station is built on the unit principle and contains four 1500-kilowatt Curtis steam turbo-generators with auxiliaries and eight water-tube boilers arranged in groups of two. The generators deliver 3-phase current, 25-cycle, 2200-volt, and are excited from a 125-volt exciter system.

By means of the substations and transmission lines described later, the Gatun hydro-electric station and the Miraflores steam station may operate in parallel in the usual manner.

Transmission System.

On account of the undesirability of crossing the canal locks with an overhead transmission line, the feeders from the Gatun hydro-electric station are run in duplicate duct lines from the station across Gatun dam, under Gatun locks in tunnels, to the step-up transformer substation located on the east side of the upper level of Gatun locks.

Gatun Substation.

In the Gatun substation (Fig. 6) the electrical energy is received at 2200 volts and transformed to 44,000 volts, at which

Fig. 3. Gatun Hydro-Electric Station.

The generator oil switches are located on the top or second gallery, from which the leads drop to the bus on the second gallery; thence to the feeder oil switches and cable.

it is transmitted, over a duplicate aerial transmission line, from Cristobal on the Atlantic Ocean to Balboa on the Pacific, a distance of about 47 miles. The Gatun substation is also used to distribute electrical energy locally to the town of Gatun, to Agua Clara water-works, and for general use. In the event that the current is generated in the Miraflores station, the Gatun substation is used to step down the pressure received nominally at 44,000 volts and distribute it, in addition to points mentioned above, to the Gatun locks. The substation is equipped with a distributing switchboard, oil switches and three 2000-kilowatt 3-phase oil- and radiator-type transformers with auxiliaries. The building is of rectangular design to accommodate four transformer units. (For further details refer to Figs. 7 and 8.)

Cristobal Substation.

The building of the Cristobal substation is a duplicate of the Gatun substation. At present, however, only two transformer units are installed. The principal peak load on the substation is the demand from the Cristobal coaling plant, and

Fig. 4. Gatun Hydro-Electric Station.

The generator leads are connected to reactance coils located on the second gallery, thence to current transformers and oil switches located in the middle and left-hand concrete compartments respectively.

the favorable steady load is that of the Mount Hope water works. The current is also used for operating the Cristobal dry-dock shops and for general use in Cristobal and Colon.

The capacity of the Cristobal coaling plant has been increased and it is very likely that the demand for coaling ships will be such that another transformer unit will be necessary to handle the peak load satisfactorily, with a unit in reserve.

Miraflores Substation.

The Miraflores substation is located adjacent to the steam station erected in 1908-9. It is in practically all respects a duplicate of the Gatun substation. The principal feeders radiate to the Miraflores locks and spillway, Pedro Miguel locks and town site, and Miraflores water purification plant. The steam-station high-tension switches and control are located in the substation. The distributed load is such that two transformer units would

Fig. 5. Gatun Hydro-Electric Station.

The circuit switches and instrument transformers are mounted in concrete compartments. The 2200-volt bus connections are insulated with varnished cambric.

have been sufficient, but, on account of the duty imposed on this substation due to shortage of water, it was necessary to transform the output of the reserve steam station.

Balboa Substation.

The Balboa substation is located near the center of load and is also a duplicate of the Gatun substation. The peak demand on this substation is severe, due to the motor-driven dry-dock pumps. These pumps are estimated to demand a maximum of about 4000 horsepower for a period of 2½ hours, whenever the dry dock is unwatered. The Balboa coaling-plant demand, although not as severe as the larger Cristobal counterpart, is nevertheless of considerable magnitude. The normal load of the Balboa shops is comparable to an ordinary machine shop working a portion of the tools only, and the abnormal demand will occur when the shops are used for repair work in times of maximum activity. The motor-driven pumps for the water-works system of Balboa, Ancon and the City of

Fig. 6. Gatun Substation.

The building is of rectangular design to accommodate four 2000-kilowatt transformer equipments.

Panama will demand a relatively constant supply ranging over many hours, similar to installations furnishing water to a diversified community. In addition to the above load there is a demand for general purposes, including the lighting system of Balboa and Ancon, and furnishing, temporarily, power for the Panama tramways system.

Gamboa Substation.

The permanent water supply for the southern end of the Canal towns is obtained from Chagres River Valley, east of the

Canal, where the Gamboa pumping plant is installed. The substation consists of two 500-kilowatt transformers and the auxiliary equipment for transforming the transmission line volt-

Fig. 7. Gatun Substation.
Oil-cooled transformers of the Radiator Type. Capacity 2000 kilowatts, 2200/ 44,000 volts.

age from 44,000 to 2200 volts, three-phase at the bus. A 2200-volt feeder is carried to the gravel wharf, where it is transformed by a rotary converter equipment to 550 volts direct current for use of the unloaders. This equipment was originally used at the Balboa sand wharf.

Darien Substation.

A high-powered wireless station is located near the railroad line about twenty-five miles from Colon, where Darien substation is erected. It is a small substation of 400 kilowatts, which transforms the transmission line pressure from 44,000 to 440 volts, three phase.

Transmission Line Structure.

The study of the type of transmission-line structure involved features not usually encountered elsewhere. As will be

Fig. 8. Gatun Substation.

Front view of main switchboard located on the ground floor.

seen from the paper presented on the Panama Railroad, the country is very rugged. To use a path for the transmission line independent of the railroad, required large expenditure for clearing, not only in first cost, but in maintenance. To follow the line of the railroad demanded that the structures should not interfere with the proper function of the railroad. The width of the embankment, especially through the lake region, precluded structures with the required base being placed on one side of the railroad line, without incurring an abnormal expense for foundations. The track-span bridges which are adopted meet the various conditions satisfactorily. It is true that more steel is required in this structure than would be necessary for a line placed entirely on one side of the railroad line, but this is compensated for by the reduced cost of foundations, low cost of erection, absence of crossing the railroad with wires, and, further, it provides a ready means for electrifying the Panama Railroad when it becomes advantageous to do so. For further details refer to Fig. 6 and to Fig. 12 of "The Reconstruction of the Panama Railroad", by Frederick Mears.

DISTRIBUTION AT LOCKS.

It has been the aim to design the distribution system for the locks on the basis of "continuity of service". In all cases where it was feasible a duplicate service has been provided, through independent-duct lines, or by separating the feeders as much as possible in single-duct lines.

Gatun Locks.

The Gatun locks are served from the hydro-electric station at 2200 volts, one set of feeders entering at the head of the locks and a second set of feeders at the foot of the lower locks. The incoming feeders connect to a switchboard, from which feeders are distributed to the transformer rooms, situated beneath the coping level of the locks. The feeders entering the head of the locks feed the successive transformer rooms, four per wall, toward the foot of the locks, and the feeders entering the foot of the lower locks feed the same transformer rooms in the opposite direction. This method should insure continuity of service under ordinary conditions, but, in the event of very extreme conditions, it is possible to remove the interlocking bar of the transformer switches and tie together the main and auxiliary buses, and thus feed the transformer room next to it over the second cable. In this extreme case, when the removal of the interlocking bars is resorted to, the transformer room nearest the incoming feeder has a choice of three feeders, and the intermediate transformer rooms have a choice of four feeders. It is inconceivable, however, that such use will have to be made to obtain continuity of service.

Transformer Rooms.

In the design of the locks, for economical reasons, the various machines were required to be placed in well defined groups at the upper and lower ends of each lock wall. For the three locks in flight at Gatun these groups are supplied by four transformer rooms per lock wall, or a total of sixteen. The groups of machines for the center wall could be supplied by four transformer rooms economically, but, since the locks are in duplicate, the transformer rooms for the center wall are likewise in duplicate. The feeders are arranged in such a manner that one flight of locks may be put out of commission without affecting the operation of the duplicate flight. Each transformer room is equipped with one 50-kilowatt single-phase lighting transformer; two 200-k.v.a. oil-cooled, three-phase transformers; a 2200-volt switchboard; a 220-volt switchboard, and protective devices. The 2200-volt switchboard is equipped with two sets of buses, either one of which may be used to connect to the transformers. A main and an auxiliary bus are also provided on the low-tension switchboard, and the low-tension feeders are connected to double-throw knife switches.

Power Feeders.

The feeders to the control boards of the motors are relatively short and are not in duplicate. The insulation of the cable, however, is of the same grade as that used for the 2200-volt cable, so that a break-down of the insulation is minimized to a great extent. Another reason for the omission of duplicate feeders is the fact that usually another machine of the group is close at hand, which makes it feasible to install temporary connections from a serviceable feeder in a short time.

Lighting.

In each transformer room a 50-kilowatt 2200-110-220-volt transformer is installed, for the purpose of furnishing the energy for the lighting of the operating tunnels, machine rooms, and general exterior illumination of the locks. The distribution center is a part of the low-tension switchboard. The feeders to the distributing cabinets are connected in the usual manner, and operated locally. The exterior lighting circuits, however, are equipped with remote-controlled switches operated

Fig. 9.   Locks Transformer Room.

from the central control house described later. For further details refer to Plates I and II and Figs. 9 to 11 inclusive.

Pedro Miguel Locks.

The description of the installation for the Gatun locks applies also to the Pedro Miguel locks, with the exception that only eight transformer rooms are required. The power is transmitted from the Miraflores substation through cables placed in underground duct lines.

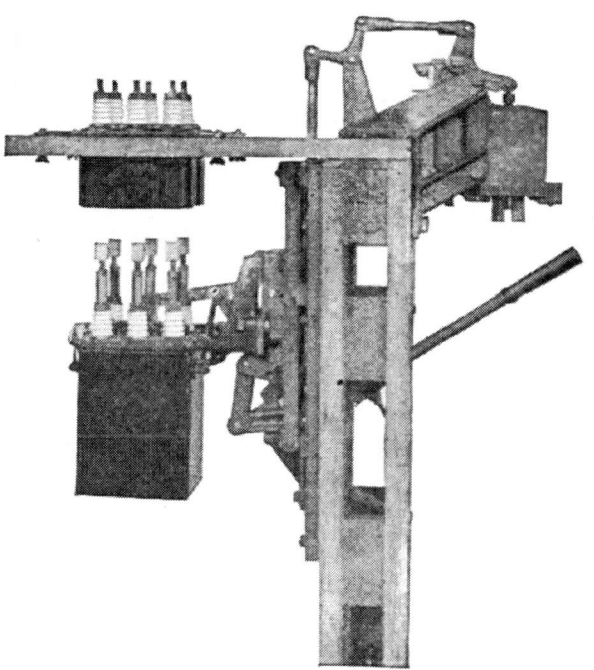

Fig. 10. Triple-Pole, Single-Throw 2500-Volt, 300-Ampere Oil Switch with Solenoid Operating Mechanism and Disconnecting Device.

The switch can not be lowered in the position shown until the oil switch is in the open circuit position, thus eliminating danger resulting from opening the circuit at the disconnecting contacts.

Miraflores Locks.

Miraflores locks consist of two duplicate locks in flight, and require therefore twelve transformer rooms to obtain the same electrical service as that described for Gatun locks. The power is derived from the Miraflores substation through cables placed in duct lines, which in their course cross the body of the Miraflores spillway dam.

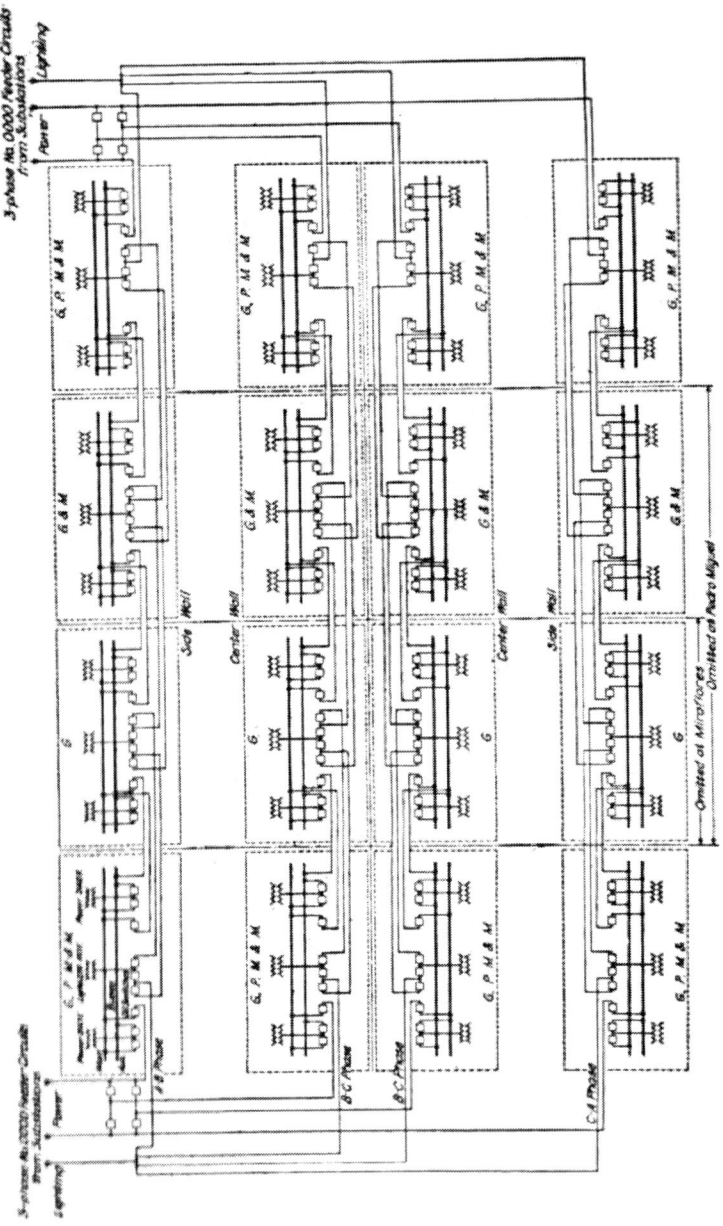

Plate I. Single Line Diagram of 2200-Volt Connections—All Locks.

MACHINERY FOR THE OPERATION OF THE LOCKS AND SPILLWAYS.

A general idea of the number of machines installed for the operation of the locks, and their relative location, may be obtained by referring to Plate III, each number representing a machine. It was required that no machinery should project above the coping of the locks. It was desired to design the machinery in such a manner that it would be accessible at all

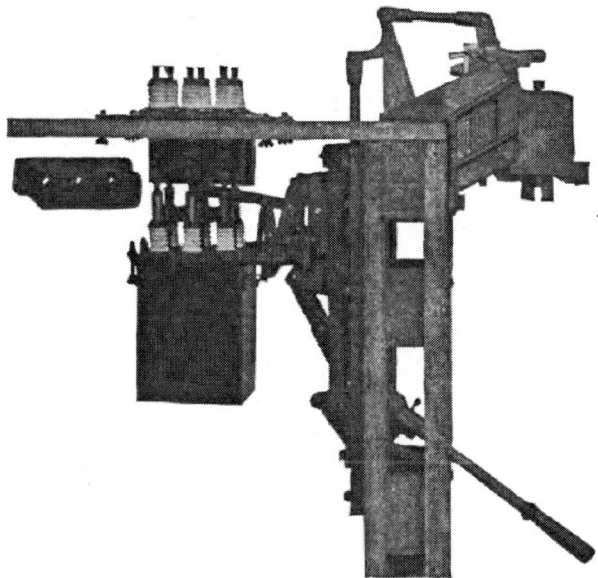

Fig. 11.

Same apparatus as shown in Fig. 10, except that the circuit is in closed position and the insulated protection of one set of terminals is removed.

times for inspection, could be installed and repaired with the aid of a crane from the top of the coping, would require the minimum amount of attention during operation, and that the least number of moving parts be submerged in water. Accordingly, the types of machines were limited to a great extent. On account of the grouping of the machines it was advisable to connect the compartments by passages below the coping. The drainage of the coping and machinery rooms required that adequate culverts be supplied, extending the entire length of the lock walls. The duct lines for the electric cables are required for practically the entire length of the lock walls. Further, it is less expensive to group the drainage culvert, duct lines and operating tunnel than it is to provide equivalent and separate means for accomplishing the desired results. The final arrangement for operating tunnel, duct line, and culvert is shown on the drawings of various machines, and is essentially an underground passageway, following the lock wall, between the extreme locations of machines. Beneath the floor of this tunnel a space is used for the duct line, and below this a square drainage culvert is installed.

Rising-Stem Valve Machines.

The rising-stem valve machine is used to manipulate the valves of the main culverts controlling the water in the locks. For economical reasons in cost of masonry, the variation in the location of the culverts, as measured from the top of the coping, is as much as twenty feet. The machines to operate the valves for these culverts should, therefore, be able to meet this condition with the least change in the individual parts. In the adopted machine this variation affected only the length of the valve stem, which was altered accordingly. The variation in the location of the culvert had no material bearing on the design of the machine as to its proportions, and it was consequently designed for the maximum conditions.

In a previous chapter describing the masonry it was seen that the valves are of a well-known type. As a result of some experiments made on the gates of the Chicago Drainage Canal regulating works, it was shown that the coefficient of friction for roller bearings was very much greater than ordinarily used. The excessive friction of the gates tested was probably due to corrosion of the bearing surfaces, to faulty manufacture, to faulty alignment, or partly to all. These conditions are likely to occur in any valve from faulty construction of the roller trains and bearing plates, or from carelessness in aligning the parts during erection. The corrosion of the steel rollers and bearing plates is a factor to be considered as always present. In view of the importance of the main culvert valves of the Panama Canal locks, and the possibility that the valves would approach a condition similar to that of the gates tested, it was considered advisable to base the estimates of power for operating the valves on the coefficient 0.04. For the side seals, which are fabricated of spring bronze and slide on planed cast steel, a coefficient of 0.25 was used.

The forces which were considered as acting on the valve, to resist the raising or lowering, were roller friction, friction of side seals, friction of stuffing boxes, pressure on top seal, weight of valve, buoyancy of valve, weight of live-roller train, and weight of machinery applied directly to the valves. The mechanical efficiency of the machine was considered of secondary importance, when compared with the safety and absolute reliability.

The length of the water course in the culverts is considerable. It was deemed essential, therefore, to avoid "water hammer", which is minimized by making the machine self locking, and by employing substantial members, as few in number as possible, between the self-locking member of the machine and the valve.

The cost of repairs on the Isthmus is considered above the average, and it was thought advisable to design all the parts with a large factor of safety.

The corrosion of ferrous metals, on account of the extreme humidity, had to be seriously considered. To minimize the effect on the machines, all small members which could not be protected adequately were required to be made of non-corrosive metals. The adopted design is shown in assembly on Plates IV, V and VI.

To allow for the easy removal of the valve, the machine is supported on cast-steel sub-bases, which overhang the valve recess, and which are securely anchored to the concrete base.

The power is transmitted by a 50-horsepower motor through miter and spur gears to two revolving screws, which actuate a cross-head by means of two bronze non-revolving nuts attached to the cross-head and spaced to straddle the valve. The valve stem is pinned to the cross-head equidistant from the screws, the non-revolving nuts are pivoted to allow movement in the plane of the cross-head, thus allowing for variation of wear in the nuts and screws. The cross-head is guided at the ends by double-flanged wheels, which run on planed rails partially imbedded in the concrete. Each revolving screw is provided with a self-aligning roller thrust bearing to take the weight of the valve and its parts during ordinary operation. When, however, the valve is held by an obstruction, and when the valve is seated, the force is counteracted by plain disc thrust bearings mounted at the top of the revolving screws. The bearings are so arranged that either set may be removed without removing the screws. At the bottom the screws are guided by a self-oiling bearing placed at the level of the bulkhead. The non-revolving nuts are lubricated with a heavy oil in a container placed on top of the nuts. In this container a scraper is mounted to remove the surplus lubricant during the closure of the valve; thus the screws are well protected from corrosion. The valve stem passes through a water-tight bulkhead which serves as a guide at this point. The lower end of the valve stem is attached to the valve by means of two pins, placed at right angles in a short connecting member, to take up slight movements of the valve in its guides. The live-roller trains operate at one half the speed of the valve. To confine them in proper relation to the valve, the upper end of each train is connected to a vertical rod, which passes through a stuffing box in the bulkhead. The upper end of the rod is fastened to a sheave. By attaching a chain to the masonry above the rod, passing the chain around the sheave on the rod, over a second sheave in line above, and a third sheave on the bulkhead, in line with the crosshead, where the other end of the chain is fastened, the roller train is constrained to move at one half the speed of the valve, and is held in the proper relative position through the entire travel.

The valve rests on a positive stop when in its closed position. Since it is impracticable to stop the machine at the moment when the valve is seated, the cross-head is so designed that the nuts can travel several inches after the valve is seated. During this interval two sets of springs are compressed, which allow sufficient time to shut off the power automatically and stop the machine. In the upward travel of the valve, a distance of six inches is allowed for stopping the machine.

The motor is equipped with a solenoid brake, which serves as a means to stop the machine in a predetermined position, after the current is cut off, with a very small variation. The machine has few moving parts which are subject to wear. The motor operates at about 480 r.p.m. which is also the highest gear speed. The bronze nuts, which are two and one half times the diameter of the screws in length, should not with ordinary attention require frequent renewal. The bulkhead is under a pressure of approximately 15 lbs. per square inch, so that the packing for the valve stems does not present any abnormal conditions. When the valve is removed for inspection and repair it will be necessary to remove the following machine parts: chain sheaves, valve stem, roller-train rods and the bulkhead. No additional parts need be removed when it is desired to lift the valve to the top of the coping.

The calculations for the machine were based on the following assumed data:

Height of valve	18'-10"
Breadth of valve	11'- 1"
Thickness of valve	20"
Area of valve under pressure	150 sq. ft.
Unbalanced area of top seal of valve at moment of closure	208 " ins.
Unbalanced area of two side seals of valve under pressure	550 " "
Rise of valve	18'- 0"
Weight of valve	20,000 lbs.
Weight of two live-roller trains	5,000 "
Weight of machinery acting on valve	7,770 "
Buoyancy of valve and immersed portions of machinery	4,540 "
Ordinary operating head, maximum	60 ft.
Operating head, lock unwatered	72 "
Weight of cubic foot water	62.5 lbs.
Coefficient of live-roller friction	0.04
Coefficient of side-seal friction	0.25
Coefficient of stuffing-box friction	0.25
Time of opening or closing valve	1 minute

Complete tests of the rising-stem valves were performed after installation on the Isthmus. Space does not permit of including these data, but it may be stated that the performance of the machine is entirely satisfactory.

Cylindrical Valve Machines.

The cylindrical valves are installed to control the lateral culverts leading from the main culvert of the center wall. The machine must be capable of raising the valve three feet. By referring to the drawing showing the design of the valve, it is seen that the lower limit of travel is its seat. To eliminate jamming of the seat, it is necessary to provide relief for the over-travel of the machine. The time for complete travel was stipulated as ten seconds. Referring to Plate VII, it is seen that the machine consists essentially of a motor, direct connected to a pinion and bevel gear actuating a screw, thereby raising the nut which is secured to the valve stem.

The weight of the valve and stem, together with the screw, is supported by a roller thrust bearing. To relieve the apparatus from severe shock when the valve reaches its seat, the screw is permitted to rise through the thrust-bearing sleeve, thus giving time for the motor to stop. The weight of the valve and stem is sufficient to close the valve without applying a downward force. Since the valve stem is of sufficient length in all cases, a single screw was adaptable, telescoping a portion of the stem. The floor of the machinery room is eight feet below the coping, and since the coping is from four to five feet above the water level, the machinery floor, and hence the valve-stem stuffing box, is under a head of only three or four feet of water. The upper portion of the valve stem serves also as an oil reservoir for lubricating the screw and preserving it from corrosion. As the stem is raised the screw enters this reservoir and forces the oil into an upper container, whence it returns when the valve is lowered. The valve stem is prevented from turning by guides. The gear casing is flooded with oil, and by means of a small gear pump the oil is forced to the roller bearing. The limit switch controlling the length of travel is geared to pinion shaft. The motor has to exert the greatest torque as the valve seal is broken. These machines are used, not only for the 120 cylindrical valves of the locks, but, by altering the length of the screws, also for the twelve auxiliary culvert valves. They have given entire satisfaction.

Miter-Gate Machines.

The miter-gate machines are used to manoeuvre the miter gates of the locks, and it was specified that they should close or open the gates in two minutes. A study of the power required to operate existing lock gates showed a wide variation in the power provided for apparently similar conditions, and the published data gave no definite basis for the design of the machine under consideration. From observation, in certain cases, it appeared that the power provided was insufficient to operate the gates within the time specified in published reports.

Personal investigations led to the belief that the acceleration of the gate was left too much to the judgment of the operators, and that this might result in straining the apparatus, or in prolonging unnecessarily the time of manoeuvering. In some well-known locks it appears that much time is lost when the gate is entering the recess and when it approaches the mitered position. It seems, therefore, that a machine for moving the gates should accelerate and retard at a predetermined rate, not dependent upon the judgment of the operator, and the extreme positions should be fixed definitely and remain so during successive operations.

For the reason that published data were at variance, it was considered advisable to carry out an independent investigation of the forces resisting the motion of a lock gate. The forces considered were: acceleration, friction of pivot, friction of collar, wind resistance, jet action, skin friction and water pressure due to difference of water level on the two sides of the gate. From these calculations curves were constructed, the ordinate as the force in pounds and the abscissa as the time in seconds from zero to 120 seconds. The forces derived for the pivot and collar friction are small in comparison to wind pressure and acceleration. The latter has a very marked influence on the difference in water level on the two sides of the gate, and this is especially true when the gate is near the recess and the mitered position. This study showed clearly that the gate recess should be designed with efficient openings for the flow of water. It also indicated that the forces increased at the mitered position, but it was not disclosed that the clearance between the lower surface of the gate and masonry had such a marked effect as determined during the test described later.

The adopted machine for operating the miter gates seems to impart an ideal motion to the gate, i. e., slow speed of gate at the ends of travel and high speed at the middle portion of travel, with a maximum force exerted by the machine at the ends of travel. The motor is allowed to come up to speed in a very few seconds.

Referring to Plate VIII, the machine consists of a large gear wheel revolving in a horizontal plane, with a vertical pin, near the periphery of the wheel, to which a strut is connected, the other end being pinned to the gate. The wheel is revolved through an arc of about 197 degrees by means of a pinion engaging the teeth on its rim, which is in turn connected by a train of gears to the motor. At the two ends of travel, the strut (or connecting rod) is on or near dead center and can exert an infinite force on the gate with very small force exerted on the rim of the wheel. The end of the strut which connects to the gate is equipped with a telescoping joint and a nest of springs, to absorb any shock and to prevent straining the gate and machine should an obstruction be encountered during the movement of the gate. The springs are mounted in such a manner that they act in compression when the strut is either lengthened or shortened. A switching device is connected to the two members having relative motion, which at a predetermined limit opens the control circuit, thus stopping the motor. When the above safety device has operated, the motor may be reversed by the control switch, thus relieving the gate.

The wheel end of the strut is equipped with a short member and a pin, placed at right angles to the main pin near the rim of the wheel, so that any slight variations in the relative movement of the gate and gear wheel will not cause any undue strains. The teeth of the large gear wheel extend only a sufficient distance around the periphery to impart the desired motion to the gate. If for any reason the limit switch fails to operate properly, the pinion disengages and further movement of the gate is checked. On the vertical shaft which carries the pinion there is mounted a bevel gear. The horizontal shaft of the bevel-gear pinion passes through the bulkhead and a spring-center spur gear is mounted on it in the motor room. The pinion on the back-gear shaft of the motor engages this spring-center spur gear. There are, therefore, four gear reductions. The limit switch is geared to the "spring-center" gear shaft.

On account of the limited distance from the top of the coping to the water level in the locks, and the space required

for the gate recess cover, the opening for the strut was forced
very close to the water level, so that the compartment containing the large gear is subjected to splashes. For this reason the
large gear wheel compartment is separated from the motor
room by a bulkhead.

Space will permit giving only a few results of tests, which
are shown in curves. Fig. 12 shows the current consumption of
the intermediate gates of the upper west chamber of the Gatun
locks. These curves were derived by means of a graphic am-
meter. The water level was changed so that the depth over the
sill varied from 20.7 feet to 62.8 feet. The two gates were
operated simultaneously during these tests. These curves show
that the maximum force is required near the mitered position
of the gates, and that the motor torque near the gate recess is
practically equal to the torque required when the gate is moving at its maximum speed. To determine what effect would be
produced by non-simultaneous operation of the gates, a series
of tests was made on the same gates, the results of which are
shown on Fig. 13. These curves show again that the maximum
torque of the motor is required near the mitered position of
the gate, but this decreases as the time interval between the
operation of the gates is increased. In other words, when one
gate remains closed while the other gate is opened or closed,
the torque of the motor remains practically constant during the
entire cycle. This seems to show that the same condition could
be obtained during the operation of the two gates simultaneously, if the passage for the water below the gate is increased. It is the opinion of the writer that by altering the
masonry below the gate the desirable low-torque curve can be
very nearly approached during simultaneous operation of the
gates. Figs. 14, 15 and 16 show various machines in the process
of erection.

Miter-Forcing Machines.

During the early studies of the miter-gate machine, the
designs followed the lines of machines in use at various locks.
With such machines it was considered advisable to adopt some
means of insuring that the gates assume perfect miter. Since
the masonry sill prevents the lower end of the gate from passing beyond the point of miter, it was deemed sufficient to force

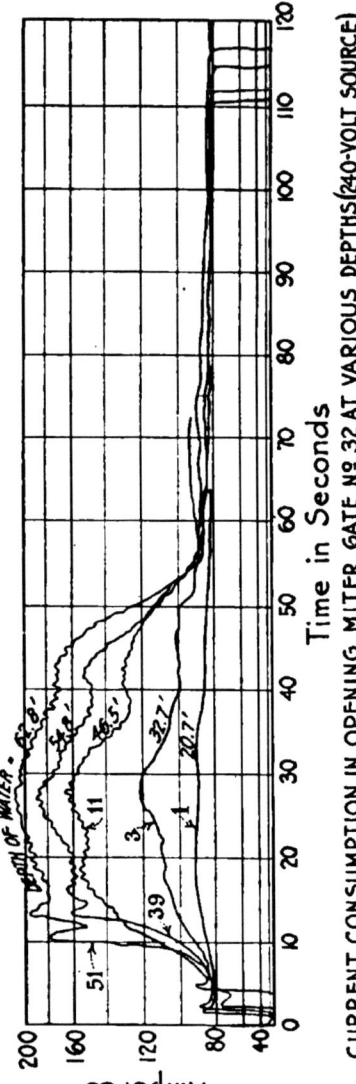

CURRENT CONSUMPTION IN OPENING MITER GATE № 32 AT VARIOUS DEPTHS (240-VOLT SOURCE)

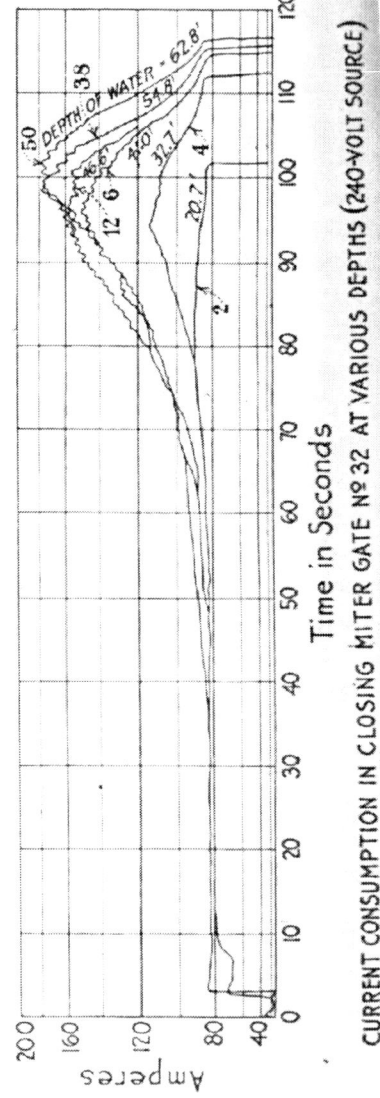

CURRENT CONSUMPTION IN CLOSING MITER GATE № 32 AT VARIOUS DEPTHS (240-VOLT SOURCE)

Fig. 12.

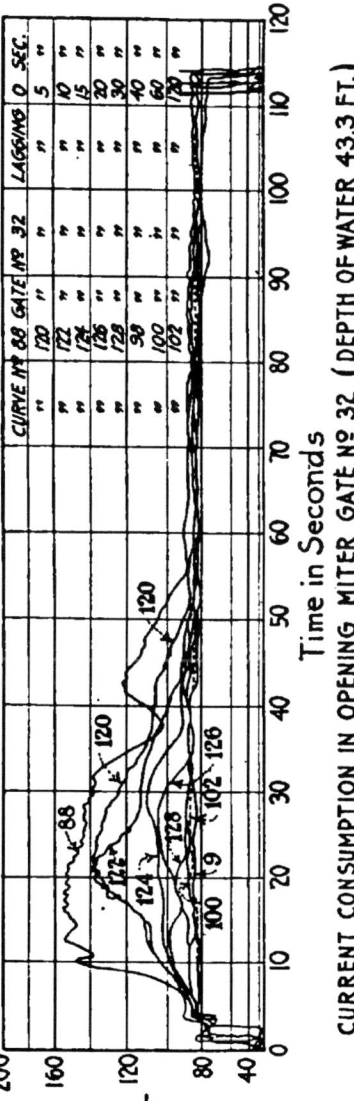

CURRENT CONSUMPTION IN OPENING MITER GATE № 32 (DEPTH OF WATER 43.3 FT.)

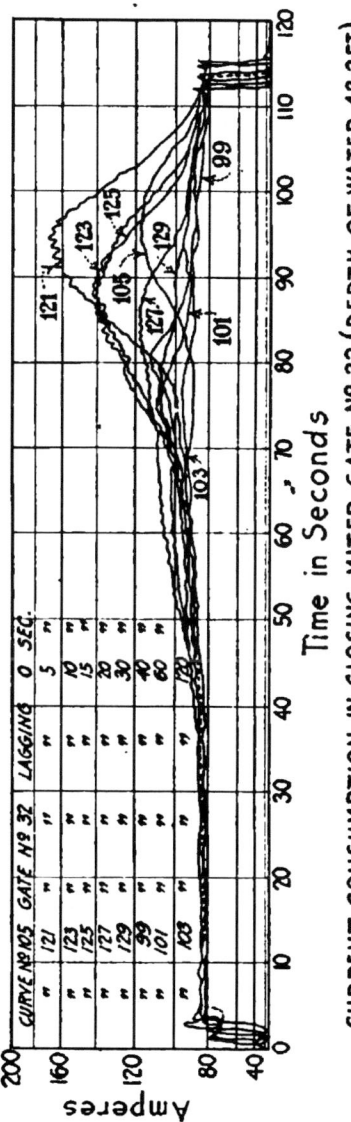

CURRENT CONSUMPTION IN CLOSING MITER GATE № 32 (DEPTH OF WATER 43.3 FT.)

Fig. 13.

Fig. 14. Miter Gate Machine.

Partial assembly of the machine for a lower guard gate. To the right of the center plate is the bulkhead beyond which is the motor room. The large pin in the foreground, two feet in diameter, is for the center pin of the horizontal crank gear.

Fig. 15. Miter Gate Machine, Lower Guard Gate.

the top of the gates into position, and thereby the best miter would be obtained when considering the gates as a whole. As long as the gates are in perfect condition a machine to force the gates into miter is not required when the miter-gate machine hereinbefore described is employed. Should the gates, however, due to some accident, be warped, then it may be very advisable to have a machine to force perfect miter at the top of the gate.

The miter forcing machine adopted for the Panama Canal is designed so that it will not only force the gates into the

Fig. 16. Gatun Upper Locks, Miter Gate Moving Machine.

Structural Steel Girders for towing-locomotive track supports in foreground. June, 1912.

miter, but it is capable of resisting a large force tending to break the miter. It consists of two principal members, one bolted to the outer end of the top girder of one of the gate leaves and provided with a large vertical pin. The second member is bolted to the outer end of the top girder of the other gate leaf and is equipped with mechanism to move a pair of jaws which embrace the pin on the other gate leaf. Referring to Plate IX, the jaws are connected by a series of toggle links to a cross-head nut actuated by means of a fixed revolving screw. The thrust of the screw is transmitted through a roller bearing to the main frame when the jaws are closed, and through a plain disc thrust bearing when the jaws are opened. The screw is revolved by a bevel gear in mesh with the pinion on the extension of the motor shaft. The motor and limit switch are in a closed compartment. The motor is equipped with a solenoid brake for bringing the machine to rest in very narrow limits, after the limit switch has opened the control circuit. The box casting which carries the machinery has two removable covers, one over the link mechanism and one over the motor space, each being provided with hand holes for inspection and oiling. The forces acting on the jaws are transmitted directly through pins to the frame, and, when the jaws are in the closed position, no strain is on the screw, due to forces acting on the jaws. In the open position, the jaws permit either gate leaf to be operated without interference between the jaws and the pin on the other leaf.

Spillway Gate Machine.

In studying the existing machines to operate crest gates, it was perceived that, in many cases, the torsional strains in the long operating shafts were not given sufficient consideration. This is especially true in the installations where the driving mechanism is placed at one end of the gate and power is transmitted to the other end by means of a long shaft. To eliminate some of the bad effects of the difference in the torsional displacement in a long shaft, the driving mechanism is placed midway between the ends of the gate supports. This necessitates invariably a strong bridge to support the concentrated load in the center of the span. The gates are usually of such weight that it is economical to counterweight them.

On account of the debris which would pass over the Gatun and Miraflores spillways, it was stipulated that the lower edge of the gate when in its raised position, should clear the highest elevation of the lake by 4½ feet, or a total travel of 22½ feet was necessary. To utilize a counterweight, as usually employed, and to take advantage of the full gate opening, require the piers to be considerably higher than required for the adopted machine.

The design of the spillway dam is such that the installation of a tunnel and counterweight pits in the body of the dam did not affect the proper stability, therefore the machinery was designed accordingly. By referring to Plate X, it is seen that the suspension of the gate is made in the usual manner. The chain attached to the end member is passed over a sheave located on top of the pier and returns through an opening in the pier and is secured to the top of a long screw, to the lower end of which the counterweight is attached. The screw passes through the threaded hub of a worm wheel, and the worm engaging the worm wheel is directly connected to a motor placed midway between the machines operating the two ends of the gate. By placing the motor centrally and driving the worm gear by extending the shaft to each, the effect of the difference in the torsional angle is practically eliminated.

On account of the debris mentioned above, it was deemed very essential that the roller trains, which ordinarily travel one half the distance of the gate, should be removed to a position protected by the gate. Accordingly, the usual method of fastening a chain to the pier, passing it around a sheave secured to the roller train and attaching it to the gate was resorted to. In addition, however, a set of sheaves was reeved into one portion of the chain. When the gate is in the lower position the sheaves are held in a fixed position to the gate. In raising the gate above the water level, a set of wheels engage with tracks which move the gate away from the pier and thus clear of the roller train. Immediately the frame of one set of sheaves is engaged with a suitable projection on the pier and the sheaves are separated, with the result that the roller train is raised rapidly to assume a protected position back of the gate. In lowering, a reverse operation takes place.

The selection of the amount of power to be applied, and consequently the time of raising or lowering the gate, was tempered by the desire to reduce the sizes of motors for the Canal to a minimum. For the spillway machines, therefore, the size and type of motors used for the cylindrical valves were adopted. These open the gates in about ten minutes. Fig. 17 shows details of the machine.

Guard Valve Machines.

At the upper end of each side wall of the locks provision is made for the entrance of the water by three openings. These openings are controlled by valves which are duplicates of the rising-stem valves. On account of economic conditions in the design of the masonry, the regular rising-stem valve machines

Fig. 17. Spillway Gate Machine, Chain and Screw.
The board in the background shows the moving elements of the machine.

were not applied in this case, because of space limitations. The adopted machine consists of a heavy chain, secured to the center of the valve, passing over a sheave directly above, then over a second sheave and down to a counterweight. The driving shaft is actuated by means of a spur and pinion, worm wheel and worm direct connected to a motor. The roller trains are held in correct relation with the valve on the same principle as adopted for the rising-stem valve, except that the chain is fastened to the counterweight, instead of to the cross-head which moves in unison with the valve. The motor is of the same size as used for the miter-gate machine, although the full rating of the motor is not required for operating these valves.

TOWING LOCOMOTIVE SYSTEM.

Experience in the operation of locks used for large ships shows that the serious accidents to the lock gates are invariably caused by the misunderstanding of signals between the navigating officer and the engine room. In order to eliminate this, and mishaps due to the use of the ship's power, and without introducing other serious elements of danger, the towing system described herein was adopted.

This system requires that the ship's power should not be used for passage through the locks. The essential requirements for the system are: to accelerate and retard the ship without rupturing the lines; to place the ship in proper relation to the locks through its course; to tow the ship through a flight of locks without change of lines; and to use a small number of skilled operators in lieu of a large number of unskilled men.

In determining the duty of the locomotives it was considered that the majority of the merchant ships using the Canal would be less than 10,000 tons displacement. The towing system contemplates the use of four locomotives as the least number per vessel, so that it was decided that these units should be capable of handling the majority of ships. For "men-of-war" and the larger merchant ships it is only necessary to add more locomotives until they can handle the vessel as practice dictates.

Locomotive Track.

To accelerate the ship to the maximum speed within a reasonable time and to be certain that the locomotives proceed in unison, it is essential that the "tractive effort" should be constant. A constant "tractive effort" cannot be secured under the prevailing conditions at the locks by means of the ordinary adhesion between rails and wheels. Moreover, some means must be provided to ascend and descend the successive lock levels.

The problem of towing the ships successfully was solved by installing tracks, along the edge of the lock walls, equipped with a rack which engages pinions on the locomotives similar to that of the rack railways used in ascending mountains. In addition, however, provision is made to counteract the lateral component of the tow-line pull. This is accomplished by shrouding the rack upon which the horizontal thrust wheels of the locomotives engage.

Fig. 18. Towing Locomotive Track; Incline on a Center-wall Return Track.

The conductors (cover plates removed) are shown to the right of the running rail. The rack is shrouded and made of cast steel sections six feet long.

During normal operation of the locks the upbound traffic will be passed through one flight and the downbound traffic through the other flight. This requires, therefore, that the locomotives should return without interfering with the following lockage. For this purpose switches are installed at the ends of the approach walls so that the locomotives proceed to the other end of the locks on "return" tracks. These tracks are not equipped with racks except at the inclines. The gauge of the tracks is the same as that of the Panama Railroad, namely, five feet. Figure 18 shows the incline on a center wall return track. The conductors are shown to the right of the running rail.

Locomotive.

The lines of the locomotives are attached to the ship as it approaches the locks, or when the ship has tied up to the center approach wall. Two locomotives are attached to the bow of the ship, one on each side, and two to the stern, one on each side. If the ship is of such capacity that four locomotives can-

Fig. 19.   Towing Locomotives.

The line is secured to a winch with a slip drum located in the center of the locomotive.

not manoeuvre it satisfactorily, additional locomotives are attached. The lines are controlled by a winch placed in the center of the locomotive and are held in proper position by a set of guide sheaves, which assume a correct relation with the line. The line may be led off on either side of the locomotive and through a wide range of angles, so that a ship with a high free-board, or a raft of piles, may be maneuvered without "fouling" of lines with the lock walls or the locomotive struc-

ture. The winch is equipped with a slip drum which may be set
to slip at any predetermined point commensurate with the
ultimate strength of the line. The original installation is supplied with 800 feet of one-inch flexible steel cable and the slip
drum is set to slip at 25,000 lbs. pull at a radius of two feet.
The variation in the slip drum is not more than five per cent
above or below the pull for which it is set. The winch is provided with a motor which will alter the length of the line at

Fig. 20. Towing Locomotives.

Four locomotives attached to the Submarine Tender "Severn". Note the
central position of the ship which is maintained throughout its course.

twelve feet per minute with a pull of 25,000 lbs. on the line.
It is also equipped with a second motor, which controls the
length of the line at sixteen times the slow rate, or about 196
feet per minute. This is used for coiling the line to take the
slack out of it after attachment to the ship and also for coiling after the ship has cast it off. The setting of the slip drum
is tested at intervals by means of a dynamometer. The working

parts of the locomotive are supported on two axles and four wheels. The wheel base is twelve feet, the over all length of the locomotive is thirty-two feet, and the total weight is 86,000 lbs.

Each axle is driven by its own 75-horsepower motor, each independently of the other. A cast-steel bracket is hinged at one end on the axle by means of journals. This bracket is provided with bearings for the transverse jack shaft and counter shaft, which is actuated by the motor secured to a substantial platform. The outer end of the bracket is supported by means of springs to the locomotive frames, in such a manner as to provide a yielding support in both the upward and downward movement of the bracket. The gears are arranged to provide a maximum speed of two miles per hour while towing or operating on inclines, and five miles per hour when returning to the starting point. This is accomplished by a shift of gears on the jack shaft, which then engages a gear secured to the axle, the rack pinion remaining idle, or it may revolve if the journal friction is sufficient to impart motion.

The two ends of the locomotive are identical and the gears may be changed from either cab. Likewise, the control of the locomotives may be effected from either cab through suitable controllers. The traction motors may be operated singly or in multiple as desired. Each motor shaft is equipped with a powerful brake mechanism, which is released by a solenoid when the controller is placed on the first notched position. These brakes may also be operated by means of a hand-wheel brake mechanism, so that the brakes may be applied gradually while the solenoid retains the brake in the off position. This feature is very valuable, as it places in the hands of the operator a means of regulating the rate of retarding the locomotive independently of the solenoid brake, the latter being set for stopping the locomotive in case of failure of the electric current.

Three-phase 25-cycle 220-volt alternating current is used for operating the locomotives, and is supplied by an underground contact system, which is installed on the side of the rails remote from the lock. Two T rails are used for two legs of the three-phase circuit, and the main-track running rails are used for the third leg. The collecting shoes are mounted in line with the axles in a flexible manner, so that the curves, both vertical and horizontal, are readily negotiated.

It will be noted from the photographs that the ends of the locomotives at the bottom have an upward slope, which is for the purpose of providing clearance when the locomotive enters an incline.

The path of the locomotive is by no means an easy one, since it has, while towing, not only to negotiate horizontal and vertical curves and inclines with a grade of 44 per cent, but also to pass, at the upper end of the locks, under a portion of

Fig. 21. Towing Locomotives.

Trial lockage of S. S. "Santa Clara" leaving the upper Miraflores locks in tow of locomotives, two of which are descending to the lower level. The control house is shown on the center wall.

the emergency dam structure without fouling the lines on the concrete projections of the emergency dam abutments or on the structure above, which projects to within one foot of the edge of the lock wall.

The operating force for the locomotives is selected from the men who are engaged on general maintenance of the locks, when no lockage is in progress, and includes such trades as locomotive cranemen, machinists, wiremen, etc. During the period of training, several minor accidents have occurred, but taking the installation as a whole it has been remarkably successful. Figures 19 to 21 inclusive show the locomotives used for various lockages.

MOTORS.

In designing the apparatus for the Panama Canal, the desirability of limiting the size and type of motors to the least number was kept in mind constantly. This has not only reduced the original cost of motors, but it affects the cost of repairs and the rapidity of substitution of motors, without being obliged to have on hand a large surplus stock. The motors installed during the early construction period were furnished with standard insulation and parts. These motors seemed to fulfill the requirements satisfactorily when they were used constantly. When, however, they were used intermittently, as, for example, on the Balboa Dock cranes, a great deal of trouble was experienced, due to the break down of insulation and corrosion of small metal parts. The commutators of direct-current motors were a source of trouble, causing repeated shut downs. The motors for the locks and spillways may not be operated daily, even months may pass without operating certain motors. It is essential, therefore, that the apparatus should be constructed in such a manner that a period of idleness does not make it inoperative.

The principal factor causing deterioration of the insulation is the extreme humidity. In order that the best motors adapted for the problem in hand might be secured, manufacturers were invited to bid on furnishing sample motors, together with a bid on furnishing a stated number, should the sample motors be satisfactory. The sample motors were subjected to a test to determine the effect of humidity, by placing all in a room to which live steam was admitted, to create an atmosphere with a high humidity, and the temperature of the room was controlled to attain 100 degrees centigrade. At stated intervals the insulation resistance was measured, and a puncture test of 1000 volts of ten seconds' duration was applied to all motors simultaneously. Some of the motors failed after a few hours' exposure in the room, while others withstood the tests for several days, and several came through the test unimpaired. At the close of this test the motors were allowed to assume the temperature of the air and be subjected to the humidity of the air. Resistance measurements were continued and some motors showed a sharp increase in value, while others were very slow in showing any signs of higher values, and still others did not show any increase until they were subjected to heating produced by running at no load.

The motors which failed were tested to determine the location of the fault and sent to the shop for repair. The motors which were insulated by impregnating the coils after assembly could not be repaired with the appliances on hand. In fact it was impossible to remove the coils without injuring the top turns of adjacent coils. The insulation invariably blistered or cracked. This was considered a very serious objection in weighing the various factors entering into the problem. The motors which withstood the tests were equipped with coils completely insulated before assembly and required no special appliances to repair them on the Isthmus. It should be stated that the motor with the highest ohmic insulation is not necessarily the best, as it may absorb moisture more readily than an insulation which shows a moderate ohmic resistance and a moderate disruptive strength. The motors selected for the locks and spillways of the Panama Canal have up to date given entire satisfaction. A list of the principal motors installed is given on the following page.

ELECTRIC CABLES.

The principal power cables are of the varnished cambric, lead-sheathed type. Special precaution was taken to exclude moisture during the installation and all ends are provided with terminals filled with insulating compound. The multi-conductor control cable is likewise of the varnished cambric lead-sheathed type. In general, very little rubber-insulated wire was used except for the lighting circuits.

The Control of Lock Machinery.

Placing locks in flight without intervening pools brings forth certain elements of danger not encountered in single lifts. In studying the problem of control, it was evident that the task of co-ordinating an operating force distributed along the three lock walls, each about 4100 feet long at Gatun, could be eliminated, and in its place a single operator could be substituted by centralizing the control circuits. By such centrali-

Summary of Motors for Locks and Spillways.

MACHINE AND OPERATION	Motors each Machine	Starting Torque	NUMBER OF MOTORS				Total Horse-Power
			Gatun	Pedro Miguel	Miraflores	Total Number	
Electric Locomotive—Towing	2-75, C	1300	32	16	32	80	6,000
Electric Locomotive—Windlass	1-20, C	280	16	8	16	40	800
Electric Locomotive—Coiling	1-20, C	280	16	8	16	40	800
Emergency Dam—Turning	2-150, Int.	3500	4	4	4	12	1,800
Emergency Dam—Wicket Girders	6-20, Int.	1000	12	12	12	36	720
Emergency Dam—Gates	6-20, Int.	1000	12	12	12	36	720
Emergency Dam—Wedges	1-25, Int.	1100	2	2	2	6	150
Miter Gate—Moving	1-25, Int.	1100	40	24	28	92	2,300
Miter Gate—Handrail	1-7, Int.	170	36	20	24	80	560
Miter Gate—Pump (Vertical)	1-8, Int.	50	40	24	28	92	552
Miter Forcing	1-7, Int.	170	20	12	14	46	332
Fender Chain—Operating (Hor.) Pump	1-70, Int.	800	16	16	16	48	3,360
Fender Chain—Valve Motor	1-¼, Int.		16	16	16	48	24
Fender Chain—Drainage (Ver.) Pump	1-6, Int.		16	16	16	48	288
Rising Stem Gate Valve	1-50, Int.	1200	56	24	36	116	5,800
Cylindrical Valve	1-7, Int.	170	60	20	40	120	840
Guard Valves—Side Walls	1-25, Int.	1100	6	6	6	18	450
Auxiliary Culvert Valve	1-7, Int.	170	4	4	4	12	84
Pump—Drainage	1-11, Int.	120	3	3	3	9	99
Pump—Culvert	1-125, C	1800	1	1	1	3	375
Pump—Portable	1-9, C		3	2	2	7	63
Pump—Tunnel	1-15, C		3	2	3	8	120
Spillway—Gate Motor	1-7, Int.	170	14		8	22	154
Spillway—Cwt. Pit Pump	1-23, Int.		2		1	3	9
Total			430	252	340	1022	28,390

C—Continuous rating at 40° rise.

Int.—Intermittent rating; 1 hr, at 65° rise.

zation it became feasible so to confine the movements of the operator, by interlocking of switches, that no damage would result by mistakes in manipulations of the control switches. In order that the description of the control system may be followed readily, it is desirable that the functions of the various machines be set forth.

Water for filling and emptying the locks is conducted through three culverts, one in the middle wall and one in each side wall. The flow of water in these culverts is controlled by rising-stem valves. These are located in the culverts at points opposite each end of each lock, so that the culvert can be shut off at any desired point, in order to fill a lock with water from above, or upstream, or to empty it by allowing the water to flow out and down to the next lock. Lateral culverts conduct the water from the main culverts, under the lock chambers, and up through openings in the lock floors. Since there are intermediate mitering lock gates for use in locking through short vessels, when the use of a whole lock of 1000 feet would be wasteful of water, rising-stem valves are also located in the side-wall culverts at points near these intermediate gates. The rising-stem valves are installed in pairs, that is, the culvert is divided into two parallel halves at each valve by a vertical wall, and a valve is placed in each half. In addition to these pairs of valves in parallel, each pair is duplicated at each change of level from one lock to the next. Thus, if the valves cannot be closed at any point on account of an obstruction in the culvert or accident to the machinery, the duplicate pair can be closed. At the upper ends of the culverts at the side walls, the duplication is accomplished by three valves in parallel, called the guard valves.

The culvert in the middle wall must serve the locks on both sides, and to control this feature cylindrical valves are placed in the lateral culverts that branch out on each side. There are ten of these on each side of the culvert at each lock. At the upper end of each upper lock there are two valves in the side wall for regulating the height of water between the upper gate and the upper guard gate. These valves are called the auxiliary culvert valves.

The mitering gates are opened and closed by a separate

motor for each leaf, and the two leaves, when closed in mitered position, are locked together at the top by the miter-forcing machine. Heavy chain fenders are stretched across the locks in front of all miter gates which can be exposed to the upper level, and also in front of the guard gates at the lower end. Lowering the chain for the legitimate passage of a vessel, and raising it again after the vessel has passed, are under the control of the operator at the control house, and each operation of raising or lowering involves the control of two motors, viz., the starting of a large motor driving the main pump supplying water under pressure, and the control of a motor-operated valve, which in turn controls the direction of movement of the chain. These two operations are combined in one, for the remote control. Each motor is stopped automatically by a limit switch when it has performed its function.

There are motors which are not controlled from the control houses, and their uses should be described briefly before proceeding. One class of these is the hand-rail motors. On the top of all mitering gates a foot-walk with hand-rails is provided. When the gates are opened and in the recesses provided for them in the lock walls, these hand-rails would interfere with the passing of the towing locomotive, except in the case of the lower guard gates. The hand-rails are therefore made to be raised and lowered. This is done by a motor under the foot-walk, controlled from the lock wall. Near the approach to each foot-walk a controller is located in the lock wall flush with the surface, this controller being operated by a foot push. If the gates are closed and the hand-rails are down and a person desires to cross on the gates, he presses the foot push and the hand-rails are raised by their motors. This is true not only of the hand-rails on the nearer gate leaf, but of the hand-rails on the farther leaf as well. After passing across, one can, if desired, press the foot push on the other side and both hand-rails will be lowered. Or, if the hand-rails are up and the gates are opened by the operator in the control house, they will be automatically lowered so as to be out of the way when the gate is in the recess. When the gates are again closed, the hand-rails will automatically rise again, if the foot controller has been left in the position to raise them. The control of the hand-rails is accomplished by means of the foot controller, a contactor panel in the machinery chamber in the lock wall and another switch geared to the gate-moving machinery, which operates the control circuit to produce the automatic lowering and raising when the gates are opened or closed. This geared switch also provides that the hand-rails cannot be raised when the gates are open and that no harm results if the foot switch is operated while the gates are in the open position.

Control House.

The control house is located on the middle wall at the lower end of the upper lock, giving a view of the upper locks upstream from the control house, and a view of the lower locks, if any, in a down-stream direction.

Contactor Panels.

The motors are started and controlled by contactor panels located near them. The contactors carry the main motor currents. These contactors are controlled from the control house. The smaller motors, including those for cylindrical valves, auxiliary culvert valves and miter forcing, are started by being thrown directly on the line. Two double-pole contactors are used, one for forward and one for reverse. In the case of larger motors for miter-gate moving, rising-stem valves and guard valves, a starting point with resistance in two legs of the three-phase circuit is provided. In all cases the contactors are operated from the control house by three wires, one for forward, one for reverse and a common return. In the case of panels having a starting point, the period during which the motor remains on the resistance is automatically controlled by a dashpot, so that the starting operation at the control house is the same,—simply energizing a forward or reverse wire as the case may be.

Indicators are used for all machines to show the operator in the control house the position of each machine at all times. In the case of certain machines, the operation of a motor lasts only a few seconds, and the indication of the position of the machine is given by the simple means of red and green lights. Such machines are the cylindrical valves, auxiliary culvert valves, and miter-forcing machines. It is never expected, in normal operation, to stop these machines at any intermediate

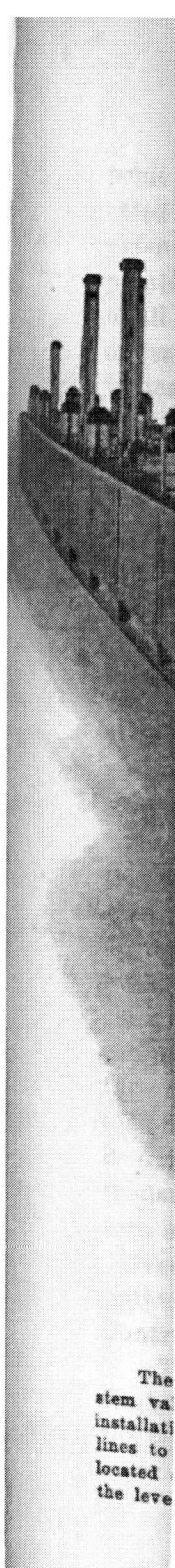

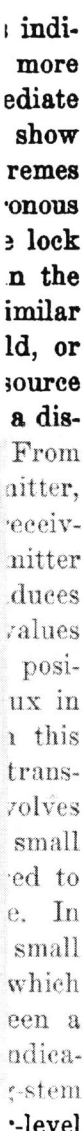

indi-
more
ediate
show
remes
onous
lock
n the
imilar
ld, or
source
a dis-
From
nitter,
eceiv-
nitter
duces
values
posi-
ux in
this
trans-
volves
small
ed to
In
small
which
een a
ndica-
stem
-level

type.
ngths

The
stem va
installati
lines to
located
the leve

hand-r
contact
anothe
operat·
and ra
switch
the ga·
is oper
Contro
Tl
lower
upstre;
if any,
Contac
Tl
locatec
rents.
The sn
iliary
throwi
used, ·
larger
guard
the th1
are op·
ward,
panels
motor
a dash
the sa1
case m
In
in the
In the
only a
machii
Such
valves.
norma·

point in their travel, and only the completed operation is indicated by the red and green lights. For machines of more extended operation, which may be stopped at intermediate points of travel, synchronous indicators are used, which show at all times the position of the machine, whether in the extremes of travel or at an intermediate point. A complete synchronous indicator consists of a transmitter at the machine in the lock wall, and a receiver, or indicator, at the switchboard in the control house. An indicator and a receiver are exactly similar and each consists essentially of a revolving bipolar field, or rotor, supplied with alternating current from the same source of excitation. Surrounding each rotor is a stator, having a distributed winding similar to that of an induction motor. From three equidistant points of this winding on the transmitter, leads run to three similar points on the winding of the receivers. The alternating current in the rotor of the transmitter (which may be considered stationary for the present) induces currents in the three wires from the stator, the relative values of these currents in the three wires depending upon the position of the field. These currents produce a magnetic flux in the receiver, which draws its rotor (free to revolve in this case) into the same angular position as the field of the transmitter. Thus, as the transmitter revolves, the receiver revolves with it, keeping the same angular position with a very small error. In the case of the transmitter, the rotor is geared to the machine the position of which it is desired to indicate. In the case of the receiver the rotor is geared to a pointer, or small model of the machine, or to some other indicating device, which it drives. This is the only important difference between a transmitter and a receiver, or indicator. Synchronous indicators are provided for miter-gate moving machines, rising-stem valves, guard valves, fender chains, and for water-level indication.

Control Boards.

The control boards are of a flat-top bench-board type. Each board is 32 inches high by 64 inches wide. The lengths for the three different boards are as follows:

Gatun	64 feet
Pedro Miguel	36 feet
Miraflores	52 feet

Fig. 23. Control Board for Miraflores Locks.

The interlocking bars shown above are connected to their respective switches and interlocked in such a manner that certain manipulations of the switches which might cause damage can not be accomplished. There is ample room for inspection, and the operating board is located on the floor directly above.

The control board for Miraflores locks is shown in Fig. 22 and the interlocking racks in Fig. 23. The handles of the various control switches are above the surface of each board, while the switch, which is of a rotary type, has its contacts beneath the board, shown in Fig. 24, and is wired from below. In a similar manner, the indicators are mounted with the greater part of their mechanism beneath the board, but with the scales and pointers above the board. The visible portions of

Fig. 24.   Control Switch and Interlock Mechanism.
The switch is of the rotary type having notched positions of "open", "closed" and "off". The interlock bars are actuated by the bell cranks.

these indicators are of different forms in order best to indicate their respective machines. (See Figs. 25 to 34 inclusive.) The miter-gate index (Figs. 25 and 26), is nearly flush with the board, and consists of a pointer swinging in a horizontal plane, and resembling the plan view of a miter-gate leaf. All these switches and indicators are located as nearly as possible in the relative positions occupied by the machines to which they apply. While the board is essentially a control board with indicators, it is made to resemble, in a measure, a plan view of the locks.

The space immediately below the flat top of the board is occupied by the switch contacts, indicator motors, and connections. Vertical shafts, operated by connecting rods from the control-switch shafts, extend downward past the electrical parts for the operation of the interlocks, as shown in Fig. 24. These interlocks are in two vertical racks, shown in Fig. 23, under each edge of the board and some distance below, so that they may be inspected and oiled from a floor which is about seven feet below the floor on which the switchboard stands. The latter floor does not extend across under the board, this space being open so that all parts on the underside of the board are accessible from the floor below. The numerous cables to the control switches and indicators also come to the board from below. Connection boards are provided for the cables, which are led up to them from each side, as are buses for supplying current to the control switches, indicators and the lamps that illuminate the dials of indicators. The indicators, transmitters and lamps are operated on 25 cycles, at 110 volts, while the control switches are designed for 220 volts. A typical wiring diagram is shown in Fig. 35. The control switchboard for the exterior illumination is shown in Fig. 36.

In general the two interlock racks contain the necessary interlocks for the switches on their respective sides of the center line of the board; but where interlocking is required between switches on different sides, it is accomplished by the aid of cross connecting rods and cranks.

Interlocking of Fender Chains and Miter Gates.

The fender chains are operated from each end by independent machines. The control of each end is interlocked with the control of the miter-gate leaf on its side of the lock, so that the chain cannot be lowered until the control switch of the miter-gate leaf has been thrown to the opening position. The miter-gate cannot be closed again until the control of the fender chain has been thrown to the raising position. In this way the assurance is obtained that the fender chain will always be in the up position to protect the gate when the gate is closed. In order to

Fig. 25. Miter Gate Index.

The Index moves in synchronism with the transmitter geared to the main machine. See also Fig. 26 for elevation of the index.

Fig. 26. Miter Gate Index.

See also Fig. 25 showing the index in plan.

Fig. 27. Miter Gate Transmitter Cover Removed.

The vertical shaft of the transmitter is actuated by a gear on the shaft of the miter gate machine passing through the bulkhead. The rack, moved by the threaded shaft, revolves the rotor which in turn moves the rotor of the index shown in Fig. 25.

avoid unnecessary complication, each end of the chain is not interlocked with both gate leaves, but with the leaf on its side of the lock only. As a rule both leaves of a miter gate, as well

Fig. 28. Chain Fender Index.

The chain of the index drops into a slot in the marble representing the lock chamber. The vertical projections likewise disappear in the slot when the chain in the lock is in its final position.

Fig. 29. Chain Fender Transmitter.

The rotor of the transmitter is revolved by a pinion and rack, the latter is actuated by a revolving screw which in turn is geared to the main shaft of the chain fender machine. Between each transmitter and index the electrical connections consist of five conductors in a lead sheathed cable.

Fig. 30. Rising Stem Valve Index.

The rising-stem valves are installed in pairs. The index consists of a cage with a reflector at the bottom shown in the right hand index, which throws the light flux on ground glass thus showing the position of the valve by an illuminated surface.

Fig. 31. Rising Stem Valve Transmitter.

The transmitter is operated by a gear secured to the main shaft of the valve machine which in turn drives the rotor through a rack and pinion.

as both ends of a fender chain, will be operated simultaneously, and further interlocking is unnecessary.

Interlocking of Miter Gates and Miter-Forcing Machine.

Each leaf of a miter gate is interlocked with the miter-forcing machine, which locks the leaves together at the top when in the closed position. This interlock is arranged so that the operator must unlock the miter-forcing machine before

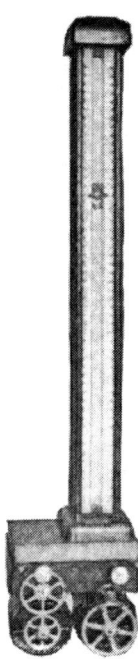

Fig. 32. Water Level Indicator.

The water-level index is equipped with two pointers, one of which is actuated by a rotor revolving through an angle of 178 degrees and the second pointer is actuated by a rotor making ten complete revolutions for the full scale. The accuracy of the water level is shown to within one twentieth of a foot through a maximum range of fifty feet.

he opens the gate. Also, the miter-forcing machine cannot be closed until the gates are closed. An electrical interlock is also provided in this case, requiring the gates to be fully closed before the miter-forcing machine can be started in the closing direction, inasmuch as it is important that the first operation be completed before the next operation starts.

Rising-Stem Valves Interlocked with Each Other.

Consider, for example, a side-wall culvert at Gatun with its principal rising-stem valves at each change of level from

Fig. 33. Water Level Transmitter.

The transmitter is operated by a large float attached to a bronze ribbon perforated to engage pegs in the rim of the driving wheel. A counterweight is attached to the other end of the bronze ribbon to insure proper engagement of ribbon and wheel. The assembly is shown in Fig. 34.

Fig. 34. Assembly of Water Level Transmitter.

one lock to the next. The control of these valves is interlocked so that if the valves are opened at one particular point,
the valves a lock length upstream or downstream cannot be
opened. Thus, the operator is limited to equalizing the water
between locks and cannot allow water to flow from the upper
lock past the middle lock into the lower lock, which operation,
if permitted, might flood the lower lock walls and machinery
chambers in them. All rising-stem valves occur in pairs side
by side, each member of a pair controlling half the opening of
the culvert. They may, therefore, be referred to as pairs. At

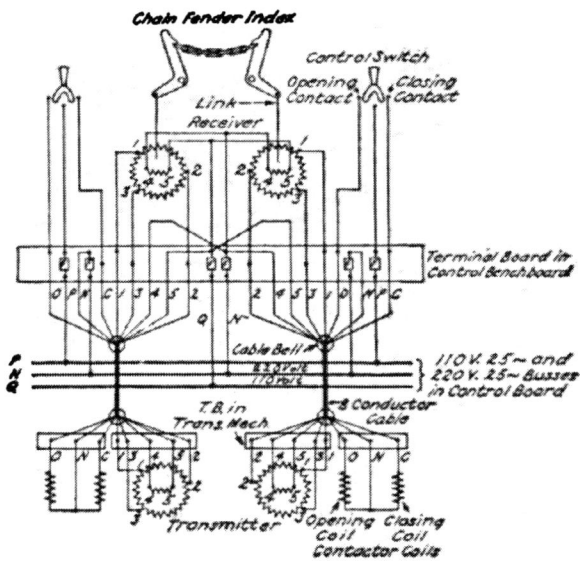

Fig. 35. Wiring for Control Switch and Position Indicators.

This shows the wiring diagram for the chain fender indicators and control
switches. This wiring is typical for all position indicators.

all points where there is a change of level from one lock to
the next, these pairs of valves are further duplicated by a
pair in series a short distance away. In regular operation one
pair can be left open as a guard pair, and the other pair will
control the flow of water. Each of the four valves of such a
group has independent control. Their control switches are
interlocked so that either pair may be opened and left open as
guard valves, and the interlocks become effective when the

operator tries to open the first valve of the second pair. Either pair may be opened first, at the choice of the operator. This effect is produced by a system of equalizing levers acting against the ends of the interlock bars, with a certain definite amount of lost motion, which is taken up on opening the first pair of valves, thus putting the interlocks in operation on the next pair.

At the upper end of each lock, three guard valves take the place of the duplicate rising-stem valves. These perform service

Fig. 36. Control Board for Exterior Lighting of Locks. Installed in the Central Control House at Each Lock.

exactly similar to the rising-stem valves, and are similarly interlocked, except that three valves in parallel in this case must conform to the same laws as the two in parallel in the other cases. If necessary to clear the interlocks at one pair of valves, in order to open another pair a lock length away, both members of the pair must be closed to accomplish it, and all three must be closed in the case of the guard valves. The same inter-

locking is effected between the successive valves of the middle
wall culverts as between those of the side wall.

Rising-Stem Valves, "Diagonal" Interlocking.

By diagonal interlocking is meant that interlocking which
is done between the rising-stem valves of the side wall and
those of the middle wall a lock length away. The result is interlocking between valves diagonally across a lock when the
cylindrical valves are open, this being needed to prevent the
flow of water from, say, the upper lock by way of a side-wall
culvert to the middle lock, thence by way of the middle-wall
culvert to the lower lock, thus allowing an operator through
carelessness to flood the lower lock walls. If the cylindrical
valves of a certain lock are closed, then this interlock is not
needed on rising-stem valves of that lock; and furthermore, its
existence would interfere with the proper use of the valves of
its twin lock on the other side of the middle wall. For this
reason this interlock is automatically removed when all ten
cylindrical valves are closed on the particular lock in question,
and is automatically applied again if one or more of the ten
cylindrical valves are opened.

Rising-Stem Valves Interlocked With Cylindrical Valves.

In the use of the middle-wall culvert, the cylindrical valves
on one side or the other must be opened before the rising-stem
valves can be opened, and the rising-stem valves must be closed
first. This interlock is applied in order to require the operator
to control the flow of water by means of the rising-stem valves.
The cylindrical valves perform a complete operation of opening
and closing in about ten seconds, and their use in regulating
the flows might cause dangerous surging. Here, as in all other
cases of interlocking on rising-stem valves, one pair of duplicates may be left open as guard valves, the other pair used as
operating valves being subject to interlocking.

The locks in most cases are divided into two parts by the
intermediate miter gates. This arrangement divides the ten
cylindrical valves into two groups of seven and three, respectively, for the long and short lengths. A selecting lever is provided for the foregoing interlocks, which may be set on
"three", "seven" or "ten", respectively, whereupon the corresponding valves are subject to that interlock, and the others

of the group of ten are locked closed if three or seven only are to be used. The failure of the operator to make his selection properly in advance will only cause him the trouble of going back and doing so, as the remaining valves are locked closed.

Interlocks on Cylindrical Valves.

The groups of cylindrical valves on opposite sides of the middle-wall culvert are interlocked with each other, so that if any valves are opened on one side, all must be closed on the other. This is to prevent careless cross filling between the locks, which operation might be combined with the regular method and produce flooding. However, there may be times when it is desirable to employ cross filling, to economize in the use of water from Lake Gatun during the dry season. For this reason, this interlock is made removable by the use of a lock and key. The key will be placed in the hands of the chief operator.

Interlocking of Rising-Stem Valves of Side Wall and Miter-Forcing Machine.

Interlocks are placed on the control switches of these machines, so that the rising-stem valves of the side wall, next above or below a miter gate, must be closed, while the miter-forcing machine is open. As the miter-forcing machine cannot be closed until the gates are closed, this means that the valves, either above or below the gate, must remain closed until the gate itself is closed, thus preventing the operator from creating a current of water around the gates while they are open, or being moved in opening or closing. This interlock is not included on the middle-wall valves, for the reason that they will be used with the locks on either side and must be free for that purpose. Furthermore, the valves of the side wall immediately at the gate which is being moved will be open to equalize water level, and the diagonal interlocking previously described will prevent the opening of the middle-wall valves a lock length above or below the gate being moved. This interlock between valves and miter-forcing machine is included on the intermediate gates, but is removable by means of a lock and key, because during the passage of large ships these gates must be left open and the valves operated independently of them. This interlock is not applied to the miter-forcing machine of the lower guard gates, for the reason that these gates open toward the sea.

There are intermediate rising-stem valves in the side walls at each intermediate gate, but no interlocks are applied to these, for the reason that they will be used in a more or less irregular manner, and no fixed laws for their operation can be laid down in advance. Moreover, they do not control the water between different lock levels, but only between different sections of the same lock, and there is not the danger from mistakes in operation as exists in the case of the other valves between lock levels. The same is true of the small auxiliary culvert valves, by means of which the water level in the space between the upper guard gate and upper main gate is regulated.

Water-Level Indicator.

The water-level indicator has an important bearing on the time in which the lockage of a ship may be accomplished, since the rate of filling or emptying the lock may be observed on the indicator. When the water levels between the two locks are very nearly equalized, the rate of change is slow; it is therefore very important for expeditious lockage that the lock gates be operated just as the water levels above and below the pair of gates are equal. The water level indicators will show these levels to an accuracy of one-twentieth of a foot.

Local Control.

The control connections are arranged in such a manner that each individual machine may be controlled locally. This arrangement provides for emergency operation, should the control circuits from the control house be out of order.

The local control was used on September 26th when the first vessel, the tug "Gatun", was passed through the locks at Gatun from the Atlantic Ocean to Gatun Lake, and on the following day on its return trip.

THE RECONSTRUCTION OF THE PANAMA RAILROAD.

By

FREDERICK MEARS, M. Am. Soc. C. E.
Formerly Chief Engineer, Panama R. R.
Member Alaska Engineering Commission
Washington, D. C., U. S. A.

INTRODUCTION.

The first attempt to establish a means of land transportation across the Isthmus of Panama was made early in the sixteenth century. The effort culminated in the construction of the stone-paved mule trail called the "Royal Road", which connected the settlement of Nombre de Dios and the Atlantic fortress of Porto Bello with old Panama, a thriving seaport on the Bay of Panama. It was completed in 1533 and used for many years. In 1536 an easier route was followed by traveling up the Chagres River to Cruces, thence over the trail to Panama.

In 1847 a French syndicate succeeded in obtaining a concession from the Government of New Granada to construct a railroad across the Isthmus of Panama. The project failed, due to the lack of the necessary funds, and the concession became void the following year. The finding of gold in California in 1848 furnished the incentive to three Americans to secure a similar concession with a view of meeting the increased traffic resulting from this discovery. This concession was exclusive, and covered means of transit across the Isthmus, whether by canal, railroad or highway.

It is not the purpose of this paper to dwell upon the early history of the Panama Railroad; suffice it to say that the new American company was organized in 1850, and, after overcoming almost insurmountable difficulties in the construction of the railroad through the dense swampy jungle and in the unhealthy climate, completed the line from ocean to ocean in 1855, antedating by fourteen years the first transcontinental railroad in the United States. The new railroad paralleled the trail of the old Spanish mule trains, and for many years did a very lucrative business. Instead of carrying golden treasure and adventure seekers, it transferred hardy pioneers and many thousand tons of manufactured goods from ocean to ocean. The railroad company later expanded and acquired a steamship line on either coast. The line on the Pacific side was soon abandoned; the eastern line continues to this day.

When the French Canal Company commenced operations on the Isthmus in 1879, they first made traffic arrangements with the Panama Railroad, and later acquired a controlling interest in the Company in order to operate the road to their advantage, and to extinguish its exclusive concession. They purchased 68,-887 shares of the 70,000 shares of stock, at $291.00 per share, and in 1883 assumed charge of the road. During the period of French control, several diversions of the railroad were made necessary in order to remove it from the prism of the Canal, the most notable of which was the change of line in the vicinity of the Culebra Cut at Rio Grande, accomplished, in 1899, at a cost of $212,873.00.

Panama Railroad Acquired by United States Government.

The United States took over the Panama Railroad, in 1904, when it acquired the property and assets of the French Canal Company, and purchased the few outstanding shares of railroad stock from private holders. It secured the steamship branch of the service at the same time.

The shipment of materials and supplies incident to the construction of the Canal, and the movement of spoil trains hauling canal excavation from Culebra Cut to the waste banks established along the old line of the railroad, greatly increased the tonnage, and made necessary the rehabilitating of the road. The Panama Railroad was handling a freight traffic of about 17,000,000 ton miles in 1904; this figure rose to 42,000,000 in 1906-7; to 150,000,000 in 1907-8; to 280,000,000 in 1908-9 and to 300,000,000 in 1909-10. The tonnage gradually declined after 1910, as the excavation from Culebra Cut was diverted to the spoil banks along the new high-level line, but it continued heavy enough to tax to the utmost the capacity of the railroad in its various transitory stages.

Rehabilitating the Old Panama Railroad.

The American canal authorities decided early to make use of the Panama Railroad as an adjunct to the Canal. Steps were immediately taken to rebuild the old railroad, in order to make it adequate for the new demands. It was found necessary to double-track the road for 37 miles of its length, to accommodate the movement of spoil trains, construction trains, and local railroad business. The old roadbed, 47.7 miles long, laid with small hardwood ties and light 56-lb. rail, was relaid with larger ties and heavier rail; weak bridges were strengthened and proper sidings were provided.

Two distinct processes were passed through in changing from the original Panama Railroad, as it existed in 1904, to the final permanent line, constructed above the levels of the artificial lakes. The first process was the rehabilitation and double-tracking of the old line, to furnish the Isthmian Canal Commission with a suitable means of handling their tonnage. The second was the construction of an entirely new railroad, built in a different location and on a higher level. The first work was no less necessary and important than the second—it was a step in the final direction. While the expense involved in the first work was insignificant compared to the final task, still it was carried on under great difficulties of commercial traffic congestion, poor equipment, inadequate side tracks and interference by Canal spoil trains. It was completed by the end of the fiscal year 1907 (June, 1907), at a cost of $1,123,477.93.

In building for the second track, advantage was taken of the large amount of spoil available from the Culebra Cut by utilizing that material to widen the existing fills sufficiently to carry another track. A few steam-shovels were employed to widen the larger cuts; but to avoid delay to traffic, old French Decauville cars (one-third cubic yard capacity) were used in most cases, the grading being done by hand.

The lack of adequate house tracks, passing tracks and storage yards on the old line necessitated the construction of sixteen house tracks and commissary tracks with a total length of 17,100 feet, 8 passing sidings having a total length of 12,300 feet, and 64,500 lineal feet of yard track at the ocean terminals. The old, small shed depots were altogether inadequate to handle the increased business, and twelve new passenger and freight depots were built at the most important points, and five were remodeled.

Due to the numerous openings required in passing through a section of country like the Chagres Valley, the new bridges of the second main track were quite an item of expense. Cooper's E-50 loading was adaptable to the maximum train load, and all bridges were built to that standard. The old main-line bridges consisted mainly of iron or steel girders under 60 feet in length, supported on masonry abutments. These girders were strengthened by driving one or more pile bents under them to shorten the span. Pile bridges were used entirely in the second track.

The crossing of the Chagres River at Barbacoas was accomplished on a bridge 650 feet long, consisting of six iron through plate-girder spans. To avoid the expense of double-tracking, a gauntlet track was laid across this bridge, suitably protected by automatic signals. Three of the old spans over the river channel were replaced by new steel-girder spans, and the three remaining iron girders were strengthened by a complete new floor system and new intermediate steel bents built up from solid foundations.

The old Panama Railroad, in its remodeled condition, handled a heavy and important business up to the very day the rising waters of Gatun Lake encroached upon its roadbed, and the results obtained from the efficiency with which this traffic was handled fully warranted the expenditure involved in its rejuvenation.

The Necessity for the High-Level Line.

The reconstruction of the Panama Railroad on a high level was made necessary by the plans of the Isthmian Canal Commission for a lock type of canal. The definite decision, which abandoned the sea-level project and adopted the high-level canal, was not reached until June, 1906. Immediately after this date preparation was made to locate and build the new railroad.

The plans for the lock type of canal contemplated the creation of two large artificial lakes as a means of passing ships over the summit level. The large lake on the Atlantic side of the Isthmus was formed by the great dam at Gatun. This lake had an area of 164 square miles and its waters inundated the roadbed of the old track to a depth of from 15 to 70 feet, through the Chagres Valley section. The Miraflores Lake, on the Pacific slope, also covered the railroad tracks for several miles.

As the right of way of the old Panama Railroad crossed and recrossed the axis of the canal at several points between the terminals, it was necessary, in order to avoid these crossings, to place the new railroad entirely on the east side of the Canal.

The old line of the railroad was laid from Colon to Gatun, a distance of seven miles, over a soft marsh, very little above tidewater. At Gatun the Chagres River was reached at an elevation of fifteen feet above mean sea-level, and the old line practically followed the river on a water grade as far as Matachin, at which point it commenced to climb over the continental divide, finally dropping down the Pacific slope, through the valley of the Rio Grande, to Panama City. The old railroad found its way across the Isthmus after the manner of any line through a virgin country, by following the line of least resistance. There were no canal problems to be taken into consideration at the time of its construction. The grade line for more than half its length was laid close to the ground, and every advantage taken of natural support.

The new line presented an entirely different problem. The engineers were required to build a railroad on a high level, in the Gatun Lake region not less than ninety-two feet above the sea, and through a country which, for the greater part of its distance, was naturally very low. The Chagres River, at a point thirty miles from Colon, was only forty-six feet above sea-level, and the tributary valleys of this stream near Gatun were all much lower, being from ten to twenty feet above mean sea-level. In building the new railroad it was not only required to remove the line from interference with the Canal prism—it was required to build an entirely different type of railroad; one which, for half its length, would be washed by the waters of Gatun and Miraflores Lakes.

THE ORIGINAL LOCATION OF THE NEW RAILROAD.

The relocated line of the Panama Railroad turned off from the old line at a point called Mindi and made the climb to Gatun on a plus 1.25% compensated grade, southbound. It was necessary for the track to attain an elevation of 95 feet above mean sea-level when Gatun was reached, in order to place it safely above Gatun Lake at elevation plus 85.0 above mean sea-level.

Under original plans the new line crossed the low Gatun Valley, from Gatun to Tiger Hill, and found support on the hills and ridges east of the old main line. An elevation of not less than 92 feet above sea-level was maintained. The Chagres River makes a sharp bend to the east at Matachin, paralleling the continental divide, and the new line crossed the river at this point and entered the north end of Culebra Cut. It was first proposed to carry the new line through the Culebra Cut on a forty-foot berm, along the east side, to reach the town of Pedro Miguel. From this point the line gradually dropped to connect with the old track at a point two miles from Panama, passing through the Miraflores Ridge by a tunnel. It was necessary for the line on the Pacific slope to maintain an elevation sufficient to hold above the proposed Sosa Lake level (elevation 55.00) until the Diablo saddle was reached at a point about one mile southeast of Corozal. From this saddle the line dropped on a minus 0.75% southbound grade to the old line. As thus located, the new line was approximately 42 miles long.

Location parties were put into the field in July and August, 1906, under the direction of Mr. J. G. Sullivan, Assistant Chief Engineer of the Isthmian Canal Commission, and the preliminary location was completed in March, 1907.

The old Panama Railroad was of five-foot gauge, single track originally, but later partially double track, to accommodate Canal work. The new Panama Railroad was located for single track, and the five-foot gauge of the old line was maintained. Decision was later made in 1913 to operate double track from Pedro Miguel to Panama, a distance of seven miles, during the period of Canal work; this section of double track will probably be retained indefinitely.

PRELIMINARY CONSTRUCTION.

The preliminary location surveys were made by forces of the Isthmian Canal Commission under Mr. John F. Stevens, Chief Engineer. In May, 1907, the construction of the relocated line was turned over to the Panama Railroad under the direction of Mr. W. G. Bierd, General Manager, with Mr. Ralph Budd, Chief Engineer, in charge of the construction. Mr. Budd continued in charge of the work until his departure from the

Fig. 1. The New Steel Bridge at Gamboa to Carry Permanent Railroad over the Chagres River. Erected in 1908 by Panama Railroad Co.

Isthmus in August, 1909, when Colonel George W. Goethals assumed its direction in his capacity as President of the Panama Railroad, and the writer was appointed to succeed Mr. Budd.

Construction was confined, during the first year, to those sections which would aid Canal plans, as follows:

1.   From Mindi to Tiger Hill, a distance of five miles.

Work on the Mindi-Tiger Hill section started in May, 1907, and consisted in building the permanent line from Mindi to Gatun, and a temporary line from Gatun to Tiger Hill, to reestablish connection with the old line at the latter point. This section of the new line was required immediately, in order that the old railroad track, which occupied a portion of the site for the Gatun Dam, might be removed from the sphere of Canal operations.

2. The permanent steel bridge over the Chagres River at Gamboa.

The steel bridge at Gamboa crosses the Chagres River at the north end of Culebra Cut, close to the site of the bridge erected by the French Canal Company. (See Figure 1.) The normal river channel at this point was about 175 feet in width; but to accommodate the excessive flood discharge of this stream, and to provide an unobstructed opening for the proposed arm of Gatun Lake, which would flood the Chagres River Valley for a distance of nine miles above the crossing, it was necessary to build a bridge 1325 feet in length. The bridge consists of one 200-foot through riveted truss of the Warren type, and thirteen 80-foot through plate-girder spans, supported by reinforced-concrete piers and abutments. It was completed in 1908, at a cost of $225,547.46.

3. Four miles of line north of Gamboa Bridge, to open dump grounds to dispose of spoil from Culebra Cut.

Immediately north of the Gamboa Bridge, the new line crossed several large valleys tributary to the Chagres River, which afforded space for many cubic yards of spoil, and their close proximity to the Culebra Cut made them advantageous dumping grounds for this material. A steam shovel and pile driver were taken across the Chagres River on temporary track and started to work before the completion of the bridge. By the time the bridge was ready for traffic, a large part of this section had been completed.

4. The Pedro Miguel-Corozal section of the line.

The work on the Pedro Miguel-Corozal section of the line consisted in the construction of two large, reinforced-concrete, arched culverts, 22 by 24 feet, one at the Pedro Miguel River and the other at the Caimitillo River; the Miraflores Tunnel and approaches; and the grading on the 65-foot level near Corozal. The culverts were built in order to make it possible to utilize Canal spoil in building the embankments between Pedro Miguel and Miraflores.

THE REVISED LOCATION.

Change in Location of Locks at the Pacific End of Canal.

Several changes in the location of the new railroad became necessary during the early period of construction. In December, 1907, the plans of the Isthmian Canal Commission for a lock and dam site near Sosa Hill on the Pacific slope were changed, and for military and engineering reasons the locks were moved inland and located at Miraflores Ridge. This change made the continuation of the line on a 65-foot level beyond Miraflores Lake unnecessary. A new location was made from Miraflores on a gradient dropping 24 feet to the mile, southbound, which permitted of a connection being made with the old main line at Corozal. This resulted in a saving of two miles in the length of the line, although, unfortunately, a large amount of work had already been accomplished under the former plan.

Abandonment of the Gatun-Tiger Hill Line.

In the preliminary soundings and borings which were made to determine what foundation existed under the swampy bottom of the Gatun Valley, and in the progress of the work on a large embankment in the immediate vicinity of Gatun Ridge (Mile 7), it became apparent that the construction of a one and a half mile long embankment from Gatun to Tiger Hill, as originally contemplated, would involve serious difficulties. An exhaustive study was made of this valley, and diamond drill borings were made at close intervals throughout the area of the proposed base of the fill. These investigations showed that the underlying strata in the Gatun River Valley consisted of a top layer of from 20 to 25 feet of fairly solid clay and sand, over alternating layers of very soft clay, decomposed wood, sand and silt, while bed-rock was from 150 to 225 feet below the general level of the ground. (See Plate I.) The elevation of this ground was from 8 to 10 feet above mean sea-level, and to build an embankment with the top but seven feet above the normal lake level would require a center height of 84 feet, a top width of 40 feet, side slopes of 1 on 2, and a total yardage of 4,250,000 cubic yards.

It was early demonstrated, by the difficulty encountered

in building the large embankment in Mile 7 (see Fig. 2), that the soft underlying strata would not permit the placing of a pressure of three or more tons to the square foot on the ground, without failure in the foundation, settlement of the filled-in material, and upheaval in the natural ground beyond the slope. It required that the supporting area be enlarged by extending the sides to a 1 on 4 or 1 on 5 slope, thereby reducing the weight per square foot of base and counteracting the tendency to "push up" beyond the base of the fill.

Fig. 2.   Large Embankment at Mile 7, Built in Three Levels.

Experience gained later in the actual construction of the immense embankments in the upper Gatun Valley, referred to in the latter part of this paper, proved conclusively that the embankment across the lower valley could never have been constructed with slopes less than 1 on 5, which would have involved handling material to the amount of 9,300,000 cubic yards. There were two other embankments on the line in wide, deep valleys (one between Tiger Hill and Lion Hill, and the other at the south point of Lion Hill) the construction of which would have involved similar difficulties.

The Chief Engineer made a report, based upon the result of these investigations, advising against the construction of the Gatun-Tiger Hill Line, but inasmuch as it was imperative that the old tracks at the Gatun Dam be removed, in furtherance of Canal plans, it was decided to build a temporary line across the Gatun Valley on a low level to connect the high line at Gatun with the old line at Tiger Hill. A steel viaduct was designed and considered for this crossing, but the idea was abandoned on the theory that it would be inexpedient to maintain this steel structure, submerged for 75 feet of its height in the waters of Gatun Lake.

New Surveys.

In the early part of 1908, locating parties were put in the field to seek another crossing of the Gatun Valley. It was known, by reference to existing topographical maps, that a supported line, swinging up the Gatun Valley and crossing the river where the foothills approached the banks, would have involved an extra distance of from 20 to 25 miles, and would have placed the line far beyond the limit of the Canal Zone. Such a location was not considered practicable.

An upper crossing of the Gatun Valley, eliminating some of the objectionable features of the lower crossing and lying within the Canal Zone limits, was found about four and a half miles east of the first location, but this line joined the original location at Bohio, and an objectionable detour was left in the line by swinging back to Bohio in the manner described. By further efforts, a low saddle was developed in the Bohio Ridge about two miles east of the original location, and the engineers finally produced the line from the upper Gatun River crossing through this gap in the hills, with very good general alignment, and joined it with the original location near Frijoles. A further change was later made between Frijoles and San Pablo by moving the line back from the edge of the proposed lake into the hills, for the purpose of securing similar advantages in shallow valley crossings and general alignment. A project was considered, at this time, to run the new main line directly from the Colon Terminal Yard to connect with the revised location at Mile 11 (Quebrancha), which route would save about five miles in distance across the Isthmus. A final location for such a connection with the Atlantic terminal city was made, but the scheme was abandoned, as it required that Gatun be placed on a branch line, which was considered decidedly objectionable.

The line as finally located over the new route made up the distance lost by the four-mile detour to the east along Gatun Ridge by securing much better general alignment from the crossing of the Quebrancha Valley (Mile 11) to Caimito (Mile 26), a common point on the Chagres River, the revised location being 780 feet longer than the original location. (See map, accompanying Gen. Goethal's introductory paper, for revised location.)

CONSTRUCTION WORK ALONG THE ACCEPTED LINE.

The adopted location turned sharply to the east at Gatun and followed the 95-ft. contour along the south slope of the Gatun Ridge for four miles, then turned south and crossed the wide Gatun Valley. While the change to this upper crossing had lessened many of the difficulties encountered on the original line, it was still an exceedingly hard problem to build a high-level line across this low valley. After leaving solid support on the Gatun Ridge, the line crossed the valleys of the Quebrancha, the Brazos, the Baja, and the Gatun River, in the order named, in a total distance of three miles. The first three streams were tributary to the Gatun River. The hills intervening between their swampy bottom-lands may be likened to stepping-stones across a wide morass. The amount of material available from the main line cuts was insignificant compared to the amount required to build the embankment.

Advantage was taken of the existence of the old railroad to build spur tracks into the new line, to carry labor, equipment, material and supplies to the work. Important connecting tracks were built at Gatun, Frijoles, Barbacoas, Matachin, and Miraflores. A large force of men was employed during the years 1908 and 1909. The energy was principally applied to the effort to reach the large embankments in the upper Gatun Valley.

The track from Gatun (Mile 7) and from Frijoles (Mile 18) was gradually pushed ahead towards this section and the

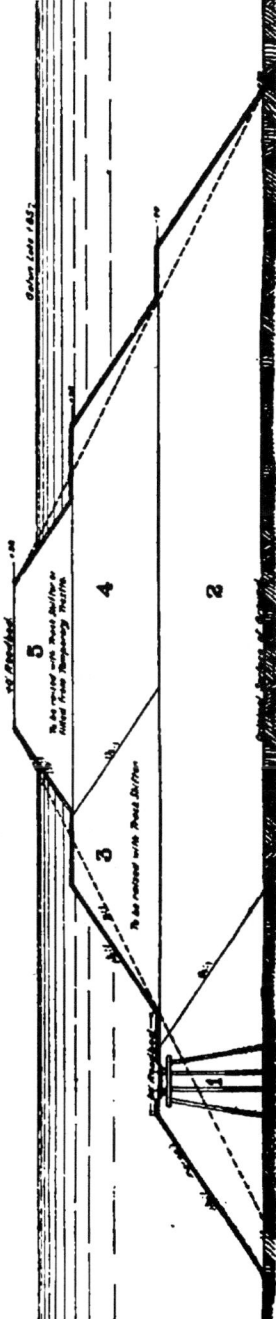

Fig. 3. Typical Section Showing Method of Making Quebrancha Embankment.

big valley was reached in January, 1910. Extensive diamond-drill borings had been taken over these swamps to determine the character of the ground. It was found that the material was closely allied to that found in the lower valley at Gatun. There were two points distinctly favorable, however: First, the floor of these swamps was at a higher elevation than was the case on the original line (the Quebrancha being at elevation plus 20.00 above mean sea-level, the Brazos at plus 35.0,

Fig. 4.   Relocation, Panama Railroad.   The Quebrancha Bottom, looking North.
Putting in First Deck of Fill to Elevation + 50.   June, 1910.

and the Baja at plus 15.0) ; and, second, bed-rock in all of the upper bottoms was found at a higher level.

It was decided to build the 1800-ft. fill over the Quebrancha Valley in three levels. A temporary trestle was driven at the east edge of the right of way at an elevation of plus 50.0 above mean sea-level (thirty feet above the natural ground) in such a manner that it would coincide with the slope of the completed fill. (See Figs. 3 and 4.)

The work proceeded in January and February of 1910

according to this scheme. The grade of the temporary construction track was raised 10 ft. when it was extended over the solid ground intervening between the Quebrancha and the Brazos, so that the temporary trestle over the latter valley was driven at an elevation of 60 above mean sea-level, the plan being to complete the Brazos embankment in two stages.

The temporary trestles over these swamps met on the 12th day of April, 1910, making track connection between Gatun and Frijoles. The efforts were then concentrated on the problem to "make the dirt fly". There were 5,000,000 cubic yards of material to be placed in these swampy valleys, three miles in extent, and formed into a permanent railroad embankment. The cry went out for heavy steam shovels, dump cars, and engines, and in a short space of time material excavated from nearby borrow pits was being placed in embankment at a rapid rate. The construction force went to work methodically to get the greatest output from each steam shovel, and to place the most yardage at the least cost. How successful they were can best be realized by reference to the monthly reports appearing in the Canal Records for that period, detailing the daily and monthly output obtained. The records of the world-famous Culebra Cut were equalled and surpassed, and one of these steam shovels, No. 257, operated by the same crew, broke all world's records, so far as known, by excavating a total of 714,777 cubic yards, place measurement, of which amount 678,079 cubic yards was solid rock, in twelve working months. This paper would not be complete if the writer at this juncture did not refer to Mr. H. P. Warren, Engineer of Construction, and to Mr. M. B. Connolly, Superintendent of Construction, who took the keenest interest in maintaining the high steam-shovel averages. Neither of these gentlemen would miss a night without securing the daily output of each steam shovel on the line and comparing it with other records, and if a steam shovel failed to make a good showing there was deep concern and immediate inquiry as to the reason why.

With this close attention to the problem of building the immense embankments, and while carrying on very heavy construction work at other parts of the line, the grade across the swampy Gatun River section was finally completed in January,

1912, but not without the most serious difficulties in the final stages. Plates 8 and 9 show the proposed sequence of operation in the construction of the Quebrancha embankment (Mile 11). The theoretical limits of the fill as originally planned are indicated by a broken line, enclosing a 40-ft. roadbed with a 1 on 2 slope. When the first deck, to elevation plus 50.0, was completed (areas 1 and 2, Fig. 3), the second deck was started at elevation plus 75.0. (See Fig. 5.) The trestle, which was

Fig. 5.   Relocation, Panama Railroad.   The Quebrancha Bottom, looking North. First Deck of Fill Completed.   Second-Deck Trestle Driven and Partly Filled. March, 1911.

used as falsework for placing this intermediate deck, was about three-quarters filled when a serious settlement occurred, accompanied by an upheaval of the natural ground beyond the toe of the slope. This movement indicated that it was necessary to spread the foundation further and counterweight the toe of the slope. By widening alternately on the lower level and filling on the intermediate level, the equilibrium of the higher mass was maintained, and the great fill was gradually brought to final grade. In this process the lower deck reached a slope of 1 on 5. The intermediate deck on the 75-foot level was filled in and widened out to a final slope before the attempt was made to raise the grade. In raising the grade, temporary false work was not used—the fill was brought up by raising the track on the center line to final grade at elevation plus 92.0. 1,000,000 cubic yards was placed in this fill. (See Fig. 6.)

The construction of the long embankment over the Brazos Valley (4800 feet long and containing 2,000,000 cubic yards)

Fig. 6. Relocation, Panama Railroad. The Quebrancha Bottom, looking North. June, 1911.

and the embankment over the Baja Valley (1500 feet long and containing 600,000 cubic yards) was handicapped by similar difficulties. In the Brazos Valley the elevation of the ground was plus 35.0 above mean sea-level and the first trestle was driven to elevation plus 60.0. (See Fig. 7.) The trestle was filled and the entire base of the embankment was placed, allowing for 1 on 2 side slope and a 40-ft. width of roadbed. A track was then laid on the center line at this 60-ft. level, and an effort was made to bring the embankment to final grade by raising

Fig. 7. Looking South over the Brazos Valley before Filling Mile 12. June, 1910.

Fig. 8. Relocation, Panama Railroad. The Brazos Bottom, looking North. First
Deck of Fill Nearly Completed.

the track on material hauled from nearby borrow-pits. (See Fig. 8.) A track shifter was used to very good advantage on this work. The dump track had nearly reached its final level when a serious settlement occurred. The upper mass dropped about 30 ft. and the movement was accompanied by the usual raising of the natural ground beyond the toe of the 1 on 2 slope, showing that the soft underlying strata had been displaced. A dump track was laid, on either side of the lower

Fig. 9.   Relocation of Panama Railroad.   The Brazos Bottom, looking North, June, 1912.

base, at elevation plus 60.0 and used to widen the base to a 1 on 3 slope before any more material was placed on the high level. The top was then raised to elevation plus 89.0 and widened to 40 ft., and allowed to stand at that level for about 18 months. (See Fig. 9.) At the end of that period the waters of the Gatun Lake had risen to within 10 feet of their final stage, submerging the slopes of the embankment on either side to a depth of 40 feet. It was assumed that the partially submerged embankment would weigh less than the dry fill and

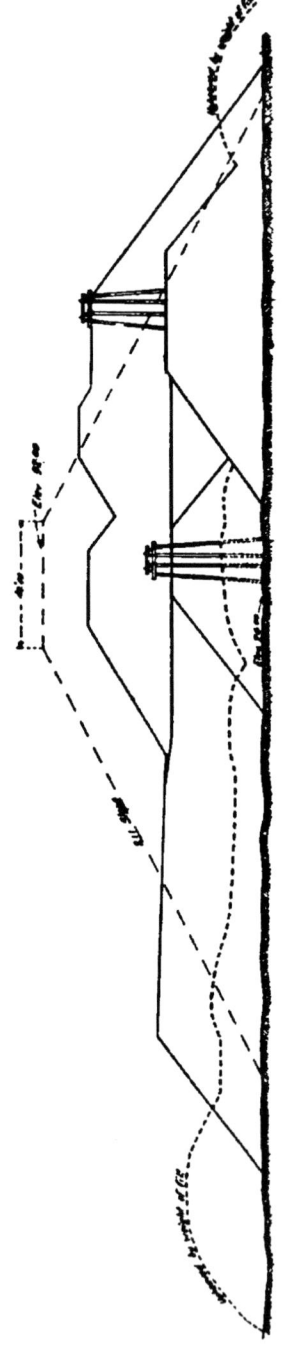

Fig. 10. Typical Cross-Section of Quebrada Baja Embankment.

that the pressure of the water along the edge of the fill would have a tendency to prevent the natural ground from raising up. Under this reasoning more weight was added to the top. The embankment was raised five feet (it having settled two feet in the 18-months' period), widened to the full 40-ft. width and was thoroughly rip-rapped with good rock along the slopes, to prevent wash by wave action, without any movement of the filled-in mass or settlement of its foundation.

Fig. 11. Relocation, Panama Railroad. The Quebrada Baja, looking North.
June, 1911.

Methods similar to those above described were employed in filling the Baja Valley, where like failure of the foundation was encountered. (Figs. 10, 11 and 12.) There was no failure in the foundation under the embankment across the Gatun River proper. A small slide occurred at the south end, near the bridge abutment, but this was due to the movement of the filled-in mass seeking equilibrium, and differed entirely from the foundation failures above referred to. (See Fig. 13.)

The question has been asked, why the large embankments in the upper Gatun Valley were not made from spoil secured

from Culebra Cut, instead of from borrow-pits. This matter
was given a good deal of thought at the time and it was considered that it would have been practically impossible to haul
sufficient material the necessary 20 or 25 miles within the time
limit given to complete the line; furthermore, actual experience
showed that this method would have been more expensive, as
the unit costs on the borrow-pit work in the Gatun Valley section were very low, in fact, material was put in place for about
the same figure it would have cost to haul it from Culebra Cut.

Fig. 12. Relocation, Panama Railroad. The Quebrada Baja, looking North.
February, 1915.

The excavation of the Culebra Cut was of supreme importance,
and, had the authorities attempted to haul this material to the
Gatun Valley section, over the single-track road, a serious
shortage in car equipment would have resulted.

It may also seem strange that solid rock was used to such
a large extent in this work. It may be said, in explanation,
that this was necessary in order to secure the amount of material needed. The engineers were forced to open their borrow-
pits in the immediate vicinity of the dumping ground, and all

of the hills in that section were of a formation of argillaceous sandstone with a shallow covering of clay. While the term "solid rock" has been used, it may be further stated, in explanation, that this sandstone was very easily drilled and cheaply handled. Its specific gravity was high. For long periods the field cost of excavating and placing this material averaged about 25c per cubic yard, which included all expenses of mining, excavating, hauling and placing.

Fig. 13. Relocation, Panama Railroad; Gatun Valley, looking South. First Deck of Fill to Elev. + 60 Completed. Trestle for Second Deck, Elev. + 92, under Construction. March, 1911.

Completing the Line.

In the limited space of this article, it was thought proper to refer more particularly to the unusual features of this railroad problem, exemplified by the building of the Gatun Valley embankments over the soft bottom lands. The railroad construction on the other sections of the line, while particularly heavy, due to the unusual elevation of the road and the mountainous country, did not present the problem that the valley section did. A glance at the table of quantities, page 39, will show the average amount of grading accomplished to June 30, 1912. It will be noted that approximately 16,000,000 cubic yards were handled, half of which was secured from Canal spoil.

There were a few small sections of the relocated line let out to private contractors on a unit-price basis, but the majority of the work was accomplished with the regular organization. Instead of doing everything by regular day labor, however, a system of "task work" was used, which resulted in securing greater efficiency out of the colored West Indian laborers. For ordinary work they were paid on a basis of ten cents for one hour's work; on railroad grading, they were paid on a basis of ten cents for each Decauville car (one-third to one-half cubic yard capacity), loaded in the cut and placed in the embankment. A tally was kept of the number of cars moved by each group of laborers, and recorded in the time-books. Under this system they performed two or three times as much work as they did on a straight hourly basis. The system corresponds somewhat to the ordinary station work, which is common in railroad grading. It was found that the West Indian laborers could not be induced to accept station work and be paid on a straight yardage basis, obtained by cross-sectioning the cut in place. They were not educated to this method of doing work, and all attempts so to educate them were failures. They insisted on being paid for each car of material moved, and they carefully kept their own record of the count.

The Miraflores Tunnel.

The Miraflores Tunnel pierced the Miraflores Ridge at an elevation of 65 ft. above mean sea-level. By June, 1908, the excavation of the tunnel bore had been practically completed, and timber lining had been placed throughout the entire length. The north 400 feet of this tunnel passed through solid rock, the south slope of which lay at an angle of 45 degrees. The excavation of the approach cut to the south portal so disturbed the equilibrium of the earth which formed the south face of the Miraflores Ridge that during July and August, 1908, the entire side-hill, stimulated by the action of the tropical rains, began moving southward along the axis of the tunnel, and also slightly eastward at an angle of 60 degrees from the direction of its axis. This carried the earth section of the tunnel with it, and literally twisted the tunnel to pieces. The timbering in the earth section, 200 feet long, collapsed in September. The rock section, 420 feet long, at the north end, was not affected, and was lined with concrete during September, October and November, 1908. Work was discontinued in the earth section until the beginning of the dry season, January 1, 1909, when the tunnel was again opened on the original center line and grade, and completed in April, 1909, at a total cost of $186,-736.37. The length of this tunnel was 636 feet from portal to portal, and the cross-section provided a width of 15 feet and a height of 21 feet 3 inches.

The Pedro Miguel-Corozal section of the line, including the Miraflores Tunnel, was formally turned over to the Panama Railroad for operation in November, 1911. The long section from Gatun to the Chagres River was turned over on February 15, 1912. These sections of the new line greatly facilitated traffic conditions on the Isthmus.

The Gold Hill Line.

It was contemplated by the accepted plans for the high-level canal, to pass the railroad through the Culebra Cut on the east berm, at a normal elevation of ten feet above the proposed water-level, but serious slides, which developed in the banks of the Canal through the Culebra Cut, caused the Chairman of the Isthmian Canal Commission to appoint a board of engineers to consider the question of removing the railroad to another location. The Board's report, approved by the Chairman, recommended that the permanent railroad be located outside the prism of Culebra Cut, and, accordingly, surveys were started in November, 1910, to seek a new route for the line.

By leaving the original location near the south end of the Chagres River bridge and climbing on a plus $1\frac{1}{4}\%$ grade, southbound, it was found possible to cross the continental divide at an elevation of plus 264.0 above mean sea-level. The line passed around the east side of Gold Hill to the upper Pedro Miguel River valley, which was followed generally in dropping down to join the old line at Pedro Miguel. Construction work was started on this diversion, $9\frac{1}{4}$ miles long, in January, 1911, and completed in May, 1912.

The necessity for leaving the Culebra Cut immediately at the bridge site, due to the serious slides which had developed in the banks of the Canal, forced the engineers to lay the line through a solid-rock ridge about one mile south of Gamboa Bridge, which required a very heavy and expensive cut. The crossing of the Agua Prieta Ridge at the summit, and the extremely heavy work encountered in the Pedro Miguel River valley, all tended to make this an expensive piece of line to construct.

While the work was very heavy, it involved no serious difficulties, except at a point near Paraiso, in the valley of the Pedro Miguel River, about three miles south of the continental divide. The river valley at this point is quite narrow, the stream being confined by precipitous sides. The angle of inclination of the underlying rock and the soft nature of the overlying clay and soil caused a serious earth-slide to develop, carrying the filled-in material with it to the far side of the Pedro Miguel River and partially damming up that stream. The attempt to construct the embankment over the original line was abandoned. By introducing more curvature, the line was benched in on the solid rock around this slide, which process involved moving about 300,000 cubic yards of additional material. Progress photographs illustrating the construction of the Gold Hill section are shown in Figs. 14 and 15.

The Gold Hill line was formally turned over to the Panama Railroad on May 25, 1912, and through trains from Colon to Panama commenced operation over this route in September, 1912.

Protecting the Submerged Slopes of Embankments.

In building the embankments throughout the line, several factors had to be taken into consideration. One of these was the possibility of failure in the supporting power of the natural ground, which has been previously described. Another was the tendency of the filled-in material to slide, *en masse*, due partially to the nature of some of the clay which it was necessary to handle, and partially to the effect of the intense rainfall in the wet season, the precipitation being in some months as high as 40 inches, with severe rains at times of from five to eight inches per hour. These disadvantageous tendencies were guarded against by

Fig. 14. Relocation, Panama Railroad, Gold Hill Line. Trestle Across Deep Valley Back of Paraiso, looking South. Highest Bent, 77 Feet. Yardage in Fill, 230,000 Cu. Yds. March, 1911.

Fig. 15. Relocation, Panama Railroad. Gold Hill Line. View up Pedro Miguel Valley Showing Heavy Pan Car Work. March, 1911.

careful
en-

the
is at
on
make
ments
on
Pro-
ment-
the water in-
tendency to
the height of
is always left
To overcome
ankments, special
sand-rock rip-rap
is carried on after
per m was under-
rows used
cars
s greater
have ruined their
consequences to these

one, not ex-
insignificant
latter part of
ary. It is an
season, in periods
and spread out

season for the maxi-
embankments
known fact
lakes would
road crossing,

Fig. 16. 20-ft. Reinforced Concrete Arch over Agua Salud Valley. Mile 28.

Fig. 17. Relocation, Panama Railroad. Double 15-ft. by 20-ft. Reinforced Concrete Box at Agua Salud River. June, 1910.

nevertheless, the construction of numerous and costly openings was required, to provide an adequate means of caring for the flood discharge during construction, and to act as equalizers after the lake was formed. Throughout the area of the lakes, a saving was made in the cost of culverts, and a better foundation was secured, by locating them on a level from 10 to 25 feet above the natural stream bed. This caused stagnant pools to form on the up-stream side of the fill, which were a source of annoyance to the Sanitary Department of the Commission, but the rising waters of the lake gradually overcame these objections.

The ordinary types of vitrified-pipe and reinforced-concrete box culverts were adopted as standard for small openings, the former class being used with success only under the lighter fills. The larger waterways were taken care of by reinforced-concrete arch culverts, of the type shown in Fig. 16, or by large flat-top boxes of the type shown in Fig. 17. They were supported on grillage piles or solid rock, as the character of the foundation dictated.

The Monte Lirio Bascule Bridge.

An adequate water opening had to be maintained at Monte Lirio to carry the flood discharge of the great Gatun Valley and to prevent any inequality in the water surface of the lake on the sides of the submerged railroad embankments. A triple, reinforced-concrete 6-ft. by 6-ft. box was placed in the Quebrancha Valley, with a floor level about 12 feet above the bed of the stream, and smaller openings were placed at other points in the Gatun Valley. A steel bridge consisting of three 100-foot plate-girder spans, supported on reinforced-concrete piers and abutments, furnished the main opening at the south end.

The back waters of Gatun Lake reach a point some distance east of Gatun, forming an arm about 25 miles in length. It was thought desirable, as a police and military measure, to provide for the use of this arm by steam-propelled tugs or larger vessels. Accordingly, the Monte Lirio Bridge was designed to provide a clear channel 80 feet wide and with a normal depth of water of 45 feet. A plan and section of this bridge are shown in Plate II and progress photographs in Fig. 18.

The new steel-girder spans installed in the Barbacoas Bridge on the old line, which are referred to in the earlier part of this paper, were made use of for the Monte Lirio Bridge. They were placed on reinforced-concrete piers and abutments, and the center span was converted into a lift span by the addition of side-trusses, counter-weights and lifting mechanism. The design adopted is known as the Strauss trunnion heel bascule. In this bridge, the lifting span moves in a vertical plane, about a horizontal axis stationary upon a pivot pier. The mov-

Fig. 18. Relocation, Panama Railroad. Side View of Bascule Bridge No. 140
Across Gatun River. August, 1913.

able span assumes a nearly vertical position when open. The bridge is opened by hand or electric power, the movable span being finely balanced with the concrete counter-weight, so as to require the least effort. The locking device is connected with a mechanical interlocking plant at the signal tower, and the approaches to the bridge are controlled by automatic and home signals.

The cost of this bridge was $83,963.56, subdivided as f[ol]-
lows:

Abutments and piers $21,381.42
Super-structure (including contract price of bascule).... 62,582.14

Permanent Track.

The roadbed section adopted for the new line is shown [on]
Plate III. A wide section was used, on account of excess[ive]
rainfall, to provide adequate side ditches to carry the wat[er]
run-off, and to make room for the numerous small slides [and]
the sedimentary deposit brought down by the water falling [on]
the slopes of the cuts. As the amount of material required [for]
the embankments was far in excess of the excavation for ma[in]
line cuts, this wide section could not be objected to on [the]
ground of additional expense.

The ordinary untreated pine or cypress cross-tie ha[s a]
short life of from three to four years on the Isthmus of Pa[na]-
ma, due to the unfavorable climatic conditions. An effort w[as]
made to secure native hard-wood cross-ties, of a variety [of]
wood known as guayacum, or lignum vitae, but with poor s[uc]-
cess. The wood is now so valuable, to furnish parts of mach[in]-
ery, etc., that it cannot be secured for cross-ties. About 8[00]
were secured and laid on the sharper curves. The balance [of]
the line was laid with creosoted pine and cypress cross-ti[es]
7 in. x 9 in. x 8½ ft., secured from the United States. A [tie]
adzing and boring machine, manufactured by the Green[lee]
Brothers, Chicago, Illinois, was set up at Cristobal and all [ties]
for permanent track were adzed and bored at the rail seat [by]
this machine. The two parallel surfaces insured a smooth s[eat]
for the tie plate, and consequently, an even wearing of the r[ail].
Ninety-pound open-hearth steel was laid with economy tie-pla[te]
and screw spikes, and the Thompson and Thompson 100% r[ail]
joint was adopted as standard. The track was ballasted wi[th]
gravel secured from the Chagres River.

The maximum grades, northbound and southbound, we[re]
1.25%, compensated for curvature at the rate of 0.04% p[er]
degree.

The maximum curve was 7 degrees, and all curves we[re]
spiralled in accordance with the following table:

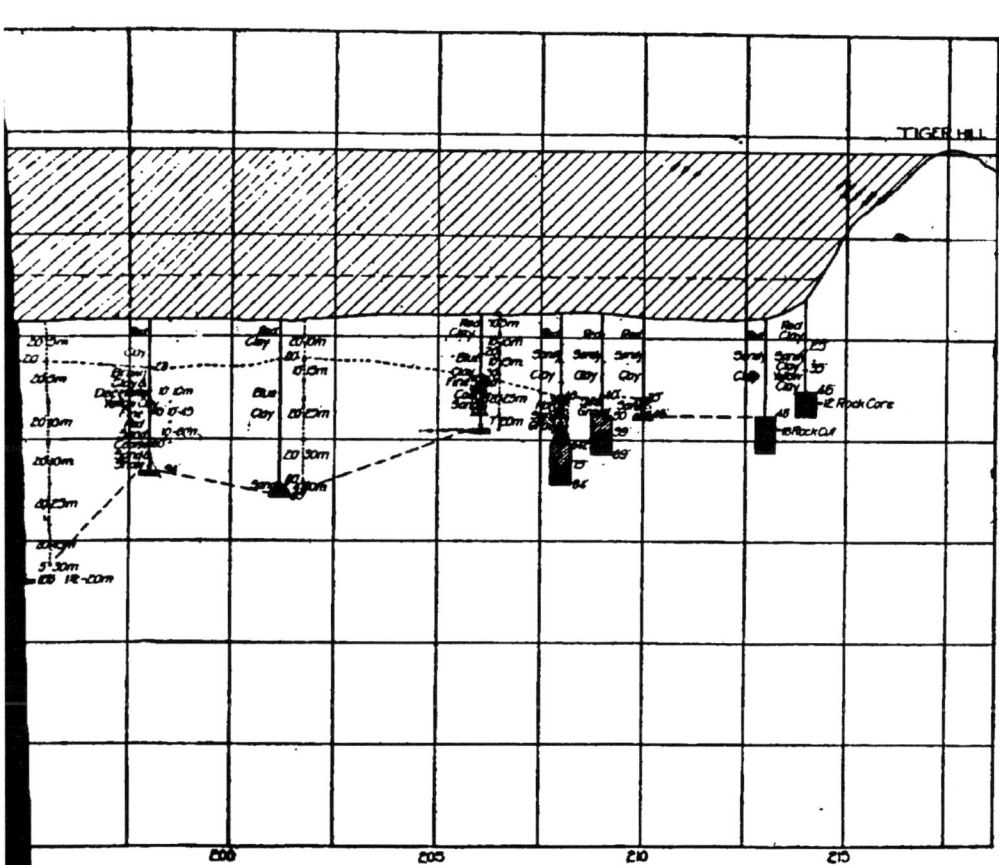

TIGER HILL

Table Showing Standard Super-elevations and Spirals for Curves.

Degree of Curve	Speed Miles per hour	Super-elevation Outer Rail in inches	Value of "a" Talbot's Spiral	Length of Spiral in feet	Distance required for attaining full Super-elevation
0° 30′	54	1 .			66
1° 00′	54	2			132
1° 30′	49	2½	1	150	165
2° 00′	46	3	1	200	198
2° 30′	47	3½	1	250	231
3° 00′	44	4	1	300	264
4° 00′	42	5	1¼	320	330
5° 00′	40	5½	1⅓	375	363
6° 00′	38	6	1½	400	396
7° 00′	35	6	1¾	400	396

TRAFFIC CONDITIONS—INTERLOCKING AND SIGNALS.

With the old Panama Railroad in use prior to February, 1912, the heaviest traffic was carried over double track. Trains were operated and spaced by manual block signals, with mechanical interlocking plants at congested points. When the old main line was abandoned and the traffic shifted to the new single track, protection was afforded in a similar way, except that the numerous block signals were replaced by automatic signals, with occasional train order signals at different points. Numerous and extensive interlocking plants were necessary to handle the traffic over the new line at junction points with the old line, or at points where the canal construction tracks entered the operated line. One of the busiest plants was that at Tower "R", at a point where the tracks from the Culebra Cut entered the main line. The train movement at this point averaged, at one time, one train for each one and two-thirds minutes for the working period of nine hours. This average is rarely exceeded in the busiest terminals of the United States.

When the formation of Miraflores Lake forced all of the Canal trains to use the single-track Miraflores Tunnel, an absolute staff system was installed, and the converging tracks at either side were interlocked with the operated line. During

Fig. 19. Relocation, Panama Railroad. Main Line Track and Automatic Signal at Mile Post 10½.

the existence of heavy traffic, it was no uncommon occurrence to pass 230 trains through the tunnel between 6 a. m. and 6 p. m., and the daily average was over 200 trains. The staff system controlled the traffic through the tunnel for a little over a year. In 1914 it was superseded by automatic-signal protection.

The automatic signals installed on the new line are the three-position, semaphore-arm type, operating in the upper right-hand quadrant. The control of the signal arm is actuated by track circuit controls ranging from four-tenths of a mile to two and a half miles, according to the grade, traffic, and other conditions. Fig. 19 shows a typical signal aspect.

In introducing automatic signals into operating problems on the Panama Railroad, rapidly changing conditions and the peculiarities of the tropical climate developed many new details never before encountered, although, in general, the best signal practice in the United States was observed. The maintenance of the automatic signals at Panama required considerably more work and a much more rigid inspection than in the United States, due to the deterioration of batteries, the corroding effects of the climate on contacts and the tendency of all iron or steel parts to rust.

HIGH-TENSION POWER-TRANSMISSION LINE. PERMANENT DUCT LINE.

In pursuance of the plans of the Canal Commission, it was necessary to pass the high-tension power-transmission line across the Isthmus from Colon to Panama. The new Panama Railroad right of way was considered the most feasible route for this line, and the final determination with respect to the type and location of transmission towers led to the adoption of wide steel towers spanning the track. These towers are located at intervals of 300 feet on tangent and 250 feet on curves, and on single track provide for approximately 15 feet clearance from the gauge of the rail and overhead clearance of 24 feet. (See Fig. 12.)

The theory was advanced in support of this type of tower that the new Panama Railroad would eventually be electrified, utilizing the power generated at the Gatun hydro-electric plant. The track-span towers would then become useful to carry an overhead power wire.

The telegraph and telephone line originally constructed for the new railroad has been replaced by an underground system, to overcome the electrical disturbance that the high-tension power wires would cause in the open-air line. A 4-way vitrified duct was laid in concrete, about 1 ft. under the surface of the ground along the right of way of the operated line. One of the ducts is used for the telegraph and telephone cable and the other for the signal cable, while the others will doubtless be leased to private cable companies.

COST OF NEW RAILROAD.

The cost of the new railroad has frequently been commented upon by persons writing of the affairs of the Isthmus.

The usual basis for these criticisms, if criticisms they may be called, is the result obtained by dividing 40 miles of railroad into $8,500,000, which gives a figure over $200,000 per mile. The original Panama Railroad, built in the 1850's, cost $7,000,000, at a time when the earning power of this amount of money was far in excess of what it is today. The old line, for the greater part of its length, had a free grade, and in the climb over the continental divide heavy construction was encountered in but few sections. The cost of the construction was high, due, mainly, to the high prices paid at that time for labor which, in turn, was due to the unhealthy climatic conditions.

The work of building the new Panama Railroad was of an entirely different character. The location, the plans, the construction and the traffic conditions were interwoven with the plans of the Isthmian Canal Commission, from the beginning to the end. The prime factor which caused the high construction cost was the unusual elevation of the line, to keep it above the waters of the lakes. The locating engineer, in reconnoitering for his line through any new country, generally seeks the aid of nature and follows the route carved out by the great drainage systems. Such a course was followed by the pioneers of the Panama Railroad, but it was denied to the later engineers. The line had to be kept unnaturally high and well back in the foothills, and thus every tributary of the Chagres River was crossed at right angles, over wide, deep valleys. There was no opportunity for development at any of these crossings, for the arms of the lake thrust out and flooded the valley below and above the line and forced the construction engineer to fill in long embankments between the points of support, which, under ordinary conditions, might have been left with wooden trestles or steel viaducts.

The minority report of the Commission of Engineers which recommended a lock type of Canal estimated the construction of a new railroad at $3,700,000. In this estimate they made no provision for the climb of 90 feet to reach Gatun. They estimated the cost of a section of line from Gatun to Bohio, 9 miles, over the Tiger Hill Line, the then accepted route, as $2,000,000. It has been shown that the least amount of material required to build the original Gatun fill on a positive foundation would have been 4,200,000 cubic yards, and that this quantity would have been more than doubled in building on the swampy bed. Thus, the estimate in the minority report for the first section was not quite half enough to build the first mile, to say nothing of the immense embankment required between Lion and Tiger Hills, between Tiger Hill and the main ridge, and through the rough country intervening between these swamps and Bohio. In all fairness, it may be said that the engineers who formulated the estimate which appears in the minority report were without information regarding the elevation or extent of these swamps, or the character of the country carrying the supported line. But, also, in justice to the engineers who abandoned the attempt to construct over the Tiger Hill route, it may be said that the line could not have been constructed on this route for many times the estimate contained in the minority report. The cost of the relocated line is given in detail in the following table, showing division of cost and unit prices to June 30, 1912:

Actual Charges to Account ''Relocation of the Panama Railroad'', September, 1906, to June 30, 1912.

Description	Mindi-Gamboa line, Paraiso-Corozal	Gold Hill line	Grand Total
Engineering	$ 308,122.61	38,296.55	346,419.16
Right-of-way and sta. grounds	543.05		543.05
Real estate	72.87		72.87
Grading	5,497,201.10	934,283.29	6,431,484.39
Tunnels	186,736.37		186,736.37
Bridges and culverts	829,592.03	79,761.48	909,353.51
Ties	99,342.05	12,980.93	112,322.98
Rails	147,506.78	62,305.09	209,811.87
Track fastenings	66,734.33	21,359.15	88,093.48
Frogs and switches	8,892.97	885.31	9,778.28
Ballast	70,013.88	11,429.45	81,456.33
Permanent track	232,328.20	19,942.86	252,271.06
Right-of-way fences	1,177.19		1,177.19
Crossings and signs	4,506.13	108.68	4,614.80
Interlocking and signals	12,307.79	77.94	12,385.73
Telegraph and telephone	75,655.27	21,134.55	96,789.82
Station buildings	35,819.71		35,819.71
Water stations	3,398.93		3,398.93
Misc. structures	2,532.01		2,532.01
General expenses	1,478.80	39.24	1,518.04
Grand totals	$7,583,962.07	$1,202,604.51	$8,786,566.58

The above amounts were paid by Canal appropriations.

There were certain other charges against the relocation of the Panama Railroad after June 30, 1912, which are not included in the above figures. They would cover such items as installing automatic signals, interlocking plants, etc. The total amount would be small.

A table showing unit cost for all construction work appears on the following page.

Fig. 20.   New Passenger Station, Panama City, Panama.

TERMINALS.

The terminals for the new railroad have been adequately planned. A new freight yard has been constructed at Balboa and Cristobal in connection with the reinforced-concrete terminal docks built at those points. A permanent station building constructed out of manufactured concrete blocks was erected at Colon in 1908 at a cost of $78,668.14, and a permanent station building was erected at Panama in 1913 at a cost of $171,120.66, including about $75,000 spent on remodelling the train sheds and tracks. (See Fig. 20.) Both of

Relocation of the Panama Railroad, September, 1906, to June 30, 1912.

(Unit Costs.)

	Mindi-Gamboa and Paraiso-Corozal Line				Gold Hill Line			
	Amount	Quantity	Unit	Unit Cost	Amount	Quantity	Unit	Unit Cost
Engineering	$ 308,122.61				$ 38,296.55			
Right of way and station grounds	543.05							
Real estate	72.87							
Grading	5,497,201.10	14,036,693.00	Cu. yd.	$0.3916	934,283.29	2,368,714	Cu. yds.	$0.3944
Shaw contract		3,154.40	"	.2500				.5700
Hardy contract		12,780.00	"	.5000		77,754	"	.3880
Hull contract							"	
Relocation forces		14,020,758.60	"			2,290,969	"	
Tunnels	186,736.37	736.00	Lin. ft.	253.7188				
Bridges and culverts	829,592.03				79,761.48			
Permanent track:								
Material	372,553.16	177,504.00	"	2.0988	108,074.62	50,917	Lin. ft.	2.1225
Labor	196,984.21	177,504.00	"	*1.1097	18,980.13	50,917	"	.3728
Total	569,537.37	177,504.00	"	$3.2085	$127,055.75	50,917	"	$2.4953

* High on account of relaying track several times and changing to 90-lb. steel.

these buildings were paid for by the Panama Railroad Company and were not charged to relocation accounts.

The main line from Diablo curve to Panama has recently been shifted, to conform to the new terminals at Balboa, and a permanent station building is in process of erection at East Balboa, near the administration headquarters.

CONCLUSION.

The relocated line of the Panama Railroad was constructed at a total cost of $8,866,392.02, from moneys appropriated by Congress for the purpose. It may be considered purely an adjunct of the Canal. The rebuilding in its new position was a necessary part of the plan, not only to furnish a system of transportation during the period of Canal construction, but to provide a suitable means of crossing the Isthmus at all times, linking the important points along the Canal one with the other. There is no other highway across the Isthmus of Panama—no road or trail which could be used by man or beast to pass between the oceans. The old Royal Road has long since been lost in the tropical jungles and no wagon road could be constructed across the Isthmus except at great expense, and then only by widening and paralleling the great fills that have been described.

The construction of the new road was fully warranted by the work that it performed as an aid to the Canal. It may never move a pound of freight after the Canal is finally completed; nevertheless, it was a necessary part of the great $350,-000,000 problem. It was necessary in construction days to furnish the avenue through which the millions of tons of spoil were hauled from the Culebra Cut; to supply the safe and systematized route over which the 45,000 Canal employees were shuttled to and from their daily tasks; to transfer the commercial freight passing over the Panama route; and to furnish a suitable system for the delivery of the thousands of tons of construction material to the various divisions and units of the Isthmian Canal Commission.

BIBLIOGRAPHY.

The annual reports of the Isthmian Canal Commission for the years 1907 to 1913, inclusive.

Several volumes of the official ''Canal Record''.

A paper entitled ''The Panama Railroad and Its Relation to the Panama Canal'' by Ralph Budd, presented before the Western Society of Engineers in 1910.

PERMANENT SHOPS, PACIFIC TERMINALS, PANAMA CANAL.

By

A. L. BELL, Assoc. Mem. Am. Soc. M. E.
Engr., Mech. Div., The Panama Canal
and
H. D. HINMAN, Assoc. M. Am. Soc. C. E.
Asst. Engr., Pacific Terminals, Isthmian Canal Commission
Balboa, Canal Zone, Panama

As a part of the terminal facilities at the Pacific end of the Canal, the construction of permanent shops for the repair of marine, canal and railroad equipment was authorized by an Act of Congress approved August 24, 1912.

The repair shops are built at Balboa within the area between the dry dock and repair wharves, and are designed to handle the various classes of work which may be required for the maintenance of the Panama Canal, for other government departments and for private companies. Briefly, they may be required to do repair work for the operating machinery of the Canal locks, for the dredging and towing fleet, the Panama Railroad, the Canal fortifications, the United States Navy, for commercial shipping and for local manufacturing and contracting companies. These varied requirements make necessary a shop capable of doing both railroad and marine work, as well as the class of work ordinarily done by jobbing establishments in the United States. The layout of buildings adopted is shown on Plate I. The longitudinal axis of the yard runs approximately northeast to southwest, but, for convenience in reference, the buildings have been considered as having their axes on an east and west, or north and south, line.

The site contains, within the area on which the buildings are erected, 36 acres, the greater part of which was low, swampy land which flooded at extreme high tide. Next to the dry dock and near the toe of Sosa Hill, which lies along the south side of this area, the ground elevation was about 18 feet above mean sea-level, and hard andesite rock reached nearly to the surface. From this locality the ground sloped northward to the repair dock, and along the waterfront was as low as 8 feet above sea-level. Toward the east, the area was low and marshy and flooded at high tide. The rock dipped toward the water-front and toward the east until it reached an elevation as low as 70 feet below mean sea-level. The surface of the underlying rock was very irregular and was broken by deep pockets, while the overlying strata consisted of several layers of black and red clay, sea shells, sand and boulders.

Preparing Site:

The site was partially occupied by the Commission settlement of Balboa as well as several buildings which formed the old native town of La Boca. The site was also obstructed by a part of the old terminal yards of the Panama Railroad, the Quartermaster's store and large quantities of old scrap iron and machinery,—all of which had to be removed. It was decided, in order to obtain drainage, to bring the total area up to elevation +17.5, and to fix the grade of the shop floors at elevation +18, the floors of the repair docks having been previously placed at elevation +17. Filling operations were begun in June, 1912, with the material excavated by steam shovels from other terminal work, such as the dry dock, and 300,000 cubic yards of earth and rock were used.

General Arrangement:

The shop buildings are grouped with a view of placing each shop as near as possible to the point where its particular output will be required. The machine shop, the forge shop, the steel storage shed, and the boiler and shipfitters' shop, all lie at the west end of the yard between Dry Dock No. 1 and the repair wharves, with their axes north and south. These buildings all have overhead crane-runway extensions at each end so arranged that material can be placed within reach of locomotive cranes on the dry-dock wall or wharves, or can be handled to and from cars on the double tracks which pass under them.

The planing mill is placed with its long axis east and west, as are all the remaining shops in the yard. This building and the lumber storage building are placed so that material can readily be transferred from one to the other or switched to the dry dock or repair wharves, if required at those points. The store-house is located centrally among the principal shop buildings and next to the repair wharves,—this arrangement makes it possible to deliver supplies to the various shop buildings promptly. The steel, iron and brass foundries with the allied buildings, the pattern storage and the coke shed, are placed on the south side of the plant. The car shop, the paint shop, and the paint house, are grouped for handling the repairs to Panama Railroad or Panama Canal cars and coaches, while the round-house and the sand house stand at the extreme east end of the yard, convenient to the line of the Panama Railroad.

Buildings:

Heretofore all shops had been constructed for use for about 10 years only. The materials to be used in the construction of these shops, however, were chosen with the idea of durability.

All the buildings are steel frame structures and the main columns of the 16 principal buildings carry loads as great as 173 tons. The 12 smaller buildings, which include the toilets, paint house and sand house, have light column loads. General design drawings of the steel for all buildings were made on the Isthmus; they showed the loads, overall dimensions, sizes of principal members, etc., but no connection details, as it was considered advisable to leave such matters to the shop practice of the contractor. No sections were used less than ⅜-inch in thickness, on account of corrosion. Bids were obtained in the United States for the preparation of detailed drawings and the fabrication and erection of the steel-work. Award was made to the United States Steel Products Company for a total of 5830 tons of structural steel, to be erected by the American Bridge Company, which covered all buildings except the shops' office, amounting to 360 tons, contract for which was later awarded to the Riter-Conley Manufacturing Company. Table No. 1 gives the floor space of each of the buildings.

Foundations:

Tests of the bearing power of the soil were made where there was a possibility of using spread footings and where the column loads were light. The results showed that the black and red Isthmian clay would not be good for more than 1000 pounds per square foot and, therefore, only one of the main buildings, the planing mill, and a few columns supporting the "lean-tos" of the other buildings, were erected on soil bearing.

When the rock was not lower than about +1, it was found practicable and most economical to excavate down to and build concrete piers on the rock. On account of the very high tide at the Pacific entrance, wood sheathing had to be used, and there was considerable delay caused by water, which came in rapidly. Where the rock was below elevation +1, untreated piles were used and cut off at elevation +5.5 or 6.5, depending upon the height at which the water stood in the soil. Plates II, III and IV show the different types of pile and concrete foundation. On the water-front end of the machine and erecting shop, and the forge shop, open caissons were sunk and filled with concrete for piers. It was considered unsafe to use there piles of the long lengths required, as the filled-in material would be in danger of sliding on the soft mud later, when the berths along the repair wharves should be excavated to —40.

There is nothing unusual in the foundation designs, and their construction was accomplished with little difficulty, except that caused by water due to high tide, and barges and other French equipment sunk and filled over along the waterfront. Fig. 1 shows the nature of the material encountered in portions of the excavation.

The expense of putting in the foundations was very much greater than the condition of the ground warranted, due to their being placed while work was being performed by other divisions on the same site.

The piles were driven by four moon-beam drivers and two swing drivers, all using drop hammers, and propelled about the site on tracks, with the exception of one swing driver which was equipped with a steam hammer and moved about on skids. There were 5382 piles driven, or 189,641 lineal feet for all the buildings, the storehouse having the largest number, viz., 1655 piles, totaling 71,052 lineal feet. Most of the piles rested on rock, but, under the shops' office, a thick layer of sand and shells was found at about elevation —7 feet, which was good enough for bearing purposes, and the piles stopped there, it being impossible to penetrate the layer.

The caisson piers were built of four-foot diameter steel cylinders which were driven to rock by a six-ton steam hammer. The material was excavated from the inside by hand, and hoisted out by steam well-drill engines. The excavation was extended down to rock, and old steel rails were placed for reinforcing the concrete with which the cylinders were filled. In some cases these rails were set and grouted in holes made in

Fig. 1. Excavation for Shop Foundations in Fill Under Buildings Nos. 1, 2, 3 and 4.

the rock foundation, to insure the pier from sliding, if a small slide should develop in the fill. The excavation for the caissons was tedious, as nearly all of them encountered old French equipment sunk in the mud along that part of the site. Oxyacetylene was used to cut this away from the caisson's shoe. To brace the piers still more, their tops were tied together with reinforced concrete beams. Twenty-three caissons, shown on Fig. 2, were used for foundations for the north end of the machine and erecting shop, the bottom resting on rock as low as 37 feet below mean sea-level. Eight caissons were used as foundations for the supports of crane-runway extensions, two of

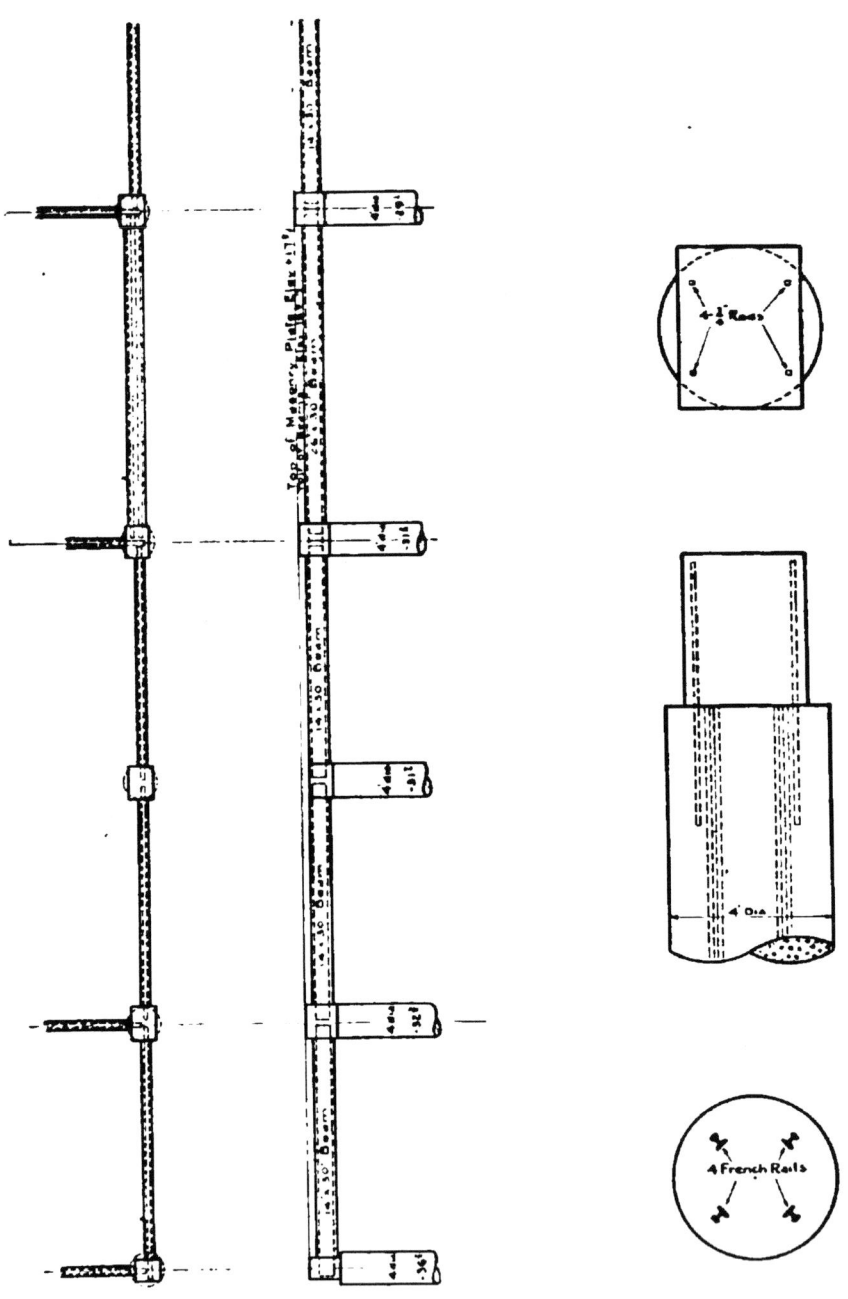

SKETCH SHOWING REINFORCING IN 4' CYLINDER

Fig. 2.   Building No. 1. Machine Erecting and Tool Shops.   Foundation Details.

which went to —48. Where piles were not used for the foundations of the crane-runway extensions of the forge shop, two similar caissons were sunk, making a total of 33 caissons. For the foundations of the transfer table connected with the machine shop, which was built over open water, 3-foot caissons were used, filled with reinforced concrete, for piers. Due to the large amount of water which entered the caissons and to the trouble of getting through the sunken steel equipment which was there, the cost of these piers was excessive. The reduction in diameter of these cylinders over those used for the main column foundations proved doubtful economy, as there was not enough room inside them to work a man to advantage. All the caisson work was performed by the open method and a great deal of pumping had to be done night and day in order that work might be carried on during low tide.

Under many of the heavy machines and under the main columns of the round-house and foundations of the turntable, pipe piles filled with concrete, and reinforced concrete piles were used. In the case of the round-house and turn-table foundations and the engine pits, pipe piles and concrete piles were used because of the soft condition of the ground, which had been made by hydraulic fill from the Inner Harbor excavation. On account of the softness of this fill, no excavation could be carried on in order to cut piles off at elevation +6.0, as would have been required had wooden piles been used. The pipe piles were made by screwing together 10-inch or 12-inch standard wrought-iron pipe, and driving it in the leads of a pile-driver, after having put a cast iron shoe on the lower end. When the pile was down to rock, four to six ⅜-inch reinforcing bars were placed in it, tied in a circular form and the pipe filled with a rich mixture of concrete. Plate V shows the design of the foundations under the roundhouse.

Owing to the variation in bearing value of the soil at different points throughout the buildings, the foundations for machines varied considerably in type. Some were carried on piles and some on concrete piers to rock, while others were on earth firm enough to support them. Fig. 3 shows the foundations for cranes in the center of the forge shop, and illustrates the use of deep piers and piles. Plate VI covers typical foundations

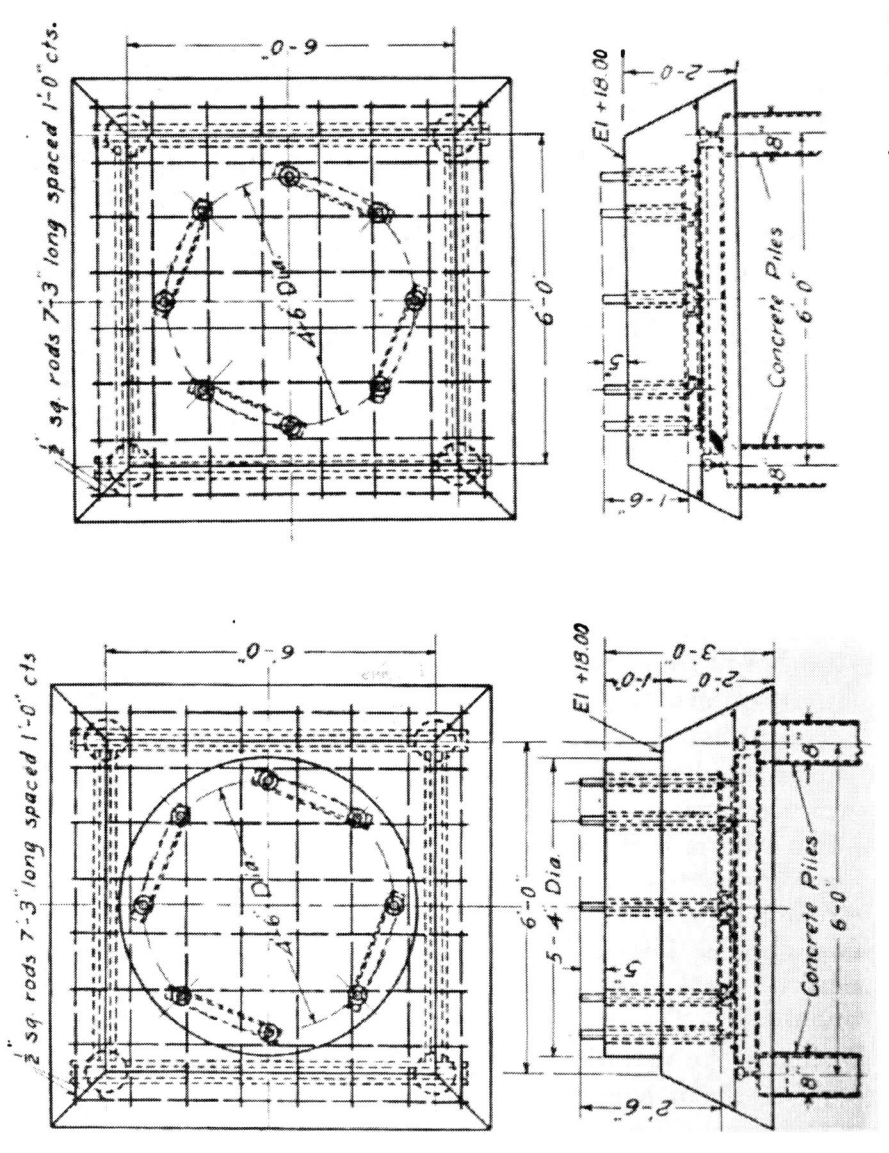

PLAN AND ELEVATION OF JIB CRANE FOUNDATIONS FOR F-46, F-49, F-53, & F-5'

PLAN AND ELEVATION OF JIB CRANE FOUNDATIONS FOR F-40 & F-42

Fig. 3. Building No. 2, Forge Shop. Jib Crane Foundations.

for machines in the north half of the east aisle of the boiler shop and shows where the earth was firm enough to support them without going down to rock foundations.

There was a total of 33,074 cubic yards of excavation for the shops' foundations and 6153 cubic yards were excavated for placing the footings for the machines. A total of 9510 cubic yards of concrete, in which there was used 204,230 pounds of steel as reinforcing, was placed for the foundations for the buildings, and 5438 cubic yards were contained in the footings for the various machines, ash pit, turntable and transfer table. In the 5438 cubic yards for machine footings, there was placed 428,989 pounds of reinforcing bars, beams and bolts.

The erection of the structural steel was somewhat unusual, in that it comprised the erection of a large number of buildings at one time on the same site, 25 being erected; and also, due to the fact that all the erection work was done with the use of locomotive cranes, alone, fitted with special, long gooseneck booms. Figure 4 shows one of these cranes being used in the erection of the roundhouse and foundry. All the track work connected with the transportation of material and locomotive

Fig. 4. Steel Work for Roundhouse in Process of Erection.

Fig. 5. Interior of Boiler Shop. Overhead Crane in Place.

cranes was done by the Panama Canal. Erection of steel began
on April 23, 1913, and was completed November 30, 1913.

Roofing:

Special inquiries were made in the United States to find a
satisfactory, durable roof covering which would resist the severe
climatic conditions on the Isthmus; and a contract was eventually entered into with the American Cement Tile Company
for the manufacture and erection of large interlocking reinforced cement tile, which were hung directly on the channel-iron
roof purlins. These tile were manufactured on the Isthmus, the
Panama Canal supplying the raw material, i. e., cement and
sand, and the contractor supplying all waterproofing, equipment
and labor. The tiles were made in varying sizes, the standard being 24 in. by 52 in., with other lengths varying down to 24
inches, where their use was necessary. Certain rows of these
tiles were made with reinforced glass panes for lighting shop
interiors, and special ridge roll and gutter tiles were cast and
applied. Figure 5 shows an interior view of the boiler shop in
which the glass insets can be clearly seen; and Fig. 6, a close
view of a section of one of the completed roofs. This type of

covering was used on all buildings except the roundhouse, the pattern storage, and the valleys in the roofs of the lumber shed, the planing mill, and the machine shop, where Barrett Specification roofing was applied. The roofs contain 7400 squares of tile, 9100 lineal feet of ridge roll, and 600 squares of Barrett roofing.

Floors:

Flooring throughout the shops varies in accordance with the work done in each. Wood blocks were used in the machine and erecting shop, and the planing mill; clay, in the foundry building; cinders, in the forge shop, boiler and shipfitters' shop, and the roundhouse; concrete, in the storehouse, paint shop, galvanizing plant, pattern storage, power plant, gas house, and toilets; and earth, in the steel storage shed, car shop, lumber storage shed, and coke shed. All tool rooms have wood-block floors laid on a concrete base; and all foremen's offices, a flooring of tongued and grooved yellow pine laid on a 2-in. planking, spiked to stringers bedded in concrete. Due to the damp climate, the wood blocks in the machine and erecting shop expanded a great deal, and the blocks in this shop, having been

Fig. 6. Cement Tile Roof at North End of Boiler Shop.

driven tightly together when laid, heaved badly, making it necessary to remove a strip one block in width across the floor about every 30 feet, the opening being filled with pitch for an expansion joint.

Closure:

The closure for the sides of the buildings was one of the features which was given great consideration. On account of the high prevailing temperature, it is necessary to have all shops as open as possible for the comfort of the workmen, and yet it is necessary to prevent the entrance of rain during the downpours of the rainy season. At one time and another, metal screening, fixed louvers, steel rolling doors and movable metal louvers were considered, and the latter were finally installed. The louver blades are manufactured of galvanized iron ⅛-inch thick. They are arranged in four rows about 5 feet long in each 21-foot bay, and are operated by a single lever which turns a shaft to which the link bar of each row is attached. The blades are 16 inches wide and give a clear space between them, when raised, of 14⅜ inches. Figure 7 shows an exterior view of the louvers in open and closed positions. The louver panels rest on the top of a 6-inch concrete wall 3 feet 6 inches high, and are carried up under the roof overhangs to prevent rain from blowing in. This type of closure is not used in all buildings, as some required total enclosure or none at all.

Power:

The machinery in the shops is entirely electrically operated, except such machines as hammers, etc., which are not adapted to this type of drive. The current used is 3-phase, 25-cycle, and is delivered to the shops at 2200 volts. The shop motors operate at 220 volts, and transformer rooms containing light and power transformers and switchboards are located near load centers in the various buildings. The main transformer rooms are placed in the machine and erecting shop, steel storage shed, planing mill, and foundry building. The machine and erecting shop has two 300-kva. 3-phase power transformers, one 140-kw. single-phase lighting transformer, two 325-kw. motor-generator sets, and a 7-panel switchboard. This equipment serves this building only. The transformer equipment in the steel storage shed, planing mill, and foundry building is practically the same in each, and consists of two 300-kva. power transformers, one 50-, 60- or 125-kw. single-phase lighting transformer, and one 3-panel switchboard. The transformers in the planing mill sup-

Fig. 7. Boiler Shop. Steel Door at End of Building Open.

ply that building only, but those in the steel storage shed supply the forge shop and the boiler and shipfitters' shop, and those in the foundry building supply the car shop, galvanizing plant, lumber-storage shed and roundhouse. All distributing cables are run through the shop tunnel in ducts laid in the wall, and are then brought up through manholes in the floor of the buildings. From the manholes, cables are run in galvanized iron conduits fastened to the roof trusses or carried on "T" iron supports attached to the steel work of the buildings above the lower chords. Drops are run down the building columns to controllers, panel boxes, etc. On account of limited space, the central switchboards were not arranged to permit control of all power and lighting circuits at the boards; instead of this, junction boxes were installed in each section of the shop, from which the power and lighting circuits for that section are distributed. The transformers are connected to the main sub-station by a single loop feeder-circuit which has ample capacity to carry the normal shop load on one side, in case of emergency. The valve and gate operating machinery on the north wall of the dry dock will be connected to the shop transformers, when it is installed.

Motors:

Four types of motors were adopted for power drives: direct-current, commutating-pole, variable-speed motors; slip-ring induction motors; squirrel-cage induction motors; and synchronous motors. Direct-current motors operate on 220-volt current, and alternating current motors on 220-volt, 3-phase, 25-cycle current. The direct-current motors drive lathes, planers, boring machines, milling machines, and other tools where a variable tool speed is desired. They have speed ranges from 350 to 1400 r. p. m.; 375 to 1125; 375 to 1500; 450 to 1800; 500 to 1500. The slip-ring, polar-wound rotor, induction motors drive machines requiring a high starting torque or that are necessarily reversible, e. g., bending rolls, low-pressure blowers, the 2-ton tropenas converter, and the transfer table. The squirrel-cage induction motors are used for all group drives and on all constant-speed machines. The synchronous motors are used for driving direct-current generators and air compressors, and are arranged for operation at 75 percent leading power factor for correcting the load factor of the plant. All motors were purchased under specifications calling for specially developed insulation similar to that used on the lock-machinery motors. The attached Table No. 2 shows the rated horsepower of all motors in each group and building for driving cranes, individual machines, and groups of machines.

Lighting:

Lighting for the shops is obtained from tungsten filament lamps, and general illumination is used throughout. This method was considered preferable to special intensified illumination at each machine or in particular sections of the shop, on account of the fact that, as all points receive approximately the same amount of light, no change in wiring or the position of lamps is required, if the arrangement of machines is changed. Lighting is all on 110- 220-volt, single-phase circuits. Feeders run from the lighting transformers to panel boxes located at convenient points throughout the shop, and from these boxes the lights in the individual sections are controlled. Branch circuits are designed for a maximum load of 3000 watts, with a drop of 3 volts. All wiring is carried in conduits attached to the roof trusses and columns, and drops are run down the columns to plug receptacles for extension lamps. Lamps themselves are 100-watt, 150-watt, 250-watt, and 500-watt, depending on their location and the intensity of illumination desired. The machine and erecting shop, for example, has a total floor space of 67,789 square feet and has a calculated illumination, in a plane 3 feet above the floor, of 7.6-foot candles in the machine shop, 8.37-foot candles in the tool department, and 7.75-foot candles in the erecting shop—this with a total of 120,425 watts in lamps. Figures 8 and 9 show interior photographs taken with natural and artificial lighting. Table No. 3 attached shows the calculated watts and foot candles in each building.

Toilets:

To provide suitable toilet facilities, urinals were placed inside some of the more important shops, and toilet buildings were located at various points throughout the yard. Buildings Nos. 17, 18, 19, 20, 21, 22, 23 and 24, shown on Plate I, are toilets, and they are fitted with slate urinals, closet and shower bath stalls, porcelain wash-bowls and steel lockers. There are two classes of toilets, one for white (or gold) employees, and the other for colored (or silver) employees. They are similar, except that those for silver men are fitted with range urinals and have no lockers. All fittings are brass, floors are concrete,

Fig. 2. Interior of Machine Shop.

and ample ventilation is secured through openings under the eaves, formed by stopping the walls when they were brought up to sufficient height to prevent the entrance of rain.

The foregoing is a statement of the general features of the shop layout and design as a whole, and there follows a somewhat more detailed description of the individual buildings and shops.

Machine and Erecting Shop:

Building No. 1 contains the machine shop, erecting shop and tool department. It consists of two high sections with a saw-tooth section between them, and a "lean-to" on the east side. The building is 358 feet 8 inches long, each high section 61 feet wide, and the sawtooth and "lean-to" 39 feet and 29 feet, respectively. A composite section is shown on Plate VII. This drawing also shows the steel rolling doors and sash at the sides of the building, the transformer room, jib and traveling cranes, drop pits, transfer table, etc.

About one-half of the north end of the west aisle is used as the erecting shop for general overhauling and heavy repairs on locomotives, steam shovels and similar equipment, and there

Fig. 9. Interior of Machine Shop by Artificial Illumination at Night.

are four engine pits for this purpose (one of them a drop pit),
—all served through steel rolling doors by a motor-driven transfer table, on to which equipment is run from the longitudinal
tracks north of the buildings. The shop is equipped with a 60-
ton electric overhead traveling crane.

The south half of this aisle is divided between the tool
and air-brake departments. The tool department includes the
tool-room for the building and also all small lathes, milling machines, tool grinders, etc. The machines are driven in groups.

The remainder of the building is the machine shop proper.
Machines of like nature have been placed together, and the
lighter and most regularly used machines are driven in groups.

The saw-tooth section at the south end contains medium
sized or light lathes and turret lathes. As there is no crane in
this section, the heavier machines are served by means of overhead trolleys carried below the roof trusses. The heavier lathes
are driven by individual motors operating on 220-volt direct
current, while the remainder of the machines are driven in
groups. Motors for group drives, the line shafts, and the coun-

ter-shafts for machines are carried on stringers formed of steel
channels. The transformer room is arranged, for economy of
space, with transformers and motor generator sets on the floor
level and with an elevated platform which supports the switchboard. North of these offices are the drill presses (also group
driven); and beyond them, near the engine pits, the wheel and
axle lathes, wheel presses, etc., all of which are equipped with
individual motors.

In the south end of the main aisle of the machine shop,
i. e., the east high section, are placed the large planers and
lathes; while at the north end, the radial drills, boring machines
(both vertical and horizontal) and large shapers, are located.
All of these machines are driven by individual motors. Machines in this aisle are served by a 60-ton and a 20-ton electric
overhead traveling crane.

Practically all the machinery in the shops has been collected
from plants which were in service during the construction
period, and none of it was especially built for motorization.

The south end of the east "lean-to" houses contains the
smaller planers, slotters and shapers. The large planers in the
main aisle are equipped with direct-connected motors operating
on 220-volt direct current, with controllers and electrical reversing apparatus, and with pendant switches which permit the operator to cut off the power at the table. The smaller planers are
group driven and have the regular belt reverse.

North of the east and west center-line track is a group of
machines, consisting of a wheel press, wheel-boring machine and
axle lathe, all served by jib cranes, on which is done all work in
connection with repairs to wheels and axles for cars or coaches;
while beyond this group are located additional boring machines
and drill presses, the milling machines and the bolt-cutting and
threading machines.

The building is supplied with compressed air, at 90- to 100-
pounds pressure; steam at from 115- to 125-pounds pressure; fuel
oil and fresh water from the distributing mains.

Forge Shop:

Building No. 2, which houses the forge, copper, tin and
pipe shop, has one high section 60 feet wide and one "lean-to"
on the east side 29 feet wide; the building is 358 feet 8 inches

long. A 25-ton electric overhead traveling crane, which serves
the high section for the entire length, can be run out of the
building at either end on runway extensions, in the same manner as for Building No. 1. Plate VIII shows a section of this
building. Its closure is of the same general type as that of
the machine shop. The wall opening between the shed overhangs or between the roofs of "lean-tos" and eaves of the main
roofs is partially closed with glazed sash. Sixty feet of the
north end of the building is allotted to the copper, tin and pipe
shop, and the remainder of the building to the forge shop.

The pipe machines are placed with their center lines perpendicular to that of the building, and pipe is run into them
through sleeves placed in the wall. All these machines are driven
in a single group by a 15-hp. motor. The main aisle of the shop
at this end contains tinsmiths' benches, on which the smaller
rolls, trimmers and groovers, which are kept in racks when not
in use, can be mounted; and also the larger hand-power machines mounted on their own frames. Next to the forge shop
in the main aisle are the tanks and forges for the coppersmiths
and a rack for odds and ends of pipe and tubing. The larger
pipe machines are served by a jib crane mounted on the outside of the northeast corner of the building, by means of which
pipe can be unloaded from cars or passed to the machines. Another jib crane handles heavy pipe over the coppersmiths' fires.
The section of the main aisle between the copper, tin and pipe
shops and the east and west center-line track is devoted to
steam-hammer work. The three largest hammers are 2000,
2500, and 2700 pounds capacity; smaller ones are placed in the
line of columns between the main aisle and the "lean-to", and
in the latter is placed a double row of blacksmiths' fires. There
are two large blacksmiths' fires for each heavy hammer, in addition to the heating furnaces. South of the east and west center-
line track, the "lean-to" houses, the foreman's office and tool
room, the power-driven hammers, bolt headers, bull-dozers and
their furnaces. In the south half of the main aisle, there are
two forges and a furnace for the spring maker on the east side,
beyond which are additional forges for handling the large
amount of special work on dump-car brake beams, levers, etc.
The forging press, capacity 500 tons, is located in the south-

west corner of the building with two furnaces, one for medium and one for heavy work, on the opposite side of the aisle. On the west side of this part of the building are located the furnaces, forges and hammers for the tool dressing plant, which consists of pre-heating, high temperature, lead bath and barium chloride furnaces, with tanks for water, oil and brine, and an air table. This equipment will eventually produce all tools used in the plant.

All forges and furnaces in this building burn crude oil. The oil is fed to the burners by gravity from tanks on the hill south of the plant. Its pressure is cut down by reducing valves on the burners from 65 to 28 or 30 pounds. The oil is a crude California grade, averaging about 17.5° Baumé, and is fed to the burners at about 85° to 88° F. without pre-heating. Two blowers, each with a capacity of approximately 3500 cubic feet of air per minute, at 6-ounce pressure, are located in the north half of the east "lean-to" next to the pipe shop, and another, of equal capacity, in the south half of the "lean-to" next to the tool room.

Steel Storage Shed:

Building No. 3, the steel storage shed, consists of a single-span section 49 feet wide and 358 feet 8 inches long. Both sides and ends are closed with hand-operated steel rolling doors. The south half of the building contains plate racks and space for storing billets and structural shapes. The north end of the building contains racks for boiler tubes, pipe and bar iron. A 20-ton electric overhead traveling crane handles material to and from cars to the various portions of the building. Near the center-line track are placed two bar-iron shears and a cold saw, and the transformer room which controls power and lighting circuits for buildings Nos. 2, 3 and 4.

Boiler and Shipfitters' Shop:

Building No. 4, the boiler and shipfitters' shop, consists of a single high section 61 feet wide, and two "lean-tos", the one on the west side 40 feet wide and that on the east 29 feet. It is 358 feet 8 inches long. The main bay is served by a 60-ton and a 20-ton electric overhead traveling crane. All of the heavy machines are served by individual jib cranes fitted with pneumatic hoists. Plate IX shows a typical section of the building. Figures 7 and 10 show the electrically-operated steel rolling doors at the ends of the building in open and closed positions. Punches and shears are placed at the south end of the building; and north of them, bending rolls and pneumatic riveters. All the rolls, punches and shears are driven by individual motors. In the south end of the east "lean-to" is a flue repairing outfit. Just south of the center-line track is located the tool room, and at the north end of this "lean-to" are situated the plate and angle furnaces, flange fires, flanging clamps and forming slabs. This shop does structural work for general construction purposes; repairs and overhauls all boilers, etc. An electric welding equipment is usually located in the building. It is, however, portable, i. e., the motor-generator set and switchboard are mounted on a truck which allows it to be loaded on cars and moved to any place where it is required. There are also facilities for oxy-acetylene welding and cutting, and the oxy-acetylene manufacturing plant, which is located in Building No. 16, between Buildings Nos. 2 and 4, contains an oxygen generating outfit, consisting of retorts for heating a mixture of potassium chloride and manganese dioxide, washers for purifying the gas, a 100-cubic-foot gasometer and a compressor, by means of which the gas is compressed directly into the portable steel oxygen tanks at a pressure of 300 pounds per square inch. Acetylene is generated by running water on calcium carbide, in a standard type generator, from which the gas passes to a gasometer, thence through purifiers to a compressor by which it is compressed to 225 pounds per square inch, in portable steel cylinders containing a cellular filling and an initial charge of acetone. This acetylene is also used for lighting certain of the aids to navigation of the canal. Acetylene welding and cutting is done, not only in the boiler shop, but at any other point in the Zone where such work is required.

Storehouse:

Building No. 5, the general storehouse, forms the main depot for all material which is stored under cover, except steel, lumber and oil. The building has two stories 120 feet wide and 400 feet long, and is totally enclosed. The main walls are made of hollow tile blocks covered with cement plaster, while the floor beams and columns are incased in concrete. A fire wall, extending across the middle of the building on each floor, is equipped with automatic fire doors on each side of all openings. There are two 15-ton electric elevators for handling freight.

Fig. 10.   Boiler Shop. Steel Door at End of Building Closed.

Wooden swing doors are placed in alternate panels on each side of the building. The first floor, placed at the track or yard level, is made of an 8-inch unreinforced concrete slab laid on the ground; and the second floor, designed for 500 pounds per

Plate 113.

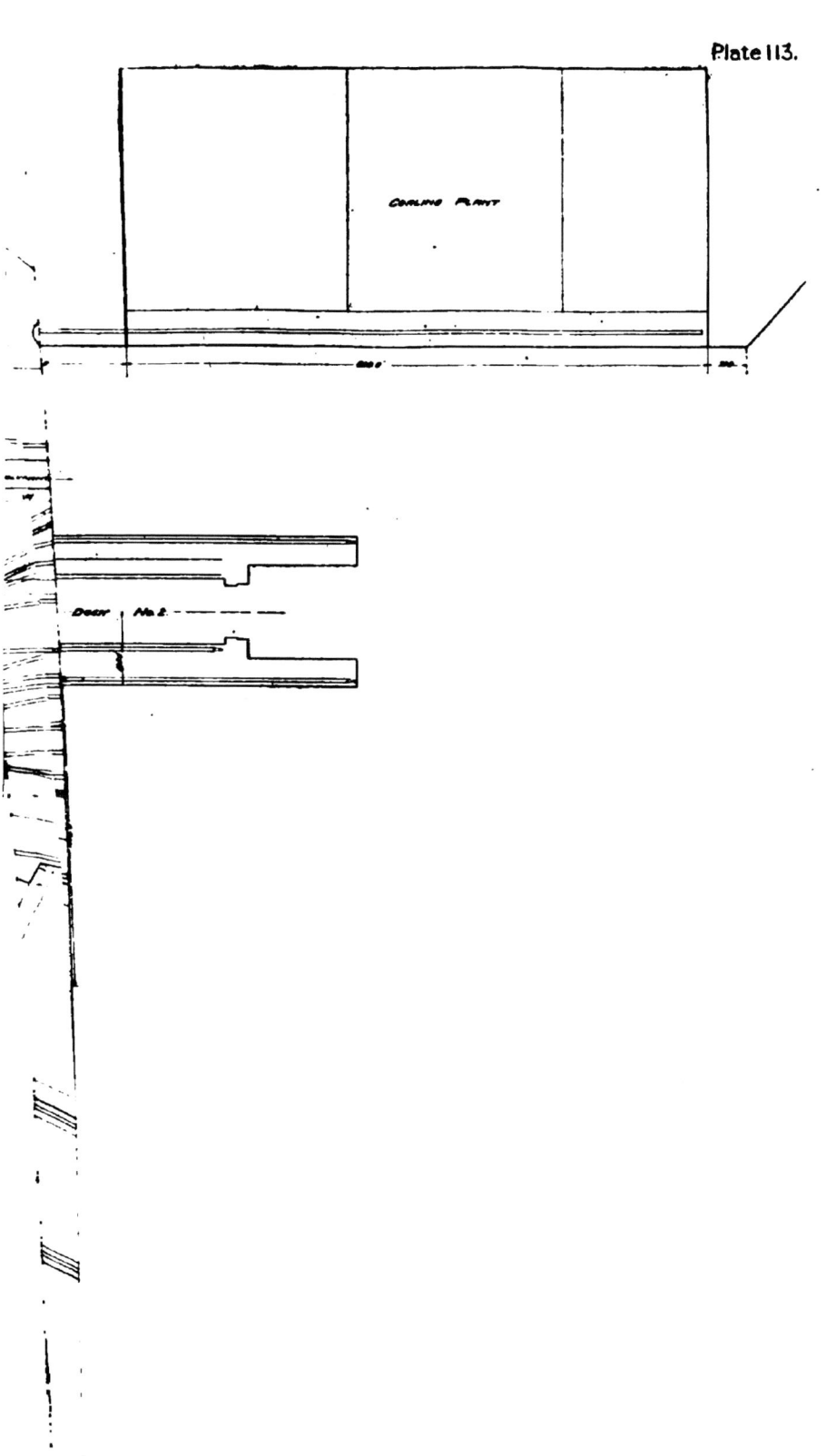

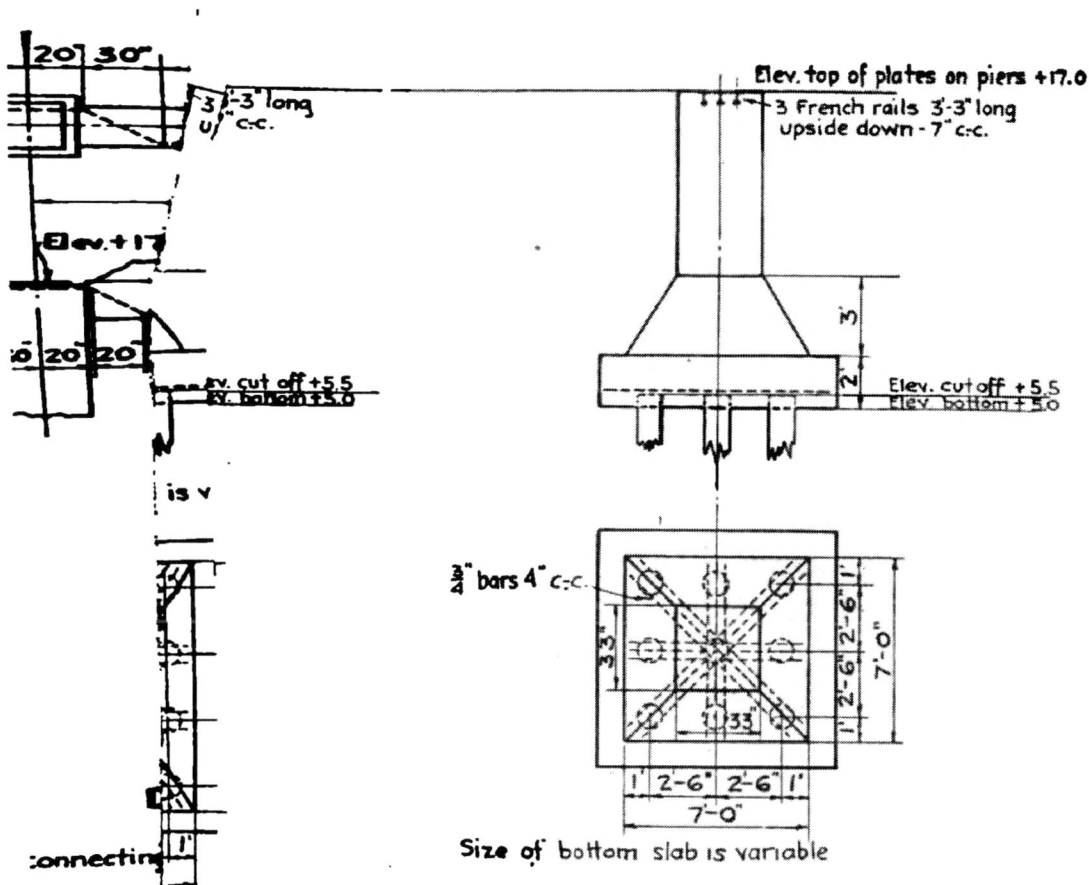

20 30"

3 3"-3" long
U c-c.

Elev. +17

6 20 20

Elev. cut off +5.5
Elev. bottom +5.0

is v

connecting

Elev. top of plates on piers +17.0

3 French rails 3'-3" long
upside down - 7" c-c.

3'

2'

Elev. cut off + 5.5
Elev. bottom + 5.0

3/4" bars 4" c-c.

3 3"

7'-0"

1' 2'-6" 2'-6" 1'

1' 2'-6" 2'-6" 1'
7'-0"

3 33

Size of bottom slab is variable

square foot, is constructed of a reinforced concrete slab carried on concrete-encased steel girders.

Paint Shop:

The paint shop, Building No. 6, is a totally enclosed structure 50 feet wide by 250 feet long. The walls are of concrete, and are fitted with a double row of glazed pivoted sash. This building is primarily for painting and varnishing passenger coaches and engines, and has two tracks, each long enough for two coaches, in the east end. Each track is equipped with two lines of adjustable scaffolds, one on each side; these are formed by telescoping wrought iron pipes in larger pipes secured to castings on the lower chord of the roof truss. The west end of the building is equipped with tanks, for washing car seats, windows, etc., and with an enclosed room 15 feet by 60 feet, in which varnishing work can be kept free from dust. Paints and oils are kept in the paint house, Building No. 26, a small building 22 feet 6 inches by 48 feet, placed just south of Building No. 6. The paint house is equipped with tanks for lye solutions for cleaning buckets, and with tanks for the stock supplies of standard paints. There are also two pigment grinding machines and two 100-gallon paint mixers, all driven by an electric motor. Both the paint house and the paint shop have concrete floors.

Car Shop:

The car shop, Building No. 7, is located east of the paint shop. This building is formed by two pitch-roof sections placed side by side, thus forming a valley in the center. The building is 122 feet wide by 317 feet long, and contains six tracks, each running the entire length of the building. The two outer tracks on each side are used for work tracks, and the center ones for material and for working space. The south track is fitted with two rows of fixed scaffolding, and is used for freight-car work. A swing cut-off saw, bench saw, rip saw and drill press are ranged along the center line of the building at the east end; all are driven with individual motors. These machines are installed for the miscellaneous work for fitting flooring, siding, etc., which cannot be economically carried to the planing mill when required. Some steel car repairing is done on tracks at the east end of the north half of the building, but most of this class of work is done on the outside tracks to the east and north. This building is closed along the north side and each end of the north half by hand-operated steel rolling doors. The south half of the building being used for freight-car work and, being not so much exposed to the rain, is left open.

Planing Mill:

The planing mill, Building No. 8, is constructed in the same general manner as the car shop. It is 122 feet wide by 480 feet long, and houses, in addition to the planing mill proper, the joiner, carpenter and pattern shops. Figure 11 shows the steel framing during erection.

The joiner carpenter shop is placed in the northeast corner, and the pattern shop in the northwest corner. All machines are driven by individual motors, except light machines used in the pattern shop, and a few morticers and stickers in the planing mill. One standard-gauge railroad track runs through the building near its center, and a narrow-gauge track, just in front of the row of car-sill working machinery, along the south side. The sides of the building are enclosed by movable metal louvers; there are two steel rolling doors on each side in bays about one-quarter the length of the building from each end, and also over the track doors. An exhaust system carries the shavings and sawdust from the machines, through vertical risers and overhead piping, to a collector on the boiler plant, where they are burned under the boilers. The building is thoroughly piped for air, steam and water. The floor is made of creosoted wood blocks laid on a half-inch of sand spread over a concrete base. The transformer room, tool room and a room containing machines for grinding saws and planer knives, are located at the middle of the north side, and a rack for templets hangs from the trusses over two bays at the east end of the south half.

Lumber Storage Shed:

The lumber storage shed, Building No. 10, is directly east of the planing mill, and is of exactly similar construction, except that all sides are open. It is 122 feet wide and 549 feet long. One track runs along each side of the building, one entirely through it, just south of the center line columns, and another through the north half as far west as the kilns. The kilns occupy a space 157 feet by 27 feet in the northwest corner. The walls are constructed of hollow concrete tile, and the roof of reinforced concrete over steel beams, supported on columns at the sides of the door openings. Blowers driven by direct-connected motors are placed on the roof of the kilns, and force through the kilns air heated by steam headers in the suction. The ducts are so arranged that air can be circulated through the kilns and back to the blower again, or discharged

Fig. 11. Looking Northwest Through Planing Mill Building.

through stacks, and a continuous fresh supply taken. A transfer table along the front of the kilns permits the shifting of stacks from one kiln to another. A screen-enclosed space in the southeast corner of the building is reserved for the storage of foundry supplies.

Pattern Storage:

The pattern storage is a two-story steel and concrete structure 60 feet wide and 120 feet long. The lower floor contains racks and open floor space for the storage of large patterns, and the second floor, racks for small patterns. The building is fitted with automatic fire extinguishers.

Foundry:

The foundry building consists of one high section 61 feet wide and two "lean-tos" each 29 feet wide. The building is 316 feet long and lies with its center line running east and west. It houses the steel, iron and brass foundries.

This building is principally closed with movable metal louvers. There are steel rolling doors over the crane openings at each end of the main aisle and over the east end of the north "lean-to". A 10-ton crane serves the east end of the north "lean-to" and handles castings to and from the cold saws and sand-blast car. This crane also handles the castings to the scales, and thence to cars for shipping.

The south "lean-to" is occupied by the foreman's office, transformer room and tool room (all enclosed with wire-screen partitions), two sand bins, the two cupolas, the converter, the blower room and the annealing furnace and mold drying oven. The blower room is built with concrete walls and roof, and houses the rotary pressure blowers for cupolas and converter, each of these blowers being driven by an individual electric motor. A charging platform, formed of steel plate laid on heavy girders, is erected at the level of the charging door in the rear of the cupolas. A pneumatic elevator serves for raising iron and charcoal to the platform, and a small landing is carried out from the front of the platform, on which skips can be landed by the overhead traveling crane, in case the elevator is out of order.

The main bay is almost entirely unoccupied by machinery or other equipment; at the west end there are placed two pneumatic molding machines, and at the east end a sand girder. This bay is served by two 25-ton electric overhead traveling cranes, the runways for which are extended on the west end across the 100-foot space between the foundry and the pattern storage.

The brass foundry occupies the west end of the north "lean-to"; and the remainder of this section of the building is occupied by benches for core makers and molders, core ovens and racks, barrel tumblers, heavy grinding wheels, cold saws, space for chipping and cleaning castings and a sand-blast plant.

Narrow-gauge cars which run on industrial tracks, into the

coke shed and between the piles of pig, can be brought into the foundry, placed on the elevator and lifted to the charging platform, where by means of an elliptical track they can be dumped immediately in front of either cupola.

Coke Shed:

Building No. 13, the coke shed, has a single-slope roof and is 18 feet wide, 168 feet long. It contains the foundry coke supply, which is unloaded by shoveling through a space between the walls and the roof, from cars run alongside the building.

Boiler House:

Building No. 14, the power plant, contains two 225-hp. horizontal return-tubular boilers, which are installed for generating steam for hammers, air-brake testing, dry kilns, vats, etc. The boilers are fitted to burn either crude oil or shavings from the planing mill. Although both boilers have been used to capacity during the construction of the dry dock for operating concrete mixers, air compressors, etc., it is expected that one of them will have ample capacity for supplying the needs of the plant itself. The building is 50 feet by 50 feet, has a concrete floor, and is closed with movable metal louvers. A branch from the main tunnel carried the steam main from the boiler house to the other shops, and the water, air, and oil lines to the plant.

Roundhouse:

Building No. 15, the roundhouse, contains 15 stalls and is 76 feet deep. It is constructed with a steel frame, all of which is cased in concrete. The roof is a reinforced-concrete slab, pitched from front to rear, covered with Barrett Specification Roofing. The two center bays are carried back to provide space for the foreman's office, tool room and a machine shop. The latter contains a lathe, grinder, drill press, boring machine, pipe machine, shaper and forcing press—all driven as a group with an electric motor. The building has a 6-foot concrete wall around the back. The projection housing the shop and office is closed with movable metal louvers. An overhead trolley fitted with an air hoist runs over the 8 center stalls over the engine pits, for handling air pumps, etc. Plate X shows a section of turntable, and Fig. 4 a view of the steel framing. The turntable is 70 feet in diameter and electrically operated. On account of the very soft ground on which it is located, the center pivot is carried on an eight-foot cylinder of concrete, sunk to bed rock; and the floor and rim walls are supported on piles. The details of this foundation are shown on Plate V.

Sand House, Cinder Pit, Oil and Water Cranes:

Southeast of the roundhouse are the sand house, cinder pit, and oil and water cranes. The sand house contains, on the first floor, a bin for the storage of wet sand and a pair of drying stoves; the dried sand is stored in an elevated bin in a tower above the wet sand bin, and is elevated by means of a compressed-air lift. The cinder pit is manufactured of reinforced concrete supported on piles; it is 40 feet long and serves two tracks. The pit is cleaned by a locomotive crane with a clamshell bucket. This arrangement was adopted on account of economy in construction, as the number of coal-burning locomotives in service will be very small as soon as construction work is completed. The regular main-line engines of the Panama Railroad are oil burning.

Galvanizing Plant:

Building No. 9, the galvanizing plant, is a concrete and steel structure, 148 feet long by 40 feet wide, divided by means of hollow-tile partition walls into three sections, for instrument repair work, lacquering, plating and polishing, and galvanizing. The building has glazed sash around the sides and ends, and a monitor with wooden louvers. All floors are of concrete except in the galvanizing section, where the floor is of cinders. The galvanizing plant is not yet in service, as the section of the building allotted to it is being temporarily used for an electrical repair shop.

Shops' Office:

Building No. 28, the shops' office, is located just east of the general storehouse. This building consists of a steel frame filled in with concrete block walls, covered on each side with cement plaster. The northwest "ells" contain private offices; and the southwest "ells", vaults and toilet rooms. There are three floors, identical except for minor details. The large single room formed by the main section of the building is divided by light wooden partitions, about 7 feet high, into smaller sections, to meet the requirements of its use. A balcony runs around the front and north side of the building on each floor. This building houses the shops' offices, and those of the store-keeper and captain of the port.

Air Compressor Plant:

Building No. 29, located just south of the dry dock, contains the shop air-compressor plant and the pumps for unwatering the dock. The air compressors are driven by 2200-volt, 3-phase, 25-cycle synchronous motors, capable of carrying 75 percent leading power factor. Rotors are mounted on the crank-shafts, and serve as fly-wheels. There are two machines installed, one with a capacity of 5000 cubic feet feed of air per minute, compressed to 110 pounds per square inch, and the other with a capacity of 2400 cubic feet. Air mains are laid around the head of the dry dock and brought into the shop tunnel at Building No. 14, and between Buildings Nos. 1 and 2. Circulating water is piped to a hot well at the boiler plant, and used as boiler feed.

Shops' Tunnel:

In order to have the air, water, oil, steam, light and power mains out of the way and easy of access, a tunnel was built along the east and west axis of the site, with such lateral tunnels as were necessary leading from it. The general plan and cross-section of the tunnel are shown on Plate XI. The main tunnel is 4 feet 6 inches wide by 6 feet high, the floor of the tunnel being below high tide. The accompanying photograph, Fig. 12, shows the method used in excavating for the tunnel. A 45-ton steam shovel was used, the tracks being removed and replaced by I-beam girders on rollers. The depth of the excavation was about 12 feet at the lowest point and the dipper stick was lengthened accordingly, so that the full depth of excavation could be made with the shovel running along on top and over the trench. This was very satisfactory and the cost of digging the tunnel was very low. As it was not certain just what the track layout in the shop yards would be, it was considered advisable to place the tunnel on a pile foundation; and piles were, therefore, driven its entire length, except where it was possible to put concrete piers in, founded on rock. The reinforced tunnel was then built on this foundation in 30-foot sections. Alternate sections were constructed, to allow shrinkage to take place, a yellow metal strip being placed in the ends of each section to form a cut-off against water entering the joints. Wherever horizontal joints were made, the metal was also inserted and allowed to project into the next layer of concrete. The outside of the tunnel was washed with alum solution, as an extra precaution against seepage of water through the walls. The floor of the tunnel has a slight slope

Fig. 12. Excavation for Shops' Tunnel, Balboa New Shops.

to allow for drainage, and shallow gutters were moulded in the concrete floor on each side. The light and power cables run through vitrified tile ducts along either side of the tunnel, and the air, oil, sewer and water pipes are suspended or supported in the clear opening of the tunnel. At each building, there is a small branch outlet with a manhole, through which the various lines are carried, to meet the needs in the building.

Yards and Tracks:

Tracks for the shops, for repair wharves adjacent to shops, and for handling and coaling locomotives, total ten miles, and

·are built on the Panama Railroad standard gauge of five feet. Of the above, about one-half mile consists of tracks to quay walls, for repairs to boats and handling of lumber and other material, and about 2½ miles are used for locomotive storage and coaling facilities. The tracks are ballasted with Ancon rock or Chagres River gravel.

The shops' floors are all at elevation + 18, and all tracks in the shops are at the same elevation. Tracks on the dry dock walls are at an elevation of + 16.50, while those on the repair wharves and leading to the Panama Railroad storage yard are at elevation + 17. For this reason the tracks between the shops' buildings and the wharves, dry dock and yard are built somewhat lower, in order to make proper connections. This also assists in the drainage system.

Generally speaking, the drainage flows both ways from a summit line along the tunnel. Tile drains with open joints are laid in trenches under the eaves of the shops, and backfilled to the ground level with broken stone. The drains are 8-inch, 10-inch and 12-inch vitrified pipe, connecting with 15-inch and 18-inch pipes, and are laid on a slope of 0.2% to 0.5%. The drainage flows out under the repair wharves or into the storm culvert behind the dry-dock walls. After the shops' site had been filled in nearly to final grade, it was finished up (to about + 18) with crushed rock and a top dressing of stone screenings. The stone was not rolled, as it was desired to make the drainage as rapid as possible. The voids in the stone are sufficient to hold a large quantity of water until the drains can carry it off, and no trouble has been experienced from standing water.

The southeasterly corner of the shops' site adjoins Balboa Townsite, and from this point a 20-foot roadway passes the easterly end of the shops to the commercial pier and small-boat landing. Another road crosses the shops' area near its middle from Sosa Hill road to the shops' office. Very little curbing is used except for the main entrance road. The grading around the building is of such character that teams will be able to go in any part of the shops' grounds not occupied by tracks. Hydrants are located at frequent intervals about the shops' yard, and, in case of fire, the water system can be changed to high pressure.

Lighting:

The shops' yard is lighted by tungsten filament lamps mounted on gooseneck iron-pipe poles. The poles are fitted with one or two goosenecks, depending on their location. When two lamps are used, they are each 250 watt, and all single lights are 400 watt. Poles are 25 feet 9 inches in total height, with the center of the lamp 23 feet 3 inches above the ground. They are spaced approximately 175 feet apart, except where yard work requires closer spacing. Reflectors are of copper, porcelain enameled. All lights are operated on 2200-volt alternating current, connected in series by armored cable laid underground. There are no overhead wires in the yard.

All the work described above was performed by the Division of Terminal Construction, Panama Canal. Lieut.-Colonel T. C. Dickson, as Inspector of Shops, was in immediate charge of the design and inspection, reporting to the Engineer of Terminal Construction, Rear-Admiral H. H. Rousseau.

BALBOA SHOPS.

Cost Per Square Foot of Floor Area to May 31, 1915.

Number	Name	Floor Area	No. of Floors	Building Cost to Date	Building Cost per sq. ft.	Machinery Cost to Date	Machinery Cost per sq. ft.	Total Cost to Date	Total Cost per sq. ft.
1	Machine Shop	67,788	1	$388,722.24	$5.74	$197,537.25	$2.91	$586,259.49	$ 8.65
2	Forge Shop	31,929	1	131,868.32	4.13	62,210.42	1.95	194,078.74	6.08
3	Machine Shop	18,090	1	96,437.46	5.33	17,035.10	0.96	113,472.56	6.29
4	Boiler Shop	46,268	1	141,145.88	3.05	75,966.55	1.64	217,112.43	4.69
5	General Storage	94,230	2	267,782.67	2.84	13,165.22	.14	280,947.89	2.98
6	Paint Shop	12,570	1	54,452.19	4.33	977.92	.08	55,430.11	4.41
7	Car Shop	38,790	1	89,921.22	2.32	2,554.65	.07	92,475.87	2.39
8	Planing Mill	48,580	1	130,362.89	2.68	39,285.09	.80	169,647.98	3.48
9	Galvanizing Plant	5,825	1	39,724.45	6.82	11,657.69	1.99	51,382.14	8.81
10	Lumber Shed	67,160	1	111,060.24	1.65	....		111,060.24	1.65
11	Pattern Storage	14,002	2	57,384.04	4.10	403.64	.03	57,787.98	4.13
12	Foundry	38,442	1	170,308.90	4.43	71,854.31	1.87	242,163.21	6.30
13	Coke Shed	3,104	1	10,111.64	3.26	6.83	.00	10,118.47	3.26
14	Boiler House	2,460	1	19,844.97	8.06	6,802.99	2.77	26,647.96	10.83
15	Round House	25,390	1	137,984.57	5.43	11,559.99	.45	149,544.56	5.88
16	Gas House	904	1	6,322.17	7.00	3,496.37	3.87	9,818.54	10.87
17-25	Toilets	10,854	1	74,227.26	6.85	....		74,227.26	6.85
26	Paint House	1,085	1	7,328.96	6.75	805.47	.75	8,134.43	7.50
27	Sand House	513	1	11,383.96	22.19	909.34	1.97	12,393.30	24.16
28	Office Building	27,624	3	164,803.89	5.96	283.03	.01	165,086.92	5.97
30	Lye House	400	1	1,531.64	3.83	413.33	1.03	1,944.97	4.86

Table No. 1—Showing the floor area, in square feet, of the various departments of the permanent shop buildings.

	Building No.	Dimensions	Ground floor area in sq. ft.	Number of floors	Total floor area in sq. ft.
I. Shops—					
1. Tool department	1	58' 6" by 105' 6.5"	6,175	1	4,174
2. Erecting shop	1	58' 6" by 253' 1.5"	14,808	1	14,808
3. Machine shop	1	130' 6" by 358' 8"	46,806	1	46,806
4. Forge shop	2	89' 1" by 274' 1"	24,416	1	24,416
5. Pipe, tin, and copper shop	2	89' 1" by 84' 4"	7,513	1	7,513
6. Boiler and shipfitters' shop	4	129' 0" by 358' 8"	46,268	1	46,268
7. Planing mill, carpenter and pattern shop	8	121' 4" by 400' 5"	48,580	1	48,580
8. Foundry (brass, iron, and steel)	12	118' 0" by 316' 6", minus 4,117 for sand bins	33,230	1	34,508
9. Paint shop	6	49' 8.5" by 252' 11.5"	12,570	1	12,570
10. Paint mixing and storage	26	22' 6" by 48' 2.5"	1,085	1	1,085
11. Car shop	7	122' 4" by 317' 1"	38,790	1	38,790
12. Galvanizing, buffing, grinding, & plating	9	39' 4.5" by 147' 11"	5,825	1	5,825
13. Oxy-acetylene	16	22' 0" by 41' 1.25"	904	1	904
II. Storehouse—					
1. General, first floor	5	118' 8" by 400' 4"	47,496		
Do.	5	118' 8" by 400' 3", minus two openings 19' 3.5" by 19' 9"	46,734	2	94,230
2. Steel, iron, and pipe storage	3	50' 4" by 359' 5"	18,090	1	18,090
3. Lumber and equipment, foundry, supplies, and dry kilns	10	122' 4" by 549' 0"	67,160	1	67,160

	No.	Dimensions	Area	No.	Total
4. Patterns	11	First floor, 58' 8" by 119' 10"	7,029	2	14,002
		Second floor, 58' 8" by 119' 10", minus 7' 2" by 7' 10"	6,973		
5. Coke	13	18' 6" by 167' 10"	3,104	1	3,104
6. Sand bins	12	27' 4.5" by 143' 8.5"	3,934	1	3,934
III. Hostling locomotives—					
1. Roundhouse	15	15 stalls	25,390	1	25,390
2. Sand house	27	19' 0" by 27' 0"	513	1	513
IV. Office	28	Each floor 50' 10" by 117' 4", and 2 wings 33' 11" by 47' 10" each	9,208	3	27,624
V. Toilets*—					
1. Seven toilet rooms for gold employees	17 to } 25 inc.	5 at 22' 0" by 48' ½"	5,285		5,285
		2 at 22' 0" by 23' 7.25"	1,038		1,038
2. Seven toilet rooms for silver employees		5 at 22' 0" by 31' 9"	3,493		3,493
		2 at 22' 0" by 23' 7.25"	1,038		1,038
VI. Power—					
1. Boiler house	14	49' 4" by 49' 10"	2,460	1	2,460
2. Compressor and pump house	29	50' by 241' and 1 wing 20' by 40' 2"	12,850	1	12,850
3. Potash vat building	30	20' by 20'			
Total					566,458

* In 9 buildings.

Table No. 2—Showing horsepower of motors and their distribution in Balboa shop buildings.

Circuit	Building No.	Cranes (horse-power)	Alternating current				Direct current (individual)		Total alternating current horse-power
			Groups		Individual				
			Number	Total horse-power	Number	Total horse-power	Number	Horse-power	
1	1	347½	21	265	18	143	29	361½	755½
2	2	67½	2	40	7	127½			
	3	83			4	30			
	4	202½	2	30	22	218			
	16		1	7½					
		353	5	77½	33	375¼			806
3	8		7	92½	30	639			
	5				2	60			
	28				2	5¼			
			7	92½	34	704¼			796¾
4	12	193	2	15	16	206½			
	10				3	15			
	7		1	7½	3	35			
		193	3	22½	22	256½			472
Extension of 4	15		1	10	1	15			
	9	25½	1	7½	6	37			
		25½	2	17½	7	52			95
Air compressor					5	2000			2000
Total								361½	4910¾

Table No. 3—Showing calculated illumination in Balboa shop buildings.

Bldg. No.	Purpose.	Dimensions	Floor space	Watts	Watts per sq. ft.	Foot candles	Lumens per watt
1.	Machine shop	130' 6" by 358' 8"	46,806	79,100	1.69	7.60	4.49
	Tool department	58' 6" by 104' 6.5"	6,174	13,825	2.24	8.37	3.74
	Erecting shop	58' 6" by 253' 1.5"	14,808	27,500	1.85	7.75	4.20
2.	Forge shop	89' 1" by 179' 2.5"	15,964	12,500	.78	2.80	3.60
	Pipe, tin, and copper shop	89' 1" by 179' 2.5"	15,964	16,750	1.05	4.50	4.30
3.	Machine shop	50' 4" by 84' 10"	4,270	6,000	1.41	6.20	4.42
	Steel storage	50' 4" by 274' 7"	13,821	5,000	.36	1.50	4.17
4.	Boiler shop	129' 0" by 358' 8"	46,268	68,400	1.48	6.10	4.12
5.	General storage —						
	First floor	118' 8" by 400' 3"	47,496	12,000	.25	1.30	5.20
	Second floor		46,734	12,600	.26	1.30	5.00
6.	Paint shop	49' 8.5" by 252' 11.5"	12,570	10,750	.86	3.99	4.65
7.	Car shop	122' 4" by 317' 1"	38,790	29,000	.76	4.02	5.33
8.	Planing mill	121' 4" by 400' 5"	48,580	56,000	1.15	6.67	5.80
	Galvanizing plant—						
9.	Plating and grinding room	39' 4.5" by 61' 3"	2,412	2,000	.83	3.48	4.19
	Galvanizing room	39' 4.5" by 86' 8"	3,413	2,500	.73	2.85	3.80
10.	Lumber and equipment shed	122' 4" by 549' 0"	67,160	5,000	.08	.31	3.88
11.	Pattern storage—						
	First floor	58' 8" by 119' 10"	7,030	1,500	.21	.90	4.29
	Second floor	58' 8" by 119' 10"	6,973	1,500	.21	.90	4.29

Table No. 3—Continued.

Bldg. No.	Purpose.	Dimensions	Floor space	Watts	Watts per sq. ft.	Foot candles	Lumens per watt
12.	Foundry—						
	Main molding floor	61' 2" by 316' 6"	19,360	22,000	1.14	4.63	4.10
	Brass molding floor and core room	28' 5" by 136' 9"	3,886	4,250	1.1	3.01	2.74
	Chipping and cleaning room	28' 5" by 179' 9"	5,108	3,250	.64	2.48	3.90
	Supply bins, etc.	28' 5" by 316' 6"	8,994	3,850	.43	1.80	4.20
13.	Coke sheds	18' 6" by 167' 10"	3,104	*	....	....	....
14.	Boiler house	49' 4" by 49' 10"	2,460	2,250	.91	3.44	3.80
15.	Roundhouse	75' 9" by 418' 5"	†25,390	14,160	.56	‡2.80	‡3.00
16.	Gas house	41' 1.25" by 22' 0"	904	700	.76	‡3.08	‡4.00
17-25	Toilets		10,854	4,560	.42	2.19	5.20
26.	Paint house	48' 2.5" by 22' 6"	1,085	480	.44	2.19	5.20
27.	Sand house	27' 0" by 19' 0"	513	300	.58	‡2.03	‡3.50
28.	Office building	117' 10" by 79' 5"	27,624	27,480	1.00	5.02	5.02
	Grand total and averages		554,242	445,205	.80	.....	.....

*No lights.
†Approximate.
‡Estimated.

TERMINAL WORKS, DRY DOCKS AND WHARVES OF THE PANAMA CANAL.

By

H. H. ROUSSEAU, Assoc. M. Am. Soc. C. E.
Civil Engineer, U. S. Navy
Engineer of Terminal Construction, The Panama Canal
Balboa Heights, Canal Zone, Panama

This paper includes a résumé of terminal projects, a general description of the Panama Canal terminal works, and as detailed a description of the breakwaters, fuel oil plants, dry docks and wharves as can be given in the allotted space. The shop facilities are treated in detail in the paper "Permanent Shops" by H. D. Hinman and A. L. Bell, and the coaling plants and floating cranes in the paper "Coaling Plants and Floating Cranes of the Panama Canal" by F. H. Cooke.

Congress authorized these terminal works; in 1902 so far as was necessary for the construction of "such safe and commodious harbors and termini" of the canal; and in 1912, as regards dry docks, repair shops, coaling plants, wharves, storehouses and all "other necessary facilities and appurtenances". Various annual appropriations have supplied funds for each project paid for by the Panama Canal, as required. The Panama Railroad has built and paid for certain terminal works out of its surplus earnings.

The Canal and accessory works have been planned and constructed so as not to exceed the cost limit of $375,200,900 fixed by Congress, in accordance with the Isthmian Canal Commission's estimate of December, 1908. Terminal requirements were not given detailed study until some time after that estimate was made. At that time it was generally assumed that the Panama Railroad would provide any required facilities in the way of permanent docks and fuel plants, out of its surplus earnings, or with loans from the United States included in canal appropriations. Canal necessities as regards permanent shops and dry docks had not then developed. The only funds for terminal works included in the estimate of December, 1908, were as follows:

Atlantic Breakwaters $11,432,000.00

Loans to the Panama Railroad for the purchase
   of equipment and the construction of wharves
   and coaling plants 8,300,000.00

       Total $19,732,000.00

Of the second item approximately $2,587,000.00 was used by the Panama Railroad for new equipment, etc., leaving about $17,-145,000 available for terminal works.

The terminal works authorized to date are estimated to cost $32,710,000, of which amount the Panama Railroad will contribute from its surplus earnings $5,855,000, and the Panama Canal $26,855,000. The excess of the latter item over the above amount of $17,145,000 is $9,710,000, which represents the sum that has been allotted from savings accruing from other items of construction work, and from the general item for contingencies, of about 5%, that was included in the estimate of 1908.

A number of items which might also be classed properly with terminal improvements have not been included in the above amounts, such as:

1. The old "French Pier" at Balboa, completed by the Panama Railroad in 1898 at a cost, including cranes, of $1,024,-000, which, with other improvements including dredging, approach, filling, new railroad yards, etc., forming "La Boca Terminal", cost the Panama Railroad originally about $2,188,-000. Since 1905, improvements to this pier, including wharf cranes recently purchased, changes in floor, etc., have resulted in an additional expenditure of about $255,000.

2. Temporary wooden docks and wharves, with dredging, built by The Panama Canal for use during the construction period, costing $526,000. All wooden and otherwise non-rat-proof wharf structures in the Canal Zone, and in Panama and Colon must be removed by January 1, 1919.

3. Such work as was necessary for the construction of the

permanent buildings and towns at the canal terminals, including filling, street improvements, water and sewer systems, quarters and other buildings. This has special application to the towns of Balboa and new La Boca.

4. The construction by the Panama Railroad of terminal freight yards, and the making of all main line and other track changes to conform to the permanent lay-out.

5. Two Panama Canal colliers, the "Ulysses" and the "Achilles", purchased to transport coal to the Isthmian coaling stations from the United States. The cost of these two colliers, $1,000,000 each, was excluded from the Canal costs that are required to be paid from the bond issue of $375,200,900.

6. Such projects as the completion of Dry Dock No. 2 and adjacent pier, together with the required excavation and dredging to give access thereto, for which the estimated cost is $1,500,000. The plans for this project have been worked out. Construction work has been suspended thereon, pending both the development of the necessity for same as well as certainty that the funds therefor will not be required more urgently elsewhere.

The following is a list of the terminal works and the estimated costs, which it is expected will be completed by July 1, 1916:

Atlantic Terminals.

		Estimated Costs		
Project Number	Description	Paid by the Panama Canal	Paid by the Panama Railroad	
1.	Cristobal Coaling Plant	$2,250,000	$1,000,000	
2.	Railroad extension to Coaling Plant		185,000	
3.	Fuel Oil Plant	200,000		
4.	Dredging Approach Channel and around Piers and Docks	500,000	300,000	
5.	West Breakwater	3,500,000		
6.	East Breakwater	3,415,000		
7.	Cristobal Mole		540,000	
8.	Piers and Docks 7, 8, 9 and 10		3,430,000	
	Total	$9,865,000	$5,455,000	$15,320,000

Pacific Terminals.

Project Number	Description	Estimated Costs		
		Paid by the Panama Canal	Paid by the Panama Railroad	
9.	Excavation, fill and other preparatory and preliminary work for Pacific Terminals	$ 1,100,000		
10.	Excavation entrance basin and removal coffer dam	900,000		
11.	Dredging inner harbor	1,300,000		
12.	Reclamation and drainage of swamp land	350,000		
13.	Balboa shops and accessories	3,600,000		
14.	Dry Dock No. 1, including 50 ton locomotive crane	2,700,000		
15.	Wharves and piers	3,500,000	$ 400,000	
16.	Coaling Plant	1,250,000		
17.	Fuel Oil Plant	250,000		
18.	Naos Island Breakwater	790,000		
	Total	$15,740,000	$ 400,000	$16,140,000

General.

19.	Two 250-ton floating cranes	$ 900,000		
20.	Two Type "A" tugs	350,000		
	Total	1,250,000		1,250,000
	Grand total	$26,855,000	$5,855,000	$32,710,000

To July 1, 1915, The Panama Canal expenditures on the foregoing twenty items had been about $19,500,000, and the Panama Railroad expenditures about $3,800,000.

Of the above, items 2 and 7, and item 8, excepting Pier 7, were designed and constructed by Lieutenant F. Mears, U. S. Army, M. Am. Soc. C. E., as Chief Engineer of the Panama Railroad.

Item 5 was designed and constructed by Brigadier General W. L. Sibert, U. S. Army, M. Am. Soc. C. E., as Division Engineer of the Atlantic Division.

The dredging included under items 4 and 11, and the fill included under item 12 were performed by Mr. W. G. Comber, M. Am. Soc. C. E., as Resident Engineer of the Dredging Division.

Item 18 was designed and constructed by Lieutenant Colonel D. D. Gaillard, U. S. Army, as Division Engineer of the Central Division, as stated hereinafter.

A part of item 15, Wharves and Pier at Balboa, was designed and constructed by Mr. S. B. Williamson, M. Am. Soc. C. E., as Division Engineer of the Pacific Division, as stated hereinafter.

The tugs, item 20, were designed by Mr. M. C. Furstenau of Philadelphia.

The remainder of the work has been designed and constructed under the supervision of the writer, as Engineer of Terminal Construction, reporting directly to Major General Geo. W. Goethals, U. S. Army, as Governor.

TERMINAL HARBORS.

The Canal terminates on the Atlantic side in Limon Bay, a coastal indentation about 2½ miles wide and 5 miles long, measured along the Canal channel inside the breakwaters. (Plate I.) The depth varies quite uniformly from the head of the bay to a point opposite Cristobal mole. The Canal channel lies about ¾ mile from the water front of Colon. The bottom is soft mud with coral formations extending to the surface along the east shore. Without the protection of breakwaters Limon Bay would be entirely open to "northers" that blow from the north or a few degrees east or west of north, occurring from November to April. These wind storms, which are usually preceded or accompanied by heavy rain, drive waves of great size and force into the bay, in the past damaging or endangering any shipping lying there. Prior to 1905 there are records of eight northers of unusual intensity that destroyed or damaged some 43 vessels, besides doing much damage to the wharves of Colon. Northers of this class usually last from three to five days and are accompanied by wind blowing from 30 to 40 miles per hour. Such northers ordinarily occur only at intervals of several years. Storms of less intensity and resulting from the same causes, but doing little or no damage, occur at the average rate of from three to five a year.

There are no currents in Limon Bay affecting appreciably either navigation or the movement of the bottom silt. Immediately after the Canal channel was cut through the bay there was considerable silting, induced by the wave action on the shore. The works which have been constructed have practically discontinued this action. The average tidal range in Limon Bay is 11 inches, mean high water being + 0.679 and mean low water — 0.246. The extreme range is 2 feet 8 inches.

At the Pacific end, the Canal passes out to Panama Bay through the old channel of the Rio Grande River. The dredged channel continues about four and one-half miles beyond the old shore line to a point opposite San José rock, where the depth is 45 feet, referred to mean sea-level. No storms that injure shipping visit the Pacific side. The most severe disturbances consist of wind squalls of comparative short duration. The maximum velocity of wind recorded at Balboa is 58 miles per hour. The usual outer anchorage of vessels is to the south of Flamenco Island. The construction of a continuous breakwater or dike from Flamenco Island to the shore has resulted in protecting the Canal channel from the littoral currents setting to the southwest, that would otherwise necessitate a large amount of maintenance work. The tidal range at Balboa, referred to the zero of the Balboa tide gauge, and based on the number of years' observations stated, is as follows:

Mean high water (7 years' record) plus 6.6

Mean low water (7 years' record) minus 5.7

Mean tidal range (7 years' record) 12.3 feet

Mean high water, ordinary Spring tides (5 years' record) plus 8.37

Mean low water, ordinary Spring tides (5 years' record) minus 7.57

Tidal range, ordinary Spring tides (5 years' record) 15.94 feet

Extreme high water, plus 11.2 feet

Extreme low water, minus 10.6 feet

Extreme tidal range, 21.8 feet

Terminal Works at Colon and Panama Prior to 1880.

At Colon, the Panama Railroad controlled the entire water front except two strips of shore line which were owned by the Royal Mail Steam Packet Company and the Pacific Mail Steamship Company. These three companies constructed a number of piers of light construction. Wooden piling was largely used for the substructure, with some metal piles, both cast iron and wrought iron or steel—some with screw discs at the point to increase the bearing area. Wooden piles have been protected from marine borers by creosoting, by sheathing them with copper, and by covering them with vitrified tile and concrete pipe. The floors of the docks were constructed of wood. Several of the pier sheds were of steel or iron, with curved top chord roof trusses and corrugated iron roofing and siding. Only three of these piers remain today. They are in poor condition, and, not being rat-proof, must be replaced with permanent construction or destroyed not later than January, 1919. Notwithstanding the damage caused to all of these wharves by the constantly recurring northers during the period from 1853 to 1880, no protective harbor works were undertaken.

At Panama, several wooden pier structures were constructed by the Panama Railroad, which were used to transfer freight to and from lighters. Panama City has never had a wharf that could be used at low water, and, since the sixteenth century and the days of old Panama, the transfer of cargoes on the Pacific side had been by lighters.

Terminal Projects and Works During the Days of the French Canal Companies—1880-1904.

The problem confronting the French in connection with terminal works was to provide as quickly as possible such facilities as were needed during the construction period, and after that to give consideration to such as would be required for the operation of the canal. The solution which naturally resulted was to erect such facilities for construction purposes as would form so far as practicable a portion of the works which would be required for the completed canal.

The following relates to the Atlantic terminal:

Several of the American delegates to the International Congress recommended, in 1879, a breakwater at Colon, extending into the bay from Manzanillo Point, where the Panama Railroad maintained a tower and light, to the west, a distance of 460 meters. Messrs. Wyse and Réclus included a similar breakwater 850 meters long in their project for a sea-level canal. In the latter part of 1881 the Commission Internationale approved the project of a breakwater 1000 meters long, constructed of rock, and armored with concrete blocks or the equivalent. This would have afforded protection to Colon wharves and piers. Before work started it was decided that the necessity of obtaining protection for assembling and mooring floating equipment of the French Canal Company was so great as to make it impossible to await the construction of this breakwater, and an alternative plan was decided upon as follows:

A temporary basin, to form a part of the permanent terminal basin of the Canal, was located between two coral reefs lying southwest of Manzanillo Island, with an entrance channel 200 meters wide. A mole composed of hard rock was built on the east reef, forming the present site of the town of Cristobal, which work started in 1881. The proposed mole on the second reef, which occupies a portion of the site of the permanent coaling plant now under construction, was never built, the protection afforded by the Cristobal mole having been found during the norther of 1883 to be sufficient. A wharf for unloading material, on the site of the present Dock 11, was started in 1881, as well as a coal dock near Folks River. The Mount Hope dry dock was excavated in the soft argillaceous sandstone, with little or no concrete lining, and having wooden miter entrance gates. Dry dock work started in 1886.

This dry dock was enlarged by the United States in 1908 to meet the requirements of canal construction work. It has performed valuable service and has been constantly busy. Its present dimensions are:

Length from head to entrance 293.0 feet

Total length from gate to head measured on center line on floor 303.5 feet

Width at entrance 49.95 feet

Width measured in body at coping level 69.33 feet.

Depth of water over sill referred to mean sea level 13.4 feet.

The dredging of the interior temporary basin, which was designed to form a part of the permanent terminal basin, was carried on from 1882 to 1885 by the American Dredging and Contracting Company. After 1885 the dredging of the basin and in the canal channel to the south was performed by another contractor, under orders to give preference to the channel work. In 1888, plans for the permanent harbor were received from Paris. Modifications recommended by the engineers on the Isthmus, including Messrs. Pioch and Dingler, led to a reconsideration of this plan. As finally approved the project is shown on Plate I.

Nothing had been undertaken on this permanent harbor plan other than dredging before the company failed, in 1889. The new French Company never performed any work on this harbor. A project including some modifications of the approved plan was considered on the Isthmus, and plans were prepared, but this project was never forwarded to Paris.

The Pacific terminal works projected in 1884 by the French were to be included between Corozal and old La Boca on the Rio Grande tidal flats and to lie between the Panama Railroad and the Canal, as shown on Plate II, with a tidal lock at Corozal. The interior basin was to be named Panama Harbor. To eliminate the effect of tides, a temporary dam and tide gate were to be located at La Boca near the shipways. The tidal gate was to be 10 meters wide to pass the construction equipment. Sluiceways were to be provided for, taking the discharge from the Rio Grande swamp. A diversion of the Rio Grande River was constructed from Pedro Miguel to the sea. The temporary dam occupied the same site as Sosa dam, later proposed for the American Canal. It was proposed to complete the north end of Panama Harbor opposite Corozal to the extent of fifty hectares. The tidal lock, wharves, storehouses, and machine shops were to be located along the east side of the basin. A dry dock of dimensions similar to those of the dry dock of the Colon project was located at the northeast corner of the basin. Each tidal lock consisted of two gate chambers 160 meters apart (524.9 feet). The gate chambers were to be 65.65 meters (215.2 feet) long and 25 meters (82 feet) wide. The width of the canal channel north of locks at the bottom was 22 meters (72.2 feet). The gate sills were placed at elevation — 12.20 meters (40 feet). The tidal locks were designed so that they could be readily removed if in actual operation they were found to be not needed.

No work was ever executed on this project except the canal channel, the old shipways and a small pier for construction use. Contracts for dredging the canal channel between Pedro Miguel and La Boca were executed in 1884, and in 1886 the French Canal Company started work on the channel from La Boca to the sea. In subsequent years this work was continued under contract. The adoption of a plan for a lock canal in 1887 and the fact that under its concession from the United States of Colombia the Panama Railroad was subject to an annual payment of $10,000 until its Pacific terminus was extended to deep water; also the completion of the channel from La Boca to the sea to a depth of nine meters in 1888, brought about the abandonment of the "Panama Harbor" project and the decision on the part of the Canal Company to build a terminal immediately at La Boca. The failure of the old French Company and the period of reorganization from 1889 to 1894 led to the deferring of any work on the La Boca Terminal until 1895, when negotiations were resumed between the French Canal Company and Panama Railroad officials, which resulted in the building of a steel pier and the dredging of a turning basin by the Panama Railroad, from 1896 to 1898. The "La Boca Terminal" cost the Panama Railroad approximately $2,188,000, of which $963,000 was for the steel pier, $61,000 for the wharf cranes, $601,000 for dredging and $89,000 for embankment and fill. The wharf, supported by large concrete cylinders carried down to rock, was constructed 302.20 meters long and 16.50 meters wide, roofed with corrugated iron on steel trusses, and provided with six hydraulic cranes of 1½ tons capacity and one hand operated crane of 15 tons capacity. A berth 350 meters long and 30 meters wide was dredged to El. — 11 meters in front of the wharf, with a turning basin 180 meters wide opposite the wharf, dredged to El. — 9.50 meters. This steel pier is still rendering good service. In 1906 considerable work was done on it, including the removal of tracks and replacing them with double depressed tracks carried on a pile trestle in the rear. The pier shed was correspondingly widened. At La Boca, the French constructed quite complete shop facilities, principally for repairs to marine equipment, including a gridiron, and shipways, which plant remained in continuous operation until it was displaced by the permanent Balboa Shops that were completed in 1915.

Terminal Work Since 1904.

The report of the Board of Consulting Engineers of 1906 recommended harbor protection at the Atlantic terminal along the lines of the French, giving due consideration to the change in the location of the American canal. The Board's plan provided for two breakwaters, approximately parallel to the channel. (Plate I.) The distance between the ends of the breakwaters at the Canal entrance was 1000 feet. The dredged channel in Limon Bay was to have a width of 500 feet. Had this plan been followed, the protected harbor would have been of inadequate size for Canal shipping of today. The minority report shifted the dredged channel in Limon Bay to the west in more easily dredged material and extended the west breakwater to the head of the bay, though it was suggested to omit the west breakwater wholly or in part and to widen the channel to 1000 feet or more.

At the Pacific terminal, the majority Board report of 1906 adopted a 300-foot channel extending in a straight line from a point north of Corozal to the tidal lock between Sosa and Ancon Hills, and thence with a slight break to deep water off Flamenco Island. This plan contemplated the use of rock excavated from the channel to form a low dike on the west side of the channel from the shore towards Flamenco to protect the channel from silting, and anticipated the advisability of using any available rock for a similar dike on the east side of the channel.

At the Pacific end the minority Board report included Lake Sosa with two-lift locks of 31 feet each, located on the west side of Sosa Hill, and a dredged channel about four miles long from Sosa locks out into Panama Bay closely following the dredged channel of the French company. The Board's report did not cover any terminal works other than to mention that the La Boca pier would probably be "of great service as a landing place during the construction of the Canal and very useful for a coaling station subsequently".

As built, the Atlantic breakwaters were located so as to shelter as large an anchorage area as practicable, and to protect the channel in Limon Bay as well. The west breakwater was authorized first. The construction of the east breakwater was deferred until the effect of the west breakwater could be observed. On the Pacific side, the removal of the double lift locks from La Boca to Miraflores was authorized in December, 1907; and leading the channel straight to sea west of Naos Island, in connection with the disposition of spoil from Culebra Cut, paved the way for active steps to be taken for the construction of the Naos Island Breakwater, which was completed in 1914.

The Panama Railroad has been largely interested in all steps taken to furnish adequate wharves and piers for permanent use at the Atlantic terminal. For several years subsequent to 1904 the railroad was handicapped by inadequate funds, and it was necessary for the Panama Canal to construct a number of temporary wooden wharves, and perform necessary dredging at each terminal, so that vessels bringing canal equipment and supplies to the Isthmus could be promptly berthed and unloaded. Canal expenditures for these temporary structures amounted to $526,000, a portion of which has been returned in the form of rentals of those docks which were used by the Panama Railroad. On the Atlantic side, these docks were located along the French canal from Cristobal point up as far as Mount Hope. At the Pacific end, the docks joined and formed an extension to the old La Boca pier.

In locating the permanent docks at the Atlantic end, attention was first directed to the French canal between Cristobal point and the dry dock shops at Mount Hope, where the French proposed their terminal harbor. The lack of ground for tracks, yards, etc., and the cost of removing the large amount of coral rock in the channel, and the depth to hard bottom on which to found piers at other points, caused the further development of the north shore line of the old French canal entrance to be abandoned, and resulted in adopting a project in the latter part of 1910, which has since been followed, of building the terminal docks and piers behind the protection of a mole jutting out from Cristobal at right angles to the Canal, parallel to the approach channel leading to Cristobal docks and located about 1000 feet to the north thereof. This plan is elastic and provides for the extension of the mole as the building of additional piers becomes necessary. This project provides room for the construction of five piers, two of which have been authorized. At the time this project was approved, the construction of the east breakwater had not been approved. So far as the protection to the canal channel and to vessels lying at the permanent wharves, and in the French canal is concerned, the east breakwater is not necessary. Its construction, which was strongly urged by the Navy Department, was authorized in 1913, principally to protect vessels lying in the outer anchorage not entirely under the lee of the west breakwater, and to ensure their communication with the shore by means of small boats in all weather. All permanent docks at the Atlantic terminal have been constructed by the Panama Railroad at its own expense, except Pier No. 16, the permanent coaling plant. This was necessary as Congress did not authorize the Panama Canal to construct any terminal docks and piers until August, 1912.

At the Pacific terminal, the pressing need of additional berthing space and the lack of authorization to construct permanent docks by the Panama Canal, led to the construction by the Panama Railroad of a reinforced concrete dock, known as "f-g", about 650 feet by 57½ feet, in 1910. This dock was located as closely as possible to deep water, and at the east end of a wooden dock that had been built by the Canal for construction purposes. This dock, with the necessary dredging, was constructed by the Panama Canal for the Panama Railroad as an open dock for use in unloading lumber, steel, etc. It was completed in July, 1912. Meanwhile the Board on Canal Fortifications in the early part of 1910, had recommended as necessary the construction of a naval repair plant, including shops, dry docks, etc., near each terminal, at Mindi on the Atlantic side, and at Diablo on the Pacific side. As these repair plants, required only for military use, would largely duplicate facilities required for canal use, an arrangement was made in 1910, satisfactory to the War and Navy departments and approved by the President, that would combine under the Canal all terminal facilities, including wharves, dry docks, shops, etc., for the joint use of all departments of the Government. This led to locating the main shop and dry dock facilities at the Pacific terminal, with the understanding that the moderate shop facilities at the Atlantic terminal and the small dry dock originally constructed by the French, would be maintained as long as necessary, and even enlarged if the future demands justified it. At Balboa the complete project provides for five 1000-foot by 200-foot piers with 300-foot slips between, of which one pier has been authorized. The depth in the approach channels and alongside of wharves at the Atlantic and Pacific sides is the same as in the adjacent canal channels, viz., — 41, referred to mean sea level, at Cristobal, and — 45 at Balboa. The interior basin at Balboa is provided for the convenient handling of vessels to the piers and docks from the canal channel and vice versa, and not as an anchorage basin.

In 1907-8, the old French dry dock at Cristobal was enlarged in order to be able to accommodate all construction equipment. This has been the only dry dock yet in use on the Isthmus. On the Pacific side, the considerable range in tide permitted under-water maintenance and repairs to be made to vessels either by beaching them or by placing them on a gridiron. Barges and other small vessels were hauled out on the shipways at Balboa. During the construction period, repair shops were located at various points where required by the work, and where the French had already constructed shop buildings and storehouses and had completely equipped repair plants in commission. These shops include the plants at Gorgona and Empire, which were principally employed to keep dry excavation plant in service. The shops at Balboa and Mount Hope were devoted especially to repairs to marine equipment. In 1904, the Panama Railroad operated its repair shops on the beach of what was originally Aspinwall, at the north end of Colon. In 1906, the railroad shops were transferred to the new plant at Cristobal. In 1913, the Panama Canal and Panama Railroad shops were consolidated, which led to the gradual closing down of the Cristobal shops. At first, the marine shops were operated under the respective divisions having supervision of construction work in their vicinity. The other shops, including Gorgona, Empire and Paraiso were operated by the Mechanical Division. During the latter days, the principle of consolidation was applied so far as practicable, and at the present time all shops are operated by the Mechanical Division.

The new Balboa plant was designed to afford the greatest convenience with the greatest operating economy. The shops and the dry dock are located on a strip of ground, made partly by filling in and partly by grading, averaging 800 feet in width, and 2700 feet in length. The details of construction of the shops are described in another paper.

The new wood-working shop, No. 8, at Balboa began operations in July, 1913, the foundry in August, 1913, and the other buildings followed at intervals.

As completed the shops compare very well with a first-class railroad or marine repair plant. The average monthly expenditures for labor and material at Balboa Shops during the past year have been $192,000. The number of employes has varied from 1500 to 2500.

All work in connection with the design and construction of the shops was performed by the Division of Terminal Construction. Lieut.Col. T. C. Dickson, Inspector of Shops, was in charge of all designing and drafting work, and of the installation of machinery, and the mechanical and electrical equipment, and of all inspection work on the Isthmus. He was assisted by Mr. A. L. Bell, Assoc. M. Am. Soc. M. E., as Mechanical Engineer. Construction work in connection with the foundations, floors, all other concrete and plaster work, etc., was performed by General Superintendent J. A. Walker, assisted by Mr. H. D. Hinman,

Assoc. M. Am. Soc. C. E., as Assistant Engineer. Me
man and Bell have prepared a joint paper on the co
of the shops as Lieut.-Col. Dickson, who is now in co
the Government proving ground at Sandy Hook, was
arrange to return to the Isthmus for this purpose.

As part of the repair plant, the Panama Canal
chased two 250-ton floating cranes for handling heavy
Floating, rather than stationary wharf cranes were sel
the principal office of these cranes as Canal accessories i
nish 500 tons lifting capacity at any lock to remove an
gate leaf in the shortest time practicable, or to assist in h
into place a new gate leaf. These cranes are useful adju
the Canal in connection with general construction and
work, and wrecking service. They have been purchased
general specifications which were based on Naval as well as
requirements. The preliminary investigation and conside
in connection with the purchase of these cranes were mad
and the general specifications based thereon were prepare
Civil Engineer F. H. Cooke, U. S. N., Assoc. M. Am. Soc. C
as Designing Engineer, Division of Terminal Construction.
Henry Schoellhorn, as Assistant Engineer, was in charge o
inspection and the approval of drawings at the manufactur
works. He also superintended the erection and tests of the cra
on the Isthmus. These cranes are described in detail by M
Cooke in a succeeding paper.

The ability of users of the Canal to purchase fuel at any
time of a satisfactory quality, in any quantity, at a reasonable
price in a convenient and rapid manner was early recognized as
a factor of great value to the Canal. During the construction
period the Panama Railroad handled all matters connected with
the purchase and supply of coal to the Canal, and to steamship
lines at the Canal terminals. Fuel oil was purchased by the
Panama Canal from the Union Oil Company. The sale of fuel
oil to steamships during the construction period was not large.
The following table gives the consumption of fuel oil by fiscal
years by the Canal and the Panama Railroad. The tons of coal
sold and used by the Panama Railroad on the Isthmus is also
given by fiscal years, as follows:

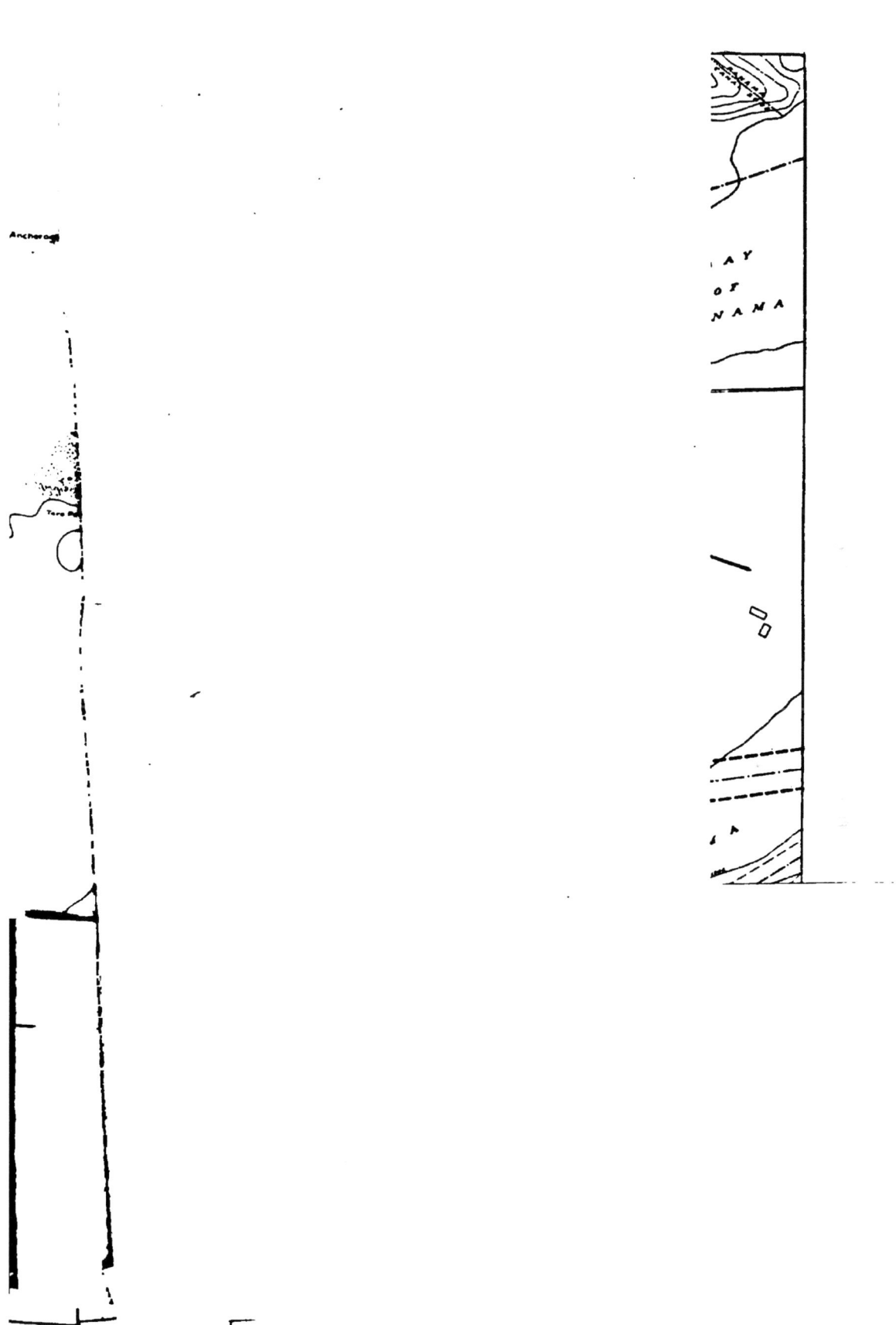

Oil.

1907	6	barrels
1908	17,405	"
1909	239,623	"
1910	1,143,539	"
1911	888,940	"
1912	694,137	"
1913	675,407	"
1914	365,859	"
1915	198,590	"
Total	4,223,506	"

Coal.

1905	75,673	tons
1906	130,383	"
1907	203,451	"
1908	368,331	"
1909	357,125	"
1910	481,039	"
1911	490,864	"
1912	491,494	"
1913	462,246	"
1914	325,646	"
1915	369,955	"
Total	3,756,207	"

The policy of consolidation, adopted in 1910, applied to the fuel plants as well as to the shops. The fuel plants have, therefore, been designed to meet Canal and Naval requirements as well as to serve commercial interests. The latter feature was approved in 1913. It resulted from the following conditions: Under existing law, the Canal cannot lease any land, or land under water, in the Canal Zone except for agricultural purposes. This was not satisfactory to coal companies, or to steamship companies desiring to establish their own coal depots on the Isthmus, as the construction of piers and other structures necessary for a coaling plant, under a revocable license, would permit the United States to terminate the license without reimbursing the owner for the value of the improvements. The situation was not a desirable one for either the Canal or the coal companies. The United States has moreover adopted the policy of retaining direct control of all water front at the terminals, including control of all water front in Colon through the Panama Railroad. The best working arrangement that could be effected therefore was to construct the Government coal plants in such a manner as would permit certain storage areas, served by the coal handling machinery in the same manner as the Canal coal pile was served, to be leased to any individual or company desiring to store and sell coal on the Isthmus. The Government furnishes all the facilities and will charge as rental an amount per square foot of area per annum, as well as a handling charge per ton both in and out of storage. This is the plan which is being followed for both the Atlantic and Pacific coaling plants. For the fuel oil plants, on account of the distance of the tank farms from the water front, and the remote possibility of the Government requiring the ground for its own uses, the leasing of lots under revocable licenses has proceeded, the United States retaining control of the water front and handling plants. The main coaling plant has been located at the Atlantic terminal in accordance with the recommendation of the Navy Department. In addition to the coal to be stored in the dry for Canal and commercial use, a pocket has been provided in each plant for the storage of coal under water, under the control of the Navy Department. The rates of handling into storage and the rates of reloading have been fixed so as to be able to equal the speed of any coaling plant in the United States, and of meeting any Naval requirement or emergency. All work in connection with the design and construction of the coaling plants has been performed by the Division of Terminal Construction. Civil Engineer F. H. Cooke, U. S. N., Assoc. M. Am. Soc. C. E., was in charge of the preparation of the specifications for the coal handling machinery for both plants, of the design and preparation of working drawings of the wharf and other structures of the Cristobal plant, and the supports for the "berm" cranes, etc., at Balboa. Assistant Engineer W. Rowland, Assoc. M. Am. Soc. C. E., was in charge of the design of the Unloader and Reloader Wharves at Balboa. Superintendent W. G. Thompson, Assoc. M. Am. Soc. C. E., has been in charge of construction work at the Cristobal plant and has acted as Chief Inspector of the erection of the coal handling machinery. At the Balboa plant construction work has been ned by General Superintendent J. A. Walker. Field engineering and inspection have been performed by Assistant Engineer H. D. Hinman, Assoc. M. Am. Soc. C. E., who also acted as assistant on construction work. These coaling plants are described in detail by Mr. Cooke in a succeeding paper.

DRY DOCKS.

Location:

The main dry dock, No. 1, at Balboa, is located under the protection of Sosa Hill. It is supported entirely on rock. Its axis is parallel to the small section of permanent dock "f-g" which had already been constructed. The coping of the dock was placed at such a distance—636.5 feet—from the face of the permanent quay wall as would permit the shop buildings to be built between them, and at the same time would not place the head of the dry dock so close to Sosa Hill as to unduly increase the excavation.

Dimensions:

The ability to dock any vessel that can pass through the Canal locks fixes the principal dimensions of this dock, which are as follows:

Length on center line from head to miter sill	1044	feet
Length on center line from head to caisson sill	1102.67	"
Width of dock at entrance	110	"
Width in body of dock at floor	113	"
Width in body of dock at coping	143	"
Elevation of top of blocks referred to mean sea level	—35	"
Elevation of floor and entrance sills referred to mean sea level	—39.5	"

Foundation:

Sosa Hill rock, on which the dry dock is founded, is a mass of dark fine-grained andesite which has welled up from below as a cooled volcanic neck. Outwards from the hill, the bedrock varies from gray to buff in color, indicating the first stages of decomposition. The strength of this lighter colored rock is entirely suitable. At different points during the excavation a number of vertical seams and pockets were encountered where local decomposition had taken place to such an extent that the material could be excavated without drilling and blasting. In general the material forming the foundation is strong, solid, and well suited for a heavy structure.

General Features:

The dock has been designed to meet all requirements of the Canal, the Navy, and commercial interests. The side altars are three feet wide, and are spaced to conform to naval requirements. The side walls are gravity walls of mass concrete. It was not practicable to excavate the rock to the desired interior dimensions and line it with concrete. Seventy-pound old rails, spaced 4 feet apart longitudinally were provided to take up the slight

Fig. 1. Condition of South Wall of Dry Dock No. 1 after Excavation by Steam Shovels to Elev. —40.

tension resulting at the level of the dock floor under the most severe assumption. The dock is closed by a pair of steel miter gates electrically operated. The design of the gates and the operating machinery is similar to that of the lock gates. The gates will open or close in less than two minutes. The sills and the hollow quoins will be granite. For the locks, the hollow quoins are metal and the sills are greenheart, attached to castings embedded in the floor masonry. The change to granite for dock was made on account of the constant exposure of the dock gates and fittings to sea water. For the same reason, the metal miter and quoin posts of the lock gates have been replaced on the dock gates (except for the quoin heel castings) by green-heart. An outer sill of granite has been provided also. The outer sill has been built to conform to the dimensions of the caisson which was purchased for use in connection with the locks. The use of this caisson, which is equipped with a pumping plant, will enable the outside of the dock gates to be examined and

Fig. 2. General View of Dry Dock, Shops, Entrance Basin and Cofferdam
from Sosa Hill.

painted. It increases the usable length of the dock about 43 feet. If necessary, the dock can thus be pumped out without using its own pumping plant. The existence of this caisson has rendered the use of miter gates practicable. The floor of the dock is level longitudinally for full length and transversely for a width of 66 feet. Access to the floor of the dock is obtained by four stair-ways on each side; one at the head and one at the entrance,— with two intermediate sets having a straight run. Slides are pro-vided in connection with the two intermediate sets. The concrete floor has a minimum thickness of one foot. Where seams or pockets of disintegrated rock occur the thickness of the floor is greater, and in some places has been increased to five feet. The keel blocks provided will be of cast iron of the wedge type, with the top block of white oak. The bilge keel blocks will be of Demerara greenheart topped with white oak, and the sliding bilge blocks will be of white oak.

At the coping level, elevation plus 16.5, along each side wall

Fig. 3.   General View of Entrance to Pier No. 19, Entrance to Dry Dock, and Shop Buildings, from Unloader Wharf, Dock No. 7.

there will be a 5-foot gauge railroad track and a 22-foot gauge crane track, the latter for a 50-ton standard locomotive crane having a reach of 87 feet. A line of bollards extends around the dock. There will be four electric-driven capstans on each side and one at the head of the dock. These capstans will develop a rope pull of 30,000 lbs. at a speed of 30 feet per minute. The dock is flooded by a culvert on each side, the sea entrance to each ⸛ert consisting of twin openings each 8 ft. by 12 ft., set 15 ft. ꝛ the dock floor, each controlled by a hydraulically operated "wagon-body" valve. Near the entrance each culvert descends below the floor level and is formed in the base of the side wall, communicating with the dock body by 17 grated openings set in the floor. This method of distributing the inflowing water was adopted to prevent detrimental longitudinal currents. The estimated time of filling the dock to mean high water level is thirty minutes. Six-inch diameter air vents lead from the top of the tunnel to the inside of the dock just above the floor level at each

Fig. 4. Setting Top Girder of North Leaf. Mitre Gates, Dry Dock No. 1.

floor outlet, i. e., at 55.5 feet intervals. To drain off any water accumulating behind the side walls, a 12- by 14-inch culvert with open joints has been built in the back of the side walls continuously around the dock, at elevation minus 27.5, with eight eight-inch connections through the side walls into the body of the dock, near the floor level, where check valves will be installed which can be readily inspected. This culvert is also connected with the interior of the pump-well by a 15-in. pipe, with a gate valve operated from the pump-well, which will enable hydrostatic

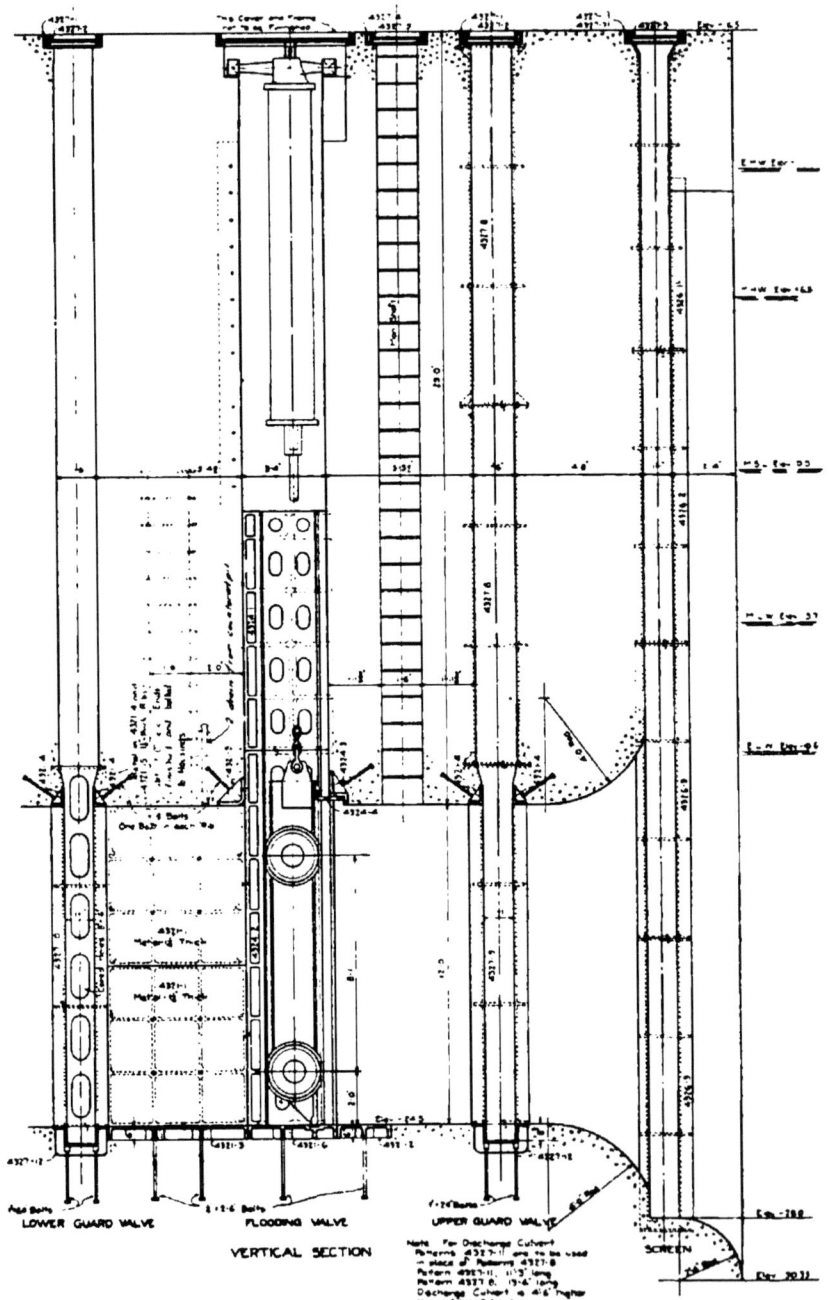

LOWER GUARD VALVE   FLOODING VALVE   UPPER GUARD VALVE   SCREEN

VERTICAL SECTION

Fig. 5. Flooding and Sluice Valves.

conditions behind the walls to be readily ascertained. The discharge through the 15-in. pipe is led to the drainage pumps.

The pump-well is located on the south side of the dry dock
near the entrance, and has been designed to serve both Dry
Dock No. 1 and Dry Dock No. 2. The logical place for this
pump-well would have been on the north or opposite side of the
entrance, but room could not be spared at that point. The pump-
well pit in plan is 99.5 ft. by 54.5 ft., with longer dimension
parallel to axis of dock. The main pump floor is at elevation
minus 37.0, and the drainage pump floor at elevation minus 58.5,
which is the lowest floor in the pit. The pump-well is excavated
largely in rock, against which the lower portions of the south
and east walls will be built.

The north wall is connected, by vertical reinforced diaphragms five feet thick and 20 feet c. to c., to the adjacent dock
wall; these diaphragms also support the seven-foot thick reinforced roof of the pump suction chamber. The discharge culvert for the main pumps is built into the south wall of the pump
well, thus reducing the amount of exposed piping. It is 12 by 14
ft. in section, and discharges at a point about 100 feet distant
from the pump well. A separate discharge culvert three feet
square is provided for the drainage pumps, parallel to the main
culvert. There are four main pumps, 54 inches discharge
diameter, volute centrifugal, single bottom suction, vertical shaft.
Each is driven by a 1000-hp., 2200-volt, three-phase motor, located vertically over the pump and supported on a floor just
above coping level. The necessary bearings for the shafting are
held by suitable intermediate supports. The combined capacity
of the main pumps is such that the dock can be emptied in about
2½ hours. There are two 20-in. drainage pumps similar to the
main pumps, each driven by a 200-hp. motor. A 3-in. bilge pump
is also provided for handling water draining into the pump
well. The main and drainage pumps are each provided with
individual suction, discharge, and non-return valves; other
valves are provided in the piping as required. All valves which
are part of the normal working of the plant are operated by
water at a pressure of 300 lbs. per sq. in., and are controlled
from a table, at which the position of each valve disc is indicated
by colored lights. The pressure water is furnished by a motor-

driven accumulator situated in the pump well. The air compressor plant is primarily for the supply of compressed air to the shops, but is housed in a continuation of the pump-well housing, the combined building being about 245 feet long by 60 feet wide. There will be two motor-driven compressors, having a capacity of 2250 and 5500 cu. ft., respectively, of free air per minute. The air thus compressed will serve the dry dock as well as the shops.

The excavation for Dry Dock No. 1, Dry Dock No. 2, the entrance basin and the coaling plant required the removal of about 1,500,000 yards of material, most of which was hard rock. This work was performed in the dry by steam shovels working inside of a clay cofferdam without sheet piling, the clay being dumped from a trestle driven from the north side of Dry Dock No. 2, across the entrance to Dry Dock Nos. 1 and 2 to the Reloader Wharf. This excavation was performed by steam shovels, the material being loaded on steel dump cars, varying in capacity from 15 to 23 cubic yards, or on lidgerwood flat cars having a capacity of about 18 cubic yards. Owing to limited space, no more than four shovels could be worked at one time, and until practically all of the steam shovel work had been completed it was impossible to commence concrete work on the dry dock. Excavation was started in January, 1913, and completed in the latter part of 1914. The excavation, including plant and division expense, cost as follows:

Dry Dock No. 1	0.990c per cu. yd.
Dry Dock No. 2	0.736c " " "
Coaling Plant	0.767c " " "
Entrance Basin	0.945c " " "

The material was hauled out on a double track leading up from the east end of the dry dock on a grade which did not exceed 5%. As excavation work progressed in the body of the dry dock, a single track trestle on a 5% grade, on approximately the center line of the dry dock, was used. The rock forming the sides of the dry dock excavation stood up very well. A great deal of the rock was of a columnar formation resembling basalt, the columns standing very straight with an upward slope to the south of about 1 horizontal to 5 vertical. A great deal of the rock that was suitable was retained in the pit for use in concrete. Several springs were encountered. They were disposed of so as to eliminate any pressure on the floor. Generally they were piped into the flooding culverts and capped with check valves. At the entrance of the dry dock, underneath the sill of the caisson, a water cut-off was provided by drilling two rows of holes, the rows four feet apart, and holes 6 feet center to center in each row, 18 feet deep, extending from a line of similar holes under the entrance pier wall on the north side, to the Unloader Wharf bank on the south side. Grout was forced into these holes under a pressure of 80 lbs. per square inch. A line of similar holes was drilled and grouted under the miter gate sill. The average amount of grout forced into the rock was 229 cubic inches per hole.

Concrete Plant:

The first concrete was placed on August 17, 1914. The main mixing plant consisted of four ½-yard cube mixers set on top of the bank, arranged in two batteries. Each battery discharged through a chute into an elevated hopper on the dry dock floor, which led directly into 2-yard bottom-dumping buckets on 3-foot gauge flat cars, handled by steam locomotives. Locomotive cranes with 75-foot booms handled the buckets from the cars and dumped the concrete into the forms. The mixers were filled by wheelbarrows from the storage pile, which was replenished by dumping cars from a raised track. The cement was delivered in bags in cars convenient to the mixers. When the wall in front of this plant was brought up within 12 feet of final elevation the plant was moved out to the edge of the wall, the mixers being dropped down on it. In order to obtain the benefit of continuous mixing, the mixing plants were customarily run continuously 8 hours per day, except for 15 minutes intermission for lunch. The labor cost alone of mixing, including direct supervision, averaged 18 cents per yard. One month's cost was as low as 12 cents per yard.

Method of Placing:

Sixty feet was adopted as the maximum length of the monoliths, and the concrete in general was laid in blocks measuring 60 feet long, the full width of the wall, and 4 feet high. The walls, therefore, consist of 60 feet monoliths, carried up from bottom to top in four-foot blocks. Generally not less than 36 hours elapsed between the pouring of successive blocks of a monolith. Water-tight joints between adjacent monoliths were secured by leaving a square key measuring 3 feet on a side diagonally between adjoining monoliths. These keyways extended from the floor level to the top. At the bottom, a horizontal key four feet high by four feet three inches wide was carried out to the face of the wall. A continuous strip of yellow metal as a water stop was carried up in opposite corners of the keyways. These water stops project about 2½ in. into the monoliths and the same

Fig. 6.   Mixing Plant on South Wall of Dry Dock No. 1, Balboa Terminals.

amount into the keys with a fold or lap to prevent breaking from the shrinkage of concrete. These keyways before being filled with concrete were used to carry the permanent compressed air and water piping down to the floor of the dock.

Forms:

In general the forms were made of ⅞-in. matched lumber, surfaced on both sides, made up in panels 15 feet long by 4 ft. 9 in. high, with vertical posts spaced 30 inches. These posts were composed of two pieces of 2- by 8-in. rough lumber. The forms were held on the wall by bolts with anchor nuts imbedded in concrete, 9 inches from the top of each lift and 18 inches from the face of the wall. Fifteen-foot sections of forms were easily handled by laborers without a crane. The 4 ft. 9 in. height gives a four-foot lift for the concrete with a 9-in. lap over the concrete below. The same form was generally used the fourteen times necessary in running up from the floor to the coping. The same sections were used many times from floor to coping on both sides. The posts were stiff enough to hold the four-foot lifts without springing out of line, and in general the dry dock walls are within an inch of the theoretical lines at all points. Up to July 1st about 128,200 cu. yds. of mass concrete and about 24,700 cu. yds. of reinforced concrete had been laid. The cost of the mass concrete, to June 1, including division expense, plant, forms, etc., has been $3.93 per yard, and for the reinforced concrete the cost has been $5.86 per yard.

Mixture:

Mass concrete has in general been mixed in the proportion of 1 to 3 to 6, or equivalent. Reinforced concrete has been mixed in the proportion of 1 to 2 to 4, or equivalent. Frequent tests were made during the progress of the work to ascertain the percentage of voids in the aggregate, and the proportion has been varied slightly from time to time to secure the best results as regards strength and density. The work was first started with Chamé sand and No. 1 and No. 2 Ancon rock, the same as used on the Pacific locks.

After the closing down of the Ancon quarry in the latter part of 1914, and also the closing down of the Chamé sand service, Chagres sand and gravel were substituted, and, when it was impossible to obtain screened gravel, run-of-bank gravel was used with such an addition when necessary of either sand or Ancon rock remaining in storage as was necessary to obtain the proper proportion of ingredients. The ½-yard mixers run full gave 0.65 of a cubic yard of concrete in place per batch. Wet concrete was used, avoiding tamping. The mixers required close watching to prevent the addition of too much water. Samples of the various materials were submitted to the Bureau of Standards at Washington for test, and following are the physical test and granulometric analyses of the various materials used in the dry dock concrete:

Physical Tests of Aggregates.

Aggregate	Weight per cubic foot Pounds	Specific Gravity	Per Cent of Voids Computed	Per Cent of Voids Observed
Chamé Sand	95.0	2.64	44.4	40.6
Chagres Sand	102.0	2.72	40.0	38.0
Ancon Screenings	80.7	2.56	49.5	50.0
Ancon Rock No. 1........	82.1	2.50	47.2	....
Ancon Rock No. 2........	82.1	2.50	47.2	45.0
Chagres Gravel Unscreened	130.5	2.78	24.8	21.7
Chagres Gravel Screened	113.5	2.81	35.4	33.5

Granulometric Analysis.

Aggregate			Per Cent Passing Sieves					
Nos.	8	10	14	20	30	40	50	100
Opening in inches..0.097		.075	.051	.034	.022	.015	0.11	.0055
Chamé Sand	99.9	99.6	99.3	96.18	78.83	59.25	46.08	9.30
Chagres River Sand	79.5	71.4	60.0	52.1	35.25	22.75	16.33	4.35
Ancon Screening....	87.8	70.8	61.3	54.3	44.5	32.9	29.2	18.3

		Per Cent Passing Screens					
Opening in inches.	3	2	1½	1	¾	½	¼
Ancon Rock No. 1...............	96.25	64.0	27.0	2.75	1.0	0	0
Ancon Rock No. 2...............	100	100	99.0	75.0	59.2	40.5	15.5
Chagres Gravel Unscreened	100		99.25	91.25	78.5	70.0	56.25	38.5
Chagres Gravel Screened....	100		94.75	87.0	65.0	50.75	33.0	12.0

Surfacing:

Vertical surfaces were given no special treatment during placing, other than to work the mortar to the face of the forms. All horizontal surfaces, including coping, altars and floor, were covered to an average depth of from 1½ to 2 inches with mortar composed of cement and specially sifted sand, mixed 1 to 2, applied at the time the concrete was placed. These surfaces were all given a "dapple" finish in the following manner: After applying the mortar and thoroughly rodding it until the water had been worked to the surface and swept off the block with a rodding stick, the surface was thoroughly floated with a wooden float, following which a wooden float was used to produce the rough or dapple surface by placing the float squarely on the surface, pressing it slightly, and lifting it directly upward from the surface. In this way the cement surface adhering to the float is slightly raised so as to give the appearance of chipped stone. This "dapple" finish is sufficiently rough to prevent slipping and makes a very suitable and satisfactory working surface. The floor was laid in blocks, in general 12 feet wide by 60 feet long.

The plans accompanying this paper give a general plan of the dock and show the principal construction details. It is expected the dock will be ready for use in April, 1916. All work on the Isthmus in connection with the construction of the dry dock, including the erection of the miter gates, and the installation of the pumping machinery and valves is being performed by the forces of the Panama Canal.

Dry Dock No. 2.

General: Provision has been made for the construction of a smaller dry dock designated as No. 2, for Canal craft and for smaller vessels in general, and for an additional pier for berthing vessels under repair on the north side of this dock. The excavation for this dry dock has been completed and the south wall and the head of the dock are under construction as a part of the approach pier to Dry Dock No. 1. All general plans, including the plans for the floating caisson by which the end of the dock will be closed, have been worked out.

In view of some doubt as to the present necessity for this dock, in addition to Dock No. 1, and of the desire to hold the funds which would be required for its completion in reserve, further work is not contemplated at the present time.

Principal Dimensions.

Width at entrance	72	feet, full height
Width on floor in body of dock	75	"
Width at coping level in body of dock	92	"
Elevation of sill and floor, referred to mean sea level	—22.83	"
Length on center line, head to caisson sill	366	"

All work in connection with the design and construction of the dry docks was performed by the Division of Terminal Construction. Civil Engineer F. H. Cooke, U. S. N., Assoc. M. Am. Soc. C. E., as designing engineer, was in immediate charge of the investigations, calculations, design, and preparation of working drawings; assisted by Assistant Engineer A. R. Brown and a force of draftsmen. Mr. Henry Goldmark, M. Am. Soc. C. E., assisted in the adaptation of the design of the Canal lock gates, of which he was the designer, for use on Dry Dock No. 1. The construction work was performed under General Superintendent J. A. Walker, assisted by Mr. H. D. Hinman, Assoc. M. Am. Soc. C. E., as Assistant Engineer, who was also in immediate charge of field engineering and inspection work connected with the dry docks. All of the foregoing reported directly to the writer as Engineer of Terminal Construction.

WHARVES AND PIERS.

Water front improvements in the way of permanent wharves and piers authorized to date comprise the following, with total length of berthing space approximately as stated:

Cristobal.

	Lineal Feet
Commercial Pier No. 7	2450
Commercial Pier No. 8	2368
Commercial Dock No. 9	1150
Commercial Dock No. 10	423
Coaling Pier No. 16	2588
Total	8979

In addition, there is a small-boat landing between Piers 8 and 9, 410 feet long. Wooden wharves and Piers Nos. 2, 3 and 4, Colon, and 11, 13 and 14, Cristobal, will be removed within the next 3½ years.

Balboa.

	Lineal Feet
Reloading Coal Dock No. 6	745
Unloading Coal Dock No. 7	1052
Entrance Dock No. 9	349
Repair Dock No. 13	290
Repair Dock No. 14	775
Commercial Dock No. 15	1146
Commercial Dock No. 16	742
Commercial Pier No. 18	2201
Total	7300

In addition to the above are the following:

	Lineal Feet
Quarantine Landing, Dock No. 1	36
Oil Crib "C", Dock No. 2, having a berthing length of about	600
Old French Pier, Dock No. 4	1109
Small-boat landings Nos. 5, 8, 17 and 19, having a combined length of about	838
Total	2583

At Cristobal there is an available depth of water of 41 feet, referred to mean sea-level, in front of all docks. The elevation of the wharves above mean sea-level varies from 10.2 to 11.5 feet. The average tidal range is 11 inches.

At Balboa the depth of water in front of all wharves and piers is 45 feet, referred to mean sea-level, or 37.4 referred to mean low water, ordinary spring tides. The elevation of the deck of the wharves above mean sea-level varies from 16.5 to 17 feet.

Character of Ground.

At Cristobal, the hard bottom, consisting generally of soft argillaceous sandstone, is found at depths from approximately 30 to 125 feet below mean sea level. Overlying the rock are strata of coral, coral sand, quicksand, clay, and mud, all of unreliable character. In all cases, therefore, foundations have been carried to hard bottom.

At Balboa, hard bottom consisting of rock, both hard andesite, and softer, partially decomposed rock and argillaceous sandstone, is found at elevations varying from about 30 feet to 92 feet below sea level, with overlying strata of soft, black mud, blue and yellow clays, and sand, none of which offer a suitable foundation for support. It is necessary, therefore, to carry all foundations to hard bottom.

Type of Construction.

The general type of construction adopted was the deck or platform type, both for piers and for quay walls, supported by cylinders of concrete that are carried down to rock. In this type of quay wall, the material under the deck is removed to the flattest practicable slope to reduce lateral pressure, and the

structure is anchored by protected steel ties extending back
into firm material. This type of structure, except for piers,
under which all material has been removed to full depth by
dredging, thus eliminating the earth pressure, is not as satisfactory and certain as the gravity type quay wall. The reasons
for its adoption have been largely the necessity of obtaining
as great an amount of berthing space as practicable with the
funds available, the great depth to hard bottom, the necessity

Fig. 7. View of Section H-I of Balboa Terminals from Headwall at Low Tide.
Shows Pier Foundations, and Pump Washing Down Mud
Slope Under Dock.

for completing the water front improvements as quickly as
possible, and of carrying on the construction with as little in-
convenience and disturbance as practicable to other adjoining
work, and the greater speed with which walls of this type
could be built.
Substructure.

The first dock work undertaken was section "f-g" (forming a part of Dock 15) at Balboa. Mr. S. B. Williamson developed for it a type of substructure consisting of concrete

shells in 6 feet sections, heavily reinforced, having an exterior diameter of 8 feet and an interior diameter of 6 feet, the bottom section being protected by a steel shoe flared out to an exterior diameter of ten feet. Adjacent sections are connected by six continuous vertical rods with long, threaded nuts at each joint to develop the full strength of the one-inch rods.

This type of cylinder is adapted for use where the surface of the ground is above water, or where the site can be coffer-dammed. Difficulties in excluding water from the joints render its use inadvisable in water.

The construction of Pier 8 and Docks 9 and 10 at Cristobal was authorized in 1911, and Lieut. Mears, Chief Engineer of the Panama Railroad, developed a type of substructure consisting of cylindrical steel forms, 4 feet in diameter for Docks 9 and 10, and 6 feet in diameter for Pier 8, manufactured in 5-foot sections and riveted up in as great lengths as convenient to handle into place. Metal ½ inch thick, with butt straps and calked joints, was used. After sinking to hard bottom and completing the excavation, the steel reinforcement is placed, and the cylinder is then filled with concrete.

The above are the two principal types of substructure that have been used. The following is the number of cylinders used in the substructure of permanent terminal works:

1st. Concrete cylinders with steel cylinders as forms:

3 feet in diameter	35
4 feet in diameter	416
6 feet in diameter	1047
8 feet in diameter	8
Total	1506

2nd. Concrete cylinders with reinforced concrete shells as forms:

8 feet in diameter	41
7 feet 6 inches in diameter	407
Total	448

About 77% of the cylinders used in the substructure were built with steel forms.

Superstructure.

Two types of construction were used for the deck.

1st. Reinforced concrete longitudinal and transverse girders.

Fig. 8.   Balboa Terminal.   Sinking Concrete Caisson Through Layer of Soft Rock.

2nd. Structural steel longitudinal and transverse girders, encased in concrete for protection against corrosion. A reinforced concrete slab was used for the deck of all structures.

Special Types.

In addition to the above types of construction there are, at Balboa, Dock 7, Unloader Wharf, and Dock 9, Entrance Pier, which were constructed inside of the cofferdam in the dry. Both of these docks have structural steel girders with a reinforced concrete slab. The substructure of the Unloader Wharf, Dock 7, consists of concrete piers 6 and 8 feet thick, spaced 25 feet center to center. The substructure of Dock 9 consists of a continuous back wall, which forms the south wall

Fig. 9. View Along Line of Bulkhead Wall of No. 1 Slip, Balboa. Caissons Sunk to Rock and Superstructure Forms Started.

of Dry Dock No. 2, with two rows of reinforced concrete piers 4 ft. 6 in. square in front of same.

Wearing Surface:

Vitrified brick, laid on edge on a sand cushion, has been provided for the decks of all docks and piers, with the following exceptions: On Docks 17 and 19, Balboa, the bricks are laid flat. On the coaling docks at each terminal and on the Entrance Pier, Dock 9, where the service on the deck will be less severe, a two-inch concrete pavement with "dapple finish"

placed simultaneously with the floor slab has been provided, similar to the finish of the dry dock floor. The first structure built, viz., wharf "f-g" at Balboa, was covered with a mortar finish, but this has not stood up as well as desired under the heavy trucking service connected with transferring cargo to and from ships.

Sheds.

At Cristobal the permanent docks and piers, except Coaling Pier 16, are shedded. The sheds consist of structural steel framework, with 6-inch concrete side and end walls. For the most part these walls have been reinforced. For more complete protection against fire and corrosion, all structural members of roof trusses of Docks 9 and 10 have been completely encased in concrete. This work was performed by contract, and was slow and expensive. The roof trusses of the other sheds have been painted and sanded. For Pier 8 and Docks 9 and 10, the roof slab, sloping ¾ in. to one foot, is of reinforced concrete three inches thick with a ¾-in. mortar finish. At intervals of 120 feet, that is, over every fourth truss, an expansion joint is located, formed by a "V"-shaped strip of No. 20 gauge copper. It has required some attention to keep these roofs entirely tight. The roof of Pier No. 7 shed is to be covered with reinforced concrete "Bonanza" tile.

At Balboa, the only shed authorized to date is for Pier 18. It is of the same general type as the Cristobal sheds, with a "Bonanza" tile roof. All door openings are closed by steel doors, either of the rolling or lifting type. The Panama Railroad has constructed a temporary open wooden shed with corrugated iron roof over its commercial wharf "f-g" (Dock 15). There is also a steel shed with corrugated iron roof over the old French pier, Dock 4, at Balboa.

General Comparison of Costs.

In order to present a comparative statement of costs of the docks and piers of different types, a general data sheet, Plate IX, has been prepared. For work remaining uncompleted, estimated costs have been used which are subject to revision.

In using the information in this table, due weight should

be given to the differences in cost not resulting from differences in type, but from such factors as working conditions, personnel, interference caused by other work in the vicinity, character of material encountered, range of tides, and from the different amounts of overtime necessary to complete the work when needed. There has also been considerable variation in prices for material dealt with generally, such as structural steel, sand, gravel, broken stone, cement, etc.

In connection with this table, typical cross-sections of the docks have been prepared and are shown on Plates X, XI and XII.

Cargo Handling Appliances.

Considerable consideration has been given to the question of the extent and character of power appliances for handling cargo to and from vessels, with which the permanent docks shall be equipped. The docks were designed, and construction was well under way, before the Canal was open for use. There was considerable difference of opinion as to the amount and character of cargo which would break bulk at the terminals after operating conditions had become normal. It was thought preferable, therefore, rather than to furnish an expensive cargo handling outfit which might not be required, or which might be unsuitable for the material to be handled, to omit any special equipment other than the following:

At Cristobal, where the tidal variation is approximately one foot, elevated columns supporting a line of overhead longitudinal girders have been supplied for Pier 8, and Docks 9 and 10. These afford, in addition to the ships' cargo booms, facilities that have proved sufficient and satisfactory. For Pier 7, this construction is varied, as shown on cross-section, but accomplishes the same purpose.

At Balboa the extreme range of tides of 21.8 feet renders it impossible for the average West Coast vessel to work its cargo, at some stages of the tide, owing to the insufficient length of cargo booms. This led to the old French pier being equipped by the Panama Railroad with its present outfit of twelve 4-ton electric cranes of the horizontal transporter type, and one pillar crane of 20 tons capacity. The shed of Pier 18 at Balboa is provided with elevated columns along each side, supporting a line of elevated longitudinal girders. At alternate columns, provision is also being made for the attachment of 65-foot booms on brackets 27.5 feet above the floor, having a capacity of three tons and operated by electric winches.

Tracks.

In general, the docks have been provided with apron tracks of standard gauge a few feet from the water front, and between the water front and the pier sheds. Pier 8 at Cristobal has been built with two depressed tracks through its center, and Docks 9 and 10 have two depressed tracks in the rear, under cover. As it is expected to use the pier sheds largely for storage, tracks have been omitted inside of the sheds of Pier 7 at Cristobal and Pier 18 at Balboa. Special tracks have been provided on the coal docks for the coal handling machinery and on Docks 9 and 13 at Balboa for the 50-ton locomotive dry dock crane.

Loads:

The standard live load that has been adopted for the docks and piers is 750 pounds per square foot. For the tracks the heaviest P.R.R. locomotive has been used with 50% additional for impact, or a 25-ton locomotive crane with 25% impact. Some of the earlier docks were designed for less load. Live loads consisting of heavy cargo have been measured on the Isthmus that have amounted to from 1000 lbs. to 1050 lbs. per square foot. The coaling plant docks and piers have been designed for especially heavy loading, resulting from the unloader and reloader towers and the stocking and reclaiming bridges. Docks 9 and 13 at Balboa have been designed for a 50-ton locomotive dry dock crane. A portion of the repair dock No. 14, Balboa, in front of the shops, has been designed for 1000 lbs. per square foot.

Specifications:

The Panama Canal standard specifications have been used so far as applicable. The specifications for steel are the standard specifications of the American Society for Testing Materials. Structural steel is limited to open-hearth steel. The unit stresses used as prescribed by standard specification No. 254 of The Panama Canal are based on a factor of safety of 4 and limit tensile stresses to 16,000 lbs. per square inch and compressive stresses to 16,000-70 $1/r$.

For reinforced concrete the Panama Canal standard specifications No. 908 were used. These specifications in general follow the last report and recommendations of the American Engineering Societies' Joint Committee on Concrete and Reinforced Concrete, with certain limitations, among them the following:

"2. Protection Against Salt-Water Corrosion. For structures subjected to salt water, salt air, or spray the surface of slab reinforcement shall be protected by at least 1½ in., beam reinforcement 2 in., and girder and column reinforcement 2½ in. of concrete.

"3. Reinforcement. Reinforcing steel shall be in accordance with I.C.C. Specifications No. 272.

"4. Allowable Stress in Steel. The allowable stress in steel under working loads shall not exceed 16,000 pounds per square inch, and no less value shall be used unless economical or constructional reasons therefor can be shown, or as hereinafter specified."

The allowed bearing pressure per square inch of cylinders on the supporting rock depended upon the character and hardness of the rock, and other conditions. In general it was limited to 150 lbs. per square inch, with a maximum of 250 lbs. per square inch. The bottoms of the cylinders were given a sufficient flare, if necessary, to accomplish this.

Assumptions for Calculations:

For the reinforced concrete deck, the slab has been considered in general semi-continuous over supports. The longitudinal beams have been considered as continuous over supports with the slab acting as the compression flange. Cross girders were considered as continuous. Moments and shears were determined by influence lines. The center to center length was used as the effective length.

For the decks having longitudinal and cross girders of structural steel, the strengthening effect of the concrete casing was disregarded. The longitudinal girders were in general designed as non-continuous. In Pier No. 8 and Docks 9 and 10 at Cristobal all steel girders were designed as non-continuous, with effective length for all girders meeting cylinders, equal to distance between outer edge of cylinders, and for other girders an effective length equal to center to center of supports.

In the coaling pier, No. 16, Cristobal, and No. 6 at Balboa, the cross girders were designed as continuous with effective length equal to center to center distance. For Pier No. 7 in Cristobal, under construction, all main girders, both transverse and longitudinal, are considered continuous over supports.

For all docks and piers, the concrete and reinforcement in the cylinders has been extended up to envelope the entire section of the main girders, so as to produce a condition of fixed supports. The deflection of any girder over a cylinder, therefore, results in a deflection of the supporting cylinders. For Pier No. 7, Cristobal, a graphical method of determining the stresses in both girders and cylinders was employed, using moduli of elasticity of 30,000,000 pounds per square inch for steel and 2,000,000 pounds per square inch for concrete. As a safeguard, and for purposes of comparison, the stresses in the girders of Pier No. 7 were also calculated with the assumption of free supports. This assumption was found to give greater stresses except over the end supports where the assumption of rigid connections gave the larger stresses. The greater stress in each case was used in proportioning the girders.

In the reinforced concrete shell and in the steel form cylinders the filler concrete was reinforced usually with from 4 to 8 old 70-lb. rails, to provide for bending caused by eccentric loading and pressure of the back fill. The allowed compressive working stress in the cylinders for concrete varied from 360 to 450 pounds per square inch, depending upon the character of the concrete. The allowed stress in tension was 50 pounds per square inch. In the coal docks of both terminals the bearing stress under girders runs as high as 1000 lbs. per square inch, and spiral reinforcement is provided.

Concrete Materials:

Atlas Portland cement was used, as for other Canal concrete. The greater part of the concrete used at Balboa employed Chamé sand and Ancon rock. Upon the closing down of Ancon quarry and the discontinuing of the Chamé sand serce, late in 1914, recourse was had to Chagres River gravel and sand. For the work at Cristobal, Chagres River gravel was used almost exclusively. In accordance with the restrictions placed on the use of run-of-bank gravel for reinforced concrete work, the standard mixture was 1:2:4; for concrete filler in reinforced concrete cylinder shells the mixture was 1:3:5. The filler used in the cylinders employing steel forms was 1:2:4 concrete. Chagres River gravel concrete weighs from 145 to 147 pounds per cubic foot.

Fig. 10. Panama R. R. New Docks at Cristobal. Foundations for Pier No. 7; a 55-ft. Steel Cylinder Ready to Be Placed.

Sinking of Cylinders:

The same general method was followed in sinking both the steel cylinders and the reinforced concrete cylinders. A standard gauge railroad track was laid between two adjacent rows of cylinders so that all cylinders could be served by a locomotive crane. Over the water this required a construction trestle, which should be about 10 feet above mean high water. The alignment of cylinders driven in the water is best controlled by wooden frames of approximately the size of the cylinder supported by additional piles, one of these frames being at the track level and one just above the water level. The alignment of the cylinders can be easily controlled by driving wooden wedges between the frame and the cylinder. In soft material cylinders were sunk to within one inch of the theoretical position. In harder material the variation was sometimes from 4 to 6 inches. In sinking the cylinders, main dependence was placed on heavy steam hammers, each mounted on a strong wooden platform designed to distribute the blow of the hammer to the cylinder casing. Steel cylinders were handled into place in as long sections as practicable, and field connections riveted and calked. The most satisfactory results were obtained by driving a steel cylinder down as far as possible before starting the excavation. It often could be driven to hard bottom at first driving. The sinking of the reinforced concrete cylindrical shells was in general more difficult than sinking the steel cylinders. To assist in this sinking, twenty-six 8-ton cast iron weights were manufactured from old scrap and rendered valuable service in sinking the concrete cylinders, either alone or in connection with the hammer.

Excavation:

The cheapest excavation in the cylinders was performed by locomotive crane and a small orange peel bucket. The general practice was to start excavation with an orange peel bucket and carry it as far as it could work economically, after which the cylinder was pumped out and kept dry while the excavation was carried down by hand. Emerson steam pumps were largely used in pumping out the cylinders. Steam was provided by some old boiler, or from a locomotive or a locomotive crane. The most satisfactory handling of excavation was by task work. The Panama Canal provided all tools, including a well drill operated by air or steam to raise the material in small buckets.

The established rates were $1 per cubic yard for excavating material not requiring blasting, and $2 per yard for hard rock. The men usually worked in gangs of three and spelled each other, one or two men being in a cylinder at one time. This method gave cheaper and quicker results than any other, and picked colored laborers accomplished as much as men of any other nationality could have performed. At these rates, the pay of some of the laborers would average as high as $2.50 (U. S. C.) per working day for an entire month. As the depths grew greater, the difficulties increased, especially in some materials as regards keeping the holes dry and keeping the cylinders true to line and shape. With steel cylinders ½ in. thick little or no difficulty was experienced from deformation of the shells. Later on, using steel cylinders ⅜ in. thick, a number of them gave some trouble by collapsing near the bottom in sinking, due either to striking a boulder or other obstruction or by the great pressure, or both. From this experience, a rough rule was formulated, to use for 6-foot cylinders, ⅜-in. metal for depths not over 60 to 75 feet; ½-in. metal for depths between 75 and 100 feet; and ⅝-in. metal for all casing driven below the 100-foot elevation. Excavation in cylinders was carried down to 125-foot depths at Cristobal. When a cylinder, which had not reached hard bottom, could not be driven further, which sometimes occurred within 5 to 15 feet from rock, the general plan followed was to drive a smaller cylinder inside of it down to hard rock. When, during excavating, any tendency was noticed for the cylinder to distort, bracing was used to prevent further movement and the cylinder was completed as quickly as possible. In sinking the cylinders, pockets of noxious gas were often encountered, and in one or two instances the colored laborers were overcome before they could be removed, and could not be revived.

A number of variations in the type of steel cylinder forms and manner of using them were worked out during the progress of construction, such as the use of removable forms above the mud line under water. These removable forms were constructed in 5-foot sections, each section being built up of two halves bolted together, with rubber, hemp or canvas gaskets between the outstanding flanges of the connecting angles. The bolt holes about 6 in. apart were slotted so that the bolts could be more easily removed under water. In practice it was found necessary to use bolts in not more than every second or third slot.

After filling with concrete, the steel forms were removed by a colored diver working in an air bell consisting of either a specially constructed metal compartment with a working platform below on which he would stand, equipped with electric light, and air connection; or, more commonly, merely an inverted old metal bucket let down by a rope with an air hose under the side. These colored divers were paid 25 cents per hour and would stay under water an hour at a time. They did

Fig. 11. Caisson Foundations for Cristobal Coaling Station.

very efficient and economical work. These removable sections were used over and over again. For any future work these recoverable 5-foot sections would be made in one piece instead of in halves, with the steel form bent so that when unbolted it would spring open two or three inches. This would save the labor of bolting and unbolting along one side.

Sealing:

After flaring out the excavation at the bottom to the required amount to reduce the bearing, cleaning up the hole, and making a final inspection, the cylinder was allowed to fill with water to relieve the pressure to an amount depending upon conditions, and sealed by filling to a height of 4 to 5 feet with rich concrete by means of a bottom-dumping bucket. Within three days the cylinder could be pumped out. Very few instances occurred of the bottom blowing up and requiring re-sealing.

Placing Reinforcement and Concrete:

Reinforcement, consisting generally of from 4 to 8 vertical 70-lb. old "T" rails, was placed by locomotive crane. The hoop reinforcing steel was bent by compressed air at the site and made up in sections, usually by task work. Small concrete spacing blocks separated the reinforcing steel from the steel cylinder the desired distance. The cylinders were filled with a concrete mixing plant consisting of a ½-yard cube mixer operated by steam, mounted on a car, and discharging directly into the cylinder. The mixer was supplied with aggregate either by wheelbarrows or through a hopper filled by a locomotive crane operating an orange peel bucket.

Plant:

It was not necessary to purchase any new plant for any of this dock work. Old plant released from Canal construction work was transferred to this work from time to time, and the dock work absorbed its share of the plant cost.

Organization.

All of this dock work was performed on the Isthmus by the forces of The Panama Canal or the Panama Railroad, except the erection of certain steel work, doors, etc., and the furnishing of the concrete for Dock Shed No. 9 at Cristobal, which was done by contract. Piers 7 and 8, and Docks 9 and 10, Cristobal, were built and paid for by the Panama Railroad, and Coaling Pier 16 by The Panama Canal. Lieut. F. Mears, U. S. A., M. Am. Soc. C. E., Chief Engineer of the Panama Railroad, designed and constructed Pier 8 and Docks 9 and 10. Mr. T. B. Mönniche, M. Am. Soc. C. E., as Engineer of Docks, Panama Railroad, designed and constructed Pier 7 at Cristobal, reporting directly to the writer.

Coaling Pier 16 is being built by the Division of Terminal Construction, Civil Engineer F. H. Cooke, U. S. N., Assoc. M. Am. Soc. C. E., being in charge of the design, and Superintendent W. G. Thompson, Assoc. M. Am. Soc. C. E., in charge of construction, both reporting directly to the writer.

At Balboa 650 feet of Dock 15 (designated as wharf "f-g") was designed and constructed (1910-1912) by Mr. S. B. Williamson, M. Am. Soc. C. E., as Division Engineer, Pacific Division. This dock was paid for by the Panama Railroad. Mr. Williamson also designed the remainder of Dock 15, 496 feet, and Dock 16, 742 feet, and started construction work on the former. Together these docks, 1238 feet in length, have been known as "g-h-i". Mr. Williamson also made the general design of Pier 18 and of small-boat landings—Docks 17 and 19. Upon Mr. Williamson's return to the United States in December, 1912, the completion of the above mentioned work was transferred to the Division of Terminal Construction, and has since been carried on with Mr. W. Rowland, Assoc. M. Am. Soc. C. E., as Assistant Engineer in charge of designing and drafting, General Superintendent J. A. Walker in charge of the construction, and Assistant Engineer H. D. Hinman, Assoc. M. Am. Soc. C. E., in charge of field engineering and inspection, as well as assistant on construction work, all reporting directly to the writer. Messrs. Walker, Hinman and Rowland have also been in charge of similar work connected with the design and construction by the Division of Terminal Construction of Docks 1, 2, 6, 7, 13 ("d-e") and 14 ("e-f").

BREAKWATERS.

Naos Island Breakwater.

The mud flats lying to the southeast of Sosa Hill offered a convenient place for the economical wasting of spoil from Culebra Cut, which led to the establishment of Balboa dump in 1907. In 1908 it was decided to connect this dump with Naos Island by a dike or breakwater, using spoil from Culebra Cut with slopes faced with selected hard stone, in order to protect the dredged channel from deterioration caused by silt-bearing tidal currents that swept from northeast to southwest across the channel. This silt was then estimated to amount to over one-half million yards per annum, and it was considered that the construction of this breakwater might lessen maintenance costs

by as much as $50,000 a year. As originally constructed this breakwater required the driving of a trestle a little over three miles long, from the main land to Naos Island. The lateral extension of the fill has merged all but 6500 feet of the original breakwater into Balboa dump. The cost of the trestle, and the difference between the cost of dumping material from the trestle and what it would have cost to waste it on Balboa dump, were the only charges made against the breakwater. Dry excavation in Culebra Cut terminated in 1913, after which it became necessary to excavate a small amount of rock from Sosa Hill to complete the breakwater fill and the protection of its slopes. Material from the dry dock excavation was also used. A single track trestle was started in 1908, and carried out to within about 2700 feet of Naos Island in September, 1911, from which point, on account of the depth of the soft mud, in some places amounting to 100 feet, and the resulting difficulties owing to the settlement of the material and failure of the trestle, a double track trestle was driven for the remaining distance. The trestle connection with Naos Island was completed in 1912, and the breakwater was completed in September, 1914. The total amount of material placed in the breakwater has been 2,138,404 yards, and the cost charged to the breakwater is $789,600. The breakwater has a width on top at elevation plus 18 feet of 40 feet, with natural slopes about 1 to 1 down to the mud line (Fig. 12), and affords communication between the Island and the mainland by means of a single standard-gauge track, an eighteen-foot highway, together with water mains, electric cables and telephone lines.

The breakwater was designed and constructed by the Central Division, Colonel D. D. Gaillard, Division Engineer, until the Central Division was abolished in October, 1913, after which the work was carried on directly under the supervision of Major General Geo. W. Goethals, as Chairman and Chief Engineer, until January 1, 1914. From that date the work was carried on to completion by the Division of Terminal Construction.

The construction of a dike of earth and rock connecting Naos, Perico and Flamenco Islands, by the Division of Fortifications, effected an extension of the Naos Island breakwater, and

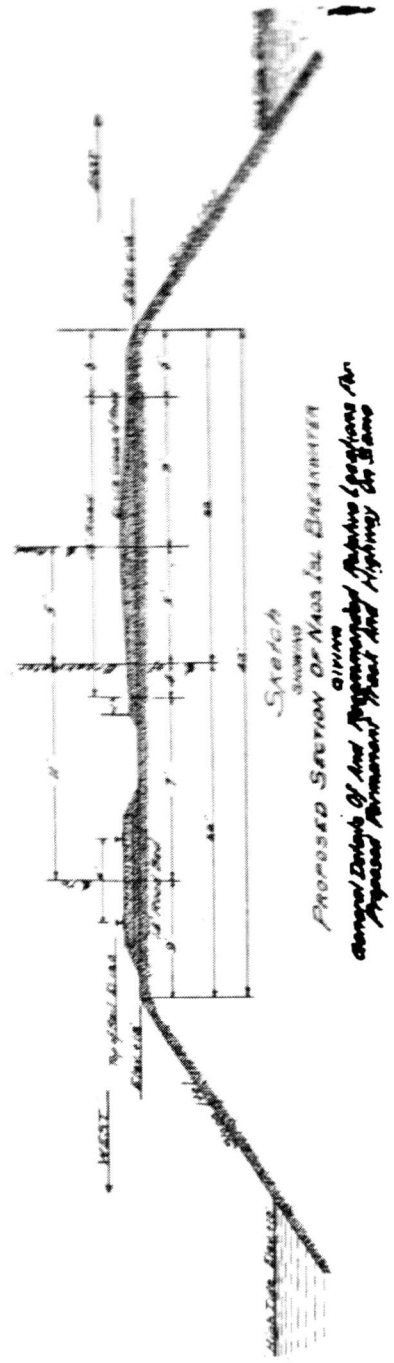

Fig. 18.

makes its effective length, measured from the old shore line, about four and three-eighths miles.

Atlantic Breakwaters.

West Breakwater. The west breakwater was authorized in 1910, extending out from Toro Point Light to within about 1,000 feet of the axis of the Canal, a straight length of 11,378 feet with a right angle "L" at the end 223 feet long—making a total center length of 11,601 feet. The depth of water at the outer end is 44 feet. On the sea side the slope is 1 on 1½ to elevation — 12 and 1 on 2, above elevation — 12. On the harbor side the slope is 1 on 1.4. The top of the breakwater at elevation + 10 has a width of 15 feet. All material above elevation — 12, and below — 12 the front face for a depth of 12 feet measured horizontally, consists of hard armor rock. The remainder is core rock. A double track trestle was built from Toro Point to within 600 feet· of the end of the breakwater, with a single track trestle the remainder of the distance. The bottom was blanketed with hard material, obtained from canal excavation and dumped from scows, in advance of the driving of the trestle, to such an extent as was practicable. A harbor was dredged at Toro Point, a wharf constructed for loading plant and supplies, quarters, hotel, office, machine shop, etc., were constructed. The trestle was driven the greater part of the time with one driver. Two 70-ton shovels excavating in the hills of Toro Point furnished enough material to enable the fill to be kept about 10 feet below sea level close behind the pile driver. This fill protected the trestle, and less than a dozen bents of the trestle were lost from storms. No unusual difficulties were encountered in the construction of the trestle. Piles 85 feet in length were used, spliced with 45-foot piles where required to obtain the proper bearing. No slides or heaving of the bottom which had been anticipated occurred. The trestle was completed in December, 1912. The best month's progress was 728 feet. The maximum settlement of the trestle due to dumping was not over three feet. It was necessary to keep a gang at work continually shimming up the tracks. The double track was kept in alignment very well. The single track trestle at the outer end required a good deal of work to keep it to line and grade. Toro Point rock being

too soft to use for armor, the best available supply was from
Porto Bello quarry, where rock was also being crushed for concrete for the Atlantic locks. The original plan contemplated
placing all the armor with derrick barges, which had been constructed for this purpose, after the core had been brought up
to —10 feet. On account of the swell this was found impracticable, and it was necessary first to create smooth water in
which the derrick barges could work by plowing Porto Bello

Fig. 13. Unloading Rock from Cars on Toro Point Breakwater.

rock from cars on the sea track of the breakwater until the
rock reached about elevation +5, after which the remainder of
the armor rock was placed by the derrick barges. A small unloading wharf was built at Toro Point on which two locomotive
cranes were placed. Unloading armor rock from barges onto
Lidgerwood cars began in October, 1911. This work was carried
on at the rate of not less than one barge per day until December, 1913, after which all rock was placed directly from the
barge into the breakwater by the derrick barges. The armor
rock was plowed off on the outside of the sea track, as dumping

between the tracks caused considerable damage to the trestle. The armor rock ran from five to twenty tons in weight. Some individual stones were handled weighing 30 tons or more. While two large derrick barges handled the large rock, a small derrick barge handled smaller armor rock to fill in the voids between the large rock. To make a more compact structure all of the trestle superstructure was removed and also the piling when practicable before the armor was completed. In dumping the core rock from the harbor track the fill did not uniformly make the required slopes. The additional material required to fill out the slopes was obtained from the canal prism excavation near Mindi and placed directly from bottom dumping scows. Very regular slopes were obtained without much difficulty. The breakwater was completed in May, 1914, at a division cost of approximately $3,493,000.00, or practically $300 per lineal foot. These figures are subject to further deduction from credits on account of Porto Bello plant. It contains the following material: 669,254 cubic yards dredged rock from the canal prism, for which no charge was made against the breakwater, 819,930 cu. yds. of core rock from Toro Point at $1.47 per yard, and 456,549 cu. yds. armor rock from Porto Bello at $5.00 per yard, total, 1,945,733 yards at $1.795 per yard. This breakwater had its first severe test in the northers of February 9 and April 3, 1915. Cross sections taken after the latter showed that the amount of additional armor which will be required to restore the breakwater to its original lines will be about 21,000 yards, measured in the solid. The points where the rock was displaced by the waves were usually where, owing to a lack of supply of large armor rock, it had been necessary to use an undesirable percentage of smaller rock, and where it had been impossible to fill the outside slope to the theoretical lines. The west breakwater was designed and constructed under Brigadier General Wm. L. Sibert, M. Am. Soc. C. E., Division Engineer, Atlantic Division, with Lt. Col. E. L. Jadwin, M. Am. Soc. C. E., in local charge to June, 1911, Lt. Col. Chester Harding, M. Am. Soc. C. E., in local charge from June, 1911, to February, 1913, Lt. Col. Wm. V. Judson, M. Am. Soc. C. E., in local charge from March, 1913, to February, 1914. The breakwater was transferred to the Division of Terminal Construction on February 1, 1914. Mr.

F. C. Stanton, M. Am. Soc. C. E., was Assistant Engineer on the breakwater work from the time it started until May, 1914, when he left the Isthmus. During the last four months he was in local charge.

East Breakwater. The east breakwater is a detached breakwater. Its outer end lies 1000 feet east of the Canal axis extended, at a point opposite the outer end of the west breakwater, giving an entrance width between the ends of the breakwaters of 2000 feet in 44 feet of water. It extends shoreward toward Coco Solo Point. The length authorized is 5290 feet, with an "L" 225 feet at the outer end, making a total center line length of 5515 feet. The inner end will lie in 40 feet of water and be 5693 feet from the shore at Coco Solo Point. The cross section of the west breakwater was adopted for the east breakwater (Plate XVI), and the method of construction adopted was to drive a double track trestle out from Coco Solo Point to the outer end of the breakwater, a distance of 10,983 feet, to blanket the bottom in advance of driving the trestle with as much material as could be obtained from the dredging work in the harbor; to plow off rock from Lidgerwood cars on each side of the trestle to about elevation —12, forming two mounds; to pump in between the two mounds, to about —15, coral rock and sand excavated by a suction dredge working behind Coco Solo Point, and handled into place by electrically-driven relay pumps located along the trestle pipe line; above —12 to plow off armor rock on the sea side to +5, to form a lee behind which the crane barges could place the remainder of the armor rock, in pieces weighing from 5 to 20 tons, and thus bring the breakwater up to the final cross section. An extension of the breakwater shoreward 1800 feet has been under consideration, and its execution will depend upon whether the necessity for further protection develops, and whether funds will be available to undertake this extension.

One of the principal factors affecting the cost of the west breakwater had been in connection with securing and placing suitable armor rock. Early attention was, therefore, given to this matter for the east breakwater. During 1913, investigations were made in regard to the character of rock at a number of points on the Isthmus, and estimates were prepared on the cost of opening up and operating a quarry. During 1913 a considerable amount of preliminary work was done by the Atlantic Division, Brigadier General W. L. Sibert, M. Am. Soc. C. E., Division Engineer, at Coco Solo, including clearing the yard, ground, extending the railroad, building a dock and small harbor for unloading piles and material, ordering material for the trestle, etc. The location, length and cross section of the breakwater were also fixed. Construction work was transferred to the Division of Terminal Construction on February 1, 1914. Two large railroad drivers using steam hammers working 8-hour "split shifts", so as to keep the drivers working 12 hours per day, were used on the trestle. From three to four 16-foot bents per day were driven. The best month's work was 1591 lineal feet of double track trestle. On the shore connection the two inner piles, that is, those under the rails of each track, were creosoted piles; the outer piles were tarred or painted with a creosote preservative to below the mud line. On the breakwater proper, uncreosoted and unpainted piles were used throughout. The bottom was very soft and consisted largely of black mud with a varying percentage of fine sand. Near the top, the silt was very soft indeed. Coral was encountered near the shore. Further out the elevation of the argillaceous rock, to which the piles in most cases were driven, varied from 70 feet to over 130 feet below sea level. This necessitated the use of spliced piles up to 130 feet in length. The standard length of the piles ordered was 85 feet. A sufficient number of 45-foot piles were ordered as splices, which were cut to the required length. The splice was made with six steel bars $3\frac{1}{2}$ in. by $\frac{1}{2}$ in. by 72 in., with six $1\frac{1}{8}$-in. holes for $\frac{1}{2}$-in. by 6-in. boat spikes. In addition to driving test piles, and taking wash borings along the line of the breakwater in advance of driving, soundings were taken with a weighted pipe, to compare the results taken with a similar pipe along the line of the west breakwater, where no slipping or heaving of the bottom occurred, and with the results obtained along the line of the Naos Island Breakwater where continual trouble of this character was encountered. A 2-in. pipe 23 feet long, filled with lead for the upper 21 feet, was used; the lower 2 feet were open, with a hole in the upper end to allow the

escape of air and water. When dropped 20 feet the average penetration of this pipe along the west breakwater was about 8 feet; along the line of Naos Island breakwater the penetration was about double; along the east breakwater the penetration was about half-way between the results obtained on the west breakwater and on the Naos Island breakwater. Making due allowance for settlement, and allowing 35% for voids in material in place in the breakwater, it was estimated that, per lineal foot of breakwater, 165 cubic yards solid measurement of core rock and 48 yards of armor rock, making a total of 213 cubic yards of material, would be required. Trestle construction commenced March 2, 1914, and had reached a length of 9498 feet of double-track trestle on February 8, 1915, costing $51.39 per foot.

On account of the suitability of the rock and the facilities available for excavating it, the quarry at Sosa Hill at the Pacific terminal was adopted as the source of supply for the core and armor rock, notwithstanding the haul of 50 miles. The rock was loaded on Lidgerwood cars, containing about 18 cubic yards, place measurement, and weighing about 40 short tons, and transported in trains of about 30 cars. There was little difficulty in maintaining with four shovels as large an output (up to 4000 yards per day) as could be dumped into place. This latter was governed by the ability to keep the trestle, where the dumping occurred, in condition to permit the passage of trains, as more or less settlement occurred in spots where the bottom was unusually soft, requiring constant attention and shimming. Up to February 9, 1915, 321,000 cubic yards of Sosa Hill rock, solid measurement, had been placed in the breakwater, and about 171,000 cubic yards of coral rock and sand had been pumped in by dredges. The dry fill, loaded on cars at Sosa Hill, cost 59 cents per cubic yard, division expense. The cost of transportation across the Isthmus was 16 cents; repairs to cars, 12 cents; dumping at Coco Solo, 6 cents; miscellaneous charges, 8 cents; making a total cost in place of $1.01. The cost for wet fill in place was 66 cents.

From February 8 to 10, 1915, a norther that came up in the night, of greater intensity than had occurred for a number of years, destroyed 4300 feet of the double-track shore-connection trestle, and about 1700 feet of the trestle on the breakwater proper, carried two pile drivers overboard and did other damage. Steps were immediately taken to obtain additional material, recover the pile drivers, salvage the material which had been washed ashore, assort it, and to redrive the shore connection. About 400 feet of single-track trestle had been redriven when a second norther of great intensity occurred on April 3 to 5, which carried away about 700 feet of shore connection trestle and 2100 feet comprising the remainder of the trestle on the breakwater. No armor rock had been placed in the breakwater. The action of the northers on the core rock that had been placed was to level it off at a depth of from 10 to 15 feet below sea level. The northers removed a considerable amount of soft material that had been deposited from dump barges to blanket the bottom in advance of the trestle driving. The effect of these two northers will be to increase the cost over what it would otherwise have been by about $360,000. The redriving of the shore trestle commenced immediately, with a view to carrying the breakwater as far as possible towards completion before the next season for northers. It was decided, in order to save time and cost, to redrive the shore connection as a single-track trestle, except for the passing track 1200 feet long, about one mile from shore. Shorter piles are being used, with wooden collars 42 inches square bolted and dapped into the piles at a proper distance from the top to enable these collars, by resting on the original bottom or on the coral fill, to assist in supporting the load. Where the condition of the bottom makes it necessary, an additional pile, making five piles per bent, is used. The two center piles are creosoted piles salvaged from the original trestle. Few piles over 85 feet in length were used. To give lateral stability and to increase the resistance of this trestle to storms, coral rock and sand were pumped in along the trestle as fast as practicable to a height of —15. In some places double collars were placed on the piles, the second collar being 10 feet above the lower collar, which, after this coral fill was made, gave additional bearing power. While the shore connection was being driven, another pile driver was carried out by barge and started in on the breakwater proper. It is expected to resume placing dry fill and to start placing armor in August. All rock two cubic yards and larger obtained from Sosa Hill quarry during the past year has been classed as armor rock, and as such has been reserved for use at the east breakwater. Each train coming under the shovel would have two cars or more reserved for armor rock, and all armor rock encountered by the shovel was loaded on these special cars, if necessary, by using chain slings handled by the shovel. This armor rock has been unloaded by cranes and stored at Coco Solo. The percentage of armor rock recovered from quarry operations has not been as large as desired, and the results of the two recent northers have shown the necessity of large masses of rock to withstand the wave action. It is expected, therefore, to manufacture about 10,000 concrete blocks measuring 7 feet on a side composed of one part cement, 2 1/3 parts sand and 7 parts Chagres River gravel, and weighing 25 short tons, with a view to placing these blocks on the outside face and slope of the breakwater and backing them up with armor rock from Sosa Hill quarry, which will be plowed off from the trestle or placed by the derrick barges. This breakwater should be completed by July, 1916. From February, 1914, when this work was transferred to the Division of Terminal Construction, to May, 1914, Assistant Engineer F. C. Stanton, M. Am. Soc. C. E., was in local charge of the work. Since May, 1914, Supervisor C. C. Snedeker has been in local charge, reporting to the writer.

FUEL OIL PLANTS.

The fuel oil handling plants at each terminal include the necessary cribs, or outlets on wharves; pipe lines between the water front and the tank farms; and the handling plants. The Panama Canal, as well as private companies, owns tanks, in the tank farms. The tanks have been located as regards elevation and distance from the handling plant and the water front, and the plants have been designed, with a view to handling oils from the storage tanks in the tank farms to or from three ships simultaneously, at a minimum rate of 1200 bbls. per hour per vessel; and to be able to make deliveries to any small Panama Canal service tanks, within a radius of eight miles, at the rate of 400 bbls. per hour. The locations selected and the general arrangement for the handling plants, tank farms, oil docks and pipe line connections are shown on Plates III and XVII. In addition to handling the commercial "topped" fuel oils, the plants are arranged to handle Diesel engine oil. Separate tanks for storing gasoline in bulk are also being provided, one at Balboa and one at Mount Hope, for use by the Panama Canal. Individuals and companies are not permitted to store gasoline, kerosene or any distillates other than Diesel engine oil, in the Canal Zone. Work on the Pacific terminal plant was started in July, 1914, and it was placed in operation in January, 1915. The Atlantic terminal plant was started in August, 1914, and was ready for operation in February, 1915. After extended investigation steam-driven pumps were adopted. The various classes of oils, the wide variation in pressure, distances, and rates of pumping, rendered less satisfactory results with electrically driven pumps more or less certain. The very satisfactory results obtained from the steam-driven pumps have entirely justified their selection. Each plant has been laid out for the installation of three boilers and three oil-pumping units. Two boilers and two pumps have been installed in each plant to date, pending the development of enough business to justify the third unit. In each plant there are two 250-hp. horizontal return-tubular boilers with boiler-feed pumps in duplicate, boiler-feed-water heater, oil heater, oil-feed pumps, etc. The fuel tanks are located so as to give a head of approximately 40 feet in supplying oil directly to the boilers by gravity. Each boiler is equipped with two 150-hp. steam atomizing "Best" burners. All boilers and accessories were obtained on the Isthmus from old retired equipment in good condition. In each engine room are two 20- and 14- by 12- by 18-in. duplex tandem-compound oil-pumping units of the outside center-packed plunger type. The nominal capacity of each pump is 1200 barrels (50,400 U. S. gallons) per hour of crude oil with asphaltum base and gravity of 16 degrees Baume at 60 degrees F (temperature of oil at time of handling 80 degrees F), against a total head (excluding suction) of 150 lbs. per square inch, with steam pressure of 125 lbs. per square inch at the throttle; and 400 bbls. (16,800 U. S. gallons) per hour of similar oil against a total head (excluding suction) of 250 lbs. per square inch. The pumps are equipped with the necessary features adapting them for handling heavy oils, including one large suction and one large discharge chamber, to permit the clearing of entrapped air or gas during operation, and an adjustable spring pressure-relief valve and by-pass pipe to permit automatically the oil to escape from discharge to suction pipe, should the discharge pressure rise above the pressure for which the valve is set. The pumps were furnished by the National Transit Company, of Oil City, Pa., at a unit cost of $3,805 delivered, including accessories such as steam, indicating and recording pressure and vacuum gauges, automatic pressure-relief valve and a complete set of oil suction and discharge valve seats, valves and valve springs. The net weight of each pump is about 36,000 lbs. A Worthington underwriters' fire pump 16 in. by 9 in. by 12 in., having a rated capacity of 750 gallons per minute, selected from old retired equipment, has also been installed in the Balboa plant, for particular use in handling Diesel engine oil, until a larger pump is necessary.

The manifold, which has been furnished for connection with each handling plant, consisting of 12-inch cast iron headers, pipe bends, valves, and fittings, accomplishes the following purposes:

(a) The suction and discharge pipe of any pump in the handling plant can be connected with the pipe line to any tank in the tank farm. The manifold can be extended indefinitely to meet the further demands resulting from the construction of additional tanks.

(b) The manifold permits oil to be taken or delivered between the tank farm and the three outlets at the water front simultaneously with or without the assistance of the pumps in the handling plant, as desired.

At the Atlantic terminal, the handling plant has been connected with the water front by one 10 in. and one 12 in. pipe line running to Dock No. 13, with provision for a third line when required. The two lines serving Dock 13 will be extended across the French canal, in a trench dredge to —45, to the new coaling plant, Pier No. 16. An 8-in. line will be laid under the deck along both sides and around the end of Pier No. 16, with a total of fourteen 8-in. outlets. It is intended to confine, so far as practicable, deliveries of fuel to Pier No. 16. It is expected to receive oil at Dock 13 indefinitely.

At the Pacific terminal a berth 75 feet wide and 2000 feet

long has been dredged adjoining the canal channel, about 2000 feet south of the old French pier, and one oil crib, "C", a reinforced concrete structure 62 feet square, supported on steel cylinders, has been built and connected with the oil-handling plant, by pipe lines laid along the bottom. A 10-in. oil line has also been laid along the face of the old French pier under the deck, with six 8-in. oil outlets.

On the Atlantic side the distributing pipes from the oil handling plant extend only between the tank farms and the water front, and the Panama Canal and Panama Railroad small distributing tanks in the immediate vicinity. On the Pacific side the Panama Canal distributes oil to various small receiving tanks as far north as Paraiso, a distance of nearly eight miles. Oil is delivered to Paraiso at the rate of 400 bbls. per hour. The Union Oil Company's trans-isthmian line has been removed. The Panama Canal does not propose to replace it, or to permit any individual or company to construct a trans-isthmian line. Individuals and companies desiring to participate in the selling of fuel oil to vessels using the Canal are permitted to lease tank sites in accordance with approved regulations, and to furnish the pipe lines as far as the handling plant. The present rate for pumping is four cents per barrel of 42 gallons, each way. On the Pacific side the tanks are located on Balboa dump. The general plan has been to grade off and roll the ground, and place the tank upon about two feet of sand saturated with fuel oil. With tanks 30 to 35 feet high, a settlement averaging 6 in. has occurred, not altogether uniform, but without affecting the tightness of the tanks appreciably. The standard size of the pipe lines at the Atlantic side is 12 in., and at the Pacific side, owing to shorter distances and greater difference in elevation, 10 in. At the Atlantic terminal, the tanks are located on the summit of a number of small hills at Mount Hope, between the Panama Railroad and the east diversion canal, which, when graded off, enable the tanks to be built on hard red clay. At the Pacific terminal, fuel oil can be easily handled either way by one pump at the rate of 2000 bbls. per hour. In handling oil to vessels it has been found that the ruling factor is the capacity of the vessel to take the oil, and not the capacity of the pump. There are at present, either completed or under construction, tanks that will enable about 150,000 tons of fuel oil to be carried in stock on the Isthmus, and there is ample room for the construction of additional storage tanks should they be necessary. The Panama Canal owns four 40,000-barrel tanks, two at each end.

The oil lines in general have been laid on the ground, and, by providing expansion joints at intervals, no special difficulties have been experienced by the pipes pulling apart or by leaky joints arising from variation in temperature. The oil purchased and stored by the Panama Canal under its present contract is California oil. On the completion of tanks which are now under construction, vessels passing through the Canal will be able to purchase California, Mexican and Oklahoma oils.

These plants were designed and constructed by the Division of Terminal Construction. Mr. F. C. Nichols, Assistant Engineer, was in charge of the designing and office work, and acted as inspector on construction work performed by other divisions. Prior to his connection with the work, Mr. A. L. Bell, Mechanical Engineer, performed important work in connection with preliminary investigations and calculations. Valuable information and assistance were received from engineers of the manufacturers of pumps, and of the handlers of oil. Special acknowledgment is due to Mr. Forrest N. Towl, M. Am. Soc. C. E., for information and suggestions offered.

The writer desires to make acknowledgment for the faithful services rendered and loyal support given by all who were associated with him on the foregoing work.

Paper No. 24

COALING PLANTS AND FLOATING CRANES OF THE PANAMA CANAL.

By

F. H. COOKE, Assoc. M. Am. Soc. C. E.
Civil Engineer, U. S. Navy
Balboa Heights, Canal Zone, Panama

COALING PLANTS.

Two coaling plants are now under construction for the Panama Canal. The larger plant, known as the Cristobal Coaling Plant, is located near the Atlantic entrance, and the smaller, known as the Balboa Coaling Plant, is located near the Pacific entrance to the Canal. At each plant work is in progress by the Panama Canal and by contractors for the coal-handling machinery proper.

Based on 45 cubic feet of coal to the ton of 2240 pounds, the completed Cristobal Coaling Plant will have a maximum storage capacity of 100,000 tons of submerged coal and 350,000 tons of dry coal. The corresponding figures for Balboa are 44,500 tons and 167,000 tons. The figures for dry storage are based on a maximum depth of 33 feet at Cristobal and 40 feet at Balboa. The total normal dry capacity is 225,000 tons at Cristobal and 91,500 tons at Balboa, based on a depth of 20 feet in each case. While it is not likely that undesirable results would follow at either plant with coal stored to the greater depths mentioned, it is probable that an effort will be made to limit the depth to the lesser figures, so far as practicable.

The foregoing figures for volume of dry storage are based on the absence of internal subdivision. Assuming the Cristobal Coaling Plant divided into 13 piles, as indicated on Plate I, the total maximum dry capacity is reduced to 311,000 tons; and assuming the Balboa Coaling Plant to be subdivided into 12 piles, as indicated on Plate II, the total maximum dry capacity is reduced to 141,000 tons.

The wet or subaqueous storage at each plant is for a reserve for the Navy. Its depth is 28 feet below mean sea-level at Cristobal and 18 feet below mean sea-level at Balboa. It is expected that this submerged coal may remain in storage for long periods of time without appreciable loss of caloric value and without danger of spontaneous combustion. The submerged stock will be covered by the dry stock, thus practically forming a foundation for the working pile of dry coal.

In June, 1913, five proposals were opened, in the Washington Office of the Isthmian Canal Commission, for furnishing coal-handling machinery and accessories for the two plants on foundations to be provided by the Government. The specifications were general, and the proposals were practically competitive designs to meet the specified conditions. The Cristobal machinery was required to develop an average unloading capacity of not less than 1000 tons of 2000 pounds per hour, and an average reclaiming capacity of not less than 2000 tons of 2000 pounds per hour. The capacities for Balboa were specified as half those for Cristobal. These two plants are markedly different from the general run of commercial coaling plants in the United States, in that the coal is both received from and delivered to vessels. The specified maximum requirements for reclaiming and reloading at Cristobal were fixed at the comparatively high figure of 2000 tons per hour, to increase the military usefulness of the plant, since this rate would enable fleet colliers to be loaded in a comparatively short time. The specifications required the reloading capacity to be obtained by the use of stocking and reclaiming bridges, a conveying system, and moving units designated as reloaders. By this means, high and expensive wharf bunkers and appurtenances were dispensed with, except that a small wharf bunker was specified for serving tugs and other small craft.

Contracts were awarded in August, 1913, one to the Hunt Construction Company, of New York, the other to Augustus Smith, C. E., of Bayonne, N. J. The successful design was that developed by Mr. Smith, the part awarded to the Hunt Con-

Fig. 1. Balboa Coaling Station, Pacific Terminals.

Fig. 2. Cristobal Coaling Station, Atlantic Terminals.

struction Company consisting of the unloading towers only, four at Cristobal and two at Balboa.

The general characteristics of each plant can be seen from Figs. 1 and 2. These are not photographs in the usual sense, since neither plant is as yet completed, but they are photographs of larger perspective drawings which Mr. Smith has had made, and which he has kindly furnished for the purposes of this article. These general characteristics can also be seen by reference to Plates I and III for Cristobal and II and IV for Balboa.

It will be seen that the Cristobal plant consists of a rectangular storage pile 1700 feet long by 307 feet wide. The length of the pile lies approximately north and south, and the northerly or off-shore part is enclosed in a U-shaped pier, which supports the coal-handling machinery and affords deep water berthing space alongside the coaling plant. The southerly part of the storage pile is beyond the final shore line.

The two long sides of the projecting pier are known as the unloader wharf and the reloader wharf, and afford berthing space, with a depth of 41 feet at mean sea-level, for a length of 1065 feet for each wharf. The tidal range at Cristobal is small, averaging about 2.65 feet; hence there will be sufficient depth for the largest ships at any stage of the tide. The north end of the pier is known as the end wharf; it affords 458 lineal feet of berthing space of similar depth, and supports the wharf bunker.

The general arrangement of the Cristobal Coaling Plant is as follows:

On the unloader wharf are four traveling unloaders, and on the reloader wharf are four traveling reloaders. The storage pile is surrounded by a double-track viaduct on which travel conveyor cars of a nominal capacity of 10 tons each. The storage pile is spanned by two moving units, known as stocking and reclaiming bridges, which travel from end to end of the storage pile. Each of these bridges supports in turn on its top chord two other moving units known as bridge diggers, whose function is to reclaim coal from storage. A wharf bunker of 1500 tons capacity, weigh scales, storage tracks at viaduct level, and an electric substation complete the general features of the plant. All parts are electrically operated except the unloaders, which are steam operated; the plant is electrically lighted throughout, and will be equipped with a telephone system and with visible and audible signals.

The general operation of the Cristobal plant will be as follows:

For unloading and stocking, coal will be taken by the unloaders and transferred to cars on the viaduct. These cars are semi-automatic and will carry the coal over one of the weigh scales, after which by means of a sliding curve they pass over one of the stocking and reclaiming bridges which have been set over that part of the storage pile to which the coal is destined. After having been dumped at the desired point, the cars continue their course, leaving the bridge by a similar sliding switch and eventually returning to the loading point to repeat the cycle. Any or all of the four unloaders may be used during this operation, and one or more vessels may be unloaded, depending on the desired rate of unloading and the number of points of deposit of coal. Since the viaduct is double track and there are two bridges, it is possible in the majority of cases to operate the conveyor cars on two independent routes.

For reclaiming and reloading, the units in use are the bridge diggers, bridges, viaduct, scales, and reloaders. The bridge diggers reclaim coal from storage, and deliver it by hoppers and chutes to the conveyor cars, which leave the bridge by a sliding curve, pass over one of the scales and dump the coal into the hopper of the desired reloader, whence it is delivered to the vessel by a system of conveyor belts, terminating in a telescopic chute, which directs the coal to the desired point in the vessel. One or more bridge diggers and one or more reloaders may be in use, according to the number and capacity of the receiving points in the vessel or vessels, and, as in the unloading operation, two independent routes may be followed by the conveyor cars for most of the operations. The discharging capacity of one reloader is equal to or greater than the reclaiming capacity of one bridge digger.

Coal destined to the wharf bunker is dumped by the conveyor cars into a hopper, which delivers to a system of belts, which finally delivers the coal into the desired compartment of the bunker by a traveling tripper. So far as the wharf bunker is concerned, this coal may be taken directly from a vessel by an unloader, or may have been reclaimed from storage by a bridge digger.

Coal can also be transferred from any point of the storage pile to any other point of the storage pile by the use of both bridges, coal being reclaimed at one bridge and dumped at the other.

The Balboa plant differs materially from the Cristobal plant in general layout, due to local differences of site. The general nature of the coal handling operations is similar to that at Cristobal, i. e., there are unloaders, reloaders, viaduct and conveyor cars; but the Cristobal bridges, with their diggers, are replaced at Balboa by four traveling double-cantilever cranes, known as berm cranes, which were originally purchased for mixing and handling concrete for the Pacific locks, and which are being re-erected and remodeled for service in the coaling plant. The viaduct at Balboa is single track, since the number of unloaders and reloaders is but half that at Cristobal, and the specified handling capacities are but half as large. The Balboa unloaders and reloaders differ from those at Cristobal in detail only, the capacities and general operation of these units being the same at the two plants. The Balboa conveyor cars have the same individual capacity as those at Cristobal and have the same running gear, but they are single-sided instead of double-sided, i. e., they dump on one side of the viaduct track only. This results from there being but a single track on the Balboa viaduct.

The storage pile at Balboa is 800 feet long and 345.5 feet wide, and is spanned by the berm cranes. As at Cristobal, one side of the storage pile is bounded by an unloader wharf, but the reloader wharf instead of lying parallel to the unloader wharf on the opposite side of the storage pile, joins the unloader wharf, forming a salient angle of about 135°. There is thus no "end wharf" at Balboa, and the wharf bunker, which is identical with that at Cristobal, is supported by the reloader wharf close to the salient angle.

The operation of unloading and stocking at Balboa is as follows:

The unloaders take coal from the vessel or vessels and deliver it to the conveyor cars, which, after having passed over one of the scales, dump the coal at a point in the storage pile along-

3 ft. 0 in. center to center, the distance center to center of the pairs of rails being 34 ft. 6 in. The speed of track travel is 50 feet per minute. Plate III indicates the general construction of the Cristobal unloaders. It will be seen that the unloaders are of the "steeple" type, and that, if required, the bucket can be run from the outer end of the water boom to the inner end of the shore boom, a distance of 162 feet. Normally but one boom will be in operation, and the guaranteed handling capacities are based on this condition. The unloaders are "double-ended", inasmuch as two operating stations are provided, one for the water boom and one for the shore boom. All the movements of the bucket, which is of 2½ tons capacity, are controlled by one man, the fatigue of whose duty is reduced to a minimum by the employment of pilot valves for admission and cut-off of steam to the engine cylinders. The water boom can be lifted to clear the upper works of vessels; the shore boom is of similar construction, but no lifting appliances are provided, since they are not required in the normal operation of the plant. The clearance line of the closed bucket is at a maximum height of 65 feet above the deck of the wharf, which is 10 ft. 6 in. above mean sea-level; the extreme travel of the bucket on the water side is 55 feet from the face of the concrete wharf, i. e., exclusive of fenders, and on the shore side it is 38 feet from the edge of the storage pile at Cristobal; thus a considerable part of the storage pile is commanded by the unloader. At Balboa the shore boom commands a strip of the storage pile 55 feet in width. This greater command is had by reason of the less width of the Balboa viaduct, and is desirable on account of the moderate capacity of the berm cranes at Balboa.

In order to deliver coal to the conveyor cars, each Cristobal unloader is provided with a belt, which transports coal from the large receiving hopper of 50 tons capacity, into which the bucket discharges, to two hoppers which overhang the viaduct, one over each track. The capacity of these latter hoppers is 15 tons each, and delivery into the conveyor cars is controlled by steam valves, worked by an operator stationed in an adjacent cab. It is also the duty of this operator to regulate the supply of coal to the overhanging hoppers, the duty of the bucket operator being confined to keeping the receiving hopper filled with coal. At Balboa, on account of there being but one viaduct track, considerably lower than that at Cristobal, it was not necessary to introduce the conveyor belt.

Each stocking and reclaiming bridge consists of two trusses, 315 ft. 0 in. center to center of end bearings, forming a through span for the passage of the conveyor cars. Each bridge supports two traveling bridge diggers running on two pairs of 80-lb. rails, each pair being 2 ft. 4 in. center to center and supported on the top chord of one of the bridge trusses, which are 23 feet center to center. There is also provided a runway, supported on brackets, for the traveling hopper and chute, which directs the coal from a bridge digger to the conveyor cars, one such hopper and chute being provided for each bridge digger. Each bridge is supported on four trucks of 16 wheels each; the maximum load on any truck, including its own weight, is approximately 1,030,000 pounds. Plate V gives a general idea of the sizes of and stresses in the principal bridge members, indicates the general construction of a truck, and shows the cross section of the bridge. Each bridge weighs approximately 1250 tons, exclusive of bridge diggers.

To minimize breakage of coal dumped into storage from the bridge, a spreader chute is provided running on a track suspended below the bottom chord. This spreader chute will be manually operated and its use will probably be confined to the first formation of a pile.

The bridge travel is controlled by the operator of one of the two bridge diggers. The maximum speed is 50 feet per minute. Each end of the bridge will be driven by a 170-hp. motor, which drives half of the wheels in each truck. Since these are induction motors, it is expected that there will be but little tendency for one end of the bridge to travel faster than the other; but should this expectation not be realized, provision has been made whereby the motor driving the more advanced end will be automatically shut off, after a predetermined limit has been reached, the other end thus being permitted to catch up. It is proposed to provide large indicating dials whereby the operator can know the extent to which the bridge is out of square; and since the driving motors are independent of each other, he can bring the bridge back to square.

The bridge diggers are traveling steel structures weighing about 125 tons each. They are required to develop a reclaiming capacity averaging 500 tons per hour each, and since the bucket is of but 5 tons capacity, the average time of one round trip must not exceed 36 seconds. The combination of bridge digger on top of bridge, supplying coal to conveyor cars running through the bridge, is one of the somewhat unusual features of the Cristobal coaling plant. The operation of each bridge digger is under the control of one operator stationed on the digger. His duty is rendered comparatively simple by the swinging boom and differential drum arrangement, developed and patented by the contractor, whereby the bucket is constrained to travel in a fixed path for the upper part of its cycle, terminating over the receiving hopper. The bucket is counterweighted, but without loss of digging capacity. Plate VI gives the general arrangement of the bridge digger machinery, and shows the principal stresses and general relationship.

The reloaders take the place of the heavy and expensive wharf bunkers seen in many coaling plants. They are traveling steel structures, weighing about 120 tons each, supported on four 4-wheel trucks running on two pairs of 100-lb. rails, 3 ft. 0 in. center to center, the distance center to center of the pairs of rails being 26 ft. 0 in. The speed of travel is 50 feet per minute. The function of the reloader is to receive coal from the conveying system and to elevate it to such a height that its delivery chute will have a sufficiently wide range of discharge. The reloaders were originally intended for loading colliers and barges, but subsequent developments have shown the desirability of also bunkering vessels by their use, and some modifications have been made in the original design, whereby it is expected that they will be efficient for bunkering vessels, as well as for the service originally intended.

Plates III and VII show the general construction of the Cristobal reloader and indicate the size of the principal members. The Balboa reloader is substantially the same in all parts except the trailing hopper, which is modified to fit the lower single-track Balboa viaduct. It will be seen that the essential parts are the receiving hopper, the approach conveyor, which parallels the viaduct, the delivery conveyor, which is supported on a hinged boom, and the delivery chute, which is telescopic and hinged to the outer end of the delivery boom. A split boom, or A-frame, is provided for handling the delivery chute and for other lifting service that may be required. The conveyor belts are 42 inches wide and are run at a speed of 225 or 450 feet per minute.

The result of all this is a delivery chute which overhangs the water. It can be lengthened and shortened, inclined outwards or inwards, and raised and lowered bodily through a very considerable range, all under the control of one operator stationed in a conveniently located cab. This operator can also stop and start the transport of coal through the reloader at will, and, by orders to an attendant at the trailing hopper, he can regulate the rates of delivery of the coal, these rates ranging from 60 tons per hour minimum to 600 tons per hour maximum.

The conveyor cars are each driven by two motors, rated at 3 hp. each, but actually of considerably higher power. Three-phase current is supplied by two trolley wires and through the track rails, and the cars are started, stopped and reversed by a conveniently located handle. The speed is 200 feet per minute and it is not necessary to board the car to start or stop it. The doors are opened and closed by hand-operated gearing, and it is necessary to board the cars to perform this operation. Each car is provided with a brake, which may be operated either by hand or foot. The cars are double-ended, a platform with the requisite handles, levers, etc., being provided at each end of the car. The cars are of steel construction throughout.

It is expected that the cars will be operated by a force of track men stationed on the viaduct, whose duty it will be to stop and "spot" the cars at the loading points, start them, weigh and dump them, different gangs performing the different operations, the cars traveling unattended from point to point. When the route to be traveled by the cars for any operation has been fixed, it is unnecessary to throw any track switches, since the cars always traverse the same route for any one operation. Cars are deflected on and off a stocking and reclaiming bridge by a curve, supported principally by the bridge structure, which slides on the rails of the inside viaduct track. There is a corresponding sliding curve in the trolley system, which assures a supply of power to the car motors at all times. About 1100 feet of storage track is provided for cars not in use, by additional viaduct structure near the south-west corner of the Cristobal plant. At Balboa there is no track built especially for storage, the layout being such that, when all of the cars are not in use, sufficient track is also not in use to accommodate the unused cars. Eighty-eight cars are being furnished for Cristobal and 34 for Balboa.

Four viaduct track scales are provided at Cristobal and two at Balboa, so located that the cars will pass over at least one of them for any operation. The scales are semi-automatic, requiring a weighman to balance the arm. When this is done, the weighman prints the weights on cards by a simple operation. It is expected to print these cards in duplicate, one being retained by the weighman, the other being placed in a convenient receptacle on the car, to be subsequently removed at the dumping point.

The wharf bunkers are identical at the two plants, neglecting differences in detail of the belt conveyors supplying them. Each has three storage pockets of 500 tons nominal capacity each. Each wharf bunker will be of steel and concrete throughout, the latter material forming the sides and floors of the pockets. Each bunker will be provided with six delivery chutes, two for each pocket, which will have a wide range of delivery. The function of the wharf bunkers is to keep available a moderate supply of coal for tugs and other small craft, thus avoiding starting up the heavy machinery for each small consumer. Advantage is taken of the structure necessary to support the wharf bunker belts, by fitting a part of it for a superintendent's office at each plant, this location affording a commanding view of practically all parts of each plant.

Twenty-five cycle three-phase power is supplied to each plant at 2300 volts, the contract work commencing with the transformation of this current in the coaling-plant substations. The motors driving the coal-handling machinery and accessories are three-phase 440-volt induction motors; the lighting is at 110 volts. It is necessary at Balboa to provide direct current for the berm cranes; and the rotary converters originally used for this purpose in the lock construction will be put into service again in the Balboa sub-station.

The contracts require the Government to furnish all sub-structures and to re-erect the Balboa berm cranes, this latter including the electrical equipment above mentioned. At Cristobal the pier formed by the unloader wharf, end wharf and reloader wharf is supported on concrete cylinders, 6 feet in diameter, sunk to rock. The cylinders are arranged in bents 30 ft. 0 in. center to center for the unloader and reloader wharves, and 31 ft. 6 in. center to center for the end wharf, the heavy wheel loads of the stocking and reclaiming bridges requiring this comparatively short spacing. The deck structure supported by these cylinders consists of structural steel girders and beams encased in concrete, and supporting a reinforced-concrete deck slab averaging 14 inches in thickness. There are 306 cylinders supporting 194,000 square feet of deck structure.

The unloader and reloader travel does not extend south of the cylinder pier structure at Cristobal, and the stocking and reclaiming bridge tracks are supported south of the pier on a pile and concrete structure. The foundations of the viaduct are also supported on pile and concrete footings, after leaving the pier structure.

At Balboa the unloader wharf is supported on concrete piers, 25 ft. 0 in. center to center, as indicated on Plate IV. The total length of the unloader wharf is 1052 feet, of which 790 feet is traversed by the unloaders. The reloader wharf at Balboa will be supported on concrete cylinders similar to the construction at Cristobal.

Permanent railway connection will be provided at each plant; at Cristobal the line crosses the French canal on a draw-bridge about 4000 feet south of the south end of the coaling plant. A standard-gauge track scale will be provided at each coaling plant for weighing the comparatively small quantity of coal which will be delivered to railway cars.

At the date of writing, approximately 60 per cent of the Cristobal substructure is completed. At Balboa the unloader wharf and berm crane tracks are practically completed, but the cylinders for the reloader wharf are not completely placed and no decking has yet been laid.

FLOATING CRANES.

Early in 1912 the Isthmian Canal Commission began to give consideration to the purchase of floating cranes, as a part of the necessary equipment of the completed Panama Canal. The conclusion was reached that two very powerful floating cranes would be necessary, to meet conditions which might require handling lock and dock gates. Cranes would also be needed for handling heavy pieces of commercial freight, for making repairs to merchant vessels, for wrecking service, and for handling the heavy guns and armament of the coast fortifications. The cranes should also meet the requirements of the Navy Department as regards lifting capacity and reach.

A study was made of the types of floating cranes in use in the United States, and the conclusion was reached that the usual American "Bridge" type of crane would not meet the conditions of service as well as cranes of the revolving type, on account of the ability of the latter type to plumb the lift without turning the pontoon. On account of the rigidity of the "Bridge" type, the utility of such cranes would be seriously limited by the comparatively narrow waterways existing within the locks, and the obstruction of the narrower parts of the Canal by such a crane would be greater. General specifications were prepared, unaccompanied by any plans, and proposals were invited, to be opened January 13, 1913.

Four proposals were received, one American, one English, one Dutch, and one German. The German bid was considerably lower than any of the others and was accepted; the cranes were constructed in Germany, a representative of the Commission being stationed at the builder's works, with authority to approve all working drawings and to inspect all material and workmanship. The cranes were towed from Germany to the Isthmus in the following state of completion: the pontoon was complete, the fixed tower was erected, the boiler and power generating plant was in the pontoon ready for service, and the revolving superstructure was complete except for the jib, counterweight arm, spindles, cross-head, winch house and hoisting machinery. Spindles and cross-head were lashed to the deck of the pontoon. The remainder of the superstructure was shipped to the Isthmus "knocked down" and was erected on the Isthmus. The cranes would have been shipped in a more advanced stage of completion had not the underwriters objected.

The jibs were erected on the east wall of the middle chamber at Gatun locks. As one was completed, the crane to which it belonged was brought into the lock chamber and the water level regulated until the correct relative height was obtained. The jib was then skidded on rollers until it projected sufficiently beyond

Fig. 3. Pinning Jib on Crane "Ajax". Middle Chamber of Gatun Locks.

the lock wall and was pinned to the superstructure. The connecting links between jib and cross-head were fitted with an extension, and by lowering the cross-head, the jib was raised to about the midway position. The jib was temporarily secured in this position, the extension removed, and after raising the cross-head sufficiently, the connecting links were pinned to the jib. Fig. 3 gives a clear idea of this operation.

At the date of writing, one crane, the "Hercules", has been tested and accepted and is in the service of the Panama Canal. The other crane, the "Ajax", is as yet incomplete, inasmuch as the new jib made to replace the jib which failed under test in December, 1914, has not yet been erected. Fig. 4 shows the "Ajax" at work in Culebra Cut in November, 1914, and Fig. 5 shows the "Hercules" holding the 300-ton test load. The new

Fig. 4. Floating Crane "Ajax" Removing Smaller Portion of Wrecked Drill Barge "Teredo". Culebra Cut.

jib of the "Ajax" will be erected with the assistance of the "Hercules", and not on the lock wall, on account of the increase in canal traffic.

Plates VIII and IX show the general characteristics of the

cranes. It will be seen that each consists of a steel pontoon carrying a fixed steel tower on the longitudinal center line of the pontoon, but comparatively close to one end of it. This steel tower, or fixed superstructure, supports the revolving steel super-

Fig. 5. Trial of Floating Crane ''Hercules''. 300 Tons Suspended at Rated Reach of 22.3 Ft.

structure, which consists of two parts, the ''bell'' and the jib. The bell is a rectangular framed structure which envelopes the tower, revolves about an axis perpendicular to the pontoon, and supports the machinery house, the operator's cab and the jib.

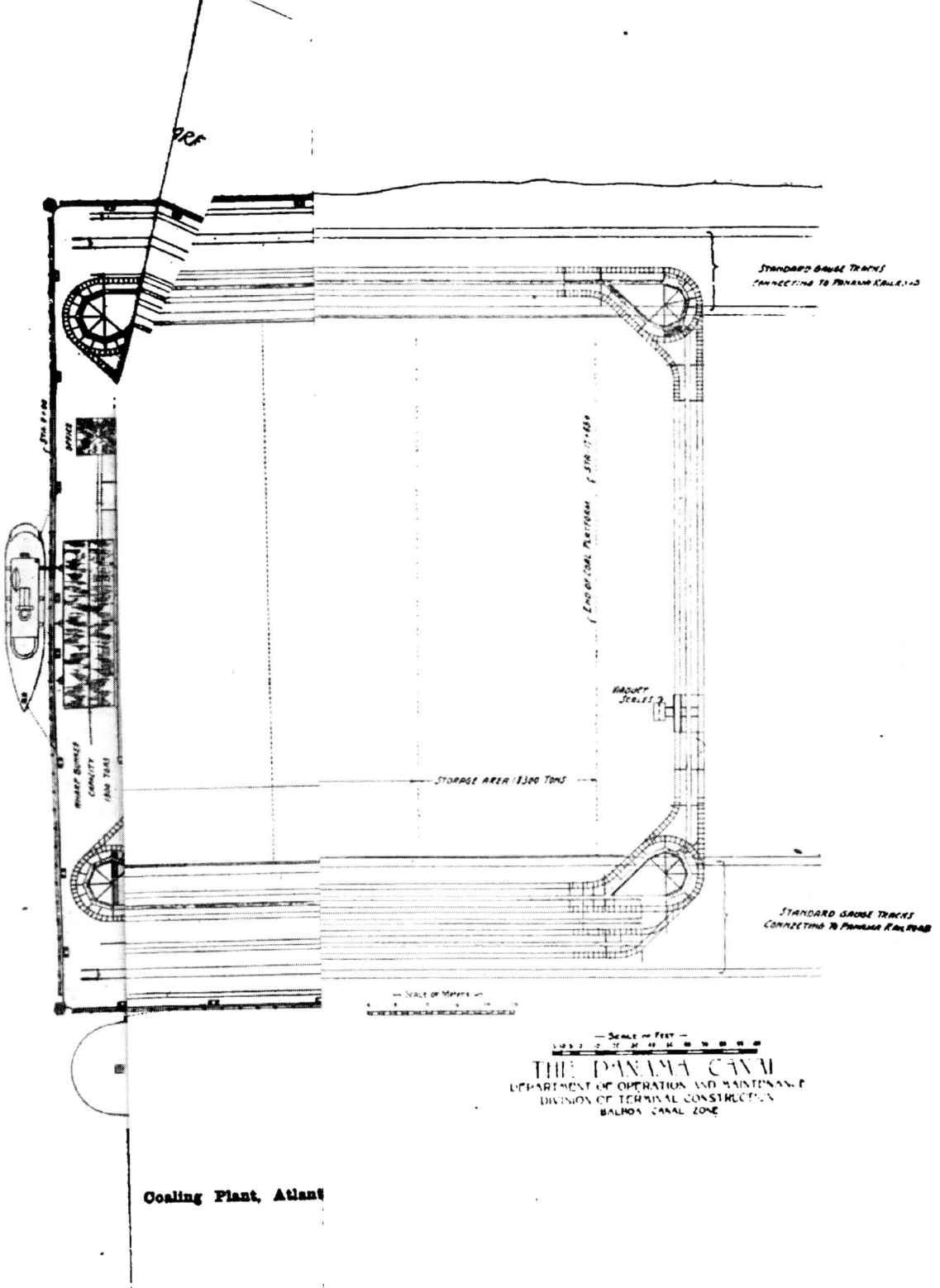

STANDARD GAUGE TRACKS
CONNECTING TO PANAMA RAILWAYS

STANDARD GAUGE TRACKS
CONNECTING TO PANAMA RAILROAD

STORAGE AREA 18300 TONS

— SCALE OF METERS —

— SCALE OF FEET —

THE PANAMA CANAL
DEPARTMENT OF OPERATION AND MAINTENANCE
DIVISION OF TERMINAL CONSTRUCTION
BALBOA CANAL ZONE

Coaling Plant, Atlant

The jib revolves about an axis perpendicular to the axis of revolution of the bell, and is caused to revolve about this axis by a pair of screw spindles which move a cross-head connected to the jib by two members or "links".

The general construction of the pontoon is indicated on Plate VIII, from which it will be seen that it is of steel construction throughout, 150 ft. 2⅜ in. (45.78 m.) long by 88 feet 9¾ in. (27.07 m.) wide, by 15 feet 9 inches (4.8 m.) deep at each side. The deck is cambered, making the center line depth 12 inches (305 mm.) greater. The main framing of the pontoon consists of four longitudinal bulkheads, continuous for its entire length, and six transverse bulkheads, all of which have continuous plate webs. These bulkheads subdivide the pontoon into 15 internal compartments and 16 external compartments; these latter are water-tight and are further subdivided to make a total of 26 such compartments, which extend completely around the periphery of the pontoon. The internal compartments are not calked and there is no double bottom. Each compartment is provided with a manhole and its floor is drained to a sump, whence any accumulation of water may be removed by a pump. The stability is such that when two adjacent water-tight compartments are flooded, the crane will still safely carry the maximum rated loads.

The principal stresses in the fixed and revolving superstructure, and the sections of the principal members, are indicated on Plate X. The fixed superstructure or tower is riveted to the pontoon framing, and, since the deck of the pontoon is practically unbroken, it acts as an efficient box girder. The average freeboard of the unloaded crane is about 8.26 feet (2516 mm.). During the acceptance tests of the "Hercules" the minimum freeboard was 2.84 feet (865 mm.) for the loaded crane without deck load, 2.23 feet (679 mm.) for the loaded crane with 300 gross tons deck load, and 1.25 feet (381 mm.) for the loaded crane without deck load but with two pontoon compartments flooded. The maximum longitudinal inclination of the pontoon is 2 degrees 5 minutes and the maximum transverse inclination is 4 degrees 34 minutes, for loads within the rated capacity of the crane. The maximum inclination observed during the overload tests of the "Hercules" was 5 degrees 25 minutes.

From the structural viewpoint, the detail of greatest importance is the "king", which transmits the loads from the revolving superstructure to the tower. This detail is indicated on Plate XI, from which it will be seen that the "king" is, in effect, a combination ball and socket and collar bearing, the former being for the vertical component and the latter for the horizontal component of the load. There is, of course, an equal and opposite horizontal component applied at the base of the tower. This component is applied through rollers which bear on a horizontal annular girder secured to the base of the tower. The rollers are attached to the bell in pairs, each pair being set in an equalizer to assure equality of bearing.

The "king" receives its load from a "king girder", located at the top of the bell, through the buttress threads indicated on Plate XI. The actual revolution takes place on a ring of conical rollers, so connected as to permit a slight degree of axial movement by any individual roller, thus distributing the load substantially uniformly on the rollers. The whole "king bearing" is immersed in an oil bath.

The stability of the crane is quite independent of moving counterweights or water ballast. There is a fixed counterweight in the after end of the pontoon, another fixed counterweight under the machinery house supported by the bell, and a third on the cross-head. By this arrangement the operator is not concerned with the amount or location of the counterweight, thus avoiding all danger of capsizing backwards, should a hoisting line or sling part when a maximum load was being handled.

An area 20 ft. by 60 ft. of the pontoon deck is made especially strong, being capable of carrying a superimposed load of 2000 lbs. per square foot. This area is intended for the reception of deck loads up to a total of 300 gross tons; thus the cranes can carry very heavy and bulky loads on their decks when desired, rendering unnecessary the use of barges, etc., for this purpose.

The motions and hoists are actuated by electric motors driving suitable shafting, gearing, and drums. Power is supplied by a steam-driven generating plant located in the after part of the pontoon below its deck. From this generating station direct current, at not more than 220 volts, is led to the machinery room and operator's cab on the bell, sliding contacts being provided

Fig. 6. Floating Crane ''Hercules'' Transferring Equipment Across Gatun Locks.

at the top of the fixed tower, on account of the rotation of the revolving superstructure. All motions and hoists are in the control of one operator stationed in the operator's cab, whence he commands an unobstructed and comprehensive view of the working area.

With the exception of the slewing mechanism, all motors and operating machinery are located in the machinery house supported by the bell, and, when the crane is in use, one machinist is stationed here to look out for bearings, lubrication, etc. He has nothing to do with the control of the various motions, except to throw certain clutches when it is desired to effect a fundamental change in the gearing.

The pontoon is not self-propelling, and is given a slight dead-rise fore and aft to facilitate towing. It is equipped with four steam capstans and with bitts, cleats and chocks for lines, and is protected by a system of wooden fenders. Each crane is electrically lighted and provided with a search light. There is speaking-tube connection between the operator's cab and the machinery house, and telephone connection between the operator's cab and the power generating station in the pontoon. The operator's cab is provided with indicators, to show the inclination of the crane, and the reach and corresponding rated capacity of the jib. Inclination indicators are also provided in the machinery house and power station, and all parts are rendered conveniently accessible by stairways, ladders and walkways.

Each crane is provided with a main hoist and an auxiliary hoist. The main hoist is fixed at the point of the jib and consists of two blocks, each of a rated capacity of 125 gross tons. These two blocks can be linked together by means of an "equalizer bar", which is equipped with a hook of 250 gross tons rated capacity; thus the two individual blocks, when so connected, form one hoist of 250 gross tons capacity, since the two blocks are lifted and lowered at equal speeds by mechanical connections with the machinery house. When the two blocks are not so connected, one may be raised or lowered, while the other is held stationary; but, if both are moved simultaneously, they must move in the same direction and at the same speed. Under the acceptance tests, the "Hercules" met the contract speed requirements without exceeding the rated capacity of the motors. These speeds are as follows:

With 250 tons load 3.5 feet per minute
With 125 tons load 7.0 feet per minute
With 62½ tons load 14.0 feet per minute.

The speed of raising or lowering the unloaded blocks was similarly found to be 20 feet per minute.

The term "hook" is used above, although for the main hoist this part, as actually furnished, is triangular in form. For the auxiliary hoist, the "hook" is double barbed. All hooks are provided with ball-bearings, so that the suspended load may be revolved without twisting the suspending lines.

Each block of the main hoist is suspended in ten parts of 2-inch (52 mm.) steel rope. The block sheaves and guide sheaves are 63 inches in diameter, while the actuating drums, which are arranged in pairs, are also 63 inches in diameter. These latter drums are indicated on Plates IX and XI, from which it will be seen that they are comparatively short, permitting only 9 wraps of line. This is of considerable advantage, inasmuch as a compact arrangement of machinery in the machinery house results; and, in order to take care of the considerable amount of rope necessary to obtain the heights and depths of the main hoist, a storage drum is provided for each pair of actuating drums, located below the machinery house floor. Each storage drum is driven by its corresponding pair of actuating drums in such manner that the rope comes to the storage drum under very little tension, thereby permitting it to be coiled in successive layers without injury, while the storage drum itself has a reciprocating axial motion which coils the rope neatly and eliminates fouling.

During the acceptance tests of the "Hercules", the following reaches were attained, without deck load or appreciable wind:

	Reach	
Load	Over side	Over end
250 tons	22.4 ft.	22.9 ft.
150 tons	62.4 ft.	61.0 ft.
100 tons	81.6 ft.	81.1 ft.

(Tons of 2240 lbs.)

The maximum height above water of hook on equalizer bar is as follows:

In 100-ton position 126 feet
In 150-ton position 154 feet
In 250-ton position 182 feet.

The term "position" refers to that combination of radius of jib and inclination of pontoon which gives the reach shown in the table above. The term "reach" means the horizontal distance from vertical through hook to face of timber fender on pontoon. There is sufficient rope provided to allow the hook on the equalizer bar to descend to a point 30 feet below the water surface, when the jib is in the 250-ton position.

The main hoist capacities above referred to are the rated capacities of the crane. The contract required the cranes to withstand test loads 20 percent in excess of the rated loads in each case.

The auxiliary hoist has a rated capacity of 15 gross tons and was tested at 33 percent excess load. As shown on Plate IX, it is swung from a carriage, or "crab", which runs on a track suspended from the lower chord of the jib. The block is hung in two parts of 1½-inch (38 mm.) steel rope. The block and guide sheaves are 51 inches in diameter, and the actuating drum is 49.5 inches in diameter by 50 inches long. The "crab" is moved along the runway by a 1⅝-inch (42 mm.) steel rope, actuated by a drum 50 inches in diameter by 30 inches long. The hoisting drum and trolleying drum are moved by one pair of electric motors, the trolleying drum being thrown into and out of mechanical connection with the motors by a clutch worked by the operator in his cab. The reeve of the hoisting rope is such that when the crab is trolleyed in or out, the block moves parallel to the runway on the jib, i. e., it is impossible to trolley and hoist simultaneously. The lack of this ability is not objectionable, and the mechanical installation is thereby rendered more compact. There is no storage drum for the auxiliary hoist, the actuating drum being of sufficient length to coil the entire line in one wrap. The hoisting and trolleying ropes are led to the jib by sheaves, so located that there is no movement of the auxiliary hoist if its lines be held stationary while the jib is luffed in or out. During the acceptance tests of the "Hercules", the fully loaded auxiliary hoist attained the contract speeds without loading the motors beyond their rated capacity, these speeds being 40 feet per minute for raising, lowering and trolleying. The corresponding speed for the unloaded hoist is 80 feet per minute. The auxiliary hoist can be operated at rated capacity with the jib at any inclination, and, since the jib is capable of complete revolution around the vertical axis, both the main hoist and auxiliary hoist command the circular area so described.

The slewing of the jib is effected by two electric motors, each actuating gearing, which terminates in a pinion, which engages a circular rack secured to the base of the bell. Plate VIII indicates the general location of the slewing mechanism, from which it will be seen that the pinions are effective at opposite ends of the same diameter of the rack, the motors and gearing being supported by the base of the fixed tower rather than by the revolving bell. This arrangement reduces the twisting stresses in the bell, but either of the two slewing units is capable of revolving the loaded superstructure, though of course at reduced speed. Between each motor and its pinion there is introduced a friction clutch which is set to a predetermined strength. The object of this clutch is to minimize the extent of damage, should the jib strike an obstruction while slewing, or be struck by a moving object, as, for example, the upper works of a ship. If the jib were held immovable by the brakes on the motors, something would probably have to give way in such a contingency; the detail here provided allows the friction to give.

In the acceptance tests the jib made one complete revolution around its vertical axis in 5 minutes under the most favorable condition, and in 8 minutes under the most unfavorable condition. In addition to the inertia of the weights to which motion must be imparted in slewing, the force required to slew is dependent on the amount of friction at the bearings at the top and bottom of the fixed tower. There is a combination of dead weights and load for which there is theoretically no resultant over-turning moment of the jib and bell, in which case the load on the tower consists of only a vertical force equivalent to the weights, i. e., there are no horizontal forces acting on the tower. The work required of the slewing mechanism is then a minimum if no wind be blowing. There is also another combination of fixed weights and suspended load which makes the horizontal forces maximum, and under these conditions the slewing mechanism must perform its severest duty.

The luffing of the jib is effected by the same pair of motors which actuates the main hoist, the luffing mechanism being thrown into and out of mechanical connection with the hoisting mechanism by a clutch worked by the operator from his cab. Plate XI shows the general arrangement of this mechanism, and also shows those parts which are in use when the hoist, only, is in operation, and when both the hoist and the luffing mechanism are being worked. The mechanical relations are such that if the jib is being luffed in, the suspended load is lowered, and vice versa; the result of this is that the load moves on practically a horizontal line, and the required power is less than what would be required were the suspended load not lowered, but lifted along with the jib. This also results in a very compact arrangement of the machinery. Plate XI also shows the detail of the thrust bearing at the bottom of each of the screw spindles, and indicates the manner in which the stresses are transmitted between the spindles and the cross-head. It is essential that uncertainties and secondary stresses be avoided to the fullest extent in this part of the mechanism. It will be seen that the thrust bearing is effective for either an upward or a downward force, since in the most nearly vertical position of the jib there may be a compressive force in the screw spindles; this force is small in comparison with the tension in the spindles. The combination of spherical and roller bearings at the lower end of the spindles effectively prevents any bending in them and reduces to a minimum the power necessary to revolve them. The connection of the spindles to the cross-head is by means of a nut which is provided with spherical bearing surfaces. The upper end of each spindle is not rigidly secured to the superstructure, but is held by a combination of springs, in such manner that it is free to move to a sufficient extent to avoid bending stresses.

The "heel" of the jib, i. e., the point where it is supported on the bell, is also provided with a spherical bearing, thus permitting elastic deformations. The revolution of the jib is, however, about a cylindrical pin, the axis of which is coincident with the axis of the spherical bearing.

In the acceptance tests of the "Hercules", the unloaded jib was fully luffed in in 9 minutes and fully luffed out in 6 minutes. The jib loaded with 100 gross tons was fully luffed in in 13.5 minutes and fully luffed out in 11 minutes.

Steam is furnished by a Scotch marine boiler at 175 pounds per square inch working pressure. The power generating station consists of one 58-kw. and one 116-kw. direct-current generator, both direct connected to one marine-type compound engine, all mounted on a single cast bedplate. The current for exciting the fields of these two generators is furnished by a 17-kw. steam-driven marine-type auxiliary set, which furnishes direct current at a constant voltage of 220. The current generated by this auxiliary set is also used in the control system and for the electric lighting. The steam engines are run condensing,—the necessary condensers, circulating system, and feed pump being provided.

The main hoist is driven by two 66-hp. motors which also drive the jib luffing mechanism when connected as above described. The auxiliary hoist is driven by two 30-hp. motors, and each slewing mechanism by one 30-hp. motor; thus there are six motors, four of which are arranged in pairs.

The speed control is effected by an adaptation of the "Ward Leonard" system, and dynamic braking is used in lowering loads.

By means of rheostatic resistances, the exciting current furnished by the 17-kw. set to the fields of the 58-kw. and 116-kw. power sets is increased or diminished, thus regulating the voltage and current furnished by the power generators, and correspondingly regulating the speed of the motors, from zero to the rated number of motor revolutions. Further speed control of the motors is effected by weakening the motor fields, a speed up to twice the rated speed being thus obtained. Plate XI indicates the general arrangement of the control apparatus in the operator's cab, from which it will be seen that there are two sets of throw-over switches and two controllers, one for the control of the 58-kw. power generator, the other for the control of the 116-kw. power generator. Each throw-over switch has three positions, marked "main hoist", "auxiliary hoist", and "slewing". Each controller has 52 points, 26 for "up" and 26 for "down". Sixteen points of each 26 are for regulating the voltage of the generator, the remaining ten points being for weakening the motor fields. "Up" and "down" of course do not apply to slewing; when the slewing motors are driven, the movement of the controller handle is in the same sense as the resultant slewing movement.

By this arrangement of control, it is not necessary to handle large currents through the controllers, and the resultant installation is very compact and convenient, and there is less wear and tear of the control equipment. The speed can be varied by small increments, which is most advantageous in handling heavy and bulky loads in cramped quarters. The operator has immediate and complete control over all motions, and can control any two motions simultaneously, as, for example, main hoist and auxiliary hoist, and either hoist combined with slewing. He can also luff in or out when the main hoist is connected. All the operations of which the crane is capable can be effected by either the 58-kw. or the 116-kw. power generator, but, for the main hoist, only half the maximum load can be handled by the smaller generator. Interlocks are provided, so that one group of motors cannot be connected to both power generators at the same time, and also so that the throw-over switch cannot be operated until its respective controller is at zero point. Large precise ammeters and voltmeters are provided in the operator's cab, so that he may know the output of each generator at any time and avoid overloading.

When the load is lowered, the motors act as generators and send current back into the line, thus tending to drive the generators and the steam engine. In order that the engine may not be overhauled, ballast resistance is automatically cut into the line, but only when one of the controllers is set for lowering and the other is not in use, or when both controllers are set for lowering. When a load is lowered simultaneously with any operation requiring power, the energy of the sinking load is utilized and resistances are not necessary.

The ability to exchange duty between the two generators, and the arrangement of motors in pairs, give considerable insurance against complete breakdown. If the 17-kw. auxiliary generator should break down, the 58-kw. power generator can be used to furnish excitation to the 116-kw. power generator. Connections are also provided for taking lighting and excitation current from an external source. Overload circuit breakers and other protective devices are provided, as well as limit switches. These latter are furnished for limiting the luffing of the jib both in and out, for limiting the trolleying of the auxiliary hoist, and the downward travel of the main hoist and the auxiliary hoist. The limit switches are automatically reset when the travel is reversed.

The "Ajax" was the first of the cranes to be completed and was offered for test December 1, 1914. The crane withstood successfully the 100-ton normal load test and met the requirements as to speeds. While the test load, increased by 20 percent as specified by the contract for the overload test, was suspended, the back of the jib collapsed, with the attendant fall of the whole jib.* The contractor expressed such confidence in his design that he offered to subject the "Hercules" to exactly the same conditions as those under which the jib of the "Ajax" collapsed. In view of the circumstances, The Panama Canal was unwilling to permit this to be done without reinforcing certain members of the jib, which point of view was also taken by the underwriters. The members were reinforced in accordance with drawings made by The Panama Canal, and, when the reinforcement was completed the "Hercules" was again offered for test. The contract required a very comprehensive and searching set of tests. The normal loads of 100 tons, 150 tons and 250 tons were suspended from the main hook with and without 300 tons deck load. All operations were performed individually and simultaneously. Two adjacent water-tight compartments were flooded and the crane remained stable with the rated loads at rated reaches and in all positions. With 10 percent excess loads, at rated reaches, complete revolutions were made. Twenty percent excess loads were suspended at rated reaches. Exhaustive tests were made with rated loads on individual main hooks, and with the auxiliary hoist and trolley. The "Hercules" met the contract requirements fully, and has since proved to be a very valuable addition to the Canal equipment.

---

* Since the foregoing was written, the "Ajax" has successfully passed acceptance tests even more comprehensive than those to which the "Hercules" was subjected, and was taken into service by the Panama Canal in the latter part of September, 1915.

AIDS TO NAVIGATION FOR THE PANAMA CANAL.

By

WALTER F. BEYER
Formerly Assistant Engineer, Isthmian Canal Commission
Milwaukee, Wis., U. S. A.

Several features pertaining to the aids to navigation for the Panama Canal, both in the layout of the system and in the construction of the various towers and beacons, are interesting, in that similar conditions, it is believed, have not obtained heretofore in the lighting and buoying of similar waterways.

In most cases, the waterways had heretofore been in existence, and were improved from time to time to meet the demands of increased commerce and deep-draft vessels by dredging channels which would connect the existing deeper waterways, thus forming a complete channel between two larger bodies of water, or between a large body of water and an inner harbor basin. The aids to navigation which had previously been in use in such waterways were merged with the newer aids established to mark the improved channels, thus necessarily limiting the scope for comprehensive and modern design.

On the Isthmus of Panama, however, an entirely new waterway from ocean to ocean was created, which permitted the establishment of an independent system of aids to navigation along that waterway, and the adoption of the newest and best ideas. Inasmuch as the general system is similar in most respects to that employed in other waterways throughout the United States, this paper will deal only with such features as are believed to be new. The system in general consists of:

16 lighted ranges (each range consisting of two towers)
46 lighted beacons
59 lighted buoys
 7 unlighted target ranges
81 spar buoys and stakes
11 reference targets

The ranges are used to establish direction on the longer tangents of the Canal, and the beacons and buoys to mark the sides and turns of the channels.

In the preparation of the project for lighting and buoying the Canal, careful consideration was given the subject of the position which the ranges should occupy with respect to the axis of the Canal. It is believed that in all the ranges heretofore established, the lines have coincided with the axes of the dredged channels. From past experience, it was found that in narrow, dredged channels, particularly such as in the St. Marys River, masters of ships passing each other would invariably turn out from the range as little as possible, thereby allowing scarcely enough room between the passing vessels for safe navigation; and in that waterway it was a common occurrence for the master of a large vessel to hold the range and force the master of the smaller vessel to turn out, thus jeopardizing the smaller vessel.

It was desired to overcome this objectionable feature on the Panama Canal and the solution appeared to be the placing of all ranges, except those at the entrances to the Canal, in such positions that the sailing lines marked by them will carry vessels from 100 to 125 feet to their starboard of the axis of the Canal; thus, in channels 500 feet wide, two passing ships, if on their ranges, will have their center lines 200 feet apart, and in channels 800 to 1000 feet wide, they will have their center lines 250 feet apart, giving ample space between the two ships, and minimizing the danger of the ships being brought together by suction. In the channels which are only 500 and 800 feet wide, the pilot, if his ship is large and difficult to handle, need not necessarily keep dead on the range ahead, but he may keep the range slightly open to his port, and thereby follow more nearly the axis of the Canal; but in passing an approaching ship, the range in this case serves to indicate how far he can safely turn out. The ranges at the entrances to the Canal were placed on the axes of their respective channels because both incoming and outgoing ships must depend upon the single range, the incoming ship using the range ahead, and the outgoing ship the same range astern. The range lights were omitted in Culebra Cut because of the topography in that region, the hills being so steep that a sufficient horizontal distance between the two lights could not be secured to make the range usable. They were also omitted on four of the shorter tangents throughout the rest of the Canal, because a ship, after making the turn into such a reach, would have to make its next turn by the time a range ahead would be of any benefit to it. However, in this short radius, target ranges, consisting of two concrete tripods, were placed at convenient points on either end of the prolongation of the axis of the Canal, primarily to mark permanently the axis for future dredging purposes and also to reference the locations of gas buoys in their vicinity; but they may also be used by day to guide ships through those passages.

When, for any reason the ranges are not visible, the pilot must depend entirely upon his compass and the side lights and unlighted spar buoys, which mark the sides of the channel. These side lights, as in other waterways, consist of lighted beacons and gas buoys, the former used wherever a foundation could be constructed, either above or below the water; and the latter, wherever there was sufficient depth of water. These beacons and buoys were placed at all turning points and at convenient intervals along the sides of the channels, in pairs, two abreast, and are in general about one mile apart. The unlighted spar buoys are placed in line with the beacons and gas buoys and midway between them.

The unreliable nature of the soil and the handling of dredges up to the toe of the Canal prism, where future dredging is required, necessitated placing all beacons and buoys from 30 to 50 feet outside the toe of the channel bank. For example, at the Atlantic and Pacific entrances, from sea to Gatun and Miraflores, respectively, where soft alluvial soil was encountered, the beacons and buoys were placed on a line 50 feet outside the toe of the channel banks, and in Gatun Lake, Culebra Cut and Miraflores Lake, they were placed 30 feet outside.

The location of the individual range towers was governed by the alignment of the Canal and the shores of Gatun Lake, Panama and Limon bays. At the time the project for providing aids to navigation was being prepared, Gatun Lake was not in existence, the small amount of water then in the Gatun Lake basin (elevation + 14 ft.) only making the heretofore existing swamps more difficult to negotiate by the surveying parties, who were subsequently to enter that field. Except in the swamp areas, all this basin was covered with large trees and dense jungle growth, presenting a formidable barrier to the men who were to deliver the material for the lighthouses and their foundations. In that part of the basin, from Gatun to the former site of Tabernilla, little excavation for the Canal was required, but a zone having the dimensions and shape of the Canal, had been cleared of all trees and jungle growth, thus forming a clear channel after the lake reached its mean level. To obtain the location of the range towers in this region, it was first necessary for the surveying parties to cut trochas, or lines, in prolongation of each tangent of the Canal up to the 85-ft. contour, that being the proposed mean lake level; then offset 100 to 125 ft. to right or left of the axis, as the case may be, and continue the line until a sufficient distance had been obtained between the proposed sites of the front and rear towers forming the range. This, in some cases, as may be seen on any map of the Canal, necessitated running lines 16,000 ft. from the point of intersection of the Canal to the rear tower, and over a rough and hilly country. The sites having been thus tentatively selected, gangs of men were set to work clearing out the trees below the 85-ft. contour, whose tops would project above the lake surface, and also the trees and undergrowth above the 85-ft. contour to a point 50 ft. in rear of the rear tower, the theoretical shape of the clearing being a polygon, the length of the base of which was the width of the Canal, the top 400 ft., and the sides from 2800 ft. to about 16,000 ft. This clearing, a total of about 1400 acres, was necessary to prevent obscuring the range lights when the lake reached its final elevation. All the sites for beacons and gas buoys in Gatun Lake were also located and cleared of jungle growth, before the water was allowed to rise. The gas buoys, being floating aids, had to be placed on stations after the waters of the lake rose, but their sites were determined and marked in advance of the filling of the lake.

In order to transport material for the towers to their sites as economically as possible, advantage was taken of the different stages of the water to which Gatun Lake rose from time to time before it reached its final level. Thus, in this region, with the water in the lake at elevation $+$ 14 ft., it was possible to deliver material and construct the towers at only 6 sites, these sites being within reach of the railroad. As rapidly as the water rose and approached a tower site, material was delivered on barges, the water course followed by the barges having in all cases been predetermined from the contours of the ground by the surveying parties, who cleared a channel about 50 ft. wide through the jungle growth. In order to increase the efficiency of the range, the site for the front tower was located as close to the point of intersection of the Canal as possible, and in four cases, submarine foundations built in the dry were used for this purpose.

Transportation of the material thus by water was the only practical way, but even then some of the sites were a considerable distance from the shore, in which case the material was handled to the site by means of improvised cable-ways, up steep hills and over valleys. Where the ground was comparatively level, Decauville track and cars were used. The material was delivered as near to the sites as practicable on barges towed by steam launches, which continually had to thread their way through the tropical forest which projected above the slowly rising waters of the lake; frequently the sites were so inaccessible that the launch could proceed no farther than within 1000 ft. of the shore, to which the barge was then poled by boatmen, passing over and around submerged stumps and snags. In the case of several of these extremely inaccessible sites, the handling of the material became a very expensive item in the construction of the structures, in some cases being in excess of the total cost of the other labor for construction.

After the preliminary examination of the probable locations for the range towers along the entire length of the Canal, it at once became apparent that two types of towers would be required, one, a rather ornate type (Plate I and Fig. 1) to be used where they were in such close proximity to the Canal, or to the Panama Railroad, that the material could be readily delivered at the site, and where it was desired that they should present a pleasing appearance to persons aboard passing ships or trains; the other type (Plate II) a simple design, with a minimum amount of material required in its construction, to be used where sites were inaccessible and the handling of material difficult.

In tropical countries, the conditions governing the design
of lighthouses are different from those of the colder countries,

Fig. 1. Range Tower Built in Accessible Places.

necessitating the elimination, as far as possible, of certain building materials, such as steel and wood, which rapidly deteriorate
in those countries, and permitting the use of concrete in bold

designs. As it was the aim to obtain permanency, minimum cost of upkeep and minimum amount of material entering into the construction of all these structures pertaining to the system of aids to navigation, concrete was the material adopted.

The tower shown on Plate I was designed so that it could be built to any height, up to 90 ft., from one set of forms. Thirteen such towers were built, the lowest being 28 ft. and the highest 87 ft. 10 in. from base to focal plane, the heights of the intermediate towers being 42, 46 and 74 feet. The walls are from 7 to 5 inches in thickness.

Owing to the frequent slight earth tremors, the stability of the towers against overturning by earthquakes was increased by adopting a heavy base section and making the shell of the tower conical with tapering wall sections, thus lowering the center of gravity. The result of the computations for the 74-ft. tower showed that the tower would be stable against winds at 100 miles per hour without reinforcing; but to provide against overturning by earthquakes, to prevent failure by fatigue in concrete and defects due to poor workmanship, reinforcing rods were used, to bind the concrete together.

All reinforcing bars overlapped at least 24 inches, the ends being securely wired to one another, and the vertical and horizontal reinforcement wired at their intersections. Round bars were used throughout and were set in at least $1\frac{1}{2}$ in. from the outer surfaces of the walls. The spacing of the vertical bars varied with the height of the tower, that for a 30-ft. tower being about 22 in. throughout, while that for a 90-ft. tower was 12 in. at the bottom, 22 in. at a point 36 ft. above the base, and 22 in. in the watch room. The circular horizontal bars were spaced 24 in. center to center from bottom to top. The reinforcement in the floors, stair landings, and lantern gallery was placed about 2 in. from the bottom and securely wired to the wall reinforcing bars.

For towers founded on clay or soft rock, the foundation slab was octagonal in plan and reinforced at the top with $\frac{5}{8}$-in. bars spaced 24 in., forming a rectilinear net, and near the bottom surface with $\frac{5}{8}$-in. bars spaced 12 in. and laid to form a diagonal net.

The mix used in all reinforced concrete consisted of one part cement, two of sand and four of broken stone; or one part of cement to four parts of sand and gravel. The latter aggregates were used in the majority of the work, the sand and gravel as obtained from river bed being in about the proper proportions to form a good, homogeneous mass. Where used in thin walls or floors, all the large pieces of gravel were removed before mixing. The concrete was carefully mixed by hand with sufficient water to make the mixture quake while being spaded in the forms. Little ramming was required, and the resulting concrete proved to be practically waterproof during heavy, driving, torrential rains.

It may be of interest to note here that in 1913, after the majority of the range towers, and especially all the high ones, had been completed, a number of quite severe earthquakes occurred at different times on the Isthmus. Some of them were of sufficient force to rock buildings and one did considerable damage to the walls and ceilings of the new Administration Building at Balboa, then under construction, but in no instance did any of the range towers suffer the least damage. Prior to these earthquakes and at a time when the highest tower, 87 ft. 10 in. from base to focal plane, located in the rock fill in the rear of the northerly end of the west wall of the upper locks at Gatun, was about completed, a white foreman and several laborers were doing some work in the lantern of the tower when a sub-aqueous blast was set off near Mindi, a point about 1¾ miles from the site of the tower, which caused the tower to vibrate both vertically and horizontally to such an extent that all fled in terror to the bottom of the tower; but before reaching there, however, the vibration had ceased. The foreman stated that he was positive the horizontal motion of the tower at the top was fully 2 ft. The tower was then carefully examined for cracks or other damage, but none could be discovered. This tower is founded on a reinforced cylindrical-caisson foundation 18 ft. in diameter, resting on bed rock, 60 ft. below grade, and it was ascertained that the rock which was blasted out at Mindi on this occasion was of the same stratum as that on which the tower is founded.

The concrete forms for this type of tower were fabricated of ⅛-in. steel plate and steel angles, the flanges of the latter being provided with ¾-in. holes for bolting the various sections together. All rivets on the sides which form the concrete surfaces were counter sunk. Each section was designed to be handled by two laborers, the outside ones for the base of the tower (Fig. 2) in such a manner that by adding or omitting vertical sections, the octagon could be increased or decreased in size to fit the base of the conical section. Also for the highest towers, where it was desirable for the sake of maintaining a proper proportion, the height of the middle panel was raised by simply inserting a two-inch plank placed on edge between the top and bottom forms of the base and securing the latter by means of long bolts. The forms for the conical section of the tower consisted of four sets of outer rings and four sets of inner rings, each ring consisting of eight segments, or staves, four feet high, bolted together along the vertical joints and clamped together by U-clamps along the horizontal joints. Two sets of these rings formed two circles, with diameters equal to the lower eight feet of the conical section for a tower 74 ft. 10 in. high, and two with diameters equal to the lower eight feet of the conical section for a 46-ft. tower, which coincides with the middle section of a 74-ft. tower. The inner ring of the first set of these forms was designed to be also used, when inverted, as the inner form for the octagonal base of the tower, in conjunction with the first forms described. The forms for the watch room, lantern, gallery brackets, and belt course were also made in sections and bolted together.

The forms for the octagonal base were first set up on a concrete foundation slab, the vertical reinforcing bars were tied to the reinforcement in the slab, and the form filled with concrete, after which the bottom ring of the conical portion of the tower was set up and filled. The second ring was then set up and clamped to the first ring, filled with concrete, and after the concrete in the lower ring had set, the forms were stripped and again set up on top of the upper ring, repeating the process until the belt course below the watch room was reached, the desired batter being given to the tower walls by omitting a segment entirely and substituting one or more narrow wooden staves for it when the ring is shifted to a higher position. Thus one set of forms answered for all towers of whatever height required. All the

Fig. 2.   Base of Tower, showing Forms in Place.

work was carried on from a scaffold tower inside the structure; the base usually being completed in one day, and the first 8 ft. of the conical section set up and poured in another day, after which the work on the conical section progressed at the rate of 4 ft. per day. Wooden forms were placed between the interior and exterior steel forms for the purpose of coring out the openings for doors and windows, which openings were later trimmed with concrete architrave moldings, sills and lintels, previously cast in units.

The concrete spiral stairways in the interior of this type of tower are believed to be unique and have the added virtue of being constructed quickly and economically. They are built up of reinforced concrete units cast at a central plant, and consist of a stair string, treads, and radial supporting beams; the center column or newel post alone being cast in place as the tower walls are being built. The stair string, in the shape of a warped surface, is cast in sections about 9 ft. long, measured along the curve of the string, and is 3 in. by 15 in. in cross section, provided on the inner surface with rebates forming seats for the stair treads. The upper and lower end of each section of string is shaped so that it will rest on the radial support beams and will also lock into the adjoining section of stair string, to which it is cemented by a bed of mortar. The stair treads are cast in the shape of 20-degree sectors, having a radius of 3 ft. 6 in. and provided with nosing and apron. After the tower walls are completed, the radial beams are set at heights of every 4 ft. extending from the center column to a slot left in the tower wall, and on these beams the sections of stair string are consecutively placed, each section being shored away from the wall by a shoulder of concrete on top of the radial beam between the outer face of the string and the inner face of the wall. The stair treads are then set in beds of mortar, the outer end resting on the seat in the string, and the inner end on a concrete lug projecting from the newel post. The stairway is thus built without scaffolding and the design permits using treads and stringers of the same dimensions in all the conical towers in spite of the fact that the higher towers have a greater diameter at the base than the lower ones. The only parts of the stairway which must vary in dimension to correspond to the batter of the tower are the radial beams.

The stairway being thus mortared together gives additional strength and stiffness to the walls of the tower; and besides presenting a pleasing appearance, it is capable of carrying heavy loads. Before being set in place, each section of stair string was tested by applying a load of 4000 lbs. on its edge. The only exposed metal on the towers consists of the gallery railing, lantern door and ventilators, all of which are made of rust-resisting iron and bronze, and the cast-iron ball ventilator at the apex of the lantern.

The forms for the tower shown on Plate II, Fig. 3, and the method of constructing them were similar to those for the towers just described. Nineteen such towers were built in isolated locations in the jungle, the lowest tower being 24 ft. and the highest 54 ft. from base to focal plane, the heights of the intermediate ones being 28, 32, 36 and 50 ft. Fifty-four feet was the height limit to which this type of tower could be safely built, and with but one exception, that height sufficed. In the latter case, the desired height was obtained by building a conical shaped base 18 ft. in diameter and 20 ft. high, with walls 8 in. thick. The foundations for these towers, like those of the preceding type, when they were founded on hard clay or other firm soil, consisted of an octagonal reinforced concrete slab; and wherever these towers were founded on concrete piers, they were secured to the latter by heavy anchor bolts.

The type of beacon adopted is shown on Plate III and is built entirely of reinforced concrete units. This type of aid to navigation was used to mark the sides of channels and cuts where it is not possible to use gas buoys; and as there were 46 required for the Canal, it at once became evident that the most economical method of building them was to cast the units at a central plant and place them on their respective foundations by means of a derrick barge, after the water had been let into Gatun Lake. Apart from its foundation, built in place, each beacon consists of three units,—the body or base, the roof, and the lantern pedestal,—all reinforced with $\frac{5}{8}$-in. round bars. In order to minimize the cost of construction, these units were cast at the central plant, located at Balboa, about one year in advance of the time they were to be used, and at the same time the stair strings, treads, buoy sinkers, window-sills, lintels, etc., were cast.

All the submarine foundations for the beacons in Gatun Lake were, like the towers, built before the water submerged their respective sites; and as soon as the water in the lake reached the

Fig. 3.   Range Towers Built in Isolated Locations.

85-ft. level, a barge distributed the material along the berm of Culebra Cut and working gangs constructed the foundations, after which the units for the beacons were deposited on the foundation and cemented together.

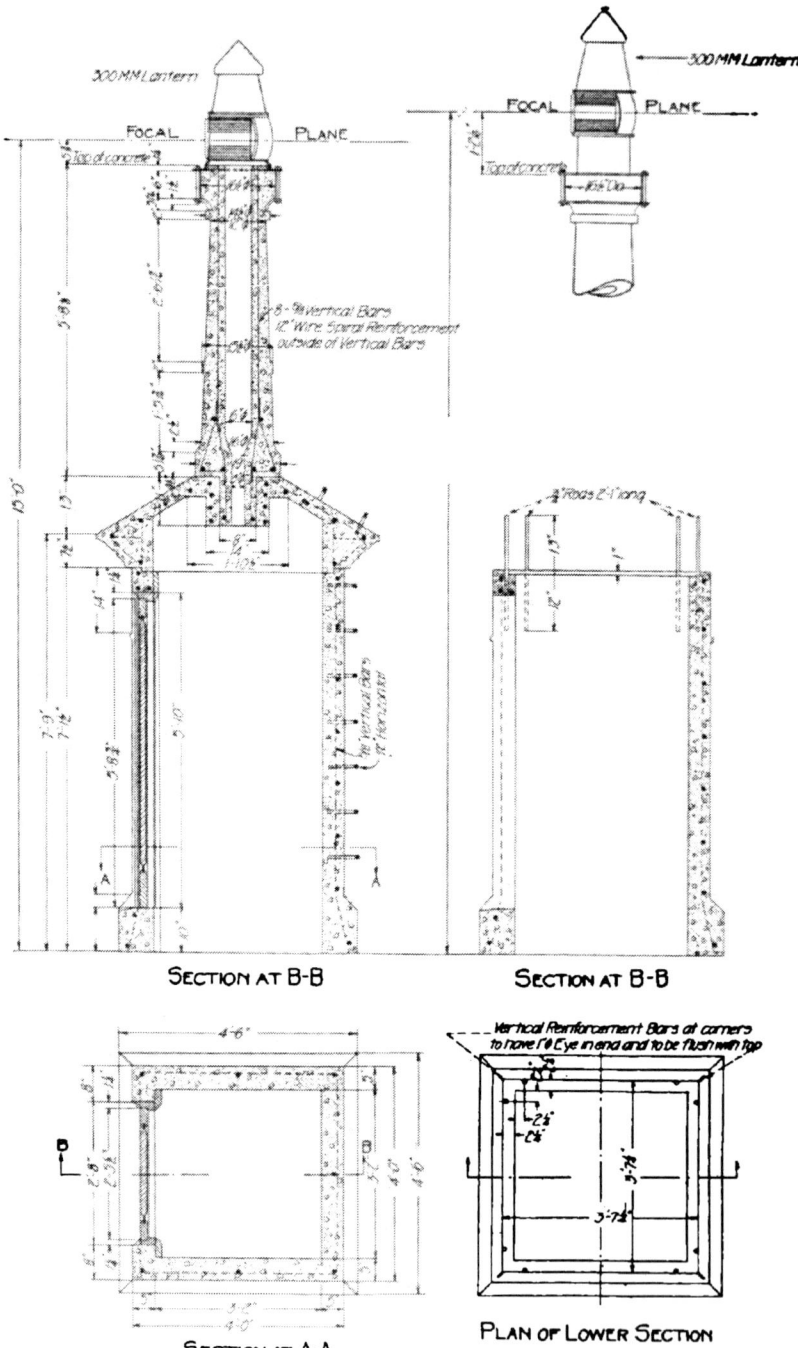

SECTION AT B-B   SECTION AT B-B

SECTION AT A-A   PLAN OF LOWER SECTION

**Plate III.   Beacons for Atlantic and Pacific Divisions, Gatun Lake and Culebra
Cut Sections.**

The Pacific end of the Canal from Balboa to Miraflores locks presented a different condition in regard to the construction of the beacons marking the sides of the channel. Here a tide with a difference of 20 ft. between high and low water was encountered, which at low tide partly exposed the sites of the beacon. The banks of the Canal at this point are composed of a soft, non-supporting mud, almost fluid on top, with underlying rock at depths of from 30 to 50 ft. below low tide, upon which only a light structure could be placed. Obviously, a pile foundation capped with a concrete deck and surmounted by the type of beacon employed elsewhere on the Canal would, at low tide, present an ungainly appearance; and a cylindrical pier founded on bearing piles would be too heavy a structure for the unstable soil. Similarly the sinking of a cylindrical foundation caisson to bed rock would be uneconomical. The structures, five in number, designed for this reach of the Canal consisted of five reinforced concrete bearing piles, forming a square 10 ft. by 10 ft. in plan, driven to refusal and cut off, according to the slope of the channel bank, at elevation from 6 to 8 ft. below mean tide. A reinforced concrete caisson 12 ft. by 12 ft. by 6 ft. high, previously constructed on shore, was launched, towed to the site, and lowered into position on the piles with the receding, or ebb, tide. A pyramidal, skeleton steel structure consisting of four legs, or posts, of 6- by 6-in. angles tied together with horizontal and diagonal braces was erected in this caisson and all members of the skeleton wrapped with wire and surrounded with wooden forms. When the ebb tide had reached a point a little below the top of the caisson, a valve at its bottom was closed and the water pumped out, after which concrete was poured into the forms. This method allowed sufficient time for the concrete to receive its initial set before the concrete was submerged in salt water. The upper part of the structure was enclosed with concrete walls and roof, and the whole surmounted by a concrete lantern pedestal. The total height of the structure is 35 ft. from base to focal plane, which gives the focal plane of the lantern a height of 17 ft. above high tide.

The locations of all gas buoys in Gatun Lake had been determined by surveying parties before the water was allowed to rise, and they were marked by stakes driven in the ground. A round of at least three or four angles was obtained by transit at each stake, using large, well defined trees which stood above the 85-ft. contour for reference objects, there being no artificial topography in this region which could be used for the purpose. Each tree was marked with painted boards nailed to a conspicuous part of the trunk, and a description of the trees entered in the field book, together with the angles; thus when the Lake rose to its final level, the gas buoys were towed to the proximity of their respective sites and with two sextants, each set to an angle equal to the one previously determined by transit, using the designated trees, the buoys were placed on their proper stations, being anchored there by concrete sinkers, each weighing 5000 lbs. These trees could not be depended upon for future use, and, therefore, artificial topography was introduced by erecting 18 concrete targets at convenient points along the shores of the lake, which, with the range towers, would give a sufficient number of distinct and permanent objects from which sextant angles could be read by a man standing on the gas buoys, and these new angles would then serve to replace the buoy on its proper station, should it ever be carried away or otherwise removed, without first placing a marker on its site.

The illuminants used in this system of aids to navigation are electric, incandescent lights and acetylene gas, the former being used whenever the aid to navigation is sufficiently accessible to warrant running a line to it. For all the lighted buoys and 26 towers and beacons which are in inaccessible places, the system using compressed acetylene gas dissolved in acetone has been adopted. As this system of acetylene gas has been frequently described in technical journals, a description of its workings will be omitted in this paper and only its application to the structures on the Canal will be treated.

The gas buoys are similar to those in general use in the United States and have lanterns 300 mm. diameter, placed on top of a pyramidal superstructure at a height of 15 ft. above water level. The body of the buoy contains four pockets, in which are placed four gas accumulators, or tanks, 9 in. in diameter and 60 in. long, filled with dissolved acetylene gas, all connected to a central tube 8 mm. outer diameter leading up to the lantern. The high pressure gas is thus led to the governor in the lantern, where it is reduced to a uniform low pressure and fed automatically to the burner. In the case of range lights and beacons, a battery of from four to six tanks similar to the foregoing is placed in the lower part of the tower or beacon, the tanks connected to a central tube which is carried up the inside of the tower to the lantern and there connected to the burner, which is identical with those used in the buoys. The capacity of a battery of tanks being accurately established, and the amount of gas consumed per hour at the burner being known, it is easily determined how long each battery of tanks will maintain a light without replenishing the tanks with gas, and thus such an installation becomes what is known as an unattended light. The length of time elapsing before the tanks are changed in those buoys, range towers, and beacons is from two months to seven and a half months, according to the characteristic of the light and the size of the burner used. The tanks are recharged at a gas plant located at Balboa, where oxygen and acetylene gas are made for use in the shops; and to make this plant available for recharging tanks for the aids to navigation, it was only necessary to add an additional gas generator, purifiers, meter, tank racks, etc., at a small cost. The plant has a capacity of twelve tanks every 48 hours, exclusive of those used for shop purposes.

The towers and beacons equipped with electric light, instead of burning continuously day and night, as in the case of the ones where acetylene gas is used, are lighted at sundown and extinguished at sunrise, the control for each circuit being located at a convenient point. All the towers and beacons from the shore of Limon Bay to and including the ones on the lock walls at Gatun are connected and are operated from switches placed in the Gatun locks. Those from Gamboa bridge to Pedro Miguel, on both sides of Culebra Cut, are on a separate circuit and operated from Pedro Miguel lock; while those from Miraflores locks to Balboa are on still another circuit. As small slides may occur in Culebra Cut, which are likely to carry away one or more of the beacons or some of the poles carrying the electric wires of this circuit and thus extinguish a considerable number of the beacon lights in the Cut, precautions were taken to minimize the number of lights which would thus be affected by broken wires. A conduit was laid below the bed of Culebra Cut, in a trench cut out of the rock, at a point nearly opposite Bas Obispo, before the water was let into the Cut, and a duplex cable pulled through it, the ends rising up on both banks through vertical conduits and connecting to the overhead wire. This cable, with the connection at Pedro Miguel lock and the wires running along the east and west banks of the Cut, formed a loop, and thus the line could be broken at any point along the Cut and still not extinguish any of the lights.

The **type of lamp** used in the electric-lighted towers and beacons is spherical and **has a spirally**-wound Tungsten filament, concentrating the light source to a sphere of ½ in. for 100-watt and ⅝ in. for 150-watt lamps. In all the electrically-lighted range towers provision is made against the extinguishment of the light by placing two lamps, one in rear of the other, behind the lens. Thus, if the front lamp burns out, the rear one will remain burning with no apparent diminution of candle power so far as the unaided eye can detect. This was determined by experiment on a dark night at points close to the range towers and also at distances of about four miles. Prior to this experiment, and before it was found that the concentrated filament lamps were to be had, a lamp-shifting device was designed by means of which a spare lamp could be automatically dropped into focus and lighted the instant the service lamp burned out. This device, however, was considered too delicate to be taken care of by negro light-keepers and was discarded in favor of the double lamp arrangement in the range tower.

The characteristic flashes are obtained by a device actuated by a 1/12-hp. motor driving a gutta percha disc, whose perimeter is fitted with brass contact plates of predetermined length, set at intervals to give the desired characteristic. The speed of the disc is uniform and is regulated by pinion and gear wheels. The resulting flashes of light have proven to be very efficient, but, of course, with such short, dark intervals as 0.3 second, which are required for the range lights, the light is not cut off so effectively as in the acetylene-gas installations having the same characteristic.

The candle power of the naked gas flame and the electric lamps is increased by the use of lenses of various types and sizes, those for the beacons and buoys being Fresnel lenses 300 mm. diameter, and those in the range tower, 12-in. diameter semaphore and fourth-order range lenses. The Fresnel lenses in the gas buoys are of ground glass and are made in France; but those for the beacons and range towers are of pressed glass, made in the United States, at a great saving in cost, and with little loss of efficiency as compared with the ground-glass lenses.

The estimated candle powers resulting from the use of the foregoing electric and gas lights in combination with the lenses are as follows:

The ranges marking the entrances to the Atlantic and Pacific ends of the Canal which lead out to sea are equipped with fourth-order range lenses and 150-watt concentrated filament lamps, producing approximately 300,000 candle power. All other ranges marking the various channels throughout the Canal are equipped with 12-in. diameter pressed-glass semaphore lenses; and in those in which 100-watt lamps are used, the resulting candle power is approximately 45,000 candles; those in which 60-watt lamps are used, 30,000 candles. Where it is necessary to use spherical mirrors in conjunction with the lenses, as for example, where it is desired to equalize the intensity of any two lights forming a range, the candle power is increased about 35%. In such cases, the spherical mirror is placed in rear of the light source and carefully adjusted.

One-hundred-watt concentrated filament lamps are used in all beacons showing a red light, which, when projected through the red glass screens, produce about 300 candle power; and 60-watt common Mazda lamps are used in all beacons showing a white light on the sides of the narrow channels, which, with their large light source produce about the same candle power as the red lights. In the range towers equipped with acetylene gas and 12-in. diameter semaphore lenses, the resulting candle power varies from 12,000 to 24,000, according to the size of burner used.

In the gas buoys and beacons equipped with 300 mm. ground-glass lens lanterns burning acetylene gas, the resulting candle power for those showing a red light and using a one-foot burner is about 125 candle power; and those showing a white light, from approximately 350 to 450 candle power, according to the size of burner used and the importance of the light.

The fact that with the use of compressed acetylene gas an almost unlimited number of characteristics,—or light characters,—could be obtained, and that similar characteristics could be obtained with electric lights by means of a simple flashing device, it became apparent that a uniform system of characteristics could be obtained by adopting flashing and intermittent lights throughout the entire length of the Canal, which would be a great improvement over a system having fixed lights. In the first place, a great saving in gas is effected by the use of flashing lights, and a smaller number of gas tanks is required, which in turn requires a smaller number of light-keepers to handle them and a smaller gas plant for recharging them. In the second place, there is no danger of the pilot confounding a flashing or intermittent light with shore lights. There are numerous red and white semaphore lights on the railroad at Cristobal and Balboa, and from Mamei to Bas Obispo, and Paraiso to Miraflores, where the railroad parallels the Canal and is in close proximity to it. In the third place, a more powerful light with the consumption of relatively less gas is obtained; and in the fourth place, a range made up of flashes of light following each other in rapid succession can be more readily picked up by the pilot, and cannot be mistaken for shore lights when the range is in the proximity of other lights.

It was at first contemplated to use only white flashing and intermittent lights throughout, but after trial, in actual practice, it was found that, while there was no chance for confusion in the straight reaches, there was at some of the bends in the Canal too much confusion, and it was then determined to have red lights on the starboard side and white on the port, leaving the ranges white as before.

For lighthouse purposes the Canal is divided into natural divisions, one extending from deep water at the Atlantic end to Gatun and known as the Atlantic section; the second from Gatun to Gamboa, known as the Gatun Lake section; the third from Gamboa to Pedro Miguel locks, known as the Culebra Cut section; the fourth from Pedro Miguel lock to Miraflores locks, known as Miraflores Lake section; and the fifth from Miraflores locks to deep water at the Pacific end known as the Pacific section.

As all the lights are unattended, it is estimated that five light-keepers, each having one assistant and several laborers, will se

in
ill
it
vo

ls-
ar

n-
be
d
st
s-

48

te
b
d
is
li
a
fi
li
tu
a
p
ir
a
b
w
t
s
p
r
c
i

i
i
t
t
l
r

d
(
t
(
t
l
l
s

be able to care for the fixed or shore lights, and one lighthouse tender all the floating aids (gas and spar buoys).

A beacon light at the outer end of the west breakwater in Limon Bay has also been established, and a similar beacon will be established at the outer end of the east breakwater when it is completed, thus marking the gap between the ends of the two breakwaters.

. The dredged channel leading from the main channel at Cristobal to the dry dock at Mt. Hope is also marked by gas and spar buoys.

Owing to the slides in Culebra Cut and the unfinished channel from Balboa to Miraflores locks, several beacons could not be constructed until the slides had ceased and the channel had been completed. In the meantime, however, temporary post lights have been placed to mark the points where it was not possible to erect the permanent lights.